And They Shall Be My People

Also by Paul Wilkes

NONFICTION

These Priests Stay

Trying Out the Dream: A Year in the Life of an American Family

Six American Families

Merton: By Those Who Knew Him Best

In Mysterious Ways: The Death and Life of a Parish Priest

Companions Along the Way

The Education of an Archbishop

FICTION

Temptations

FOR CHILDREN

Fitzgo, the Wild Dog of Central Park

My Book of Bedtime Prayers

And They Shall Be My People

My People

An American Rabbi and His Congregation

Paul Wilkes

THE ATLANTIC MONTHLY PRESS
NEW YORK

Published simultaneously in Canada
Printed in the United States of America

FIRST EDITION

Library of Congress Cataloging-in-Publication Data

Wilkes, Paul.
   And they shall be my people: an American rabbi and his
congregation / Paul Wilkes.—1st ed.
   ISBN 0-87113-561-2
   1. Rosenbaum, Jay.   2. Rabbis—Massachusetts—Worcester—
Biography.   3. Judaism—Massachusetts—Worcester.   I. Title.
BM755.R548W55   1994   296.8'342'092—dc20   94-7679

DESIGN BY LAURA HOUGH

The Atlantic Monthly Press
841 Broadway
New York, NY 10003

10 9 8 7 6 5 4 3 2 1

For my beloved father-in-law
Lawrence Gochberg

"I myself found fully grown carob trees in the world; as my fathers planted for me before I was
born: so do I plant for those who will come after me."   Jerusalem Talmud Ta'anith 23a

Preface

This is the story of a rabbi and his congregation. The year-long period I spent with them begins just after the High Holiday season has ended.

This might seem an odd choice, for the High Holidays—which begin with Rosh Hashanah and end eight days later with Yom Kippur—mark the holiest time of the year for Jews. It is the time when the greatest number of Jews formally acknowledge their religious belief by attendance at synagogue services. Their congregation, their Jewishness, their rabbi take a central—albeit momentary for most—role in their lives. It is at this time of year that Jews are most willing to be public about their faith as they participate in venerable rituals and observe practices thousands of years old. And it is a time when their rabbi's words, if not always heeded, are at least heard. Non-Jews are once again made aware of the Jews in their midst, perhaps when a fellow employee takes off from work to attend services or a newspaper photograph features Jewish ritual. A certain line is drawn between Jew and non-Jew.

But of course the rabbi, together with his formally affiliated congregants, has a life throughout the rest of the year. So does every Jew in America. The line quickly fades. Even those who triumphantly proclaim their Jewishness during the High Holidays can blend back easily into a society where they are once again a minority. Their rabbi fades into the background of lives lived not in the embrace and confinement of ghetto or *shtetl*, but in a free and open society. As the months move along, some grow closer to their religious belief or cultural identity as Jews, others drift farther away, while still others consciously decide to turn their backs. Far more seem to do little about it.

For no other religious group in America is the gap between observance and assimilation wider or deeper than it is for the Jews—and for good reason. No other religion makes as many demands—demands that a small number of Jews embrace with total orthodoxy, others attempt to balance within a secular life, and still others completely ignore.

The rabbi written about in these pages is not well known outside his congregation, and while he is certainly admired by his people, Rabbi Jay Rosenbaum has done nothing in particular to distinguish himself outside this small world. He is not the author of a popular book; he is not sought out by talk-show hosts to convey the "Jewish point of view"; he is not renowned by any means. He is the rabbi at Congregation Beth Israel, a midsize Conservative synagogue in Worcester, Massachusetts.

I came to know Rabbi Rosenbaum and his congregation by a somewhat circuitous route. When I began this project, I had written a good deal about religion and religious belief in America, usually centering on the Catholic church. I myself am Catholic. I had recently written about a Catholic priest, Father Joseph Greer, and his parish in Natick, Massachusetts, and thought it would be interesting to go on to study a Protestant congregation in similar detail. So I set about visiting various Protestant churches in my area of central Massachusetts.

I talked to male and female ministers and found them variously enthusiastic or pessimistic about their work, some aflame, some defeated. Good people, all of them, but none—and this is most probably my oversight and not their lack—kindled that spark that must be there if a writer is to spend the amount of time necessary to research and write in depth about so complex an issue as religious belief. It had taken me many months to find Father Greer, so I plunged ahead and scheduled another round of preliminary interviews with another group of ministers.

About this time, at a routine doctor's visit, I confided my frustration to my children's pediatrician, Dr. Arnold Gurwitz, who is Jew-

ish. He mentioned Rabbi Rosenbaum in passing; although he was not
a member of Rabbi Rosenbaum's congregation, he noted that the rabbi
had earned a very good reputation among the Worcester Jewish community. Not long after, Rabbi Rosenbaum's name came up again in a
casual conversation I had with a woman I know who is a member of
the rabbi's synagogue. She was, she admitted, one of those members
who only sees the rabbi during the major Jewish holidays, or when a
life-cycle event within her family—a birth, a bar mitzvah, a marriage,
a death—necessitates attendance at the synagogue or a visit from the
rabbi. Nonetheless, she spoke highly of her rabbi, describing him as an
extraordinarily good man trying his best to serve a congregation she
called "a tough nut to crack." To her, Rabbi Rosenbaum represented
what was best in a profession that in her opinion most non-Jews (and
few Jews) little understood.

And so I went to meet Rabbi Rosenbaum.

I was immediately taken with his great breadth of Judaic
knowledge and his intense concern for the souls of his people, as well
as for the souls of the many alienated, unaffiliated Jews he had yet to
reach in the Worcester area. He was at once an informed, modern
scholar capable of giving an interesting, contemporary exegesis of ancient truths and a beleaguered Old Testament figure, gnashing his
teeth about the inability of his people to embrace and live out those
truths. I liked him immediately; he was a study in confidence and conflict. He seemed absolutely sure of his calling in life, although I could
sense his deep-seated frustration that he was not more effective than
he was.

After that initial meeting, I did some background reading and
quickly found that Rabbi Rosenbaum's concerns are deeply felt across
Jewish America. In an essay in *Commentary* entitled "The Future of
American Jewry," Irving Kristol characterized American Jews as "nervously at home" in America, a country that has given them an enormous degree of success and influence while exacting the heavy price of
their unique identity. The secular humanistic and overtly Christian
culture in America, so strong and so appealingly mainstream, is continuing to erode Jewish substance. Kristol predicted a time when "reli-

gious orientation, like sexual orientation, will be largely a matter of taste. We are seeing, rather, the end of a major phase of American Jewish history . . . [and] American Jews, living in their suburban co-coons, are likely to be the last to know what is happening to them."

In a recent issue of *Moment*, a magazine of Jewish culture and opinion, Joshua O. Haberman, a Washington rabbi, addressed the plight of the two-thirds of American Jews who are not affiliated with a synagogue, the so-called cultural or ethnic Jews. "Because of their di-minished Jewish social contact and sharply reduced participation in the Jewish community," Haberman wrote, "their sense of belonging is most often based on little more than fading Jewish memories. Predict-ably, they will drift to the periphery of Jewish life and, sooner or later, will melt into the gentile majority. If this happens—and it is happen-ing now in our open society—we shall see in the decades ahead the largest voluntary exodus from Judaism in history—unless present trends are reversed."

The end of an era? The last to know? A *voluntary* exodus?

I returned to Rabbi Rosenbaum's office and, after another long conversation, impulsively asked if I might follow him about on his rounds, not only to find out what a rabbi does each day, but to see how he addressed these larger issues of Jewish assimilation and indifference. What I really wanted to find out—as I told Rabbi Rosenbaum—was what was happening in his own inner life as a Jew, and in the inner lives of his people, in these days when a conventional religious life seems such a precarious vocation to sustain. How were his people liv-ing out Judaism? What did Judaism mean to them? And to him?

I told the rabbi that I would try to be as unobtrusive as I could, but that I would like to feel free to ask him for his reflections on the events that would occur in the days ahead. I also told him that, on occasion, I would follow some tangents of my own, asking some of the people with whom he would have contact for their own reflections.

At about the time we met, Rabbi Rosenbaum was planning an evening meeting at which he was going to propose a congregational trip to Israel the following summer. It seemed as good a time as any to begin.

AUTHOR'S NOTE

In a few places, where it seemed appropriate to protect the identities of the individuals concerned, I have used pseudonyms, indicated by an asterisk. All other names, place-names, and events are factual.

And They Shall Be My People

I

To Rabbi Jay Rosenbaum, the twenty-three men and women arrayed before him in the library of Congregation Beth Israel on an unseasonably balmy November night in Worcester, Massachusetts, represented nothing less than the seeds of new life. That they were somewhat older seeds, and fewer in number than he had hoped—over sixty people had originally expressed interest—seemed not to disturb him. These twenty-three were the hope for a season of growth to Rabbi Rosenbaum, the promise of renewed commitment to the observant Jewish life within his synagogue—in essence, the beginning of a new era at Beth Israel. He stood proudly before them, a generous and confident smile on his face, as if they were a mighty legion awaiting his call to service.

Bookshelves containing an impressively wide range of volumes, from current Jewish fiction to ancient Talmudic commentary, Jewish history, philosophy, and thought—none of which, the rabbi would have to admit, circulated particularly well—surrounded the small group seated on gray metal folding chairs. From the walls, portraits of two of Beth Israel's former presidents—one of them looking most impressive, a Bible firmly clutched in his right hand—gazed out impassively over the gathering. No former rabbis were in evidence. In American synagogues, such memories are typically carried in the heart, not committed to canvas.

The rabbi warmly introduced Channy Greenberg, who had just arrived from New York to represent Kenes Tours, her travel agency, which was ready to organize a trip to Israel the following sum-

mer for members of Beth Israel. The trip, which was to be "Personally
Escorted by Rabbi and Mrs. Jay Rosenbaum," looked, in the impressive
color brochure she handed out, much closer to reality than it actually
was.

Just a few minutes into her presentation, Mrs. Greenberg's enthusiasm seemed to overwhelm her, necessitating a pause after her de-
scription of day six of the two-week trip. "I have made sixty-five,
seventy trips to Israel," she confided, sotto voce, nodding her head
knowingly, "but each one is new, each one different. You will have
two weeks of incredible experiences and"—she hesitated in her reverie—"a lifetime of memories."

In her twenty-minute presentation, Mrs. Greenberg, an attractive, effervescent woman with dark hair, dark eyes, and wearing a fashionable dark wool suit, beckoned the Beth Israel congregants to travel
with her along the road that Joshua trod as he entered the Holy
Land—up the steep incline to the fortress at Masada, where Jewish
zealots committed suicide rather than yield to the Romans; to Cae-
sarea and the Western Wall; to mount the Golan Heights, so crucial to
Israel's security; to wait on the tarmac to greet a planeload of newly
arrived Russian emigrés; to visit a kibbutz, to spend a night in a Bedouin encampment, to hear a briefing at a military base on the Jordanian border; to walk the quiet halls of Yad Vashem and honor those
who died in the Holocaust; and to explore the Museum of the Diaspora, where they could embark on a computer-assisted journey into
their own Jewish pasts. "And not one *Shabbos*, but two"—her voice
was now flavored by both remembrance and reverence—"two will be
spent in Jerusalem.

"As for practical things: once you take your luggage off the
trolley at Ben-Gurion Airport, you will not have to touch your bags
again. We take care of everything, so you can enjoy yourself. Transpor-
tation, guide, everything. And, spiritually, ah!" she concluded. "There
you are truly blessed." Looking to her left, she slowly, deferentially,
extended a hand toward Rabbi Rosenbaum. "Your *own* rabbi will be
with you. With him, you will have the spiritual dimension for your trip
of a lifetime."

Rabbi Rosenbaum's response at the end of Mrs. Greenberg's presentation was immediate. "I'm ready. Let's go tomorrow," he said, a boyish grin spreading across his face as if, indeed, a lifelong wish had been granted. But, judging by the tone and number of the questions that followed, his congregants—a few single women in their forties, three couples of child-rearing age, the rest couples in their sixties or seventies—were considerably more cautious. Their spiritual guide might be ready to lead them into the Promised Land, but they were not yet sure they wanted to follow. Exactly how observant would they be expected to be on *Shabbos?* What clothes should they bring? What plans were there for activities to occupy the young children? What about weather, credit cards, bottled water, food, their digestive tracts, currency exchange, shopping time, free days, and—some shuffling of feet here—what about that night in a Bedouin encampment? A *Bedouin encampment?*

Moses may have led the Jews out of bondage in Egypt to wander forty years in the desert, but the Jews of Beth Israel in Worcester, who would be transported via El Al jet and chartered bus to stay in luxury hotels, wanted their spiritual guide to know, up front, that they would not take kindly to spending a single night on the sand. To their credit, there were no questions about the dangers they might encounter in a land that lives daily in various stages of military alert. But, equally, to the rabbi's quiet consternation, neither was there a single question or comment about the religious dimension of the trip.

A beeper sounded near the back of the room. Dr. Howard Fixler, an internist, pulled it from his belt, looked at the encoded message, and put it back in place. Channy Greenberg was now fielding questions about whether or not men would need to bring a jacket; could—and should—Israel bonds be cashed in to pay for expenses. One woman asked in a serious voice if Cheerios were sold in Israel, as if this were the manna needed to sustain her family in the desert wilderness. Howie Fixler's beeper sounded again. Patting his wife, Jody, on the knee, he shrugged with a certain resignation to the rabbi and left the room to return the call.

Howie and Jody Fixler were exactly the kind of people the

rabbi wanted on the trip, and he was happy they had come. They were young, marginally observant Jews who he sensed were ready for a deeper commitment. But Howie was one of the few who could boast hair beneath his *kippah*—or at least hair not yet totally gray. It wasn't that the others in the room—couples like Murray and Freda Rosenberg, and widows like Marion Blumberg and Rose Goldstein—were not good and loyal members of Beth Israel; on the contrary, they were solid, observant congregants. But they represented the dying breed of American Jew, second-generation sons and daughters of the immigrants who had come to Worcester and other American cities around the turn of the century. They were born Jews, had married Jews, and would die Jews. It was Howie Fixler's generation that represented the future of American Judaism.

When he had outlined this trip to Mrs. Greenberg, the rabbi had taken great pains to include the needs of both groups. He often felt the older and the younger members of his synagogue had little to do with one another and did not share common goals. He was determined that traveling together on this trip would begin to bridge that gap. But even before this inaugural meeting, he had heard that some older couples were adamant that they would not be along if they were expected to travel through Israel on a bus loaded with children. He was also aware that another proposed trip was competing with his own. Dr. Charles Mills, another of his stalwart members—and like Howie Fixler, an internist—was organizing a trip exclusively for couples with young children. Even before the rabbi had his chance to present his hopes for the congregational trip, a certain factionalism had already set in.

Before Rabbi Rosenbaum came to Beth Israel, a few congregational trips had been attempted; the response had always been poor. Notwithstanding the current state of the economy and reports from other rabbis that similar efforts had only recently failed (including a proposed trip by the Worcester Reform synagogue, Temple Emanuel), Rabbi Rosenbaum felt he could wait no longer. This was the year to go to Israel.

He had been at Beth Israel for six years, had started a slew of new programs, had brought in excellent speakers, and had begun to reverse the demographic trend, attracting younger families into what had been an aging, somewhat moribund synagogue. He was loved and respected by virtually all of his people; he was well known in Worcester as a community leader, devoted to social action, and was considered an exemplary Jew. By any rabbinical measurement, he was also a success: more homes—perhaps a fifth of the congregation—kept a kosher kitchen; forty people—by today's standards an incredible number of men (and a few women)—were qualified Torah readers; six *havurot* groups met regularly for study and prayer. Sabbath attendance was up; his sermons were spiritually insightful, contemporary, and often provocative. At life-cycle services for birth, bar mitzvah, wedding, or funeral, Jay Rosenbaum could be counted upon to make the moment memorable.

But it was not enough. The time had come to move beyond the small victories and to ask for more, much more, not only *from* his people, but *for* himself. He had readied his people; it was now time to make the quantum leap of faith. The longer he waited, the more difficult it would become, both for him to ask and for his people to respond. His successes, he feared, had bred a certain complacency; the people of Beth Israel were, for the most part, content with their level of Judaic commitment. But Rabbi Rosenbaum was far from satisfied.

He wanted his people to live more intensely Jewish lives, to break out of the cycle of spotty attendance, of High Holiday, wedding, or bar mitzvah frenzy, of the casual observance of *halakha*, Jewish law. He wanted to take them to the birthplace of Judaism, to have them walk where the prophets walked, to see the places told of in the Torah, to witness living Judaism as the state of Israel struggled to be a light unto the nations. In essence, he wanted to make the ancient come alive for his people of 1990s America. He wanted them to hear the voice of God, calling out to them to keep His commandments, the *mitzvot.*

And then, after the trip, the rabbi hoped for them to return dedicated to the ideal of creating a Jewishly observant community—

not in the Hasidic *shtetl* of Crown Heights or in an Orthodox enclave like Forest Hills—but in the midst of a midsize, postindustrial Massachusetts city. It would be a community that honored the Sabbath not only by coming together for services, but in being *shomer Shabbat*—forgoing travel, work, and modern conveniences on this holy day each week. In doing so, the rabbi hoped, the Jews of Beth Israel would find mutual support as they lived within a society where Saturday more typically meant Little League, lawn mowing, and trips to beach, ski slope, or shopping mall.

In recent years, Rabbi Rosenbaum had felt increasingly compelled toward this gamble by both communal dreams and selfish motives. In his own effort to live an observant Jewish life in Worcester, he found that he was often alone. His children did not have playmates from *shomer Shabbat* families. He and his wife, Janine, did not have a circle of friends who had made *Shabbos* the precursor of heaven it was supposed to be; too often it was little more than a burden to be endured.

And there was also the issue of his next contract with Beth Israel. Jay Rosenbaum had two years remaining on his current three-year contract. If he signed another contract, it would signal his intention to spend the rest of his rabbinic life in Worcester. Would he stay at Beth Israel and live in the midst of tepid observance, or go on to pursue a more intensely Jewish life elsewhere, in a place where modern Orthodox and Conservative Jews had grouped together around their synagogues—for instance in Newton or Brookline, nearer Boston? Or near his mother, in Forest Hills, New York?

Ironically, Jay Rosenbaum had discovered that being the rabbi of a Conservative congregation was exactly what was standing in the way of a fully religious life for himself and his family.

The subtle nudges of assimilation that rabbis like Jay Rosenbaum constantly battle—both in their congregations and in their personal lives—are proving a far more insidious threat to the identity and faith of American Jews than the gauntlet of blows the Jewish people have weathered throughout history. In one of our first conversations, the rabbi showed me a recent study by the Council of Jewish Federations that reported that, since 1985, 52 percent of American Jews have married non-Jews. Of the children born to intermarried couples, the study reported, over 90 percent in turn married outside the faith. Synagogue attendance is down across the country; so is the number of people who donate to Jewish philanthropies. American Jewry—just forty years ago a homogeneous monolith, within which intermarriage was virtually unheard of—finds itself fragmented, diluted, and faced with an enigmatic, precarious future. Once some 4 percent of the American population, Jews now represent a mere 2.5 percent; low birth rates and a high percentage of Jews who never marry, coupled with the breakup of traditional Jewish neighborhoods and the relentless undertow of a predominantly Christian nation, have conspired to make the maintenance of a Jewish identity ever more difficult.

The fate of the Jewish people has frequently been in question throughout their four-thousand-year history; the findings of social scientists, sifted and processed by computer, are only the latest troubling omen. Yet while statistics may present what many regard as a problem, to Rabbi Rosenbaum they also make clear the solution. Even though half of all American Jews have intermarried, the percentage of intermarriage drops in inverse proportion to the level of Jewish education and observance. The rabbi's solution is straightforward: if an American born a Jew is to remain a Jew, he or she must *live* as a Jew, within America. Cultural Judaism, ethnic Jewish identity, High Holiday attendance, and *Yiddishkeit* memories are simply not enough to sustain them.

"Are you sure, Rabbi? Rabbi!"

The question was insistent and a bit testy, as a group of older congregants cornered the rabbi at a table at the rear of the library where an urn of hot water and packets of instant coffee and tea bags provided the humble refreshment for the evening's meeting. Jay Rosenbaum smiled, as is his fashion when either complimented or attacked. "Of course we can have two itineraries. The kids will be taken care of by a counselor for activities they wouldn't get much out of. It's done all the time. Those are minor details that can be easily worked out. Okay? I'll be in touch on the phone and by mail. Let's get the hundred-and-fifty-dollar deposits in so we can start planning. I can't wait."

The room emptied quickly, and a few minutes later Rabbi Rosenbaum found himself looking out over rows of misaligned chairs. Collecting his file folder, which contained the list of those present at the meeting, and the pile of extra brochures, he turned out the light and locked the library door. Striding purposefully across the foyer that leads to the sanctuary, he then proceeded down a dimly lit hall to his office. He went around to his side of the desk, set down the file folder, and, like a mindful shopkeeper, scanned the stacks of papers and books to see if there was anything needing his attention before he closed up for the night. He then looked up at me, standing quietly on the other side of the desk. At first he appeared vaguely uncomfortable; it was not usual, I assumed, for someone to be in his office, except on official business. Then I saw another look come over his face.

It was a somewhat mannered look, as if a consequence of conscious effort. It seemed strange, and, as I did not yet know the rabbi well, it puzzled me. He appeared sure, almost cocky. I took this to be the look of a seasoned professional who could not afford to allow the vagaries of the moment to register on his face. But when he spoke, his words did not reflect the confidence he seemed to demonstrate.

"Spiritual life? We were talking about that, weren't we?" he began, answering a question I actually hadn't asked, but one that he must often consider, both in thought and in conversation. "Sure, everybody's seeking that, an inner life, some way to make sense out of their lives. And here it is, right in front of them. It's called Judaism. Is it difficult? Yes, but worth it. Judaism is a beautiful, total, wonderful, fulfilling way to live a life." He took his coat out of the closet and, hesitating with but one arm in a sleeve, continued. "My job? My job is to convince people of that, that their lives can be transformed in Judaism. That by cutting things out, they actually get more from their lives. A tough one to sell to modern-day Americans, believe me, tough. But going to Israel together will be a big step. Where else can you go and be a Jew all the time? Where you can be comfortable being a Jew? Where the plumber is Jewish and bus driver is Jewish and the lady at the ice-cream stand is Jewish? Israel. In America, the culture is always going against you. Israel. We just have to go. I know they'll come home different people. I just know it."

As the rabbi was leaving Beth Israel, Channy Greenberg was arriving at the Worcester Marriott, her lodging for the night. She was pleased with the rabbi's enthusiasm for the presentation she had made, but she was equally famished. An observant Orthodox Jew, she keeps a kosher kitchen and eats only kosher food when she is away from home. Rabbi Rosenbaum had picked her up at the airport, and one of the congregants had brought her to the Marriott. Neither had thought to ask her if she had eaten, or was hungry. Situated as she was at a hotel with a nonkosher restaurant, and in a downtown area she didn't know, Channy Greenberg bought another bag of potato chips from a vending machine and went to bed.

2

Rabbi Rosenbaum's day begins—as any observant Jew's must—with prayer. For the rabbi, *Shacharit*, the first public prayer of the new day, takes place in a small chapel at the rear of the synagogue at seven o'clock. Although he customarily sits in a pew near the front, at this service Rabbi Rosenbaum is no more than an ordinary, practicing Jew, one of a *minyan* of at least ten men, which for centuries was the necessary number and proper sex needed to conduct a Jewish prayer service. As of 1988, by a congregational vote, women of Beth Israel have been deemed worthy of being counted. It is rare that ten congregants do not show up—only the winter migration south causes problems—and if this happens certain public prayers are not said.

> *Praised are You, Lord our God, King of the universe*
> > *who enables His creatures to distinguish between night and day,*
> > *who made me in His image,*
> > *who made me a Jew,*
> > *who made me free,*
> > *who gives sight to the blind . . .*

The Beth Israel chapel is a low-ceilinged rectangular room. The left wall is red brick, the right is mostly windows, over which vertical blinds and gauzy drapes are drawn, casting the room in a muted mauve light. The textured white stucco ceiling has a single undulation to it, as if a gentle wave were washing over the heads of those present. At the front is the Ark—which to non-Jewish eyes might appear to be a large dark oak vanity with sliding doors—where the Torahs are kept. Except for the first words of the Ten Commandments, written in bold, gilded Hebrew script on the Ark and woven into a decorative tapestry, it is room universal enough to serve almost any religious group. At the back is a clock; instead of the usual numbers, the letters B E T H I S R A E L have been arrayed about the periphery, marking ten of the twelve hours of the day.

The synagogue's chapel, dating from the 1950s, generally reflects the era in which it was constructed, when Judaism was quietly entering the American mainstream. It was a time when Jews wanted their synagogues to be discreet and tasteful—certainly nothing like the richly ornamented and embarrassingly Old World synagogues that the first European immigrants built.

> *. . . who provides for all my needs,*
> *who guides us on our path,*
> *who strengthens the people Israel with courage,*
> *who crowns the people Israel with glory,*
> *who restores vigor to the weary.*

At the lectern on a blustery morning in December, Robert Weintraub—who, before he retired, owned a popular delicatessen on Water Street, Worcester's Delancey Street—was leading the group in prayer. A younger person will occasionally attend, usually to say *Kaddish* on the anniversary of a loved one's death, but the morning *minyan* at Beth Israel is usually made up of retired men like Mr. Weintraub, this morning eleven of them, in addition to the rabbi and a lone woman. Sam Cooper, who started the first automatic car wash in Worcester, is a regular, as is Yael Cohen, who was a men's clothing salesman; Dr. Sam Zaritt, a retired dentist; Dr. Earle Halsband, an oral surgeon; Stanley Baker, a used-car dealer; and Paul Gubb, who for years sold the Sweetlife grocery line. Another regular is Murray Rosenberg, a retired carpenter and one of those present at the meeting about the proposed congregational trip to Israel a few weeks before.

Each man wore a *kippah*, or skullcap, most a *tallit*, or prayer shawl. Some, like the rabbi, wore *tefillin*. In the Books of Exodus and Deuteronomy there are injunctions not only to read the words of God daily, but to have the words bound upon the arm and head. *Tefillin* do that literally. One tiny box, containing the three specific passages commanding this act, is placed upon the forehead and held in place by a leather strap; another is affixed to the upper arm by a strap, which is then wrapped about the forearm and palm. It is always the weaker of a person's arms that is thus bound—the one more in need of strengthening by God's word.

Drawn heavily from the Psalms and recited entirely in Hebrew, morning prayer is a wonderful mix of request ("Let no evil impulse control us"); humility ("Not upon our merit do we rely in our supplication, but upon Your limitless love"); thanks ("Lord, I cried out to You and You healed me"); adoration ("Acclaim the Lord, praise His name"); and ultimately exhortation to go forth into the day with confidence ("They stumble and fall, but we rise and stand firm").

As is typical of Jewish services, *Shacharit* is at once a religious and social occasion. "Reverence" would not accurately describe the mood in the chapel, for the men talked readily to one another as the prayers droned on. Neither, perhaps, would "relevance" apply. Although each of those gathered can read Hebrew and are able to recognize oft-used phrases, most would be hard-pressed to translate the prayers they were saying. They spoke more or less by rote, chanting the familiar daily ritual that no doubt meant different things to each of them.

After prayer, the men took a few minutes to socialize, their conversations finally unhampered by the formalities of their religious lives. One man, who had left in midprayer, explained on his return that his diuretic had insistently kicked in; a shoulder was acting up, a son had gotten a new job, a grandchild had been born. Murray Rosenberg, still as thin and wiry as when he was working twelve-hour days, turned his wonderfully craggy face to his friends and exclaimed, somewhat impatiently, "I gotta get going! With you guys shooting the bull, it'll be lunchtime before I get out of here."

As some of the men headed for the Newport Creamery, a restaurant up on Park Avenue, Murray traveled to his modest home on Sussex Lane, a working-class neighborhood that used to be home to far more Jewish families than live there today. In fact, statues of the Blessed Virgin and Saint Francis grace more than one well-tended front yard. Some weeks later, when I sat with him in his immaculately clean kitchen—a study in gleaming linoleum and tile, inhabited by appliances that looked as new as the day they left the store—Murray offered a characteristically straightforward view of the daily practice of morning prayer.

"Look, I was raised Orthodox; this is like a duty to me," he said. "So a lot of 'em don't do it anymore. I do. You know, I talk all the time, but I don't like to talk during the service; I try to say the prayers and say them with feeling. These other guys I'm praying with? *Machers*, most of them, bigwigs, and here is Murray, the last Jewish carpenter in Worcester. But I knew their fathers, and their fathers were rag peddlers and junk dealers. My father was a master carpenter, the best in Worcester. So these *machers* made more bucks than me, got more prestige. They might think they own this synagogue. But in *minyan* we're all Jews, all the same. Prayer? Basically I believe in prayer. I'm out there on the golf course and I get a pain. I pray right away. I say 'God! What's going on here? Help me!' "

While Murray, prayer never far from his thoughts, goes about his day (a few lines of bowling in winter, golf in warmer weather), the other morning congregants, informally called the "minyanaires," extend that communion of prayer over a leisurely cup of coffee at the Newport Creamery. But Rabbi Rosenbaum, after these forty minutes spent with his mind on God, must immediately address the needs of a young family and the day's work. While he acknowledges the obligation of a Jew to pray, he looks at morning *minyan* another way.

"The Hebrew word for describing the spirit of Jewish prayer is *kavana*, which could be translated as 'direction' or 'intention,' but actually means 'aim,' like an arrow, before you take a shot," he told me in the first of what would be many conversations about his life and belief. "You focus your energy on a point. Who steps up to the line in any game and just throws? What about your life? When you start a day with prayer, you aim at seeking the noblest outlet for your energy. People do exercise as a daily routine. Why not prayer?"

That December morning, the rabbi drove back to his home on Longworth Street, a cul-de-sac about a mile from the synagogue. Parking his Ford Taurus station wagon within, the rabbi hurried through his attached garage, which was still stacked with the boxes of his father's papers he had hoped to sort out soon after the move to Worcester six years ago. The house he hurried into was *his* house, a crucial distinction, as any modern-day rabbi would attest.

It has only been in the past two decades that rabbis have been paid enough to own a house. In times not long past, these spiritual guardians lived by the largess (and at the mercy) of their congregation in the home that came with the job. And, if there are tales of the Talmud and tales of the Hasidim, there are also tales of the rabbi's house —where rusted rain gutters, a chronically leaking toilet, peeling wallpaper, or crumbling front steps finally drove the rabbi from his pulpit. In the old days, every repair or renovation had to be approved by a housing committee. Even when the rabbi had the patience of Job, the work never got done as expeditiously as it might have had he been the homeowner. Jay's father, also a rabbi, lived in a congregation-owned house for over two decades and raised his family there. When Jay's father died of cancer in 1978, his mother was asked to move out of that home the following month.

The Rosenbaums' home in Worcester is a comfortable new split-level three-bedroom house in a newer subdevelopment. Of the ten houses on Longworth, three are occupied by Jews. If the unpacked boxes in the garage signal a certain unsettled quality to their lives here, the decor itself and the absence of any distinguishing interior-decorating touches add to that impression. The rugs and furniture are muted grays and browns. The highly polished coffee table is devoid of accent pieces. A reproduction of a nondescript landscape hangs on the wall, centered above the couch. The photos displayed on the mantel and on the bookshelves fall somewhat equally into two categories—family and synagogue events. It seems to be a house only recently moved into, one whose occupants either were not sure how long they would be staying or who hadn't yet found the energy, time, or interest to imbue it with their own distinctive mark. Before the fireplace rests a huge, plastic Fisher-Price doll house.

Janine Rosenbaum, Jay's wife, drowsy from rising a short while before, was standing at the top of the stairs as he came up from the lower level. Janine, who is forty-one years old, is a substantial, earthy woman, with an olive complexion and silky dark hair parted down the middle. She was wearing a loose-fitting cotton shift, whose long sleeves covered part of the plastic braces that extended from her palms to her forearms. The rabbi, still on the run, mentioned that he would be home at the regular time, sometime after five, but right after dinner he would be leaving for a meeting. He answered a question about a spider posed by his daughter, Shoshanah, who is three, and encouraged six-year-old David to bolt down his scrambled eggs so that they could return to the synagogue, where David attends full-day kindergarten at the Solomon Schechter Day School. Not more than ten minutes after he had pulled in, they were backing out of the garage.

Congregation Beth Israel, where the rabbi was again headed, is on Worcester's west side, an area of moderate to expensive, mostly newer single-family homes. The synagogue is just off Salisbury Street, a winding road dotted with churches and dominated by Assumption College, a small Catholic liberal-arts institution. Beth Israel, by membership, is the second-largest synagogue in Worcester—the Reform temple, Emanuel, is larger—and a notch beneath another Reform temple, Sinai, in the assumed wealth of its congregants. There is also a tiny and dying Orthodox congregation in Worcester, Shaari Torah East, near downtown; Shaari Torah West, its daughter synagogue on the west side; and Tifereth Israel, the small but active home for members of the ultra-Orthodox Lubavitcher sect. These three synagogues, because of their stricter religious views and practices, have little religious contact with the rest of Worcester Jewry.

Beth Israel counts 530 families as members and has an annual budget of $660,000. Members are required to pay $650 a year in dues, and while some balk at this, others voluntarily pay more. The synagogue is a stolid red-brick structure, initially a single story tall; library, foyer, and administrative offices surround a cement courtyard. Leading to the courtyard, four ocher-colored columns give the strange impression of the entryway to a Minoan temple. Beyond the courtyard, the sanctuary (which is marked by a narrow swath of multicolored glass panes that seem almost fortresslike in their parsimony) abruptly rises to two and a half stories, then drops a half story for the auditorium, which accommodates the larger numbers that attend the Jewish High Holiday services. An attached two-story wing, with broad expanses of windows, houses the Solomon Schechter Day School classrooms, which are also used in the after-school religious program.

Beth Israel was built in 1959, near the end of a boom in synagogue construction all across America, necessitated by an upwardly mobile and inwardly confident Jewish population. It was a time when the campus concept was in vogue for growing Jewish congregations, a time when the predominant architectural fashion was to embrace the mood of the day, eschewing any outward signal of the building's religious function. Except for a distinctive aluminum sculpture on the front wall—an abstract menorah over which is juxtaposed a stretch of razor wire (despite the powerful imagery and ready reference to the Holocaust death camps, it is there in fact to prevent access to the roof)—Beth Israel could easily pass for another low-slung office building.

Shortly after eight, the rabbi pulled into his reserved spot and kissed David, who ran off to his classroom. A few minutes later, he was seated at his desk. His office, about ten feet square, with a small private bathroom adjoining, is lined with books in both English and Hebrew, which he speaks, reads, and writes fluently. A stack of toddlers' toys brightens one corner with its clutter; it was strategically introduced a few months ago so that parents visiting the rabbi with small children in tow might be able to concentrate better with their little ones occupied. His office door is always closed, simply because it opens up on a busy corridor, along which are the office of his executive director, Richard Sobel, and, at the end, the administrative office, where one full-time and one part-time secretary work. Although Sobel is Jewish, the secretaries are not, the result of a conscious decision in many synagogues to ensure that congregation business remains confidential. While there may be differences about how people express their religious beliefs, the Worcester Jewish community is extraordinarily close-knit. Virtually every Worcester Jew is acquainted with, related to, or—at a minimum—knows something about every other Worcester Jew. If such facts as who comes into the synagogue to see the rabbi, what child has been suspended from bar mitzvah classes, or what divorce (and its ease or stickiness) is about to be granted, are to be known at all, the rabbi would just as soon have the repositories of the information be Peggy St. John and Linda Ducharme, the secretaries, young working mothers who have little or no social interaction with Jews outside of their office time.

Squarely in the middle of the rabbi's Formica-topped desk sat his day book, opened, but as it could never hold all the projects under way, the people he needs to see or call, and the specific tasks he must address, the rabbi had a companion list of things he hoped to accomplish that day. There was also a separate sheet that would key him to such general areas as "social action," "life-cycle," "ritual," "youth," and "administration." There was still another, separate, list of pastoral activities tucked into the day book—calling upon him to pay visits to the sick, to bereaved families, and to contact people he has not seen in the synagogue recently or others who he has heard might need his attention. Also, on a stack to the side rested his prayer book—the *siddur*—some Torah commentaries, and, on a lined pad, the beginnings of his jottings for the week's sermon.

As a rabbi, Jay Rosenbaum is expected to be not only the spiritual leader of his congregation; he must also be a principal representative of the Jewish community in the secular world. Toward this end, Rabbi Rosenbaum is involved in a cornucopia of causes—trying to re-open Worcester public library branches, working to improve a middle school in one of the city's poorest areas, and drawing attention to the needs of the homeless, to name just a few. Then, of course, there are the community-wide functions of the Worcester Jewish Federation, ranging from the celebration of certain Jewish holidays and Israel-oriented events to assisting Russian Jews arriving in the area. He is occasionally called upon for counseling, but most of his congregants prefer the professional services of a therapist. Also, for the infrequent seeker, he is available to answer questions about the basic tenets and requirements of Judaism.

But what is expected to take most of his time—and is the main purpose for which his congregation hired him—is tending to the religious and personal needs of the people of Beth Israel. "Rabbi" translates as "teacher," a role he is expected to carry out through a smooth and affecting *Shabbos* service, life-cycle events, the preparation of children for their bar or bat mitzvah, and continuing education for adults. Because of the significant number of Russian Jewish emigrés in Worcester, Rabbi Rosenbaum's province has expanded; in essence, he has two "congregations." One is the dues-paying members of Beth Israel; the other, a shadow group, is the Russians, whom he wants to introduce to Judaism, something denied them in their homeland. Additionally, as the resident expert on *halakha*, he is called on to arbitrate and interpret the ancient codes as they apply to Jews in modern-day America—at least for those interested or concerned enough to inquire.

This plethora of religious and community responsibilities adds up to considerably more than a full-time job. The rabbi's average work week is sixty hours.

Rabbi Jay Rosenbaum is forty-two years old. He was ordained twelve years ago after graduating from Jewish Theological Seminary in New York, which has trained virtually all of America's Conservative rabbis, past and present. Beth Israel is Rabbi Rosenbaum's second congregation; his first six years were spent at Ahavath Israel in Ewing, New Jersey, a congregation of 150 families. While there was a certain wariness within the Worcester congregation about hiring this young man—scholarly and a vegetarian, possessing a seemingly impressive record, but not especially sparkling or charismatic in person—it appeared a good fit at the time. The search committee said that while they wanted a rabbi who was reasonable and open to suggestions, they did not want one they could push around. Rabbi Rosenbaum assured them he would not be so moved. Throughout the interviewing process the search committee was struck again and again by a certain innate goodness they saw in Rabbi Rosenbaum. And, beyond his personal traits and intellectual prowess, the committee was pleased that Jay Rosenbaum was a member of the Union of Traditional Judaism, and thus part of the right wing of the Conservative Movement. Beth Israel had always prided itself on a certain conservatism in its services and practice; one longtime member told me that Worcester Jews feel religious merely by virtue of being members of this particular synagogue, even if they don't practice. Of course, Rabbi Rosenbaum would disapprove of such a convenient—and basically meaningless—compromise.

The rabbi stands about five feet ten inches tall and has the beginnings of a slight paunch—too many hours at his desk and at meetings and not enough time swimming (his only form of exercise), he admits. He is given to light-colored shirts and acceptable ties; he has at least a dozen knitted *kippot,* selected to match the day's attire (today's was dark blue, to complement his blue blazer). He wears a *kippah* constantly, whether in the sanctuary, at his desk, or shopping for groceries at the Big D with Janine. He wears roundish, silver-rimmed glasses, and, when he speaks, his voice sounds as if he is chronically congested, which he is not. His hands are delicately sculpted, his palms uncallused. His brown hair and trimmed beard are flecked with gray; he has a perfect set of teeth, which are often displayed, as he is a man with a propensity for smiling. That ready asset was in gleaming evidence on this morning as he opened the office door to greet his eight-fifteen appointment.

He ushered Adam Winter and his pregnant wife, Lynne, into the office. He shook their hands warmly and hung their coats in his closet before he returned to his side of the desk. Like many who make their appointments at this hour, Adam and Lynne have come to see the rabbi on their way to work. Adam nervously pulled out a chair for his wife, then sensing he had distanced her unnecessarily from the rabbi's desk, nudged her closer as she sat.

Adam's story began, as many an American Jew's might, with an Orthodox grandmother and grandfather, living in Flatbush. "But then my parents rejected it all," Adam told the rabbi. "I remember the day my mother used the dishwasher for *fleishig* and milk; that was the turning point." A huge man, bearlike in the way he sat crouched over on his chair, Adam had the face of an innocent. He had trouble maintaining eye contact with the rabbi, more a product of native shyness, I thought, than of embarrassment with his tale. "I went on to my bar mitzvah and actually spent six months on an Orthodox kibbutz in Israel; I could live it there, but when I came back to America, I knew I couldn't go on."

"Flatbush!" the rabbi interjected as Adam paused. "Good to meet a *landsman*. "I went to the Yeshiva High School of Flatbush on Avenue J and East Sixteenth."

"I got my degree at Pace," Adam continued methodically, not pursuing the connection, "came to Boston as an office manager, and eventually became a programmer. I guess I kept doing Jewish things, like Israeli dancing at MIT and then going to some *havurah* services, but I met Lynne and, well . . . we wanted to get married." His voice struck a lower pitch. "It seemed to suit everybody. We had a priest and Marrying Sam, the rabbi; found him in the Yellow Pages. Right after we were married, I attended synagogue services every once in a while, and I went to church with Lynne. I guess we were trying to figure out which way to go. But Christ? I tried, but I never could accept that. So many people told us just to get married and when we were ready to have children, then to talk about religion. Well, we've been doing a lot of talking and the baby is due in a couple months." His voice dropped still lower. "And my parents said, no matter what, the baby can't be Jewish because of Lynne. My mother, by the way, who now claims she's an atheist."

"The spiritual aspects of religion were always strong in my family; still are," Lynne began as Adam paused. A large woman with close-cropped curly hair, wearing a patterned maternity blouse draped over what would certainly be a substantial child, she seemed eager to present her side. "There were seven of us and both my parents were active in our Catholic upbringing; it went beyond just going to church on Sunday. We had a sense of who God was. There is a spiritual side to me; it's something I need. So when I go to services with Adam, it's all worship to me, not uncomfortable at all the way Adam feels when he's in church and hears about Christ. So I think we can do it. We can raise the child Jewish."

Here was the point of the Winters' visit to Rabbi Rosenbaum. Although they were members of suburban Boston's B'nai Shalom, a Reform synagogue in Westborough that suited their "comfort level," with its services in English and openness to the intermarried, events far outside that community and their control had breached that peace. "As you know, Israel is threatening to change the law of return so that converts and children of Reform Jews will no longer be considered Jews," Adam said. "I don't know what the future holds, but I want my child to be born a Jew. I . . . we want to raise him or her as a Jew; we've decided that." While not dues-paying members of Beth Israel, couples like the Winters represent at once the vexing problems of intermarriage and the hoped-for opportunity that the child of such a union could be raised Jewish. Because Lynne had no desire to convert to Judaism, the couple would be categorically spurned by the Orthodox; on the other hand, Reform temples have many such mixed marriages. Conservative Judaism's stance is a question of strategy rather than ideology: how best to respond to the Jewish partner in a mixed marriage? For Rabbi Rosenbaum, it meant making a fairly fast decision: Did this foray into his office have meaning, or was it merely the product of a guilty conscience? Did the child in question stand a chance of being raised as a Jew or was this no more than window dressing?

While the Orthodox, some 16 percent of practicing Jews in America, hew to the absolute authority of religious texts—conducting all services only in Hebrew and observing all major holidays—Reform Jews, approximately 35 percent, have shorter services, worship largely in English, and insist that reason and modern scholarship can shed light on the sacred texts, bringing about new interpretations in belief and religious practice. Conservative Judaism—at 43 percent the largest segment of American Judaism—has taken the middle ground, holding on to the extensive use of Hebrew in synagogue and some of the religious practices of the Orthodox, but remaining open to new insights and innovation. "Tradition and change" is their motto, and living on the edge of uncertainty is their destiny. A uniquely American expression of Judaism, the Conservative Movement bears the greatest share of the challenges inherent in seeking to live a life both fully American, yet fully Jewish. In its early days and its period of greatest growth—the post–World War II baby boom era of the 1950s— Conservative Judaism did not even consider accepting intermarried couples, nor did it have to, as there were so few. Times have changed, and intermarriage, now far more common, is a topic vigorously under debate within the Conservative Movement. Yet the Conservative Jews are nearly alone in this concern; the Orthodox, knowing where they stand, have no reason to debate the issue, while the Reform Movement long ago abandoned the dispute, accepting non-Jewish partners as inevitable.

Their differences on intermarriage and many tenets and practices notwithstanding, the three main branches of the religion are in total agreement on one concept: each believes itself to be the most authentic expression of modern-day Judaism.

The rabbi directed his first question to Lynne. "What about Christmas," he asked, "when you go to church and your child goes to synagogue? Will your child be exposed to Christianity? How will you reconcile that? There are major differences in belief and practice, are there not?" His questions did not appear at all inquisitorial, but rather seemed to be offered more as prompts for an examination of conscience.

"I think I can reinforce that there are many ways of relating to God," she replied quickly, without needing to contemplate a tactful answer. "Yes, when the child's cousins receive First Communion, we will celebrate with them, and I'm sure the child will learn a lot of Catholicism along the way, but it's not something I'm going to push. The important thing is for our child to know about God and have some relationship with Him."

"*Shabbos?*" the rabbi asked.

"We tried to light the *Shabbat* candles on Friday night," Adam replied, "but it's really a woman's job and Lynne wasn't comfortable with that. In fact, I'm not comfortable with it; my parents never did it."

A smile crept over the rabbi's face. The couple did not respond in kind. "Good! At least you're being honest about this. Not trying to impress the rabbi." And then he enthusiastically went on, as if he had decided to give this couple the benefit of the doubt, at least initially. "There are historical reasons for welcoming the Sabbath by lighting the candle, but don't worry about that for now. It is a lovely time, a ceremonial time; candles create a mood. You can have a romantic dinner. *Shabbos* is a day to rest, to pray, a time to make love: the Orthodox say three times! A time to relax after the week. There is a difference between having a family meal together and going to a Celtics game. Don't for now think of it in terms of Jewish law—you're not at that point yet. Just start with some simple observance, something with a Jewish component. Make this day special."

"Sundays were always a family day for us," Lynne said in reply. "I think I can move that to Saturday." Finally she, too, smiled.

The couple's story unfolded further. Lynne had taken a basic Hebrew course; they had attended intermarried couples' groups. She acknowledged that Christmas—this Christmas, every Christmas—would be tough.

Rabbi Rosenbaum leaned over his desk toward them. "It was tough for me and my father was a rabbi," he confided in a low voice, his eyebrows arching. "My kids have it tough. It is a basically Christian world out there; all Jews feel isolated at Christmas. It's a tough balancing act, but you're doing the right things. You're talking about it; Lynne, you are trying to learn. This child, all your children, God willing, will take their cues from you. If you do something by rote, they'll know. If it is out of conviction and means something to you, it will mean something to them."

The Winters had been with the rabbi well over an hour. As they talked, he had been making an assessment. Would they really make a serious effort to give the child a Jewish education and perform the rituals of Jewish life? The rabbi has enough Jews in name only in his congregation, but he also knows that the road to the observant life is often a winding path through the lands of nonobservance and tepid faith. The rabbi has fought Jewish birth rituals when he realized they meant nothing more than window dressing to the requesting parents or (more often) grandparents. But to do so in this case would certainly push the Winters even farther to the periphery of Jewish life.

The rabbi drew a breath and released it slowly. A decision was imminent; their workday and his own demanded it. "I don't know you well at all, but I see this is not something you came to casually," the rabbi finally pronounced. "Adam, I think your Jewish background is stronger than you think. It won't let you alone. Yes, I will help your child through the steps of conversion. If it's a boy, he will have a *Brit Milah l'shem gerut*, a circumcision for the sake of conversion, because we can't put an eight-day-old baby through the *mikvah*. I'll give you the name of an excellent *mohel*. And then, when the boy is seven or eight months old, you'll come to the *mikvah* for the actual conversion. For a girl, just the *mikvah*. Okay?" The couple grinned to each other and Adam reached for his wife's hand.

"Call me when the happy event occurs."

The rabbi was already late for his weekly meeting with his cantor, but when the Winters left, he closed his eyes slightly and knowingly nodded his head.

"Those two people are a microcosm of the American Jewish experience," he told me, leaning back in his chair, his hands behind his head. "Before marriage, I do everything I can to discourage them. *Everything.* After marriage, I try to be as welcoming as I can be. What else? It's done. But these people struck me as taking it seriously. Most don't. It takes a great effort to be a Jew today, to come to *shul*, to observe *Shabbat*. We're Americans; we don't like to be told we have to do anything. And we're up against some pretty stiff competition. After all, what else did Jews have to do on *Shabbat* in nineteenth-century Poland? It was easy to be observant.

"The key is that modern Judaism must offer an alternative— and not just try to force on people the obligation to be observant," he continued, ever the teacher. "Guilt isn't a great motivator. Nobody responds to guilt anymore. In the old days, the rabbi said and the people did, often begrudgingly. Of course, those days are long gone. And so, younger rabbis like myself have two main jobs: first, to break down the professional role of the rabbi—the distance at which people held their rabbi in the old days—and show them that we are all in this together. To be honest about the fact that it's hard for me to be observant, as it is for them. But, yes, that it's well worth it. Second, I have to convert them. Yes *convert.* I know that's a very Christian phrase, but what we are talking about isn't just fine-tuning. We're talking major, major work, the reorienting of a life-style."

In Rabbi Rosenbaum's first congregation, he was rabbi, cantor, and executive director; now, with a larger congregation and budget, he has the luxury of a full-time cantor, Stephen Freedman. It is a luxury not only to have Freedman, as Conservative cantors are in short supply, but moreover that Freedman happens to be young and good. Congregations used to look for a Jewish Pavarotti, the rabbi told me; now they want a cantor with a strong but pleasant voice so they can sing along. Cantor Freedman fits the bill exactly.

The rabbi meets with Freedman to evaluate the previous week's *Shabbos* service, plan for the next, and discuss any problems in ritual. The cantor is a handsome, trim young man of thirty-two. His dark beard and burning, dark eyes impart a certain Old Testament urgency, but a gentle sprinkling of facial freckles are reminiscent of that good little boy in every grade-school class who was constantly incensed by his loutish classmates. Cantor Freedman began by reporting that he had been hearing some grumbling from congregants about the service dragging and spilling over its expected three hours. "The *Gabbai* has to get people up to the *bimah* quicker," he said, referring to the person who assigns the readings, "so there are no lapses. But I am not—repeat *not*—going to ask them to speed up the readings," he added emphatically. "Sure, we could shave ten minutes, but there goes the beauty. If we want more people to participate, it takes longer; that's that." While in many Conservative synagogues the majority of the readings are read or sung by the rabbi and cantor, here at Beth

Israel Rosenbaum and Freedman have been working hard to expand the number of those who read. Most Conservative Jews were trained to read Hebrew for their bar or bat mitzvah, but often their education in the ancient language ends with their descent from the *bimah* in their thirteenth year.

"Another thing—*tefillin* for the seventh graders when we have *minyan*," the cantor continued. "We've bent over backward to accommodate the Reform kids from Temple Emanuel and Temple Sinai when we have it with them, made it optional, but now our kids think it's always optional and nobody's wearing *tefillin*. We're not talking prayer in public school; this is a Conservative day school. They have to play by our rules."

"Right; mandatory, Steve," the rabbi agreed. "And this is a good chance to educate the parents about *tallitot*; most of them don't know why we use them. The grandparents know; the kids know; the parents? Now, what to do about the service; that's tougher."

"All right, I'll send a letter to all the readers to ask them to speed it up a bit. But don't count on it."

The rabbi glanced down at his watch. "Speaking of time, I'm off to see the Russians."

The rabbi and cantor have developed a good working relationship, although they do not often socialize together. On his days off, the cantor leaves his *kippah* at home and goes out into Worcester as just another young father. He has a number of non-Jewish friends. He and his wife, Marion, keep a kosher home and are quite serious about their Judaic observance, but Steve Freedman would never claim to be—nor would he want to be—the totally dedicated Jew that Rabbi Rosenbaum is.

Over the past thirteen years, more than seven hundred Russian Jews have been brought to Worcester under a plan worked out by the Hebrew Immigrant Aid Society, an agency that has assisted Jewish immigrants since 1880. HIAS apportions the Russians to geographical areas, depending on the size of the resident American Jewish population, Russian family members already there, and the amount of money

the local Jewish Federation can raise to help support them. Functioning somewhat like a classic settlement house, the Worcester Jewish
Federation finds housing for the new arrivals and tries to help them
find work. While the Federation addresses most of the immigrants' secular needs, Rabbi Rosenbaum has made it one of the year's priorities to
concentrate on the religious education of this, his shadow congregation. Not knowing exactly how to go about this task, the rabbi began
by proposing to meet weekly with as many Russians as want to join
him for what he calls "News, Views, and Schmooze."

Some forty or fifty people were present in a large conference
room at Temple Emanuel, where an acculturation class had just ended,
when the rabbi first presented his idea to the Russians. He offered
them a chance to practice their English by talking about current hap-
penings in America and the world, and—the rabbi added with a
smile—Judaism. The rabbi's ready smile and willingness to help with
their English seemed to engage them, and there were many nods of
approval at his proposal. But later, when he moved to a smaller room
to inaugurate the first session of "News, Views, and Schmooze," only
five people followed him. The next week there was only one—Simon
Mats, a forty-year-old computer expert, who had been in America one
month.

On this day, a week later, there were two men in the room
when the rabbi entered. They quickly rose to greet him, their broad
Slavic faces conveying both respect and a certain nervousness. Both
were dressed in suits made of heavy wools not often seen in America,
shirts of a drab, synthetic fiber, and lumpily knotted ties. "Last week
Simon and I had a wonderful talk about his town, Bobruysk, a suburb
of Minsk, yes, Simon? I'm happy to see more of you today," the rabbi
began. He asked Abram Korotkevich, who had arrived in Worcester
just the week before, to introduce himself, which Abram did in an English far more halting than Simon's. "We can talk about anything you
like here. Maybe you can tell me something about you and your lives
in Russia." Abram immediately looked in Simon's direction, his eyes
pleading for a reprieve.

"My education, good," Simon began slowly, translating Russian thoughts into English words, "our lives, not good. We are Jews; we don't even understand what this is, but we are Jews. Like what happens my father. He in Russian army, captured by Nazis, spend three year in prisoner camp. He get out after war and KGB says: 'What, you out? You, Jew. Nazis kill Jews, so you must be spy.' So they put him back in jail. It like that, always suspecting us. But I had friend, Christian friend. He had books, Solzhenitsyn, books like that. But he write poems about 'the situation' and KGB find them. KGB ask me if I know him. We work together in summers at cement plant collective. I tell KGB nothing. But, my friend, he believe in God. God? I could not explain this thing, God, in rational way, but he believe and, yes, I find I believe, too. But he was dissident and they make him pay. But he lives. Why? I no explain. I am here with my family. Why? I think I survive because this God exists. It depend not on our efforts," he concluded, smiling warmly at both the thought and his ability to convey it, his normally pink cheeks drawn up in two tiny rosebuds. "In August 1991, it look like civil war; army on streets in Moscow. But then it go away. During this time, my thoughts about God jump and I am here."

"Yes, there is a mystery to it," the rabbi said in response to this eloquent, if broken, soliloquy. He talked slowly, and a bit loudly—as if his small audience were deficient not only in this language, but in hearing as well. "But there is something within the human spirit that surges toward freedom, toward goodness. And why? With all the hate around you, the economic problems, the meat shortage; how can this be?" Simon and Abram nodded knowingly. "I brought the Bible. Excuse me, but as a rabbi I find the stories in here often tell us a lot about what's happening today," he said, lifting the book off the table. "Maybe we will find time to have me read you a story. Hanukkah is coming; maybe next time we can talk about that. What do you know about Hanukkah?"

"Ah," Simon said, "Hanukkah gelt. I could get ice cream, go to movies. Yes, we light menorah, eight candles. I don't know much about it, but we keep some tradition. Without that, I am empty. But I know little tradition; I can't give my children. It is lost. For now."

"No, no, not lost," the rabbi gently admonished, "just put

aside. Like here in Worcester. When the Jews came, they all lived together in triple-decker houses. They did better; they wanted more room, so everybody spread out. It's hard to be a Jew by yourself. You are not alone, Simon."

The promised hour was over, and the men rose to leave. "Good, we got a good start today," the rabbi said, shaking hands with both of them. "A lot of people in America feel something is missing from their lives, too. We Jews can practice our traditions freely here, but many have turned their backs on them. Some made money, some had nice homes, the best of whatever they wanted; they moved out of the old neighborhoods and forgot they were Jews. Many are saying that is not progress, my friends. We are a people, Jews, but we have to figure out how to be Americans *and* Jews. We haven't figured it out yet; maybe you, the newest American Jews, can help us out. Next week, okay?"

On the surface, the rabbi's work with the Russians might appear uncomplicated: here are fellow Jews, the latest in a long line of immigrants to America, in need of the requisite adaptive social services. While the work is both labor-intensive for the rabbi and fraught with organizational problems—Sue Miller, the Federation's social worker, has conveyed to the rabbi her frustration and her anger at organizing events no one attends—Rabbi Rosenbaum is willing to put up with such difficulties. But he knows full well that in giving more time to the Russians with "News, Views, and Schmooze" he is embarking on a precarious venture. Congregation Beth Israel is noted for its generosity toward the Russians and concern for their plight, expressed concretely by pledges of money and time to the Worcester Jewish Federation for Operation Exodus; BI had the highest percentage of people of any local synagogue manning the phones on three pledge nights for the drive to raise money for bringing the Russians out. But with this goes their grousing that so few of the Russians have affiliated themselves with any of the temples and synagogues of Worcester. The rabbi has heard it many times and from a variety of congregants: we helped them get settled, we are helping them to become Jews; can't they join a synagogue to show their thanks? It is one thing not to attend services—many members know that well—but it is another not to join the synagogue and eventually pay dues.

By one-thirty, the rabbi was back in his car, headed toward Beth Israel and a full afternoon's schedule. Our conversation quickly turned to the Russians.

"I always try to put the Russians in context, because if I didn't, I'd be more frustrated than I am. When the Jews came from Eastern Europe at the turn of the century, they had been steeped in Judaism; many of them lived in Jewish ghettos or enclaves. They cut off their *peyos* and jumped into American life. These Russians are totally different, not at all the classic Jewish immigrants. Judaism has not been their salvation; it's been their curse. They suspect everybody and everything. So I have to proceed slowly—and with great patience. But this is virgin territory, the hope of American Judaism.

"I'm well aware that Judaism isn't a priority to the Russians right now. They're not seeking God; they want jobs. These people might have been persecuted in Russia, but at least they had good jobs. They want to work. They want to move out of tiny apartments. Joining a synagogue is the last thing on their minds. If it helps them get a job, they'll do it. They see it probably won't, so they don't. My job is not to get them on the books as members, but to make Judaism so appealing that they'll want to join. How to do that, how to do that—it's a question that keeps me up at night. And meanwhile I have to hold off my own members who want me to pay more attention to *them*. And, by the by, hope that maybe a couple of Russians *will* join."

Awaiting the rabbi on his return were a stack of pink phone message slips. It was a fairly average group: minyanaire Yael Cohen asking for an appointment so he might discuss his granddaughter's new attachment to a Lubavitcher group at the University of Texas, where she is attending college; Mattie Castiel and Aaron Mendel have had their baby, a boy, and request the *Bris* be held in the requisite eight days; two members are angry because of the tone of the letter the synagogue has sent out to those behind in their dues; a man who is civilly divorcing his wife (and whom the rabbi suspects might be withholding the

Jewish divorce in order to get a better settlement) has finally agreed to come in; a woman rabbi who wants Jay and two other Jewish males to officiate at a ritual conversion of an adult woman that will take place the following month at the *mikvah* in Worcester. There was also a call from Janine.

The day's mail had brought, along with pleas from the United States Holocaust Memorial Museum, the Friends of the Israel Defense Force, assorted travel agents, summer camp directors, Judaica purveyors, and asset managers (all of these go into the wastebasket unopened), a flurry of newsletters from Jewish agencies and other synagogues, and four invitations to Worcester-area events, all of which fall on days the rabbi is already booked.

There was a single personal letter—from a college student who was one of the rabbi's first bar mitzvah boys at Beth Israel. It was a long letter, three pages, single-spaced; the rabbi smiled as he read the line "The Torah is a crock of shit."

"At least he cares enough to take on the Torah," the rabbi said as he put the letter on a stack of correspondence to be answered. "A starting point." He took out a lined pad; it was time to begin preparing his sermon.

The evening before, quite by accident, his weekly dilemma had been solved: the theme for his *Shabbat* sermon had come to him. Once a *Shabbat* is over and his sermon has been delivered, Rabbi Rosenbaum must immediately move on to the next week's, which he will write out—in longhand—during blocks of time he usually sets aside on Wednesday and Thursday. He knows the scriptural readings for the weeks of the year almost by heart and usually uses the *parasha*, or weekly portion, as a springboard. But an article in *Newsweek* magazine about multiculturalism and a "usable past" got him thinking, and a sermon theme of "Reclaiming the Past" quickly coalesced in his mind. Now he would have to figure out how to craft and shape this idea into a twenty-minute sermon.

Puzzling over a blank sheet about how to begin, he came upon a strategy. He would first hold up popular contemporary Jewish heroes—like Sandy Koufax, Albert Einstein, and Leonard Bernstein.

And then, in effect, he would take them down a notch, putting them in their place. What is particularly Jewish about a fastball, the theory of relativity, or a musical score, he would ask. Then he would present Moses, Abraham, and Isaac as the authentic role models for the modern-day Jew. His office quiet and no one due for an appointment, he scribbled quickly, filling three pages.

As the afternoon hastened on, the rabbi attended to the small details that absorb so much—too much, he laments—of his time. He returned a series of phone calls, then went in to check with the office staff on the mailing of small aluminum-foil menorahs and sets of eight candles to Beth Israel college students. By then, the flow of his thoughts on his sermon had been interrupted, so when Michael Halzel, the principal of the Solomon Schechter Day School, found the rabbi in the administrative office and asked if he might see him immediately, the rabbi acquiesced. From the look of irritation on Halzel's face, and the clipped way he uttered "board" and "rent," the rabbi sensed that this was to be but the latest chapter in the thorny and continuing problem of how much rent the school was being required to pay to Beth Israel. And, equally—from Halzel's point of view—how the Beth Israel board had no sympathy for the school, which was running a budget deficit.

Of the 550 Conservative synagogues in America, only about 70 have full-time day schools. It is a prestigious accomplishment for Beth Israel to house a religious school, providing the optimum training ground for young Jews, the rabbi continually tells his board. In response, the board confronts the rabbi with the financial burden such a tenant places upon the synagogue. God may rain down blessings upon the Jewish people, but fuel oil is not included in His benevolence.

"Jay, look, every time we want to use the sanctuary for a service or a function and the heat is turned up, the board is charging us!" Halzel snapped once the rabbi's door was closed. "Does this show they want us here? Tell me, Jay, does it?"

At five o'clock the rabbi had accomplished perhaps half the tasks he had assigned himself for that day, seen the various staff people who had to see him, and returned the most pressing phone calls. If he did not leave now, he would be further cutting into the short amount of time he would spend with his family. There was just one more thing to be done. Marc Smith, a congregant who is the resident director of Foothills Theatre, Worcester's small but accomplished theater company, had a bowel obstruction and was in the intensive care unit of St. Vincent's Hospital. The rabbi had to see him.

Smith, a huge man whose large stomach mounded the crisp white hospital sheets, had oxygen tubes inserted in his nose and a tangle of intravenous tubes radiating from both arms, yet he managed to greet the rabbi with a huge, if tired, smile.

"Jay, sorry I had to cop out on that lunch, but as soon as I get out of here . . ."

"Whoa—let's just get you better first," the rabbi replied.

"Now about that Rosh Hashanah sermon . . ."

"You liked it, right? Agreed with everything your rabbi had to say?"

"Of course not. Look, I'm bringing in a new Gardner McKay play—more compelling than a lot of this religious hocus-pocus."

Some men of the cloth might be taken aback at such an attack, but to Rabbi Rosenbaum, these were welcome words—an opening volley in a game in which too many of his congregants are not willing to engage.

"Look, I like good theater, but give me a chance to get *my* act up on stage for review," the rabbi countered.

"Jay, what am I going to do? I'm one of your three-day-a-year Jews. I'm basically a Zionist, a socialist. Religion isn't compelling."

"So try the Bible. Great script, written by the ultimate source. Compelling as anything."

Their Talmudic debate cut short by a nurse who arrived to take Smith's vital signs and replace two bottles of saline solution, the rabbi was soon back in his car and finally headed for home. He was smiling.

"At the heart of Judaism is the parry and thrust of debate, chewing on a text, talking it over, arguing it over," he said as we picked our way through Worcester's modest rush-hour traffic. "There are many tales of fistfights breaking out in the old *yeshivot* over disagreements in interpretation. If you look at a published version of the Torah, you will see a small amount of the text—and the rest of the space devoted to various interpretations, often completely at odds with one another. Marc Smith can say his plays have more truth and that college kid can call the Torah a crock, but they're thinking about it. Judaism has a hold on them or else they wouldn't squirm."

By the time he arrived home, his children had already started eating, an eggplant parmesan that Janine had made. The rabbi slid into his place at the table, reached for a piece of bread, with which he starts every family meal, and quickly breathed a *motzi,* or prayer. As he stuffed the food into his mouth, he nodded readily, listening attentively to Shoshanah's story of how her doll had cut her finger that day and heard David retell in stop-action detail a kickball triumph. After the meal, he helped clear the dishes and then went into the living room to sit on the couch with Shoshanah and David. The rabbi had been in the house less than an hour when he got up, put on his coat, kissed both the children and his wife, and was out the door. Tonight, it was a meeting of the early childhood committee to discuss the problems in the nursery school.

When he returned at nine-thirty, the children were in bed and Janine was watching television.

"How are they feeling today, honey?" he asked as he plopped down beside her, motioning toward the plastic braces on her arms.

"The same," she said with a tired smile.

"We have to try that other doctor in Boston."

"We'll see."

"There's got to be something."

"Jay, I never see you."

3

It was a cold, brilliantly sunny Sunday morning in Worcester. Inside the new four-bedroom home at 14 Holly Circle in an upper-middle-class subdevelopment, about a mile and a half up Salisbury Street from Congregation Beth Israel, Mattie Castiel and her mother, Raquel, were arranging the serving dishes and platters upon a fine white linen tablecloth that had been spread over a table pushed against a wall in the dining room. The table was covered by a sumptuous array of food: breads and pastries, elegant almond *tishpishti* and baklava; *borekes*, a Sephardic delicacy, filled with spinach, potato, and cheese; pounds of lox sliced so exquisitely thin they were almost translucent; baskets full of plump bagels; and an imposing mound of cream cheese. Two fine, huge smoked whitefish rested on beds of crisp lettuce, their dull eyes staring at the ceiling.

In a way, the meal being laid out for the morning's guests was symbolic of exactly who Mattie and her husband, Aaron Mendel, were—unabashedly Jewish and yet not completely so. This spread, for all its abundance, was not kosher.

Outside the Mendel-Castiel home, a few cars bearing families on their way to Christian worship wound their way through the streets of the subdevelopment on their way to Salisbury Street. They were met, uncharacteristically for this day and hour, by considerably more cars coming in the opposite direction. Soon, Mattie and Aaron's driveway was full; the curb in front of their house, and that of neighbors on either side, was lined with cars. One of them was a Ford Taurus station wagon, Rabbi Rosenbaum's car.

Like his counterparts in the Catholic and Protestant clergy, Rabbi Rosenbaum is called upon to mark and individualize life-cycle events for members of his congregation. Perhaps this has even heavier weight in the lives of American Jews, who know at least something of their rich heritage—and whose living memory might encompass that devout *zayde* or *bubbe* from the old country—but who, for the most part, do not attend a synagogue with much regularity. Thus the rabbi often officiates at ritual circumcisions, weddings, and funerals for people whose faces he might recognize and can match with a name, but whose lives and souls are unknown to him.

Nonetheless, Rabbi Rosenbaum covets the opportunity to meet these marginally observant Jews under such circumstances. At High Holidays, when most Jews dutifully appear at synagogue, or during chance, fitful meetings at supermarket, drugstore, or movie theater, they will inevitably display their guilt for not being at *Shabbat* services more regularly. Rabbi Rosenbaum finds such encounters useless at best, frustrating at worst. Instead, he prefers these more intimate events, which take place in the familiar surroundings of a Jew's own home—a setting in which the rabbi is a welcome and somewhat prestigious guest who can be shown off to friends and family as perhaps a more integral part of their lives than he actually is. Rabbi Rosenbaum is always mindful of the Jewish teaching that the home is *mikdash m'at*—a miniature sanctuary—because so much ritual is set there. The home is a temple, as holy a place as any in which formal worship takes place, where far more time is spent and where far more opportunities are presented to live Jewishly.

Ideally, the rabbi would hope, these are moments of conversion within the *mikdash m'at*; at a minimum, they present a time when he, if only for a few minutes, has the undivided attention of those involved. He especially tries to make the most of such opportunities with his younger members. Because of the demographics of his congregation, this is only sound strategy. Thirty-five people died and were bid farewell, while twelve newborns were welcomed into the congregation last year. And Beth Israel hosted only six weddings.

Today's *Brit Milah*, while an occasion to do exactly what the rabbi feels is his calling, proved to be something of a burden at the end of another trying week. A low-grade viral infection, though not bad enough to confine him to bed, had sapped Rabbi Rosenbaum's energy for the past week. Out every evening at meetings, he had yet to get even one full night's sleep. Synagogue finances, the ailing nursery school, Schechter, liturgy—each occupied an evening. And, with the onset of colder weather, the pain in Janine's hands and wrists had intensified. The rabbi had tried to help her more around the house with such simple chores as emptying the dishwasher and taking out the garbage, but his time at home was so limited, it seemed he always left her with household work undone and the children to be readied for bed.

Janine suffers from de Quervain's disease, a rare condition affecting soft tissue, which has manifested itself in an acute inflammation of the tendons in her forearms. The plastic supports that she wears, which extend from her palms to the middle of her forearms, help to stabilize the tendons and moderate what has become chronic pain. To lift a child or a shopping bag is sometimes impossible, and always painful. Each Friday morning, it is the rabbi who takes the heavy Dansk dishes from the sideboard in preparation for setting the *Shabbat* table. Janine can barely close her hand with enough force to hold a pencil. She is not one to complain in public, and surely not to people at the synagogue; but the rabbi is well aware that his wife contends with constant and disabling pain.

Professionally, it had been an equally difficult week for the rabbi. When he arrived for his weekly "News, Views, and Schmooze," after an hour of preparation, not a single Russian was there. His class for twelve-year-olds preparing for their bar or bat mitzvahs was devoted to discipline, not education. (This week, a group of boys had conspired to take a vow of silence in the class, making teaching extraordinarily enervating.) Yesterday's *Shabbat*—a day of rest for the observant Jew—left the rabbi, as usual, exhausted.

This afternoon, the rabbi and his family had planned to drive down to Long Island for a wedding of one of Janine's best friends from Seattle, her hometown. Although he regularly teaches a Sunday-morning adult religious-education class, the rabbi could have had at least a partially recuperative lazy morning in bed before the class, then a leisurely drive south to New York. But the birth of Aaron and Mattie's baby had changed all that, for a *Brit Milah* required more than merely his presence; his words for this first act of a Jewish life had to be carefully prepared and shaped so as to be specific to this couple and this child.

He was presiding over the ritual circumcision of Zachary, the second son of Mattie and Aaron, both physicians in their early thirties. While it would focus on one child, this celebration in upper-middle-class Worcester brought together an extraordinary mosaic of Jewish lineage. Mattie, a dark-haired, sturdily built woman with animated features and flashing eyes, comes from a family of Sephardim that traces its roots over the past few hundred years from Spain to Turkey, then on to Cuba and Los Angeles. Quick exits, new homelands, and new languages to learn; small fortunes made and left behind; always having to stay ahead of the hot breath of anti-Semitism in its myriad varieties—Mattie's family had experienced all of this and more. Aaron, a gentler, quieter complement to his wife's higher velocity, is Ashkenazi: the czar, pogroms, *shtetl* life in Russia and Romania, a voyage in steerage to America make up his family's history, leading finally to their settling in Ann Arbor, Michigan. Rich strands of Jewish history, lived and remembered, were woven together in this sun-streaked living room, finally knit together in eight-pound Zachary—who was dressed somewhat outrageously for the occasion in a miniature one-piece black tuxedo jumpsuit, complete with a drawn-on starched shirt and a red bow tie.

As people mingled and conversation filled the air, an observer might have assumed that they knew one another well—that the Jewish camaraderie that so many non-Jews admire was being renewed and relived once more. Actually, the majority of the thirty-five people here were neither family members nor old friends. Except for a few of Mattie's and Aaron's friends from the hospital, most were members of Congregation Beth Israel—people whose names, if he were asked to introduce them, Aaron would be hard-pressed to remember. Mattie, at least, knew the names of all the Beth Israel women present, for it was through a BI program for young mothers that she—and, less directly, her husband—have been gently drawn into synagogue life.

At Rabbi Rosenbaum's initiation, Beth Israel has not only extended a welcoming hand to the Russians; the synagogue has also embarked upon an effort to reach an entirely different kind of Jewish immigrant. No, Mattie and Aaron have not come from another country; they are quite proficient in English and hardly need material support or housing. But these itinerant young professionals are being offered (some, with candor, would say lured into) the Jewish community they might never have known, or had left behind. No longer is a young couple with newborns simply invited by letter or phone call to attend a synagogue; at Beth Israel, they are "targeted."

Rabbi Rosenbaum's strategy, called Jewish Family Place, is a three-pronged campaign. It begins with "Baby Brunch," which welcomes newborns and their mothers; moves on to "Mommy and Me," for toddlers twelve to twenty-four months old; and then offers "B.I. Buddies" for two-year-olds. The religious content of each program is purposely underplayed; instead, the format offers a series of guided discussion groups to talk over the obvious—the bearing and rearing of children—while providing companionship for young mothers who are suddenly out of the workforce and homebound with infant children. Karen Rosen, a Beth Israel member, coordinates these programs; she was here this Sunday morning with her husband, Paul, a social worker and psychologist. Other young mothers who had gotten to know Mattie in the group had also come, as had Rhonda Mills, who assists Karen. Rhonda was accompanied by her husband, Dr. Charles Mills, the organizer of the competing Israel trip for young couples.

Even though Charlie and the rabbi greeted each other cursorily when the Millses arrived, the rabbi seemed not especially eager to engage either of them in further conversation.

The ceremony to be performed this morning—with the assistance of a *mohel*, a urologist named Stuart Jaffe—will relive the first major covenant of the Jewish people with the God who chose them.

By distinctively marking the penis of all male children—cutting off the foreskin—the Jews set themselves apart and promised to be faithful to their God, as He, in turn, would be faithful to them.

"As we stand here in this lovely house, I think it's important to note that we could be killed for doing what we are about to do . . ."

The room immediately fell silent at these words.

". . . that is, if we were in Hitler's Germany, or Stalin's Russia, or Haman's Persia, or any other of the hundreds of places throughout Jewish history when ritual observances were forbidden and punished," Dr. Jaffe continued. Putting his surgical duties aside and momentarily (but adroitly, and with obvious relish) crossing over into rabbinic territory, the *mohel* went on. "We perform the *Brit Milah* to once again renew our covenant with God, to distinctively mark this child as God's own." Handily embracing the half-dozen or so Christian friends present, Dr. Jaffe noted that "the event is even more holy at this time of year, seeing that the Christian world will, in not too many weeks, celebrate the feast of the circumcision of Christ, on New Year's Day."

After Dr. Jaffe finished his short monologue, the rabbi also sought to acknowledge the Christians present, though in a much different manner. "We look down at this tiny baby, Zachary, with awe and great, great respect," the rabbi began, "as we know that any male child could be the *mashiach*, the Messiah. Zachary. Zechariah!" the rabbi said, proclaiming the Hebrew name triumphantly. "What a great name! We all know the story of Zechariah. It was at the time of the building of the Second Temple; the Jewish people were discouraged about their progress and were constantly under attack from their enemies. But Zechariah had a vision of a menorah burning brightly. The menorah was the symbol of hope, of light, he told the people; proof that God was with them. And the people went on, encouraged and strengthened by his words. The temple was completed. Let this Zechariah see the light within his home," the rabbi said, taking in the room and its occupants with a grand sweep of his arms, "as he begins to grow and to study to take his place as part of the Jewish people. And soon we will call upon him to bring light into the world."

A white tablecloth had been spread on the dining-room table in preparation for the ritual. Taking Zachary from his mother's arms, Dr. Jaffe laid him squarely in the middle. Employing a clamp called a *Mogen* to hold back the shaft of the penis so that only the foreskin was exposed, Dr. Jaffe finished his preparations and looked up. Knowing what was to come next, the more squeamish eased back from the table. The *mohel*'s rubber-gloved finger soaked with wine provided both an age-old anesthetic and gave Zachary something to chew on. With a deft flick of the scalpel proffered by Dr. Jaffe, Aaron Mendel, an obstetrician by trade, marked his son as a Jew.

First there was a whimper, then a full-lunged wail; finally, led by the rabbi, a thunderous round of applause. Their arms wrapped around each other's waists, Mattie and Aaron looked down at their baby boy, their faces beaming. He was crying and so were they.

Thousands of years ago, when God made his pact with the first Jews, the wandering Israelites, He constantly asked of them, will you keep My timeless laws, or will you abandon Me and live by the whims of the secular world? Long gone for American Jews are the days of being forced for survival's sake to deny their religious heritage. In modern-day America, the choices for a Jew are not between actions obviously sacrilegious and those obviously righteous. It is not that Jews must choose again between the lesser of two evils, but rather between the greater of two goods. It is not the Cossacks or the SS beating down the door that will make the observant Jewish life difficult for Mattie and Aaron. Outside their door is a more complex challenge: their own ambitions to perform well in their chosen fields, the classic modern dilemma of the two-career family. And for Mattie and Aaron, two altruistic young healers who have readily cared for the poor and indigent in their practices and who see medicine as *their* calling, being called to live the life of an observant Jew is at best inconvenient, at worst unwelcome. And on top of these conflicts come the pressures of living in a dominantly Christian world and the fear of being considered "too Jewish" because of their religious practices.

When I later visited Mattie and Aaron, talking to each alone as the other spouse was at work, they revealed conflicting emotions about the possibility of the more intensely Jewish life they knew Rabbi Rosenbaum hoped they would now lead.

"Oh, we tried, we tried to eat kosher for a week," Mattie told me one afternoon as the hum of her microwave signaled the preparation of a meal for a family continually pressed for time. "Then it got to be too much trouble; we went out and got a pepperoni pizza. We do light the *Shabbos* candle on Friday, something I never did when I was a kid. I'd like to do more of the Jewish things, but we just don't have the time. And so many of the traditions are so outmoded; they just don't make sense anymore. I'd like to get more involved, but when I went to a meeting of the Sisterhood at BI, they asked what my husband did and it stopped there. Even most of the mothers in 'Mommy and Me' don't work now. It's an interesting group, from the JAPs to some pretty regular women. But I have so little in common with them. Listen, I can't just drop out of medicine and hope I can drop back in. My training is better than Aaron's. I've struggled too hard for this; I had to overcome the machismo in Cuba, and even here. But, believe me, it depresses me to think of going back to work, which I'm going to do in about five weeks. We're going to try to be as Jewish as we can."

I visited with Aaron one evening. When he had finally gotten his children to sleep, he readily described himself as religious. "As long as I don't have to define what 'religious' is," he added, smiling. "I'm a cultural Jew, but believe me, I'm not going to tempt fate and not have a *Bris*. It's been here for centuries. I joined Beth Israel before my first son was born, so we could have a *Bris,* so we could go there on High Holidays. I went to morning *minyan* once, but I felt out of place; I get lost saying those prayers. I really didn't have a very good religious upbringing. And on Saturdays, when we both have a day off, I don't want to spend it in *shul*. I want to be doing something with my family. We don't get enough time together now."

Rabbi Rosenbaum, the man who had so artfully initiated their son into Jewish life, had his own conflicts about the morning.

"Zachary's *Brit Milah*, for the people attending, is a chance to be part of an ancient Jewish rite, something wonderful, something rich

in tradition," he told me later. "But if it is nothing more than a ceremony and a chance for some good food? This is what keeps rabbis up at
night, believe me. Just about every Jew wants to be a Jew—when *they*
want to be a Jew. They are selective. At birth, they want to be a Jew;
when a boy or girl comes of age, they want *them* to be Jews, when they
marry, when they die. But what about the rest of their lives? Judaism
isn't just selective ritual; if it is, it's just window dressing. Judaism has
to be lived, every day.

"In seminary, we called an occasion like this *Brit Milah* a
'teaching moment.' Some of the older rabbis invoke guilt on these
powerful, beautiful occasions, wagging their fingers at the unobser-
vant. That never seemed right to me, and I don't think it's especially
productive. Instead, I try to speak to the young couple—although I'm
very aware that they are on the edges of Jewish life—as though they
were at the very center, as if the observant life that I'm holding up and
celebrating in my remarks is already theirs. Maybe I'm fooling myself,
but if I didn't somehow ask for something more, push for something
more, I couldn't do these. I'd be fooling them and fooling myself.

"How will they do? Realistically? They are very nice, decent
people. They will be members; they will pay their dues. I will see them
at major holidays. I don't think it will be much more than that. But I'm
always hoping."

At the *Bris,* another drama unfolded as young Zachary, after no more
than a minute of crying, grew quiet and contentedly began sucking on
a pacifier, freeing the guests to move into the next room to confront
the huge banquet set out for them. The guests continued to mingle
quite easily, with one pointed exception. I noticed that each time the
rabbi and Charlie Mills came within speaking distance of each other,
they seemed to drift by, never making contact. Once, I gathered, they
would have eagerly sought each other out on such an occasion. But
now, I began to suspect, the two-trip conflict had cooled their relationship.

The synagogue grapevine—as the rabbi learned after the previous day's *Shabbat* services—had it that Charlie and the young organiz-

ers of the other Israel trip already had sixteen people signed up. As of yesterday, the rabbi had only three people who had expressed serious interest, none of whom had yet sent in the $150 deposit. While Rabbi Rosenbaum is not a man to carry grudges, neither is he a saint. He moved past Charlie Mills's turned back once more and poured himself a cup of coffee. He sampled none of the food; this is not a kosher home.

The rabbi spoke briefly with Dr. Joel Kaufman, a neurologist, another of the young doctors in his congregation. They vowed—as they have vowed before—to meet to discuss what they both know is a continuing problem at Beth Israel: the small, continuing drop in the number of members and the resulting ever-larger deficits. Finally, with some embarrassment at his lack of availability, Dr. Kaufman paged through his pocket datebook and finally found a Tuesday afternoon in which an hour was free.

"Unless you hear from me, we're on," the rabbi replied, jotting down the date and time on a paper napkin.

Together with Charlie and Rhonda Mills, Joel Kaufman and his wife, Carol, represented two of the rabbi's success stories. Joel and Carol were both born into observant families, but in their early adult-hood their own Jewish religious lives had become attenuated. They joined Beth Israel, as many a young couple does, so that their children would have at least a basic Judaic education and a place for their bar or bat mitzvah. But the Kaufmans, taken with the new vigor Rabbi Rosenbaum brought to Beth Israel, became active in the synagogue. Joel served on numerous committees; Carol was this year's president of Hadassah, the Jewish women's service organization. They attend *Shabbat* services regularly and keep a kosher home.

Charlie Mills is a convert to Judaism—his father is an Episco-pal priest—and, while he and Rhonda keep a kosher home, they are less active in the synagogue, attending *Shabbat* services perhaps once a month. Both the Millses and Kaufmans are members of a *havurah*—a sort of home-based synagogue group that meets two Saturday after-noons a month for worship and fellowship. Charlie, while an ardent young convert passionate about Judaism, finds *Shabbat* services enervating and tedious; he feels he has little in common with the mostly older members of the congregation who attend regularly.

Some of the guests had already begun to leave when the rabbi, coat in hand, turned to find himself face to face with Charlie Mills.

"You know, Jay, I feel a little guilty about this," Charlie blurted out. He is a tall man, with rich brown curly hair and an elastic face that accentuated his look of little-boy sheepishness. On this occasion, Charlie looked like the kid ready to confess to his father that he had just broken the picture window with the BB gun he was not to use without permission.

"Guilty, Charlie?" the rabbi asked nonchalantly as he put on his coat.

"The trip, Jay, the trip."

"Oh, the trip. You have different interests, Charlie." The rabbi shrugged, pulling on his gloves. "Don't worry about it."

"Really?"

"Really."

It seemed a simple enough exchange, but, of course, there was far more to it than either man was then willing to reveal. Charlie Mills would later express his reservations with thoughtful candor.

"After our last Federation trip to Israel, some of us younger couples started talking about a trip where we could take our kids and just have a great time," he said. "The *shul* wasn't really doing much about a trip, although I knew Jay wanted to get back to Israel pretty bad, as he hadn't been there in twenty years. So, our theme is the family. Jay's is the congregation, and I'm sorry we seem to be in competition, but I don't want a trip where we have to play to the oldsters at BI—we do that all the time anyhow. I was on the board of directors for a while; all they do is argue about petty things: High Holiday seats, stuff like that. Look, I love Jay. I admire Jay. We are lucky to have him as a rabbi and he shouldn't have to pay for the trip himself. No rabbi does when he takes a group along. Twenty-five people should sign up; I hope they do, and then he and his family go for free. But, honestly, I wonder if I would have a good time with him on the trip, have fun with him. I see him as a man without really close friends. You can't seem to get to know him, to get beneath the surface of the guy."

A few minutes later, the rabbi bid good-bye to Mattie and Aaron, patted the sleeping Zachary on the head, and headed back to Beth Israel. Before going into the chapel to conduct his class, the rabbi stopped in his office to call Janine. He had left this morning before a decision could be made.

"I know the airfare is three hundred and twenty-nine dollars," was his initial response.

"No, it's not silly; fly," his second.

"We don't spend money on frivolous things," he continued.

"Go. Please. C'mon, honey, I want you to."

"It'll kill me if I have to drive down there today and drive back tomorrow. I can't seem to shake this thing I have," the rabbi said, his brows knitting together. He massaged his forehead.

"Don't worry about the kids. I can handle that.

"You deserve it; sometimes . . .

"We'll get the furniture too."

Nothing was more precious to Janine than Seattle and her Seattle friends—Jay Rosenbaum knew that well. His wife made few demands on him and, in turn, often had to fill in around his schedule, canceling family outings when life-cycle events occurred or when synagogue business had to be quickly attended to. He did not want to disappoint her again today. But neither could he physically make the four-hour trip to New York and not suffer for it throughout the next week. And with Janine's arms in constant pain, he would not let her drive by herself.

Finally, Janine agreed; she would fly from the Worcester airport to La Guardia that afternoon.

The rabbi was a few minutes late for the morning's adult education class: "Basic Jewish Practices: How to Do Them and Why." Five men and two women were present. He was once more smiling, radiant, as if the task of convincing this tiny class of the worth of Jewish practice was the purest pleasure. The rabbi withdrew his *tefillin* and *tallit* from their velvet pouch.

"Numbers are very important in Judaism," he began, unwinding the leather strap and then wrapping it around his left arm. "Seven times you wind the leather strap around your forearm—why? It takes away the uniqueness by having a prescribed number. It becomes generic, ordinary. It is obeying a commandment from God, quite simply. At *minyan,* we begin with a verse of ten Hebrew words, no more, no less—they translate as 'God opens His hand and satisfies every living thing with His favor.' Numbers tell you you don't have to wait for an inspiration to pray; you just pray." He smiled broadly. "The feeling will come.

"We wrap *tefillin* about the arm to symbolize that God is our power. It shows that we are slaves to no man; we are servants of God only. And when we wrap the leather three times around the finger, we say, 'I will betroth You.' Each morning God and the Jewish people are getting married. It's a beautiful symbolic act."

His tiny audience nodded appreciatively but said nothing. Finally one of the men, in his thirties and prematurely bald, screwed up his nose. "Kind of outdated, isn't it?"

"Some say that, but I look at these rituals in another way," the rabbi replied. "These rituals bind us together, as they have bound Jews together for thousands of years. To think that this has been going on for so long; there is a certain power in just knowing that. And, my little contribution, my wrapping the *tefillin*, will be built upon in centuries to come. It provides a structure in your life. Think of the Jews wandering in the wilderness. They had just been freed from captivity. They could have just wandered off. Instead, they moved in a tight formation, with the ark in the middle. They had discipline, a common purpose.

"I prefer the large *tallit*," the rabbi continued, unfurling his white prayer shawl, which is accented with rich blue stripes and threads of blue and silver. "It's a symbol of God's protection. I like being wrapped in it." He swirled the *tallit* behind him, then pulled it up from his shoulders to cover his head. "I have this image of God as an eagle," the rabbi continued, his voice muffled and only a small piece of beard peeking out, "protecting me, hovering overhead. He doesn't expect us to fly solo."

Again the group was silent. Finally a woman spoke.

"When the feeling comes, what will it feel like? Will I know I'm feeling it? Will I, Rabbi?"

4

The rabbi awoke on the morning of 7 Tevet—known to the rest of the country as the fourteenth day of December—with a terrible cold and issues of life and death burning in his mind. Jacob. Dr. Kevorkian. Euthanasia. Life-support systems. Somebody's Aunt Bessie begging to die.

It was a Saturday morning, *Shabbos* morning, and Rabbi Rosenbaum was once again ready to do his part to keep the challenge of Judaism before his people. If there were intellectual issues burning in his mind, his nasal passages were equally aflame. His throat had been etched raw overnight; his head was pounding and his joints ached. The infection, viral or bacterial, that had been simmering for the past few weeks had found its full force. That his heart was heavy with disappointment at the congregation's meager response to his Israel trip was a separate issue entirely. Early, and repeatedly, Jay Rosenbaum had learned from his father that disappointment was the constant companion of the ancient prophets—and the modern-day rabbi's portion as well.

Dressed in one of his half-dozen dark, conservatively cut suits, he softly closed the bedroom door on his still slumbering wife and headed for the kitchen. He passed the dining-room table, set the day before for the *Shabbos* meal with the Rosenbaums' Dansk china. Because they are vegetarians, the Rosenbaums do not need to maintain two sets of dishes for milk and meat products; during the week they use utilitarian, break-proof plastic plates. The best is reserved for *Shabbos*. One of the burners on the stove was on, as was the oven, set to two hundred degrees, keeping warm the tamale pie Janine had baked the afternoon before. Lights were burning in Shoshanah's room and the bathroom. The lights in David's room and the living room were on a timer and had gone off automatically last night. All that remained of the *Shabbos* candle, which had been lit at sundown on Friday, was a charred piece of wick at the bottom of its glass holder on the mantel above the fireplace in the living room.

The rabbi made himself a cup of tea and ate a small piece of honey cake. He put on an overcoat, then slipped on another jacket, as well as another pair of pants—these made of waterproof Gore-Tex—and over-the-ankle rubber boots. Janine and the children would follow later, in an hour or so. Shortly after eight o'clock, the rabbi stepped out of his front door and into the cold, pouring rain. It was the beginning of the day that was, as Abraham Heschel extolled, "A reminder of every man's royalty; an abolition of the distinction between master and slave, rich and poor, success and failure . . . the Sabbath is . . . the presence of eternity, a moment of majesty, the radiance of joy."

After I had been through several *Shabbosim* with the rabbi, I asked about his sentiments on this day. He immediately struck what would become a familiar chord, the liberation that can come from religious prescriptions, most pertinent on *Shabbos*.

"If you can't turn on a switch, you can't get in a car, can't light a fire, you're bound to have your normal life altered—and with all those restrictions comes the holiness, the differentness of this day," he said. "There is a certain atmosphere about *Shabbat* that no other day of the week has. I need to do this, to observe Jewish law totally on this day. It is the baseline for me. Now, I must admit, it's not always the great spiritual day it should be. And I know it's tougher yet on Janine—she has to do most of the preparation—but without this pause at the end of the week, how can Jews be Jews? But you have to work at it, not just observe the ritual; it doesn't come automatically. But properly done, and done with feeling, *Shabbat* is a condensed version of the highest ideals of the Jewish people. In a word: perfection."

Rabbi Rosenbaum's path that morning, as it is every Sabbath morning, took him out Longworth, right on Amherst, and another right on Kennecott, which turns into Jamesbury near the synagogue. He passed the homes of a number of his congregants—the Silvers, the Fishers, the Goffs, Mrs. Pulda. Some families of Beth Israel consciously bought houses within walking distance of their *shul*, but the number, the rabbi estimates, is not high. Even the Silvers, who are very active at the synagogue, drive to services. No, it is more about finding the right house, the affordable house, the right school district, the correct number of bedrooms and garage spaces that today motivates the Jews of Beth Israel—like most Jews in America—in their search for a dwelling.

Of course, it was not always so.

When the first substantial number of Jews arrived in Worcester in 1875, the ground that Rabbi Rosenbaum covered this morning was owned by the Ellsworths, a family of sturdy Yankee Protestants who farmed the gently rolling land extending from Beaver Brook to the narrow dirt way called Salisbury Street. Not only would no Jew have had reason to venture this distance from the city limits; few others traveled so far out of what was then Worcester's hub.

Many of the early Jews of Worcester had come from the Pale— the western section of czarist Russia designated as the only place Jews could live in the kingdom. In this swath of Eastern Europe, which takes in parts of modern-day Russia, Poland, Ukraine, and Lithuania, Jews led precarious lives. They were forced to withstand the pogroms that arbitrarily swept over the land in the wake of the assassination of Alexander II in 1881 and to live under impossible economic restrictions. A Jew could not work in industry, agriculture, or the government; as a result, most were village merchants, tailors, craftsmen, or itinerant peddlers.

In the three decades before World War I, fully one-third of all Europe's Jews came to America; they made up one-tenth of all United States immigrants of that period. By the time this incredible exodus of Jews abated, America found itself home to the largest number of Jews ever assembled anywhere in the world.

Dire poverty fueled their great migration from the Pale and

Eastern Europe, but if the Jews of the *shtetls* of Smolyan, Utian, Roki-
shuk, and Balbirishuk had little to carry in their rucksacks and bun-
dles, they brought a rich legacy to the east side of Worcester, a legacy
forged through thousands of years of tradition and generations of living
in close-knit villages. And, within that tradition, nothing was more
precious than *Shabbat*. For six days a week, they toiled to earn their
humble fare. On the Sabbath, they were reminded of their royal kin-
ship with God. *Shabbat* confirmed the sacredness of every Jew. Special
food and dress, combined with the mandate to rest, to study, and to
worship, provided refreshment, insight, and the inspiration to go on as
Jews. Temporal powers may have overtly ruled their lives, but in their
Jewish community, on every *Shabbat* as they attended *shul* and reveled
in the *Yiddishkeit* of their villages, the Jews were royalty once again.

   And so, when the Jews came to Worcester—usually encouraged by one of their own brave villagers (most often a single young
man) who had ventured before them and sent back glowing reports of
the business possibilities in a booming industrial city—they transplanted their *shtetl* life from muddy village streets to Water Street,
which had been the home of waves of immigrants before them.

   As the Swedes and Irish moved out, Jewish clothing stores and
furniture stores, tailor shops and barbershops sprung up along Water
Street; Jewish butchers, junk men, freight handlers, and tanners
crowded into the tenements above the stores and then spilled out into
triple-deckers on the surrounding streets to accommodate growing
families. There were already eight small synagogues in Worcester,
three within walking distance of Water Street, when a group of successful men in their thirties and forties—most of them in the clothing
industry—borrowed from the elegant design of Congregation Kehilath
Jeshurun on New York City's East Side to build a monument to their
faith and prosperity. Shaari Torah, dedicated in 1904, would prove to
be the true mother synagogue of Worcester: Orthodox, of course (Reform Jews were lesser in number in America and mostly of German
extraction, and the Conservative Movement was still twenty to thirty
years away from widespread popular appeal), but not "old country" Orthodox as the other Worcester synagogues had been. Shaari Torah

would address the needs of a younger generation; not only Hebrew, but "the American language" would be heard within its walls, its founders declared.

As the Jews of Water Street and Shaari Torah grew more economically and socially secure, they left their crowded tenements and the triple-deckers around Water Street—places that had once seemed so spacious—and made for Worcester's west side, to rent apartments or buy modest homes. Here on the better side of town, America's openness to new thought and new expressions of belief spawned a Jewish religious diversity that the European Jews could never have imagined. A new synagogue founded in 1921 was called—transitionally, it would prove—"non-Orthodox." It was Temple Emanuel, and would be the first Reform congregation. A second Orthodox synagogue was founded on the west side a few years later to take care of the ever-growing number of Jews who lived there. This was Congregation Beth Israel. Twenty years later, in 1954, BI would acknowledge its progressive leanings and affiliate itself with the newly formed and burgeoning Conservative Movement.

As the miracle of America's interstate highway system found its way to the heart of Worcester in the late 1950s, Shaari Torah, the still grand east side synagogue, saw its neighborhood cut in half by a broad swath of asphalt. Two other synagogues were demolished outright. But it was not just a system of roads that speeded Shaari Torah's demise. The triple-deckers, tiny homes, and tenements on Water Street were by now almost totally bereft of Jews; attendance at services had fallen precipitously. Finally, attempting to reclaim some of the west siders who had become Reform or Conservative Jews, were no longer affiliated with a *shul,* or, regardless of their belief, would no longer venture for services and education classes into a neighborhood now considered dangerous, Shaari Torah bowed to the inevitable and bought a *used* synagogue on the west side in 1959. The synagogue by the interstate was to be known as Shaari Torah East, the new group, Shaari Torah West. The west side building was owned by Congregation Beth Israel, which, while Shaari Torah was losing members, had been riding the tide bringing hundreds of Worcester Jews—tired of the rigors of Orthodoxy and finding their children reluctant to worship and learn in such an uncompromising atmosphere—to a new and uniquely American expression of Judaism.

Beth Israel's original building had been in keeping with the spirit of prevailing religious architecture, which quietly and consciously resembled many of the Catholic churches of the 1920s. Its stately amber brick facade looked out over Pleasant Street, a busy main thoroughfare. But in post–World War II America, up-and-coming congregations no longer considered it propitious or necessary to situate a synagogue in public view. And so the new Beth Israel was tucked away in a growing, more prosperous and residential Worcester neighborhood. The synagogue itself occupied just one space within a complex holding classrooms, offices, childcare rooms, and a huge auditorium. It was, in effect, a modern Jewish house of worship and social center all in one. Included in the design of the sixteen acres that Beth Israel had purchased on Jamesbury Drive was a consideration anomalous to previous generations of American Jews: generous room for parking lots.

As Rabbi Rosenbaum approached the building at eight twenty-five that Saturday morning, there were still no cars in any of the synagogue's three main parking lots. But he was well aware that before his opening words at nine o'clock, and then as the service progressed, the cars would come. Acknowledging that suburban sprawl had replaced the urban compactness of the old Jewish neighborhoods, the Rabbinical Assembly of the Conservative Movement issued a ruling in 1955 permitting observant Jews to drive to synagogue on *Shabbos* if the distance was too great to walk—stipulating that should be the only use of a car that day. Driving on *Shabbos* is something of a moot point among the Beth Israel congregants; the rabbi estimates that not more than four or five families (in addition to his own) routinely leave their car or cars in the garage throughout the Sabbath.

While the level of Jewish observance in Worcester is cause for concern among all Worcester rabbis, the city is generally considered a place where Jews like to live. There has not been a noticeable Jewish flight out of the city to suburban communities, and generations of Jewish families have been—and still are—city residents. In fact, there are virtually the same number of Jewish families in Worcester today as there were a century ago. A substantial number of Jews are among the most influential people in Worcester; it is a city with a noticeable "Jewish presence." One day, as I traveled back to the synagogue with the rabbi, after he had attended to some matters at the Jewish Community Center, he talked about the Jews of his city.

"When you realize what an impact the Jews of Worcester have made, and continue to make, on this city, it's amazing," he told me. "What are we, maybe six, seven percent of the population? But Jews are leaders in philanthropies, in culture, in education, in business, in politics; Worcester's had three Jewish mayors, including the current one, Jordan Levy, who is a member of BI, but not especially involved. We have John Honig, who has a large garment factory; Carlton Palley, who's big in the candy business; Joe Freilich, also quite wealthy—but none are active in the *shul*. Our impact is far beyond our numbers. Jews are the movers and shakers in Worcester, but do we see them as being practicing Jews? Sadly, no.

"But ask any of these movers and shakers if they consider themselves Jewish. They would be offended by the question. 'Of course I'm Jewish!' Yet, except for the big Jewish holidays and the life-cycle events in their own families, they really could be anything. Their Jewishness is to some extent tribal, and to some extent bigotry. Jews are better than other people, they would say—and usually the most non-religious would say this loudest. 'We have strong families; we educate our kids.' But I tell them, 'How long can that last when there's no "we"?' I tell them, 'If you're Jewish you have to do something about it.' Then they go nuts when their son or daughter comes home with a non-Jewish partner."

At nine o'clock, his *tallit* draped over his shoulders, but thrown back to leave his hands free, the rabbi stood before the sanctuary lectern on the *bimah* to begin the service. The *bimah* is a raised platform where the rabbi, Cantor Freedman, the first of the lay readers, and the synagogue president, Dr. Manouch Darvish, a children's dentist, sit together overlooking 476 theater-type seats upholstered in a light blue fabric. That day, about 60 of the seats were occupied.

Beth Israel congregants dress well for the weekly *Shabbat* services—the men in suits and virtually all the women in fine, often large, hats that harken back to the fashion of another decade. They were all gathered in a sanctuary that is roughly as high as it is long and wide, done in light tan brick and blond wood. The stained-glass windows, in a line a third of the way down from the ceiling, appear from the inside to have been randomly placed; no design or form is apparent. On the wall near the rear of the sanctuary are memorial nameplates in raised bronze—placed here after a donation of $250 or more—each with its own small bulb, which is lighted on the anniversary of the named person's death. On the wall behind the *bimah* are large Hebrew letters, the first words of each of the Ten Commandments. Beneath the letters, and at the top of a three-step approach, stands the Ark.

While air-conditioning might cool the sanctuary in summer and forced air warm it in winter, while indirect lighting may illuminate the space and finely woven carpeting grace the floors, at the doors of the Ark, modernity stops. Here, behind a folding door, itself faced with a rich velour fabric, five Torahs reside. Each is a complete rendition of the first five books of the Bible—Genesis, Exodus, Leviticus, Numbers, and Deuteronomy. Each has been hand lettered, in Hebrew, on a parchment scroll, little different from the way the first Torah was transcribed. And, regardless of architectural fashion or its place within the "campus," the sanctuary faces east. East toward Jerusalem, the Holy City. East toward Israel—as the Torah proclaims—the only true home of the Jew.

With the words of the *Birchot Hashachar* and *P'sukei D'zimra*, the *Shabbat* service was under way. As Rabbi Rosenbaum led the prayer, he peered intently at the *siddur* before him. When he was not reading, however, he allowed his gaze to wander over the faces of the people before him. He knew quite a bit about the regulars—both about their exterior and interior lives. For instance, he knew that Gene

Lewis, whom he regards as an extremely ethical businessman, had some years ago fought an ugly lawsuit after he was sued by the town near Worcester where his chemical plant is located. Lewis, who loved Israel so much he was ready to make *aliyah* in the 1950s and move there, decided against it when the Israelis wanted to debrief him about top-secret chemical processes he worked on during World War II. Lewis successfully fought the lawsuit, handed the business over to his children, and continues to be active both here at Beth Israel and in state and national Jewish organizations. This man, in the rabbi's mind, was a gracious and generous man, a good and righteous Jew. He knew that Murray Rosenberg, who has done beautiful carpentry work for Beth Israel and faithfully attends morning *minyan*, had a wife and children who were not nearly as enthusiastic about Judaism as he was. Murray loved to lead the *minyan*, but his Hebrew was so coarse that the more sophisticated members of the old guard found it openly offensive. Murray—outspoken, but solid and good indeed.

He knew that Bruce Herzberg—at forty-three, one of the younger regulars—was a secular Jew ten years ago, and a marginal member of the Reform synagogue, Temple Sinai. Stirred by his own inner yearnings and brought along by the rabbi's gentle urging, Bruce had become one of the few *shomer Shabbat* of Congregation Beth Israel. He and his wife, Patricia Bizzell (she was born a Christian, but has converted), adopted two Korean girls, who attend Schechter. It was hardly a classic Jewish family, but now a fervently observant Jewish family nonetheless. The rabbi knew that Abe Kravitz, a retired kosher butcher and, at eighty, one of the oldest members, wants—and needs—to stay involved at the synagogue and can be called on to pre pare, serve, or clean up after any event requiring food. He knew that David Strebnick, in his early forties—unmarried, a bit of a Peter Pan, and the seemingly perennial bachelor—was finally talking about getting married to the woman he'd been dating for eighteen years. (Strebnick's beautiful voice and skill as a guitar player have made Beth Israel's Purim presentation a Worcester classic.) And he knows a lot about Judy Wolfe, one of the few women who are here for the entire service. Judy Wolfe, who, with the rabbi's help, has struggled to come to terms with what she considers the inequities toward women inherent in Judaism. Judy Wolfe, who would unabashedly and un-equivocally state—to anyone within hearing distance—that Rabbi Rosenbaum has changed her life and made her a kosher, observant, and happy Jew.

Such were the rambling thoughts of the rabbi as he looked out over his small flock on this Saturday morning.

And there, *davening* with gusto, rising up on the balls of his feet and bowing low—a gesture known as *shukeling*—was Carl Aframe. Carl is a successful bankruptcy lawyer, a man the rabbi does not know especially well, but who has been attending more regularly—and is one of those signed up with Charlie Mills on the proposed family trip to Israel next summer. He is known as one of the most successful and most aggressive bankruptcy lawyers in Worcester, a voluble, outgoing man who loves an audience, loves to work a crowd. But here in *shul*, he seemed alone, standing where he did, many seats and rows away from the other congregants. His face bears mute evidence of the ravages of adolescent acne, but he is a handsome man; his greenish blue eyes open wide, intent upon the Hebrew words in his *siddur*.

When I later went to visit Carl in his attractive suite of offices in a downtown building, I found there were other scars, not so readily visible, that had been visited upon him in his youth as a Jew in Worcester.

"I have a problem with that place Beth Israel, but you know what? My hunger for Judaism is just too strong," he said. "I need to be there, to pray. And I need to really emotionally get into it, to *shukel*; I'd like to put the *tallit* over my head and just get buried in it, but peo-ple would start to talk about this religious fanatic, Aframe. They prob-ably talk about me anyhow. Let them. This is Worcester.

"Worcester is a many-tiered society for Jews. My family? My father was Abe Aframe, a cattle dealer; he drove a truck, picked up cattle, went to the auctions. He had manure on his boots. We were on the bottom tier and it hurt. I decided early on I was going to show everybody; I was going to make it in Jewish Worcester. I went to law school; I set up my own practice. I can buy six-hundred-dollar suits.

But it turned out to be hollow. What else was there in life? So I went to Alan Ullman, this rabbi who doesn't have a congregation, but is really into educating Jewish adults—and Alan really breathed life into the Torah for me. He became my guru, my gateway back to Judaism.

"That's fine for inspiration, but you need a congregation to worship with—and this is mine. I don't think it's a congregation with a lot of people who have really deep religious feelings—it's the acceptable thing for a Jew to do. I'm getting into it more and more. As for my rabbi, Jay? Listen, this is one wonderful guy. But he's a bit wooden about it. Is he a rabbi, and maybe not a human being? So, for Israel I signed on with Charlie. Listen, Jay has to pay attention to the old guard here—they're tough, and demanding. I just didn't want to go to Israel and have to have him catering to them. I wanted a religious experience. And I wanted to have some fun."

Carl Aframe sat down as the service moved on. The Conservative *Shabbat* morning service he was a part of is a wonderful and rich blend of praise and baleful cries to God, marching orders to greatness, and repeated thanks—for delivering the Jewish people, for giving them the continuing guidance of the Torah, and for the grace of another *Shabbat* to rest and open their minds and hearts to God. The majority of the service is in Hebrew; many prayers and readings heard in English are also spoken in Hebrew. As was evident at morning *minyan*, the reverence and contemplation of the weekly religious experience of the Christian world is foreign to the Jewish experience of worship. Every Jewish religious event is also a social event, an ingathering of God's chosen. Accordingly, there is nothing wrong with talking to the person next to you; nothing wrong with having an extended conversation that weaves, like a piece of sturdy twine through a fine tapestry, in and out of the service. And there is no stigma attached to coming late, timing one's arrival so as to be seated for what is considered the "good part," the Torah reading and the rabbi's sermon—in other words, the last half of the three-hour service.

Despite the apparent casualness, the Conservative service has a unique decorum about it. In Orthodox synagogues, services can be noisy, nearly unmanageable affairs that often require the cantor (who typically leads the service) or a lay reader to pound on the lectern to regain order. Conservative services—marrying the old world and the new—are actually *conducted* by a rabbi, but are more like American Protestant services (except for the casual conversations) than classic Jewish worship. Aesthetics and convention—middle-class American, and not Jewish norms—prevail. And the service is supposed to move along crisply.

At the center of the service is the reading of the week's Torah portion, or *parasha*. Beth Israel prides itself on being a traditional Conservative synagogue, reading the full portion each week so that, by the end of a year, the Torah has been read through completely. More lenient congregations read but a *parasha*, a third as long, each week, completing the Torah in three years and their weekly service in two hours.

When the Torah is taken from the Ark (it is a considerable honor in itself to be asked to open the Ark and retrieve the scroll) at about nine forty-five, and again when it is returned after the readings about an hour later, it is paraded through the aisles of the synagogue as congregants show their respect by touching it with the edge of their *tallit* or prayer book, then kissing the edge that has come in contact with the Torah. Touching the Torah directly is considered irreverent. The *parasha* is divided into seven sections, each of which can have its own reader—if, as at Beth Israel, there are enough qualified readers— who receives an *aliya*, or is "called up" to read the word of God. This is not arbitrarily done; the readers are notified well in advance and are expected to practice their part. Nor is the invitation to read an honor given to everyone; indeed, some Beth Israel congregants would maintain that the old guard has too much say in who is chosen and who is not. To be able to read at this length and with some fluency in Hebrew is considered an accomplishment; and so, when Edward Siff, a school administrator, completed his section on this morning, he was congratulated with handshakes and pats on the shoulder as he returned to his seat.

Once the Torah reading and an additional reading called the

Haftorah—taken from the prophetic books of the Bible, such as Isaiah and Jeremiah, and bearing on the Torah reading—have been completed, Rabbi Rosenbaum steps to the lectern to deliver his sermon. It was now close to eleven o'clock.

Before him were 146 people, almost equally divided, with perhaps a few more women than men. Each man wore a *kippah*, of which there were a rich assortment in evidence: some were of a single color, made of a synthetic material resembling satin, and are more than likely from a bar mitzvah, which would be noted in an inscription on the inside. Others were of rich brown and blue knits; still others had intricate gold and silver thread patterns, perhaps a souvenir of an Israel trip or a visit to a good Judaica shop. Covering most men's—and a few women's—shoulders were *tallitot*, some brought along for the service, some borrowed from the prayer-shawl rack outside the sanctuary doors.

The day's *parasha*, taken from Genesis and called *Vayiggash* (each is named by the first Hebrew word of the reading), is a sprawling document, within which the rabbi had sought to find a passage or theme to tie in with something topical. In the past, he had used the story of Abraham and Isaac to summon his people to a more observant life, and placed before them Maimonides, Abrabanel, and Heschel as contemporary Jewish guides, while scolding Alan Dershowitz and his book *Chutzpah* for failing to put forward Jews who live observant lives while confronting contemporary issues. He had even retold the story of the worship of the golden calf in the context of the debate over Robert Mapplethorpe's photography exhibition to dramatize that art's beauty could never be considered without its moral content. His congregants expect a mix of religion and modern realities—Jewishly based, informed, and interesting. And they don't want to be preached at or down to.

All week long Rabbi Rosenbaum is a teacher—in the Solomon Schechter nursery; in bar mitzvah, Hebrew high school, and adult-education classes; in talks to the retired at the Jewish Home or to the Russians. Nonetheless, *Shabbat* calls him in a special way, on a special day, and with the greatest number of his people gathered. On this *Shabbat*, the rabbi began by quoting Jacob, first in Hebrew, then in

English: "It is enough; Joseph my son is yet alive; I will go and see him before I die." Pointing out that Jacob was by then quite old and might be expected to think that death was at hand, the rabbi argued, "There is a big difference between Jacob *accepting* death, knowing his beloved Joseph was alive, and saying he actually *wanted* to die, and die now—when he was happy, and ahead of the game in a life that had seen so much pain; die now as there was no other frontier in his life that he wanted to conquer. Accepting death. *Wanting* it to happen. Very different. We all have to think: does our own desire for a peaceful death give us the moral right to somehow arrange for it?" A pause was called for on the page before him and the rabbi looked out over the congregation.

The hinge between the ancient world and the modern was a silence of five seconds. The inspiration for this part of the sermon was still fresh in his mind.

Benjamin Hillman* had been a loyal member of Beth Israel for years; he had helped to raise the money for the new synagogue and had served as its president for many terms. A slender, peppy man, he had built his printing firm into one of the biggest in Worcester. He had substantial real estate holdings and was a generous benefactor. Just two days ago, the rabbi had paid a call to the Hillmans' sprawling home on one of the west side's best streets. Ushered through the foyer by their black maid, the rabbi found Mirna Hillman at the other end of an expanse of living room, just a tiny dot of a woman, dwarfed by a grand piano. But even at a distance the look on her face was unmistakable. Indeed, as their son (who had called the rabbi) had said, his mother was deeply depressed.

The rabbi had talked quietly to Mirna for ten minutes as she sat, unmoving, dressed in an expensive silk dress, a single strand of pearls at her neck, her head bowed between the arms of the aluminum walker she now required to move about her home. He conveyed the congregation's concern about Bennie, assuring her that he was remem-

*Throughout the text, asterisks denote pseudonyms.

bered in their prayers and was often recalled for all the good work he had done for Beth Israel. As she hobbled into the bedroom, leading the rabbi, they were greeted by her husband's somewhat startled, sweetly vague smile, indicating that he knew some sort of friend had come but could not figure out exactly who. He looked quite healthy, pink cheeked. Only his eyes were cloudy.

"Why should she have to go through this day after day? She can't put up with it much longer," Rachel, the wife of Benjamin's son, pronounced angrily when the rabbi came back into the living room. "They ought to have a pill for this; let poor Bennie out of his misery. This Alzheimer's will kill her before it kills him."

"One shudders to think what would have happened if deathmaster and euthanasia peddler Derek Humphry would have been around to hear Jacob's fateful words." The rabbi continued with his sermon as he planted his feet firmly on the carpeting behind the lectern. " 'Here, Jacob—with my compliments—is a copy of *Final Exit,* my best-selling book. It made number one on *The New York Times* bestseller list; with all the wonderful publicity from my good friend Dr. Kevorkian, it'll get there again. In it you will find a quick and painless release from your ordeal.' Or what if Dr. Kevorkian were there in Jacob's time? 'I'll help you out of your misery, old man. I have heard your cry and I understand completely. I have the solution in this little machine that will quickly, painlessly send you on your way.'

"As a matter of fact, neither of these men was there, and Jacob went on to live seventeen more years. Thank goodness. But today we face questions about life and death that Jacob didn't have to think about. We have made great medical advances, we have conquered many diseases, and we wonder when we can simply say that enough is enough." The rabbi hesitated for emphasis, then went on: "Jewish law is clear and reasonable—if a person is dying, you cannot unnecessarily extend that life. We are not to fight death at any cost. On the other hand, if the person—regardless of condition or appearances—is not in immediate danger of death, then we must try to save them. Medical advances have made this more complicated; we have life-support ma-

chines that Jacob's age did not have. But this much is clear: there is
no reason to take a life. Ever. Especially when a person says, 'I'm too
sick or too depressed, I *want* to die.' How easy it is to lose your bearings
at a time like that. Many of us have been faced with friends and relatives who are terminally ill; we wonder what is best for them. But we
have to think clearly in situations like that and remember that for a
Jew suicide and murder—regardless of what people in the general
society say—cannot be moral solutions to the wide variety of human
sufferings.

"And let us always be careful that the hope for a peaceful passing for the dying is not simply motivated by the desire for a more
peaceful and trouble-free life for the living."

The sermon had taken its usual twenty minutes, and the *Shabbat* service moved on toward its culmination:

The happy, joyous tone of the *Amidah:*

> . . . Our God and God of our ancestors, accept our
> *Shabbat* offering of rest. Add holiness to our lives with
> Your *mitzvot* and let Your Torah be our portion. Fill our
> lives with Your goodness and gladden us with Your tri-
> umph. . . . Lovingly and willingly, Lord our God, grant
> that we inherit Your holy gift of *Shabbat* forever, so that
> Your people Israel who hallow Your name will always
> find rest on this day. . . .

The marching tone and call to arms of the *Aleinu:*

> We rise to our duty to praise the Lord of all, to acclaim
> the Creator. He made our lot unlike that of any other
> people, assigning to us a unique destiny. . . . And so we
> hope in You, Lord our God . . . perfecting earth by Your
> kingship. . . . Sovereignty is Yours in glory, now and for-
> ever. . . .

The amazingly positive tone of the *Mourner's Kaddish*, sung entirely in Hebrew and in which there is no mention of death, only affirmations of life and God's goodness:

> *Yitgadal v'yitkadash sh'mei.* . . . Magnified and sanctified be God's name: in the world which He created according to His will, may His kingdom be established. . . .

The service seemed to move along more briskly now. Responses were louder; there was less talking among the congregants. A long morning's adoration was coming to a close and with it came both a sense of relief and of satisfaction.

For the final song, the *Adon Olam*, the younger children—who had been in nursery or classroom, depending on their age (or hanging out in the halls and foyer, depending on their interest)—streamed onto the *bimah*. David and Shoshanah Rosenbaum joined their father, who was standing some distance behind the lectern. Shoshanah, struck with a sudden shyness, tucked herself into the shroud of his *tallit* and peeked out. David, a *kippah* decorated with a swirl of Ninja Turtles chasing one another atop his bristly blond hair, stood bolt upright in his place of honor.

At the conclusion of the service, the sliding doors at the rear were opened to reveal a large auditorium, which extends the sanctuary and is large enough to accommodate the rest of the twelve hundred people who flock to Beth Israel for the Jewish High Holy Days. Sweet rolls, challah, juice, pickled herring, gefilte fish and its horseradish companion, together with tiny paper cups filled with wine to toast *Shabbat*, had been set out for a light snack called *Oneg*. At least for the moment, the rabbi seemed to have shaken off his flu. He smiled warmly, greeting such regulars as Joel and Carol Kaufman, Steve and Esther Levine, and looked about for faces rarely seen or not familiar at all. He makes it a point to talk to as many BI strangers as he can. He was pleased to see the Fixlers—Howie, Jody, and their two children—

who have been coming more often and are the one young couple who have shown strong interest in the Israel trip. Howie Fixler is a quiet, unassuming man with piercing black eyes and robust, dark skin that looks perennially tanned; he offered a small, yet welcoming smile to those who greeted him, but he was not usually the one to initiate a conversation.

Jay Rosenbaum did not yet know Howie Fixler well. He knew he was an internist who specialized in rehabilitation, but the rabbi never saw Howie at work and rarely met people who were his patients. On the other hand, Howie knew much more about his rabbi, a man constantly in the public eye, whose personality and actions are critiqued constantly by congregants and noncongregants alike. Howie can speak perceptively of the man to whom he has—only recently—entrusted the care of his soul.

"Jay has a tough job; I mean *tough*," he told me. "Trying to balance the money people and the vision/service people. 'We're not against that,' the money people say, 'but how are we going to pay for it?' Everybody wants from him and most of the time he gives, but then some member's father-in-law dies—even though he didn't live here—and the rabbi doesn't call and a nose is out of joint. He gives such wonderful sermons, too. I leave here and I just feel great. My kids want to go to a movie, but I'd like to really just bask in the glow of *Shabbat*. I don't think most of the people really give a hoot about religion, the kind of religion that Jay is presenting to them. Maybe because they somehow can't get to him. On an individual basis, sometimes he doesn't come through. There's a piece missing. If only he'd let people in a little more on himself, I think that would be better."

At the *Oneg*, Rabbi Rosenbaum had moved on to the Lewises and to a couple visiting them from out of town who had come to services. Sometime *Shabbat* regulars or even the casual guest will want to discuss the sermon; that seemed not to be the case today. Except for a round of compliments, the sermon had not stirred anyone to deal immediately with its specifics. The rabbi was used to this sort of nonresponse, and, while it always gave him pause (had he made his points?;

was he clear?), he knew from experience that scattered seeds will sprout as they will; he had little control over the soil upon which they had been sown. And, after all, Judaism is not a religion of exhortation, but of practice, not of altar-call conversions, but of incremental steps toward God. The rabbi hurried by Janine, who was being cornered by an irate mother whose requested caterer for a bar mitzvah couldn't be sanctioned because the caterer was not kosher. Janine kept a fixed smile on her face and took another bite of challah.

By one o'clock the last of the congregants had gone. The rabbi put on his Gore-Tex suit for the walk home; Janine carried an umbrella for herself and David, while Shoshanah had the canopy of her stroller to keep her dry. The Rosenbaums trudged silently along the empty, rain-slicked Worcester sidewalks. An occasional car passed; the rabbi waved to one of them, containing a member who had not been in *shul* that morning.

Once the rabbi arrived home and took off his dripping clothes, the achiness returned. He took a long nap. Meanwhile, Janine played board games with the children. I wondered what her sentiments on *Shabbat* might be. I needed only to ask.

"When I was a little girl growing up in Seattle, we were Orthodox and we went from house to house on *Shabbat*; it was wonderful," she said with a smile of remembrance. "I loved *Shabbat*. But then you are the rabbi's wife." Her face suddenly darkened. "What you did before out of conviction and a pure desire becomes expected of you. I'm *supposed* to go to all the services. I'm *supposed* to look good all the time, have a smile on my face even when some witch is using me to funnel a complaint to the rabbi that she won't tell him herself. Our *Shabbat* routine? Ha! We don't have one. We don't rest. Jay is exhausted; we eat, he naps, and he goes back to *shul*. How am I going to say this? Let me just say it. Being the rabbi's wife has bled religion out of me. He believes it, lives it. I'm like the corporate wife. It's just a job for me. That's sad to say, isn't it?"

I was taken aback both by the depth of Janine's feelings and by her honesty with me. But then, I was *not* a member of the congregation; I was *not* a Worcester Jew. I quickly realized that I was one of the few people she knew outside of those groups. To whom could she say such things and not have them come back immediately to haunt her?

An hour before sundown, the rabbi returned for *Havdalah* service to end *Shabbat*. Twenty people were present. By seven o'clock he was back home; the children were watching their weekly rental movie on a television set that had been off-limits for the past twenty-four hours. Another Saturday had passed for America, another *Shabbat* for the Rosenbaums.

One hundred and forty-six adults attended synagogue that morning, representing some 10 percent of Rabbi Rosenbaum's congregation. That turnout reflected a considerable improvement over the sparse audience that greeted the rabbi when he arrived six years ago. And the rabbi knew that his 10 percent—while it was a statistic that placed Jews decidedly behind Catholics and Protestants in weekly attendance—was actually better than most Conservative congregations. But he was not foolish enough to take pride in being better in a not very competitive field, and neither was he content to think that mere attendance was enough for those who would then go out and spend the rest of this day as if it were simply an American Saturday.

Whether the words of the *parasha,* God's word—or perhaps no more than a kind word from one congregant to another—have made their impact felt this day, he didn't know. And whether his own words in the sermon have had any effect on his people, he was equally uncertain. As for the impact on Bennie Hillman's family, whose anguish had never been far from his thoughts, he was sure. None of them had been present to consider the insights and guidance he had wrested from the ancient texts.

5

Mosher was not about to share his sunflower seed with Kosher. Rabbi Rosenbaum peered intently into the wire cage where, on a bed of fragrant cedar shavings, a nasty family squabble was going at full tilt. He waited patiently, hoping for a peaceful resolution. Although he is constantly using real-life experiences to underscore Judaic truths, or finding a Bible story leaping to mind that will build upon an ordinary occurrence, on this gray, suddenly calamitous morning, all the rabbi could do was smile and shake his head at the gerbil's greed. The nursery-school children were gathered around him; amidst the clatter their teacher beckoned the rabbi to read a story to them from the book under his arm.

The rabbi had not gotten home until after ten the night before. After hearing of Janine's day and then relating only the choicest tales of the Beth Israel executive board—the Rosenbaums howled with laughter at the amount of time spent discussing what action should be taken on the synagogue's disposable *kippot*, which are made in China (China being the leading arms supplier to the Arab states)—he fell asleep, exhausted. His mind was a tired blur at morning *minyan*, and a string of brush fires demanding his attention had hardly started the day well. The menorah mailing had missed a few well-placed Beth Israel college students (good schools *and* dues-paying parents—a double whammy); the office photocopier was on the blink; an outraged mother of the bride insisted, loudly and at length, that the restaurant she'd chosen would do just fine, even though the food would not be kosher. And then, just before the rabbi walked over to the nursery,

Naomi Levine* paid an unexpected visit. Two months ago, she had come to the rabbi to say that not only had her husband been unemployed for some time, but an illness had put her in the hospital just when she had finally found a job. She tearfully admitted her utter disgrace at having to beg, but they could not pay their rent or buy food. The rabbi had been able to see that five hundred dollars was sent her way; this morning, Mrs. Levine expressed her gratitude. She also expressed puzzlement. She produced a stern dunning letter from the executive director noting that her synagogue dues had not been paid. Rabbi Rosenbaum's face flushed as he read the letter, which he crumpled into a ball—muttering, "Forget about it"—and tossed into his wastebasket. He offered an apology for the letter and for having to leave immediately, as he was already late for his nursery-school visit.

So there in the nursery he stood, confronted not only by an avaricious gerbil and not enough three- and four-year-olds to sustain the nursery, but also by the beaming face of his director, Fran Smith, searching his own face for the affirmation he did not feel in his heart.

The Beth Israel nursery school the rabbi was visiting this morning was the keystone of early childhood education at the synagogue—and one of his most nagging problems. The number of children enrolled had been dropping steadily in the past few years. At one time, the nursery routinely enrolled thirty-two children a year; this year there were twenty-six; and the projection for next year dropped precipitously to seventeen. The rabbi was well aware that the young couples of his congregation, as well as Jewish families unaffiliated with a synagogue, were overwhelmingly choosing the newly refurbished Temple Emanuel nursery. The problem was not just that his nursery needed a paint job and some new toys—and the rabbi knew it.

Fran Smith had headed the Beth Israel nursery for twenty years and had done a generally outstanding job. But, while her motherly approach might have had an appeal in years past—her voice was always sweet and well modulated and she was constantly on her knees, trying to be accessible to her students—it was apparent that more and more parents were choosing Emanuel instead because of its young, energetic teachers. Fran, whose husband had been disabled by a stroke, needed the job; the rabbi had been reluctant to urge her to retire, considering such pressure unethical. But the group of nursery-school toddlers represented something far more than income for the synagogue or a job for Fran. To Rabbi Rosenbaum, they were the future of Beth Israel. Last night at the executive board, his rhetoric swelling to match the fervent conviction in his heart, he had called the nursery school Beth Israel's "crown jewel." It was the place where young Jews started their religious training and often was the prelude to entrance into Solomon Schechter Day School. Schechter, in turn, produced the most religiously active teenagers as well as those who went on to participate in Hillel at their colleges. It was a crucial first step for the children—and often the path back for their parents, many of whom had lapsed in their religious practices. When children came home filled with questions and newfound pride in their Jewishness, these young parents were forced to reassess a way of life they all too often had moved away from. The executive board acknowledged the nursery school's importance but said categorically that unless the nursery carried itself financially, it would have to close. There were too many drains on a budget that was already running a deficit.

The search committee, in interviewing and then hiring Jay Rosenbaum six years before, had made it clear that he needed to attract young couples if the synagogue was to prosper. He had reminded the executive board of this mandate on more than one occasion, and he had done so again last night. He said that the closing of the nursery school would jeopardize the very future of Beth Israel. The point he was trying to get across was unambiguous; if the nursery went, so might this rabbi.

"It's hard, very hard, to translate the needs and sentiments of the people who work in the synagogue every day to the board, and vice versa," the rabbi told me as we walked to the nursery that morning. "Last night there was all this talk about who was paying their dues on time and who wasn't paying for their High Holiday seats. Should we demand they pay for their seats *before* the High Holidays? One hundred and twenty-five dollars for a permanent seat; seventy-five dollars for a temporary seat? Is a rabbi to be concerned about such things? Of course we have to have money to operate—but am I supposed to be some kind of policeman, somebody who rations out his services depending on who pays and who doesn't?

"Schechter is running scared; they are facing a hundred-thousand-dollar deficit. They ask for a reduction in their rent, fifteen hundred dollars. It's more symbolic than anything else—they want the board to say, 'We care about you; you are important to this synagogue. Let us help this little bit.' But the board too often looks at such things as strictly business decisions. Schechter is a tenant and should pay its way, goes their thinking. Well, if the synagogue is a business, they have the wrong man in charge. I just can't make those kind of cold-blooded decisions." I saw in the rabbi's face and heard in his tone a rare indignant note. "So, I try to be the peacemaker, to show the board how necessary the day school and nursery are. Feelings get hurt very easily. I spend a good amount of my time just trying to make people feel good and wanted. I'm trying to make Fran Smith feel good and at the same time save the nursery school from closing. A balancing act, believe me."

"Mine, Rabbi! Try mine!" The nursery-school children proudly displayed their Hanukkah candles, made of construction paper, with a sliding section that allowed them to appear lighted. The rabbi gathered the children around him in a circle of chairs. "What holiday is coming up?" he asked as if it were a mystery to him. "No, not Passover. Yes, Hanukkah! I almost forgot. And we will eat . . . ? Yes, latkes. How many days in Hanukkah? What games do we play? The dreidel? How many of you have heard of Brooklyn? This is a story from Brooklyn . . ."

The rabbi began the Isaac Bashevis Singer story of the parakeet that flies into Jacob and Esther's Brooklyn flat just as they are about to eat their Hanukkah latkes. The bird picks at a dreidel, loves the proffered latkes, and squawks, "*Shalom*, Sarah." It is a sign to Esther that this Hebrew-speaking Jewish parakeet should not be kept in a cage because Hanukkah is about freedom, and that if its rightful owners are not found, it has a permanent home with them. Their son

David goes off to college, meets a Sarah who says she lost a parakeet many years before—and so the parakeet is reunited with its owner, who marries David. Latke-loving parakeet and good Jewish couple live happily ever after. The children cheer.

"Now, what would have happened if that parakeet had flown into a non-Jewish home?" the rabbi posited. Silence. Fidgeting. Finally, one little girl kicked one of her sneakers into the leg of her chair and stood up abruptly. "He wouldn't have any latkes to eat!" she offered. "He would have starved to death!"

"Very good," the rabbi replied. "A Jewish home is many things—and latkes are a very important part—for people *and* for parakeets. Okay, I've got to get going."

As he quietly closed the nursery door, the rabbi glanced back at it, much the same as a father might after paying a nostalgic visit to the familiar room of a son or daughter who has since left home and gone on to another life. For a moment he stood there, transfixed, seemingly lost in his own thoughts about what he might do to preserve this "crown jewel." Then, glancing down at his watch, the rabbi quickened his pace toward his office. He took a few minutes to proofread and sign some correspondence, return some phone calls, and have a light midmorning snack. Rabbi Rosenbaum neither takes a lunch break in his office nor goes out; instead, he grazes throughout the day. At that moment, it was half a tuna-fish sandwich; also in his lunch today were a container of Dannon coffee yogurt, a granola bar, an apple, cucumber spears, and a small bag of Cape Cod potato chips. Just before eleven, he slid behind the wheel of his Ford Taurus station wagon to spread still more word about the joys of living the Jewish life to priority group number two.

The session of "News, Views, and Schmooze" began with three people present—Simon Mats, Abram Korotkevich, and Larisa Kalyuzhny, all of them sitting perfectly straight in their chairs, eager to begin. Larisa's lipstick was a brilliant red not often seen on American women past the age of seventeen, but it added a colorful accent to the otherwise muted tones of the men's heavy wool suits. Larisa is from Odessa, where, she asserted, there are more Jews than in Moscow—

and where, she added, the Jews were watched constantly. Attendance at services in Odessa was a dangerous adventure—for those braver than herself, she admitted.

Soon the small group was expanded when Olga and Vladimir Volfson, both medical doctors from Vilnius entered the room and apologized profusely for their tardiness. After Olga and Vladimir told something about life in Lithuania and the anti-Jewish persecution they witnessed and endured, the rabbi launched into a Hanukkah mini-course.

The Greek culture was sweeping through the civilized world two thousand years ago, he told them, and Jews were not exempt from falling under its spell. Nakedness seemed in vogue and the modesty Judaism had always taught seemed terribly old-fashioned. "Not that the Jews needed so much convincing," the rabbi said, affecting a Yiddish accent. "This was fun, observance wasn't always fun." But when pigs were slaughtered on the altars and pagan statues brought into the Holy Temple in Jerusalem for Jews to worship, he continued, Mattathias and then Judah the Maccabean (heads nodded with recognition at a familiar name) fought back to preserve the Jewish way of life. After they won the final battle, the Jews wanted to light the menorah to begin to purify the temple, but they only had enough oil for one day. Miraculously, that tiny bit of oil burned for eight days. Hanukkah would soon be celebrated once again, the rabbi continued, memorializing that rededication of the temple, but, more important, symbolizing a revival in the lives of Jewish people everywhere.

"So what does this have to say to us in modern times?" The rabbi hesitated for effect, but the Russians thought he was actually posing a question. Heads dropped, eye contact was lost. "*You!*" he shouted. The heads jerked up. "You, the Soviet Jews, are like living Hanukkah candles, bringing light into the world. You had the courage to rise up against these forces to remain Jews. Everything about you said 'No, no, no' and you said 'Yes, yes, yes.' Sharansky"—"Natan," they mouthed affectionately, almost in unison—"and so many others stood for the light in Judaism that represents the soul, the soul that has strength, the soul that wants freedom and righteousness. This is stronger than any army, stronger . . ."

Abram Korotkevich's lips were moving. The rabbi stopped in midsentence. The room was suddenly quiet.

"The spirit," Abram said, hesitantly. *"Da,* the spirit; it is alive. *Da."* He smiled broadly—exposing a mouth chock full of silvery fillings—as much with the thought as with his ability to express it in the language of his new promised land.

"Spoken like a true rabbi," Rabbi Rosenbaum brightened. "As we will say on Hanukkah, 'Not by might, not by power, but by my spirit, saith the Lord.' Now, *now,"* his voice descended to a lower pitch and graver tone as he reached the end of his hour, "it's not the Greeks, but what we in America call 'the prevailing culture' that says, 'Who needs to be Jewish anyhow?' We should have been wiped out years ago. We should not be sitting here. But we are. How do we explain that?"

Again, silence, but this time, with this question before them, none of the Russians was looking down.

"We are Jews, sitting here together, are we not?"

Indeed we are, their smiles conveyed.

Rabbi Rosenbaum quickly scanned the agenda on the sheet before him. Fourteen items. The usual stuff. He had just left the Russians at Temple Emanuel and was now seated at another long table, this time of fine mahogany, not institutional oak.

Across from him was Rabbi Seth Bernstein of Temple Sinai, in whose spacious, well-appointed office the meeting was being held. To his right was James Simon, the new head rabbi at Temple Emanuel, and his assistant rabbi, Stuart Gershon. Although there are two other congregational rabbis in Worcester, they are Orthodox and never attend these monthly meetings of what is grandly called the Rabbinical Council of Central Massachusetts. The Orthodox view Rabbi Rosenbaum's Conservative synagogue and the two Reform temples as inadequate expressions of Judaic belief; for the Orthodox to acknowledge their legitimacy, or to join in their programs, would be akin to apostasy.

Rabbi Bernstein is a diminutive, fast-talking man; Rabbi Simon, with his tie pulled down and his fingers dancing over the keyboard of his pocket electronic calendar, could pass for a successful Worcester lawyer ready to discuss a case. Rabbi Gershon, bedecked in a beautiful patterned tie, looked more like a stockbroker on his lunch break, his portable phone at his feet, ever ready to take calls from his clients. There was a certain ease within the room—despite the brisk pace, as this meeting was allotted, religiously, no more than an hour—of seasoned professionals methodically going about their work. The first item on the agenda was the question of how to work with the Jewish Community Center and this year's *Yom Ha'atzmaut* celebration—which commemorates Israel's independence—so that the event would not be completely secular. "I hate to bring up the 'c' word; let it not pass my lips," Rabbi Bernstein offered. "I don't want to lose any friends over there. And, God willing, the 'f' word. That one I can say out loud: 'fun.' How about making it some fun so people want to come?"

"Right, fun," Rabbi Rosenbaum affirmed. "And we have to make it clear that this is not a turf war, a question of ownership, just a question of the 'c' word—excuse the expression—'content.' " The rabbis chuckled at its sound.

The relationship between synagogues and their local Jewish Federations is unique among religious groups in America. Indeed, as each participant in the relationship seeks to fulfill its mission, there is sometimes another "c" word—"conflict." The Jewish Federation is the agency that addresses Jewish needs and interests within a given geographical area and is the major fund-raiser for Jewish causes. Often, as in Worcester, the local chapter maintains a Jewish Community Center for recreation, social events, day care, and education. In the past, the unquestioned mission of the Federation was to serve as a cultural nexus for Jews and the rallying point for the support of Israel; fully half of the Worcester Federation budget is sent to Israel under the auspices of the United Jewish Appeal. The Federation conducts an annual drive to sell Israel bonds; across the country, millions of dollars are raised each year. Most Federations have typically been run by either secular Jews or members of a Reform temple, with the result that religion was either not a major consideration or was merely given some sort of lip service to appease the local rabbis.

Over the past decade or so, this situation has changed dramatically. Alarmed by a rising intermarriage rate and challenged by the fact that an exponential growth in Jewish wealth has been accompanied by an actual drop in the number of Jews giving to Jewish causes, Federations across America have changed their approach. They now seek to make and keep Jews religiously literate, to educate young Jewish community leaders—in essence to raise the community's spiritual, not merely cultural, consciousness. They too have found that cultural Judaism is not enough to maintain Jewish identity. Sometimes, the Federation's new-found religious zeal seems to step onto synagogue territory; at other times, they are criticized for their secularism. This was the case when the Worcester Jewish Community Center wanted to open its athletic facilities on *Shabbat,* a move that Rabbi Rosenbaum and the other Worcester rabbis successfully resisted. While each has need of the other, a delicate balancing act between Federation and synagogue goes on in Worcester—and in cities across America.

The meeting at Temple Sinai droned on (should we invite Moslem clergy to ecumenical functions?; what should we do about the Lubavitcher rabbi who doesn't want his name on the letterhead?) when, serendipitously, items one and six on the agenda coalesced in Rabbi Rosenbaum's mind. Suddenly, as if divinely revealed to him, he saw the possibility of something more than an individual program or an innovative angle to lure people to the synagogues of Worcester. Instead, he had a plan, a sustained assault on that elusive target, priority group number two.

"Leonid Feldman!" the rabbi blurted out, pointing with one index finger to "Soviet Jewry Update" and to "Hadassah Wedding" with the other. "We have a kickoff lecture with Feldman for the Russians. Soon. Feldman's a Russian, a former atheist and good Communist party man; now he's a Conservative rabbi. And then, leading up to the wedding, we have an event each month with the Russians doing the basics: Passover seder, observing *Shabbat,* the meaning of *Purim* and *Shavuot,* things like that."

"Just right," resonated Rabbi Bernstein, "hands-on stuff. I have a feeling the Russians are embarrassed by how little they know. We have to start from square one."

"Oh boy, do they feel embarrassed," Rabbi Gershon agreed.

The culminating event was already well known to all of them. In May, a Jewish wedding was to be held for a prototypical Russian couple—one of the many who had been allowed only a civil ceremony in the Soviet Union. Within a few minutes, the rabbis expanded this celebration into a mass wedding for as many Russian couples as wished to take part. Not only would the wedding have religious significance; it would serve as the year's chief fund-raiser for the local chapter of Hadassah. "We'll build up to it, and meanwhile we have to keep on getting the Russians invited to spend Jewish holidays with our people—so they can see what it's about."

"Great idea," Rabbi Simon said. "Capital. Let's punch in some dates," he continued, his pocket computer calendar at the ready.

Many of Rabbi Rosenbaum's evenings—too many, he complains, and Janine will more than agree—are taken up with meetings. It is not unusual for his calendar to be filled on all four possible weekday nights (Friday night is part of *Shabbat* and therefore inviolable). But on a certain December evening, it was not Jewish organization or Worcester's needs, but Jewish tradition that would prevail. Ziva and Levi Rosenhand, who live a block from the Rosenbaums on Cricket Lane, were hosting a Hanukkah celebration. It was just the kind of affair that the rabbi cherished and would like to see more of: enjoyable, spontaneous, and Jewish. Such nights were the precursors of what life could always be like in the observant Jewish community he wanted so badly to establish in his small corner of America.

Ziva, of Iranian ancestry, and Levi were both born in Israel. While neither are openly religious or members of Beth Israel, they are two of the Rosenbaums' closest friends. This night they have opened their home to their neighbors—including a good sprinkling of Catholics. They have also invited one of the Russian families—Simon and Zina Mats and their four-year-old son, Eugene. It turned into a wonderful, noisy evening, with plenty of good Middle Eastern food—falafel, tabbouleh, hummus, baba ghanouj—children running about with minimal parental intervention, presents to be opened, and a Hanukkah service presided over and richly embellished by the rabbi. With his questions—and the children's well-informed answers—Rabbi Rosenbaum retold the story of the Maccabees' triumph over the Greeks and the miracle of the menorah.

The men had come in sport shirts and slacks, the women in more dressy clothes; although they were not all close friends, they mixed easily. But one man seemed out of place, as if he had wandered in on the wrong party. Clad in a jogging suit, he stood fixedly by a counter in the kitchen, continually looking at his watch. He wolfed down his food as if there would not be enough to go around. His name was Peter Hellman.* Our somewhat disjointed conversation—he kept looking over my shoulder at the clock on the wall, and I sensed I was keeping him from leaving—revolved around Jewish holidays and observance. He unabashedly told me that he never attends *Shabbos* services, found them boring, and could persevere perhaps an hour in *shul* at High Holiday time. Keep a kosher home? Downright stupid, he said; of course not. And yet, he proudly admitted, he had sent both of his sons to Solomon Schechter Day School and was continuing their Jewish education post–bar mitzvah. "American Jews?" he asked, as if of himself. "Will there be any, except for the Hasidim, in fifty years? That's a real question. That's the . . . Squash!" he interrupted himself in midsentence. "That's my real passion." And with that he was gone for his eight o'clock match.

I wanted to have more than such a truncated conversation about this seeming paradox he was living—extensive Jewish education for his sons coupled with his own lack of faith—so over lunch sometime later I asked Peter Hellman how typical he might be. "Hanukkah is wonderful, a good time," he explained over a plate of grilled shrimp at the Legal Seafood restaurant in downtown Worcester. "But to sit around all Saturday, go to *shul* and listen to Hebrew? To what end? As for synagogue attendance, I'm a twelve-hour-a-year Jew. The obligations of Judaism demand a life-style and a considerable amount of time every day observing its rituals. That's the *last* thing I would want to do, to tie myself down to something like that.

"Now, don't get me wrong. Everything about me is Jewish, and Judaism is something I want to preserve; that's why my boys received the education they did. I would rather have them shaped by the Torah than U2 or the Rolling Stones. They need a Jewish education just to stay even. I'm more assimilated than my parents; my boys would be more assimilated than me if I didn't do something about it. People without a religious faith lack something in their character; they are usually boring and dull. Judaism is a combination of a people and a religion. I feel an obligation of loyalty to the people; I'm one of them. That's what I want to preserve, and the only way to preserve it is through the religion—even though I don't believe in it. What's wrong with being formed by Judaism and yet not living it? For my sons, I'm keeping their options open; the great Jewish transmission belt goes on. And I wouldn't be totally happy if my boys didn't marry Jewish girls, because—notwithstanding the fact that most of my best friends are Christians—there will always be a gulf between me and Christians.

"Let's look at the average Jew who, for instance, may be a small businessman; on *Shabbos* he needs to hear that he should spend more time with his family and less in the business. That there is a deeper meaning to life than just earning a living. I don't need to hear that: I live in the world of ideas. I'm not making or selling something, and I don't want to spend my time with people who are. I'm happy to hear that religion means something to them. Good for them! But my life doesn't need that kind of enriching. I'm stimulated all the time; I'm constantly studying great thoughts. I have my family, my reading, and my daily squash game. I don't need the companionship of God in my life. But check in with me if I have cancer in a couple years and then see what I say.

"Confusing? Perhaps. But I know a lot of Jews—I'm not much different from most members of Beth Israel."

* * *

This one reluctant congregant and his committed rabbi surely represent two quite divergent views of ethnic and religious belief. But the Jews of Beth Israel are certainly not alone in trying to sort out how (or *if*) to live as Jews, a life in which so much of daily routine is necessarily prescribed and proscribed, and also as Americans, where freedom of choice, expression, and movement are preciously held tenets.

From the novels of Philip Roth to the pages of various Jewish publications, reflection and debate about the meaning of Jewish identity continues. What does it mean to be a Jew in America? Should Jews attempt to live a life that appears so at odds with mainstream American culture? Perhaps no other religious group has found the American soil so fertile for their personal aspirations, yet so antagonistic to the demands of their religious practice. The major portion of the history of the Jews in America is little more than a hundred years old, yet within that century this religion of millennia has undergone profound change as it has been lived out by the largest group of Jews gathered anywhere in the world.

The Jewish experience in America has proved to be absolutely unlike the experience of Jews in any other country; it is at once rich and full of ambiguity. The Jews who came to America found their world upended; for some it was paradise, for others, hell. Respected rabbis lived in cold-water tenements, *schnoring* for their daily bread. Scholars who had been the pride of their Jewish communities in Europe were reduced to paupers. But the brassy, good-for-nothing, scrappy kid who came to America with holes in the soles of his shoes and a burning desire to succeed could achieve his dreams. He grew out his hair, worked hard, ate what he wanted, often changed his name to one with an American ring to it, and blended in quickly. The premium once placed on Judaic learning, on living the observant Jewish life, seemed to have no value here.

Being Jewish in Europe provided a community, continuity, and a transcendental dimension to life. This could still be had in America for those who desired it. But many found that the benefits of observant Jewish life did not outweigh the drawbacks. The restrictions placed upon where a person could live, what they could eat, with whom they could socialize—restrictions that had been part of both their religious and social culture virtually everywhere in Europe—seemingly had no value, no purpose here. For many, their newfound liberty to progress as far as their own drive would take them far outshone the comfort—and limitations—of the Old World Jewish order.

But, whether they held fast to the religion of their ancestors or blended into secular society, Jews were destined to be successful in America. There may be many reasons, but certainly important was the singular advantage of their history, which had at times plagued them and made them objects of derision, but which ultimately helped them in a country that had little history—at least not enough to have spawned its own brand of anti-Semitism. For generations the Jews, the landless, had been engaged in buying, selling, lending, and other occu- pations that had coincidentally come to form the backbone of the American middle-class social order. Knowing they could be exiled at any time from their homeland of the moment, the Jews had over the centuries acquired habits of care, foresight, and delayed gratification. While many immigrants were illiterate, Jews were usually schooled in Hebrew as part of their religious training. Literacy, even in a language that had little place in America, gave them the tools for learning the new lingua franca—a crucial head start—while also insuring their ability to preserve their own identity. At least initially.

As Jews became economically successful and their children found their way into the professions during the first half of the twen- tieth century, an amazing transformation took place—one that would provide the grist for Roth's novels, Isaac Bashevis Singer's stories, and the ingredients of the current Jewish conundrum. Mainstream Ameri- can values became Jewish values. The ethos and standards of a nation no more than two hundred years old were embraced as the values of a people thousands of years old. "For example, the myth of the Jewish- American princess was born," Silvia Barak Fishman of the Center for Modern Jewish Studies told me when I visited her office at Bran- deis University, outside Boston. "Second-generation Jews wanted to groom their daughters to be real Americans, and to them the real

American girl was Daisy Buchanan of *The Great Gatsby:* well educated, refined, who didn't work and looked terrific all the time. There was nothing Jewish about it at all. Jewish women have always prided themselves on being hardworking and levelheaded. Every Yiddish word that is a compliment for a woman describes her as competent. On the other hand, *tzatzkeleh* implies a woman is an ornament; it's an insult."

While many Jews could not shed their Jewishness soon enough when they first came to America, after World War II the number of Jews proclaiming their Jewishness grew rapidly; synagogue affiliation grew from 20 percent in 1930 to 60 percent of all American Jews in the 1950s and early 1960s. Some of this return to Jewishness could have been guilt: the Holocaust had occurred and American Jews had been incapable of doing much to stop it. But equally, American Jews, now second and third generation, were finally at home, safe from persecution, and—except for tasteless anti-Semitic jokes and the occasional desecration of a synagogue or cemetery—were unlikely to be bothered. As America became mobile, Conservative and Reform synagogues were built at an unrelenting pace to accommodate Jews leaving the cities for the suburbs. In what is now considered a golden age of American Jewry, 80 percent of Jewish children were receiving some sort of religious education. Intermarriage was still virtually unknown; Jews tended not only to worship, but socialize with other Jews. In their classic work of 1963, *Beyond the Melting Pot,* Nathan Glazer and Daniel Patrick Moynihan reported that Jews were the most endogamous of U.S. ethnic groups; Jewish survival, it seemed, was assured. Yet what appeared to be a dramatic religious revival did not bring with it a return to observance of Jewish law or the study of sacred texts. Instead, there was a return to what came to be known as "Jewish group feeling." Peter Hellman, as well as the other Jews of Worcester now in their thirties and forties—that troubling group Rabbi Rosenbaum has so much difficulty reaching—could enjoy being Jews in the company of other Jews. For the most part, they were solidly middle- or upper-class; they did not have to prove anything anymore. The new synagogues could have been mistaken for country clubs, where dances and social gatherings were primary events and *Shabbat* services were sometimes relegated to Friday night, so as not to interfere with the weekend. The synagogue, once a Jew's second home, the place where honor was gratefully rendered to God, had taken on the characteristics of a secular, voluntary association. Will Herbeg, in his well-known study, *Protestant, Catholic, Jew,* said insightfully that while Judaism was seemingly accepted by American Jews, it was also in the process of being diluted.

With the upheavals of the later 1960s and the 1970s, the Jewish ties that had bound the post–World War II generation together frayed and loosened. Being "too" Jewish was once again out of fashion—as it had been during the years of mass Jewish migration to America. But while in those days marrying anyone other than a Jew was unthinkable, now intermarriage with gentiles became more frequent. And now the Jewish partner in such a marriage—once considered an outsider and an embarrassment by non-Jews—was looked upon as a good catch, a person with family values, education, a good earning potential. As for the Jew marrying outside the faith—well, they probably hadn't been *that* Jewish anyhow. As with all mainstream religions, Judaism suffered in the turbulent wake of these chaotic years. The community pressures that brought people to synagogue in the 1950s were gone. Religious Judaism—shed of its cloak of social respectability—was now scrutinized in the harsh light of a new age of reason. Intermarriage rates began their climb to the current level of over 50 percent. Jewish young men and women actually avoided each other, expressing a "toxic feeling" about Jews of the opposite sex. Jews tended to not marry at all or marry later than the national average; when they did marry, they tended to have fewer children. Many Jews moved to smaller towns, which had no significant Jewish population and thus a lower consciousness of Jewish presence. The rich Jewish heritage in America continued to erode.

"Setting aside those who have always been more or less observant in their beliefs and a small number of Jews returning to their religion, we are now faced with a far larger number of American Jews—an inordinate number of whom are very successful—who have nothing more to prove and are looking for meaning in their lives," Silvia Fishman told me. "Deep within themselves, they don't want the same situation to happen to their children, so they want to transmit some sense of meaning and Jewish identity to their sons and daughters—whom they are shocked to find are embarrassingly American. But they are not willing to become more observant, to really live more Jewishly. They think the Jewishness they remembered from their grandparents will be automatically transmitted to their children, as if it's in their DNA. Of course, they are living on memories."

The celebrants back at the Rosenhand home continued spreading the warmth of Hanukkah into the later evening hours. Children opened presents (most of them quite modest; a small Lego set or a book, for example) as the grown-ups talked national and Israeli politics, Worcester schools, and the anemic economy and job market. When one of the children set up an ersatz basketball hoop over a door, threatening a handsome table lamp, wallpaper, and unmarred paint, not a single parent voiced the slightest concern. Even the occasional shuddering of the door and the *thump* of a slam dunk did nothing to bring the children's fun to an end.

There was nothing overtly religious about the evening once the rabbi had finished his Hanukkah portion. There was a sense of a real community, of family fun strengthened by a true affinity among the people there. I was the only stranger, but I was made to feel welcome; it was understood that just by my presence I had earned a place among them.

When someone asked what I did, I told her about my travels with the rabbi. Others overheard and I was immediately surrounded. "Ah, now we'll find out what he does all day," one man said, loud enough for the rabbi to hear. The rabbi ducked his head as if a missile were headed his way, and smiled. "Seriously though," the man confided in a more quiet voice, "you couldn't have picked a better man. The best rabbi I ever had." The others agreed.

6

It had not exactly been the vacation the rabbi had hoped for. Strangely, however, he had found spending a week in bed was exactly what he had needed. When he, Janine, David, and Shoshanah arrived at Janine's parents' home in Seattle in late December on their annual winter trip, the rabbi thought it was only the accumulated fatigue—albeit magnified—of the past few months that he had felt. Instead, it was an old-fashioned case of the flu. "My mind just shut down," the rabbi explained to me upon his return. "I just hibernated."

But the time in Seattle was well spent on other accounts. Janine, he knows, is never happier than when she is back in her home town and able to be with her parents, Victor and Deborah Guttman, who are in their eighties. She is very close to them, with ties and memories that few daughters have.

Both Victor and Deborah were born in Europe. With the Nazi tide rising, Victor escaped from his native Czechoslovakia and joined the French Resistance. His parents and five brothers and sisters held on, hoping the scourge would pass. All eventually died in the death camps. Deborah, who was born in Poland, lost her first husband, her parents, and four brothers and sisters in the Holocaust. Uncles, aunts, cousins also perished. When the Guttmans arrived in America in 1951, they were people without a country and without a family—except for their eighteen-month-old daughter, Janine, who had been born in a refugee camp in Paris. The Guttmans eventually moved to Seattle, joined an Orthodox synagogue, and lived an observant life. But, from a young age Janine has been aware of her parents' tenuous relationship to a God who spared them yet allowed so many of their loved ones to perish.

Janine's Worcester friends know little of her family background, but they have often heard her talk of Seattle, extolling the city's cosmopolitan atmosphere, the wilderness areas nearby, the wonderful beaches, the temperate weather, the many people she knows there. But there is more to Seattle for Janine than the sum of its assets. It is also a place that is *not* home to her husband's synagogue; it is a place with, as she told me, "the beauty of anonymity." There are no congregants to see what she is wearing, what she is putting into her shopping cart, what she is saying to her children. There are no congregants to corner her, to register their complaints, to pass a word they hope will reach the rabbi's ear. "Worcester is *his* life," Janine told me one day; "Seattle is *my* life. *Our* life?" She laughed at her own question.

And now, refreshed and once again healthy, Rabbi Rosenbaum was at his desk in the middle of his first week back at work. The mountain of mail had been plowed through, most of the calls returned, and a fresh list and fresh list of lists had been made. In a separate category was an imperative: CALL ON ISRAEL TRIP. He had been putting off following up on those who had attended the first meeting of the proposed congregational trip to Israel, hoping that the native appeal of two weeks in the Holy Land with fellow Beth Israel members (and their rabbi) would ultimately attract the needed number. That had not happened. Now, some two months after that meeting, and well past the deadline for down payments, only eleven people had signed up.

But one of them was the man walking into his office. Howie Fixler, in fact, represented six of those eleven. Howie, Jody, and their two children, as well as Jody's parents, who lived in upstate New York, would be going on the trip.

Since Dr. Fixler had taken over the chairmanship of the education committee earlier in the year, the rabbi had been impressed with his willingness to tackle the many time-consuming and difficult problems involved in Beth Israel's efforts to religiously educate children and adults. Perhaps more important, the rabbi knew that Howie was his sympathetic, dependable confidant as he sorted out his most nagging problem: what to do about the failing nursery. Howie was equally opposed to firing Fran Smith, or to making her life so difficult that she would have to resign. But he also agreed with the rabbi that something had to be done, and done soon.

Dr. Fixler was a busy man—the rabbi knew that; what doctor wasn't?—but the young internist clearly had made providing Judaic studies for his and other synagogue children a priority in his life. He was one of a handful of younger Jews in the congregation in whom the rabbi sensed a readiness for a deeper Judaic commitment. The rabbi wished only that there were more of them.

"Packing yet?" the rabbi asked as they stood at the door after twenty minutes together discussing staffing at Beth Israel's afternoon Hebrew-school program.

"Packing?"

"For Israel."

"Oh, we have a little time left. Say, we're going to get enough, aren't we? I'm really looking forward to this."

"Sure, sure. No problem," the rabbi replied quickly, although not totally honestly.

When I called Dr. Fixler and asked to talk with him, I was taken with his ready accessibility; when I arrived for our lunch appointment, I was surprised to find him already waiting. While he gives a somewhat impassive initial impression, I found him warm and open. It was immediately obvious that his Judaism had become very important to him.

"It's amazing; all my friends think I've turned into this religious fanatic," he said with a self-conscious grin on his face. "Just because I'm talking up the Israel trip, just because I'm talking up my new interest in Judaism. Me? We don't even keep a kosher house. My kids don't go to Schechter. I've just come inches and I've got miles to go. I don't know what it is, but I haven't been able to go further. Maybe I can't.

"But I look at Jay as sort of a role model. I'm in medicine and, believe me, I don't look up to a lot of people there. I haven't found great solace among my colleagues; they don't seem to see medicine as a higher calling. They're more interested in who their next patient is and how they are going to be paid for the treatment. Religion fulfills that need, that need for a higher purpose in life, of getting away from the day to day. And Jay is really doing it, at great personal sacrifice. But I look at him and ask, Is he happy? I honestly don't know the man well enough to know if he's happy at it. I'd like to be closer to him; I wish he'd confide more, but maybe he can't. He confides the synagogue business with me, but I'd like to hear about him.

"Maybe in Israel. Israel? This trip has to happen. It's the next natural step on this journey of mine, wherever I'm going to. And I guess I have to do what I don't want to do. I've got to talk to Charlie Mills. I've been avoiding him; I'm mad as hell at him for organizing that other trip. For Israel to happen, it has to happen as a congregation. The next time I run into him, we have to have this out."

If only Rabbi Rosenbaum had known of Howie Fixler's growing faith and his desire to serve as mediator. It is not often that the rabbi feels that congregants are taking charge of troubling synagogue situations. More often, he must provide the impetus.

The rabbi had an especially busy morning to confront, at the end of which Bertha Levin was due in to harangue him (which he has already surmised from the tone of her phone call) about the fact that the synagogue is not doing enough to find jobs for the Russian Jews. Bertha, one of the first of the new Russian emigrés to arrive in Worcester, is now a successful real-estate broker and the unofficial doyenne of the growing community of Russian Jews. Last month, the rabbi prevailed upon her—in what he admits was the first time he ever *asked* someone to join his synagogue—and he knows that Bertha will not be shy about prevailing upon him now. She did so *before* she was a member.

But all in all, the morning seemed to be moving along well when Sue Miller, the coordinator of Russian emigré activities for the Jewish Federation, returned the rabbi's call.

"Am I hearing this correctly, Sue?" he said, his voice a study in uninflected bafflement.

"Yes, I am hearing this correctly," he answered his own question. "Sinai, Emanuel, and Beth Israel can somehow come up with the money, but the Federation cannot come up with a thousand bucks to bring the one Russian that our Worcester Russians will listen to. The Russians you work with and try to help adjust to American life and hope that they will become affiliated Jews. These are the same Russians, am I correct?" The rabbi's tone was evolving into that of an older brother who cannot believe that his younger sibling will not return a baseball glove *he* had so kindly lent him in the first place. "You cannot find one thousand dollars to bring Rabbi Leonid Feldman to Worcester—Rabbi Feldman whom I got to come here at less than his usual fee? What am I doing this for; it's not even my job!" He paused for her answer. "I hope that works out, Sue. Please. I've already been talking it up with the Russians. They're expecting Feldman. This one would kill what little credibility we have; we don't want to lose him. Okay?"

No sooner had the rabbi hung up than the intercom buzzer sounded. Peggy St. John, the synagogue's full-time secretary, told him that Richard Perlman was on the line. After a sigh of resignation, the rabbi reached for the telephone. When Richard or his brother Robert called, Rabbi Rosenbaum knew that whatever was on his schedule, whatever professional or personal plans he had made, were about to be preempted.

"Martha Epstein?" the rabbi confirmed, writing the name at the top of a fresh sheet on a yellow legal pad. "Thanks, Dickie."

In the midst of a morning in which he had wrestled with such temporal banalities as travel expenses for a guest speaker and the color of the paper a flyer should be printed on, Rabbi Rosenbaum was suddenly confronted with perhaps the deepest mystery of a life—its end. Martha Epstein had died that morning, and Jewish law dictates that she must be buried before the sun sets a second time. In the case of Mrs. Epstein, whom he barely knew, the rabbi's first, and somewhat daunting, task was to find out what sort of woman she was, so that he might eulogize her properly. The following morning he would be called upon to play a signal role, explaining the meaning of her life to family and friends. As a representative of their religious faith, the faith in whose ritual she would be sent from this life, he hoped to underscore how—or if—Mrs. Epstein's Jewishness made her what she was.

Mrs. Epstein marked the sixth Beth Israel congregant to die in the past few months, two of them while the rabbi was on vacation. Of the four he buried, the rabbi knew only one of them well enough—Benjamin Hillman, who died two weeks after the rabbi's visit—to be able to speak personally about him. In a congregation of some 1,500 people, where the average weekly attendance at synagogue is between 125 and 150—and where the crowds at High Holidays provide little more than a chance to exchange greetings of the season—it is likely that Rabbi Rosenbaum will have only a blank slate upon which to etch what is expected to be a lasting memory.

At two o'clock, the late Martha Epstein's unmarried son, Alan, and her sister, Eva Sherman, sat across the desk from the rabbi. Most often, the rabbi will go to the home to discuss funeral plans, but for some reason Alan and Eva had insisted on coming to his office instead. After bringing them coffee, the rabbi asked them to tell him their fondest memories of Martha, a good way to start, he has discovered. "What can I tell you?" Eva began, her hands raised before her. "She was a wonderful person. I couldn't say a bad word about her. She was beautiful. We shopped together; not a day went by that we didn't talk on the phone. Wonderful, she was wonderful. All her customers at the Paris Curtain Shop loved her. The Greek woman who ran it said, 'You're a Jew? No, you're too pretty to be a Jew.' She was gorgeous."

The rabbi turned to Alan. Although Eva, an attractive, birdlike woman, had been able to talk about her sister without breaking down, Alan, a heavyset man who was wearing a T-shirt despite the cold weather outside, had a considerably harder time controlling his emotions. "We had a clean house, too clean sometimes; you could have come in with white gloves," he uttered, barely able to choke back his tears at the thought. "My father never made any money; they lived a simple life. She worked all the time; she had to. She was a great cook; cooked for everybody in the neighborhood. What can I say? She was a wonderful mother."

"She graduated from high school, didn't she?" the rabbi inquired, almost pleadingly. "What did she excel at?"

"She excelled at prettiness," her sister answered. "And she
loved to sell."

"What did she love about it?" the rabbi asked.

"She loved people."

It was a rabbi's nightmare. "Wonderful mother." "Wonderful
sister." "Clean house." The scant material, rendered in the rabbi's almost illegible scrawl, amounted to a small entry at the top of the vast
expanse of yellow pad before him. He plodded on through the desolate
terrain unfolding before him, jotting down material he knew he could
not use.

At ten o'clock the next morning, friends and relatives of Martha Epstein gathered in the blond-paneled chapel of Perlman's Funeral
Home on Main Street. In front of them, over a small *bimah*, burned a
menorah with a Star of David at the apex and the eternal flame, the
Ner Tamid, above it. A single, tasteful flower arrangement of lilies and
white roses was in place before a closed casket made of pine, containing the unembalmed body of Martha Epstein. Yesterday afternoon, her
body had been washed and clad in a simple white shroud by the
women of Worcester's *Chevra Kadisha*, or "holy society." This task had
not been left to outsiders—hired out, as we might say today—and the
Chevra Kadisha had made sure that the body was not left alone at any
time, as Jewish law requires. Everything was exactly Jewish: in death,
none are alone; in burial, all are equal. The container in which the
mortal remains of a Jew are interred must be simple and unadorned. It
is the same with floral tributes—once forbidden and still discouraged,
but which are now finding their way into perhaps half of all Jewish
funerals. If mourners wish to honor the dead, the preference is for a
donation to a cause helping the living.

Most of the men in attendance had taken a *kippah* from a bas-
ket outside the chapel, disposable *kippot* of the thin black cloth that
mark Jews who wear them ceremonially and rarely. These *kippot* sat
akimbo on many a head; on others they rose to an alarming point as

the creased skullcaps, newly released from their folded state, refused to obey on such short notice. A few *kippot* rested snugly on heads that had borne them many times before.

The service is begun with Cantor Freedman's softly lilting Hebrew prayer, after which the rabbi read the Twenty-third Psalm, first in Hebrew (*"Adonai ro'i lo echsar . . ."*), then in English ("The Lord is my shepherd . . ."). Reading Psalms Fifteen and Ninety, which bespeak the comfort and safety of believing and dwelling in God, Rabbi Rosenbaum blessed the remains and then intoned a portion of the thirty-first chapter of Proverbs. The formal prayers completed, he looked out over Martha Epstein's family and friends, ready to explain the meaning of her life to them. Eva Sherman was seated in the third row; Alan, wearing sunglasses to cover his red, swollen eyes, was in the first row, next to his brother, who had flown in from California.

The day before, after he had spent an hour with Martha's son and sister, the rabbi had taken his notes home, frustrated that no theme had yet come to him. Then, as he was ready to go to bed, the inspiration came. He hurriedly mapped out his sermon.

"Two verses will be read throughout the Jewish world this *Shabbat,* and, knowing Martha, as we hear them at *Shabbat* services, we know we must use both to tell about her," the rabbi began confidently. "For Martha Epstein was a classic Jewish woman. The verse from the Song of Songs speaks of her beauty; Proverbs Thirty-one tells of her moral virtues—for she was *eishet chayil,* a woman of valor. She was a beautiful person, both outside and inside. She was a good Jewish homemaker, and a good businesswoman. She did before she was asked. Wonderful smells came from her kitchen—her *hamantashen* on Purim were legendary—and when you went to her at the Paris Curtain Shop, you knew you would be treated fairly, professionally; she knew her business well. In today's world, we approach a salesperson with caution: will they try to sell us something we don't need or want? Not Martha Epstein. She didn't pressure her customers. She had no tolerance for sham. She was a human being first, a mensch. Judaism teaches that a person is not tested in a house of prayer, not in a place of study, but in everyday life. And Martha passed that test. At the gate of heaven, we will all be asked, Did you deal honestly with others? Martha Epstein can answer yes."

Most of the congregation was dry-eyed. Alan sobbed.

"We live in a world where we constantly want more. Martha Epstein—Marisha bat Isaac—was happy with her portion in life. And she always had time for others. Her sister Eva could share her grief with Martha after Eva's husband died. The man next door—Martha brought him cake for Passover. She lived simply and nobly, and she left this world a better place. As we say in the prayer, 'Wherever people gather, her deeds will be praised.' We all can draw strength from her memory and we can learn from her example," the rabbi said, ending his ten-minute disquisition on the life of one Martha Epstein.

The half-hour service completed, the casket bearing the body of Martha Epstein—accompanied by the chanting of Psalm Ninety-one ("Dwelling in the shelter of the most high . . .")—was borne to the Perlman brothers' hearse. Some twenty cars followed the hearse as it traveled slowly down Main Street, across Webster Square, and onto Stafford Street. It was a gray, bitterly cold day, another in the long string of unseasonably cold days that had been visited upon Worcester early that winter. The route to the Orthodox cemetery on the outskirts of Worcester—also named *Chevra Kadisha*—took the cortege through what once was a thriving industrial corridor but which has experienced its own death. Vacant factories and their broken windows—like so many mouths agape, yet silent in mourning—stood mutely as members of Martha Epstein's last cordon. The last quarter mile to the cemetery covered a tortuously potholed dirt road. The cortege slowed to a crawl.

Although a Jew's interment usually takes no more than fifteen minutes, Mrs. Epstein's was unexpectedly interrupted. Looking for his wife's tombstone, Abraham Lutsk, an older member of the congregation and a friend of the Epsteins, shuffled along the frozen ground and, leaning heavily against one of the taller tombstones for support, toppled it. His leg was gashed and bleeding profusely. He was quickly propped up on the fallen tombstone, head down to reduce the loss of blood, and one of the handful of people in the crowd who had a cellular telephone called for an ambulance. After the ambulance arrived and Mr. Lutsk was safely on his way to the hospital, the rabbi, flexing his toes within his shoes to stave off the cold, intoned the prayers of interment. Shovelfuls of soil—strewn with the rocks indigenous to this part of New England—thumped loudly on the lid of the pine box. And Martha Epstein—not an openly observant Jew, a salesclerk, wife, and mother—was finally, and with great dignity, laid to rest.

Back in their car for the drive back to the synagogue, the rabbi and cantor remained silent for a short time, a carryover from the somber occasion at which they had just officiated, marking the end of a life they really knew so little about. It is at moments like these that men like the rabbi and cantor often reflect: could we have reached her before she died; did we do right by her today; what about when our day comes—what will they have to say about us? Finally, Rabbi Rosenbaum turned to Cantor Freedman. His face was still drawn.

"Rehearsals, Steve," he said. "Rehearsals every Sunday night; we've got to be ready."

Martha Epstein had been buried. The feast of Purim was now only weeks away. It was to the future, no longer the past, that they must devote their energies. "I know it's a pain in the butt, but we need all the time we can get to get those lyrics down."

"Time!" the cantor replied, with a gravity proper to both funerals and the demands made of the congregation's leaders of worship.

"Funerals lay waste to a rabbi's life, believe me."

"Yeah," the cantor said, "I could go for a few more weddings myself."

"Let's not add up the divorces, okay, Steve?"

"What are we wearing?"

"White shirts, open. Maybe have some *tsitsit* hanging down for the heck of it. Cordovan penny loafers. Cool?"

"Cool."

In the days ahead, the notation CALL ON ISRAEL TRIP was transferred from one of the rabbi's lists of things to accomplish to the next. A week later, it had evolved into MUST CALL ON ISRAEL TRIP. But along with this self-proclaimed first priority for the year—the one he was having the greatest difficulty finding time to address—were a myriad of other projects, needs, obligations, and problems. The range was considerable.

The organizational—Tactfully introduce, then gently incorporate Karen Rosen as an unofficial codirector to "jump start" the nursery school, while preventing such a move from appearing threatening to Fran Smith.

The long range—Prepare a master plan for Beth Israel's future—addressing stagnant budgets, rising deficits, and declining membership—making sure he had the executive board's backing for such an effort.

The financial—Find someone who can be approached for the money to refurbish the nursery. Could the Hillman family be inspired to have their lately departed Bennie memorialized with a plaque? (Beth Israel was already overlaid with plaques, but there were still pressing needs—and wall space could surely be found to acknowledge the generous.)

The pedagogic—Preview, then select an appropriate (and short—the attention span of teenagers must be taken into account) section from the movie Brooklyn Bridge to entice high-school students into taking a religious-education course. (Also, spend more time—alone and out of class—with twelve-year-old Eddie Rabb so that he might see the wisdom in the Book of Leviticus and better prepare his bar mitzvah talk.)

The diplomatic—Somehow blunt Bertha Levin's simmering rage at the Worcester Jewish Federation's inability to get jobs for Russian Jews (while encouraging Sue Miller to do exactly that).

The pastoral—Schedule another casual meeting at Friendly's Restaurant to talk over Marc Smith's incipient agnosticism and try to talk about what Judaism could do for his life. (Also find some nice Jewish girls for Josh Israel, a new medical student in town, to meet.)

The educational—Organize a "Torah-thon" for a crash course in Jewish literacy. (A six-week course might not draw as many, given that Beth Israel congregants, in the rabbi's words, "like to take a pill and have it over with quick.")

The Talmudic—Render these opinions:

Q: *Does a family have to sit shiva for a crotchety stepmother who's been technically dead in a coma for months?*
A: Yes, but only two nights.

Q: *Can the teenage grandson of the priestly Cohen line go to the cemetery for the unveiling of his grandfather's tombstone?*
A: Yes, but stay on the periphery.

While in detail these tasks might be different from those performed by Christian clergy, their broad scope encompassed what might be expected of others in any ministry. But what I was discovering in the months I had spent with Rabbi Rosenbaum was an entire sphere of duties that need never be addressed by his colleagues in the Catholic and Protestant clergies: the demands of a ritually observant life. Because of its precision and stipulations, Jewish ritual life is, while enormously edifying, enormously time-consuming for the observant Jew: prayers three times a day, the meticulous preparations for the many holidays and the weekly *Shabbat,* the care of keeping kosher, continuous Torah reading and study—and more besides. It was certainly difficult enough for a layperson; far more for the rabbi, who was expected not only to live by the ancient edicts, but to stand with and support others as they made the attempt.

Halakha, Jewish law, set forth in 613 *mitzvot,* covers every aspect of life, from the Ten Commandments to the practice of leaving the gleanings of a harvested field for the poor to the divine command that stipulates that the truly religious Jew should actually live in Israel, the Promised Land. Not only does *halakha* imbue modern-day human events with a religious meaning, a reaffirmation of God's presence in the insignificant and momentous occasions of a person's life; more than this, the codes also served the very human requirement of ensuring justice. Indeed, they doubled as the civil laws of the ancient Jews. And *halakha* certainly has provided the continuity that is at the core of Jewish survival. Rabbi Rosenbaum often reminds his people of the strength of this divinely inspired and mandated uniformity.

As Rabbi Rosenbaum launched into the new year—Christian-based though it may be—two such ritual events were on his calendar: the conversion of a non-Jewish woman and the divorce of another.

While Reform Judaism does not demand it, the Conservative Movement has hewn to the Orthodox practice of baptism by total immersion for those who wish to convert to Judaism. This takes place in a *mikvah*, the ritual bathhouse to which women who keep the laws of family purity, *taharat hamishpachah*, go on the seventh day after their menstruation is complete, to be cleansed for future intercourse. In Worcester, the *mikvah* is a rather ordinary-looking small frame house on Huntley Street, maintained and supervised, as in most cities, by the Orthodox.

On the winter's morning on which is scheduled the conversion of Penny Gould—a woman in her midthirties, born and raised a Presbyterian, who had married a Jew and was already keeping a kosher kitchen—Rabbi Rosenbaum and Rabbi Jonina Skoff arrived at the Huntley Street *mikvah* to find it locked. When they drove over to the Lubavitcher yeshiva a few blocks away to talk to the keepers of the *mikvah*, they found a young bearded rabbi there who had just put on his *tefillin* for morning prayer. He was not disposed to unwrap in order to unlock. Finally, the *mikvah* attendant was located, Penny Gould took a shower, and the conversion was ready to begin—an hour later than planned.

Inside the Huntley Street house are separate dressing rooms and showers for men and women, each leading into two separate baths, divided by a wall. The *mikvah* resembles a moderately deep (about four feet), quite large (six by eight feet) ceramic-tiled bathtub, with stairs cut into one side. A portion of the water must be rainwater. It is heated and then covered by a tufted plastic insulating sheet to keep its temperature in the low to mid-eighties.

Halakha prescribes that, while certain prayers are recited, the person, nude, must immerse entirely in the water, with feet off the floor of the bath, if only for an instant. The embrace of Judaism implies a total conversion of manners, so the convert simulates a return to the womb and rebirth. The ritual is tactile, enfolding—and perhaps, for an instant, frightening and dark. But then, through eyes blurred with water, comes light—soft fluorescent in the Worcester *mikvah*—and the implication of new life. *Halakha* requires that three authorized men sign the conversion document but prohibits them from seeing a woman nude in the bath. With Penny Gould and Rabbi Skoff on the other side of the partition separating the men's from the women's bath, Rabbi Rosenbaum, Rabbi Nathaniel Ezray, and Cantor Freedman inclined their ears toward the partition.

"She's in the water now," Rabbi Skoff called out. A splashing noise was heard. "Ready? She's submerging now." There was a noise, as if a huge bowl or pot were being plunged into dishwater. "She's in."

"Blessed are Thou, Lord God of all creation . . . who has commanded us concerning the immersion of proselytes," Rabbi Rosenbaum intoned.

"Twice; three times," Rabbi Skoff's voice came through the partition, and Penny Gould was launched as a Jew with the Hebrew name of Ruth Bat Avraham—Ruth, daughter of Abraham. Like all converts, Penny had the venerable patriarch as her adopted father.

It was an experience that would not easily be forgotten by Penny Gould—as evidenced by the contented glow on her face as she emerged from the dressing room. Her husband—for whom she had converted and who had not even worn a *kippah* as his wife took on her own mantle of Jewishness—looked down at his watch. He seemed impatient to get moving on with his day now that this had been attended to.

Three men stood somberly before Rabbi Rosenbaum, who was seated at his desk. Off to the side, near the bookcase, stood a woman, dressed rather smartly for the occasion in a blue jacket and bright pink silk blouse. She was silent, but smiling.

"What is your purpose here?" the men said gravely, in unison.

"I am the appointed agent of . . . ," the rabbi replied, with equal gravity.

If the conversion rite borders on the mystical, Jewish divorce traditions might appear somewhat utilitarian by comparison. Each has its roots in a primitive culture far from modern-day Worcester, where Rabbi Rosenbaum performs them.

Jewish law roundly celebrates the joining of man and woman in marriage, but unlike most other religious faiths, Judaism does not turn its head when they are divorced. Here, too, a ritual is called for. When a couple is married, the man signs a *ketubah*, vowing to provide "food, clothing, and necessities and live with you according to universal custom." When he is to be divorced from his wife, another instrument, the *get*, is required. Although the Jewish divorce of Judith and Larry Gluck was scheduled for eight o'clock on a January morning in Rabbi Rosenbaum's office—so that Judy could make it to work more or less on time—it had all the elements of a ceremony that could have taken place in the desert thousands of years ago.

Even if the husband were present this morning—which he was not, as is usual in modern practice—the *get* would still be presented by a third party, called a *shaliach*, who acts as the agent of the husband. It is a humane way of delivering a divorce decree. According to Jewish law, this presentation must take place during daylight hours—a protection against impostors—and before three adult Jewish men, not necessarily rabbis, called *bet din*. Actually, a rabbi is not needed, but is customarily the *shaliach*, to assure the ritual is properly executed.

The *get* itself is ingeniously "coded" with a hole punched in a certain place, the location of which is revealed to the *shaliach* and the *bet din* through a separate letter from the rabbi who prepared the document. For today's document, it was over *"Yisrael"* in the last line. This is to assure that the document, in Aramaic—which few people of the time, and fewer still in Worcester, could read—is the one drawn for this occasion.

The three men of the *bet din*—in this case, Cantor Freedman, Richard Sobel, the synagogue's executive director, and Yael Cohen, who lives nearby, have the responsibility to make sure there is no coercion, implied or real. Following a printed sheet, the *bet din* addressed a series of questions to the *shaliach* determining everything from the proper names of the couple about to be divorced, that the husband is still living, has not annulled the *get*, did not specify a time in which it had to be delivered, and that the wife has not been forced into accepting. "Have you undertaken any vow or oath, subjected yourself to threat of excommunication, made a solemn promise by handshake, or any other such solemn agreement or obligation that would force you now to accept this *get* even against your own free will?" they inquired of Judy Gluck.

In preparation for the actual reception of the *get*, the *bet din* asked Judy to remove all rings so that there might not be anything between her flesh and the document. She is a petite woman, given to bursts of nervous laughter on this important morning. She extended both hands, palms up, and once the *shaliach* placed the document upon her hands, she lifted it above her head. She walked a few steps—not a simple task in the crowded office—so that the *bet din* and anyone else present could readily see that she had accepted the document and, to underscore her acceptance, had symbolically taken it with her. Additionally, as rabbis over the centuries have contended, this also provides firm statement of her new independence.

By nine o'clock, with a warm hug from the rabbi, Judy was free to go off and start her new life. A certain rebirth had occurred here as well; certainly there was none of the coldness of the judge's chamber, the lawyer's office, or the registered letter that typically attend a civil divorce. Hopefully, Judy Gluck will marry—Jewishly—again.

Penny Gould's conversion, and the Glucks' divorce, took a certain amount of time to transact, but the phone calls to make the arrangements, the preparation of documents, rounding up of witnesses, and accomplishing other details added up to considerably more time. If all the hours were added up and compressed, each would have occupied Rabbi Rosenbaum for much of a working day. And this rather generous ritual outpouring—as was the case for Martha Epstein's fu-

neral—was for people at the periphery, at best, of Beth Israel. Penny
Gould was not even a member of his congregation; neither Judy Gluck
nor Martha Epstein were active members of Beth Israel.

I wanted to hear the rabbi's rationale for preserving these time-
consuming traditions. After all, Worcester is not the desert and Jews
are no longer a wandering tribe; dietary, civil, and social conditions
are hardly the same. Why was it necessary in modern-day America to
keep these ancient ways? And why should a rabbi perform elaborate
religious rituals for those whose Judaism appears to be such an occasional part of their lives? It was difficult to set aside time in the rabbi's
day at the synagogue to talk at length, so finally I found the one place
in Worcester where we could have some privacy—and some lunch. It
was the Annapurna Indian restaurant, which, because it only serves
vegetarian food, could be considered kosher.

"To understand what we do today, it's necessary to go back, all
the way back to Creation," the rabbi said as he began to address a
plateful of various dishes, all made with artichokes. "In the first eleven
chapters of Genesis, we see God experimenting with man. Adam and
Eve sin, Noah has to take to the ark; God is finding out that this thing
called man is more unpredictable than He imagined. So, in Genesis
Twelve, God calls a stop and changes plans. He will set down some
rules, work through a certain people, and through them, reach the rest
of humanity. How to do that? First, God knows man can't do it alone;
he needs a community of support, people who at least know the rules,
whether or not they choose to play by them. But within this community is a chance to test moral ideas, to see how to live in harmony,
ethically.

"The laws, the *mitzvot,* give your life a structure, make it more
meaningful. The rituals draw a person closer to God, connecting people to other people who have the same goals. That's what gives it extra
power and gives you confidence; you are part of a community of history. On the other hand, anything worthwhile, anything that requires
you to focus, anything that tests you, is a pain in the neck: it's pressure-
filled, anxiety-provoking. But it is ultimately exhilarating. Like a great
work of art, or literature—something beautiful existed within that per-

son, but had they not concentrated on it, it would never have been produced. If you want satisfaction, you have to put up with the pressure; anything done well requires discipline.

"It's very important *not* to look at the law, the *mitzvot,* as arbitrary, a test of one's obedience to God's will, or a throwback to ancient practices. Why have observant Jews down through the ages survived the horrors they've faced? Because of the framework of their lives. We don't have to reinvent the wheel in every generation; that's why we hold to Jewish law. How is a person to live in this very secular age without some structure? Most of my congregants would say it's a structure they don't need. They would say they have enough pressures in their lives. But Jewish practice is not something superimposed on your life. You build your life upon *it.*

"I hear the same rationale: Why have a kosher home? We don't have to worry about sanitation anymore. Why walk to synagogue? We don't live in a tiny village where everyone walked anyhow. Why attend *shul* regularly? I meditate; I take care of the planet; I have my own spirituality.

"When I perform a ritual with people whose lives are not exactly steeped in Judaic practice, I am hoping against hope that something within that ritual will spark something deep within them. True spirituality, lasting spirituality. Of course it bothers me when I feel I'm being used as a ritual high priest, pulled out of the closet and dusted off when it's convenient. But I hope that this contact with Judaism at a critical point in a person's life will illustrate that this is something you can have every day, in every action you do.

"It's why I want to go to Israel, dammit, so my congregants can see a totally Jewish society—economic policy, army, cab drivers, *Shabbat*—every part of life is Jewish. To see what Jewish values mean. Now, Israel is far from a perfect society, but where on earth has any nation been fairer to the people who hate them? No political figure has ever been assassinated for their beliefs in Israel. I think Jewish laws are working better in modern Israel than they ever did in biblical times. It proves again that the laws handed down are still valid.

"Now I just have to get enough people to go. We have to go. I have to go. I may need it more than they do. *This week*, for sure, I'm going to start making those calls."

The range of affinity for Jewish observance was certainly quite wide within Congregation Beth Israel. For someone like Charlie Mills—who told me his attraction to Judaism began when he was a student at Harvard and found "something intact and wonderful" in the Jewish students he knew who led observant lives— eating kosher makes every morsel a blessing; observing *Shabbat* (although not necessarily in the synagogue) gives a holy texture to the rest of the week as he anticipates this day. Yet, for Peter Hellman, Judaic law presents burdens he has no intention of shouldering.

Even in the Rosenbaum house itself—the house set upon the mountain, the light unto the congregation, where proper observance is paramount—following the ancient laws had different meanings for the two adult inhabitants, I was learning. For the rabbi, observance meant the fulfilling of a religious obligation, following God's edicts. For Janine, it was part of a cultural heritage she had, a cultural heritage she would not squander even though, as she had told me, its religious component had been "bled" out of her.

7

"Jay, you're doing a terrific job, just terrific. Our programs and special events are the best; your sermons—terrific. Rave reviews, all around. But . . ."

"But." The rabbi mouthed the single word then sat back in his chair, the tips of his fingers touching one another and his lips in a pensive pose.

"That's what we're here to discuss, that 'but.' "

"I know that."

"We're on a dangerous trajectory, Jay, a very, very dangerous trajectory."

"I know that too."

"Every year, twenty or twenty-five members come in—but we lose thirty. Our budget is stagnant. The numbers just aren't there, Jay; the kind of support we need isn't there." Dr. Joel Kaufman, a tall, affable, prematurely balding man, had a broad smile on his face, but his look was hardly in sync with his sobering words. "We're not doing well getting new members. We're stressing *our* values, not looking at prospective members' needs. We have no way of knowing what their needs are. We're flying blind. We need outside help."

The rabbi shifted in his chair. "This isn't going to work if it's the work of a professional staff, and not our staff who—"

"I disagree," Dr. Kaufman interjected.

"The best advertising is word of mouth, our people recommending the synagogue to others. That way—"

"I disagree with that, too. Our members are not finding new members. Our membership committee is totally ineffective."

"We need to take the list from the day school and follow up on nonmembers, go to our young families; who do they know? The phone book. We need a committee to—"

"Again, I disagree. A committee that meets once a month, takes the summer off, and we'll-have-this-same-meeting-next-year. It took me four months to get here today."

"Well, what is effective?" the rabbi shot back, a rare tone of irritation rising in his voice.

"Outside professional help. Long-term planning is the answer. A needs assessment. Jay, a marketing plan. We have to run this like a real business, with a goal—say a hundred new members, so we can have the budget to do innovative things. What will it take to get a hundred new members? Maybe we need to hire a mercenary outfit who we pay for every new member they bring to us. We have fixed costs. If we pay such an outfit two hundred dollars for every family they bring us, we've netted four hundred dollars in the first year alone."

"I don't like the tone of this."

"Pretty soon, we won't have a choice."

It had hardly been a propitious day in the life and career of Rabbi Jay Rosenbaum when Dr. Kaufman finally came to call. Reservations for the Israel trip remained stubbornly fixed at eleven, even after a round of belated, but certainly enthusiastic follow-up calls, which had in turn followed a mailing and a number of in-person reminders after *Shabbat* services. Channy Greenberg had called this morning to see if she should go ahead with preliminary plans; June was the busy season for tours, and she wanted to be assured of adequate hotel space. The rabbi, in essence, answered with a lie: "It looks good; it looks good. Just give me a little more time to round up a couple more people."

More immediate plans were also in jeopardy: the Worcester Jewish Federation, which Rabbi Rosenbaum thought would quickly come to their senses about supporting the talk by Rabbi Leonid Feldman, was still balking at paying its share of the expenses, claiming to have no money left in its budget. The stack of twelve to fifteen messages sitting next to his phone this morning seemed to grow even as he

returned calls. The rabbi had jammed down his lunch of a cold tem-
pehburger while listening to still another irate congregant on the telephone (it was necessary to time his bites carefully), trying to convince
him that her now deceased mother cared little for Judaism—and actually had cared little for her—so why should she have to sit shiva for the
full seven days in order to mourn a loveless woman. Couldn't the rabbi
show some flexibility, some compassion?

His daily trials notwithstanding, the rabbi had looked forward to today's meeting with Dr. Kaufman. The young neurologist's
concerns about Congregation Beth Israel were deeply shared by the
rabbi. Yet it was rare that such an exchange took place at the synagogue. Rabbi Rosenbaum was more often confronted by one of the
chorus of peripheral members whose only contact with him was to
register a complaint or ask for a variance. But Joel Kaufman was different; he was active in the congregation, a member of the executive
board, the assistant treasurer, and regularly attended *Shabbat* services
with his wife and family. As medical director of the local Fallon
Community Health Plan—a health maintenance organization—Dr.
Kaufman was also considered something of a marketing whiz. He was
a man who not only talked about problems; he was someone who
could find solutions. But, the rabbi was discovering, he and Joel
Kaufman had greatly different visions for the future course of Congregation Beth Israel.

"Let me give you my list," the rabbi said, his voice retaining
the irritation, but lowering an octave, "and see where we are." Dr.
Kaufman, who had been hunched forward over the desk, leaned back.
"Number one: early childhood; our numbers in the nursery school are
going down. If we lose that, we're in trouble; it's what attracts young
families. Two, membership. We agree that's soft. Three, fund-raising.
Something new beyond sending out dunning letters for dues. And
four, youth; we're losing kids after bar and bat mitzvah; we have nothing to offer them, nothing to hold them."

"Needs assessment," Dr. Kaufman countered. "*First.* Both to
see if we're meeting our members' needs, and to listen to those unaffiliated Jews out there to see what they need."

"What they *need* might not be what we want to *be*," the rabbi replied. His voice was rising again.

"Jay, let's just *see*. Let's not make any premature judgments. Maybe this will cost us five thousand, ten thousand, but then we'll know. Focus groups? A survey? We need to develop a plan, put a price tag on it, and present it to the executive committee."

"That's going to be a tough sell," the rabbi said. "They feel we're stretched to the limit now."

"Twenty thousand, maybe. If we wait five years and do it out of desperation, it might be too late. By the way, I've been over to Temple Emanuel's nursery school. It'll knock your socks off; bright, appealing. A heck of a lot of our members' kids are there."

"And our own people don't think anything is wrong with that."

"Face it, our place isn't as appealing. And it has a—excuse me—old feel to it."

"I know. I know. We're working on that."

"Goals, dates; we have to figure out who's going to make this happen. We have to have a preliminary plan ready soon, if we want to get it before the executive committee in time for them to take some action before summer."

The rabbi had begun to sink into his chair, defying both his balky back and the orthopedic roll that strives in vain to provide him some surcease. After a moment of thoughtful silence, he straightened slightly and extended his arm over the desk. "Let me have your notes and I'll put them together with mine and draft a plan."

Dr. Kaufman pulled out his datebook. "In two weeks?"

"Fine."

"No hard feelings, right?"

"Of course not."

It seemed so simple and straightforward not that many years ago. Religious preference and affiliation were conveniently proscribed by family and neighborhood and were supported and regularly nudged along by prevailing social pressures. What your parents were, religiously, so were you. Your place of worship was the nearest church or temple. The sweeping scale of America's post–World War II internal migrations, and the social upheavals of the 1960s and 1970s, put an end to all that. It was not that people needed spiritual solace any less as they became freer to choose with whom and where (and if) they would worship. The plethora of new religious and quasi-religious movements—as well as the many secular approaches to human fulfillment—indicated that the need was every bit as critical.

Rabbi Rosenbaum knew well that Jews in the 1990s were having difficulty sorting out the meaning of their own lives, meanwhile trying to instill a set of values in their children at a time when there were so many other conflicting messages presented to the young. But his was just one voice, calling out with the promise of solace amidst a cacophony of spiritual hucksters. And if he was to have an opportunity to be heard above the din—to gain people's attention—he knew that he must, in essence, "market" religious belief, wrap it in an attractive, no-cost, no-obligation introductory package so that nonaffiliated Jews would at least sample his wares. His many innovative programs—from Baby Brunch to his popular yearly Purim presentation—were stunning successes. Yet, as Joel Kaufman pointed out, membership continued to slip.

"When they start out with that 'You're doing a terrific job, Rabbi,' you don't even hear it," the rabbi told me when we talked about his meeting with Joel Kaufman. "You're waiting to see what's on the other side of the 'but . . .'

"Look, I'm not afraid to admit to Joel Kaufman, or anybody else who is willing to listen, that everything isn't going right—and that we have to open up this synagogue to scrutiny. But, man, it hurts to get raked over the coals like that. Joel and I are on the same wavelength; our methodology is different. It's hard to be confronted with shortcomings, but I wasn't going to just sit there, happily taking on another task. I wanted to make it clear I don't want this dumped in my lap. I barely have a free night now; I'm shuffling stuff around that I should be attending to. I'm putting in sixty-hour weeks, and my one day off is often eaten up with a funeral or a *Bris* or an appointment with somebody who can't make it any other day. Janine's howling mad about how much time I spend here, and I don't blame her. She's getting the short end of the stick. Yes, it's important to have a growing congregation, but I'm not a superhero. I have a family; I have a life outside the *shul*. Sort of.

"Judaism isn't the center of Jews' lives, as it once was; people have other interests that take their time and money. To bring them back, to convince them this is worth it—it's a big job. And meanwhile, keeping the present folks happy. And getting them more involved. Also a big job."

It is a quandary rabbis across America know well. Do they put their energy into outreach, working on the marginal members of their congregations, trying to increase membership by gathering unaffiliated Jews back into the fold? Or do they devote themselves to "inreach"—a newly popular term in rabbinic circles—concentrating on that quarter or so of the congregation who are already active members in hopes of making religion so compelling a necessity, so sweet a food for their souls, that Judaism and its practices become central to their lives? Rabbi Rosenbaum and his colleagues in the rabbinate find that while they may be Old Testament prophets, proclaiming one of history's most enduring messages, they are working with—as did Moses, Abraham, and Jacob—a "stiff-necked people," no longer kvetching about a diet of manna perhaps, but still a legion of very finicky eaters, picking and choosing among the rich offerings the rabbis place before them.

But even as they devote considerable time and effort to their work, rabbis like Jay Rosenbaum find themselves losing an inexorable war of sheer numbers. At its peak in the early 1960s, the Conservative Movement—which had been constructing as many as fifty new synagogues a year—had some 800 affiliated congregations. Today, there are about 785 congregations, and the years ahead will see a steady drop in that number as few new synagogues are built and many more are forced to close in areas that no longer have enough Jews to sustain them. But even more telling is the level of weekly *Shabbat* morning attendance, which has fallen dramatically since the Conservative heyday in the 1950s and 1960s. As for the Friday-night services that usher in *Shabbat,* and used to be well attended—these have fallen off even more.

The tactics of "inreach" or "outreach" aside, Rabbi Rosenbaum was well aware that a meeting like the one he had just held with Dr. Kaufman was not only about the future of his congregation; it was at least as much about his own future with Beth Israel. It was not that declining numbers would necessarily lead to terminal dissatisfaction with him, although congregational love affairs with their rabbis can suddenly and inexplicably turn cold. But a static budget limited the congregation's ability to pay both his ever-increasing salary (he was now receiving $67,000 a year, plus very generous benefits) and to provide the kind of programming that a young, enterprising rabbi like Jay Rosenbaum wanted. Worcester fell into the "mature city" category; it was not experiencing population growth, and it certainly had no specific draw for Jews. Beth Israel was finding itself on the wrong end of a buyer's market in spirituality, which for Jews today—confronted with a dizzying array of choices—certainly did not necessarily mean affiliating with a synagogue. And Jay Rosenbaum was facing the fact that he was now forty-two years old; either he moved on soon, or he remained in place, in essence offering himself to Beth Israel for the rest of his rabbinic life.

When Rabbi Rosenbaum was presented with his most recent three-year contract a year ago, it contained a unique clause, designed to address the problem of the budget deficits Beth Israel had carried the past few years. If he could increase membership—and therefore receipts—he and his professional staff would earn a bonus. In essence, he was being offered a "finders' fee" for new members—a bounty.

Although the rabbi verbally agreed to the rest of the three-page document, he refused to sign it. He found the idea of profit-sharing repugnant. A year later, with the clause removed, he finally signed the contract.

"So, why do I put up with all this?" the rabbi asked himself in my presence after one uniformly frustrating day. "Janine asks me that three times a week, sometimes three times a night. What can I say? I love this stuff. And it's the last thing I ever thought I'd be doing with my life."

Jay Rosenbaum was born in the Bronx and was three years old when his family moved to Levittown, thus joining the mass migration from city to suburb of post–World War II America. Shortly after settling on Long Island, his father, unhappy with his work as an advertising copywriter—selling the virtues of everything from beer to deodorant—decided on a dramatic career change. Nathan Rosenbaum, who had come within a year of completing his studies for the Orthodox rabbinate, took on a small, struggling Conservative congregation in North Bellmore and went back to Jewish Theological Seminary to qualify for ordination as a Conservative rabbi.

Nathan Rosenbaum's move to the Conservative branch was in keeping with a larger trend that was shaping American Judaism, yet hardly disruptive of what was already a very observant Jewish life for his family. Although Nathan had been raised in an Orthodox home, he—like so many Jews of post–World War II America—could no longer abide by Orthodoxy's unquestioning, literal acceptance of the Torah and Jewish law. Conservative Judaism offered a life that was at once religiously rigorous yet enlivened with the possibility of new insights into old teachings—and open to modern scholarship. The Conservative Movement's seminary, Jewish Theological, was a towering institution of religious study. Abraham Joshua Heschel, Louis Ginzberg, Saul Lieberman, and Mordecai Kaplan were among the foremost Judaic scholars of the day—and all were members of the JTS faculty.

Although Jay admired his father—for his ease with people, his ability to bury and circumcise and marry with a deep humanity, and the deep natural religiosity that shone through his work—Nathan Rosenbaum's son knew from a young age that the rabbinate was not for him. It was a flame that consumed his father. He would not be so burnt. He wanted to be a good Jew, and that was that.

Young Jay attended Hebrew Academy in West Hempstead and, because there was no high school on Long Island with a sufficiently intense Jewish curriculum, had to travel back into the city to attend Flatbush's Yeshiva High School, an Orthodox institution. Although Jay and his two younger sisters, Risa and Rachel, had non-Jewish playmates on their block in North Bellmore, they never really socialized with them or their families. On Jewish holidays, on the Sabbath, at summer camp, for youth dances and field trips, Jews gathered together, to the exclusion of their Christian friends and neighbors, who were doing the same thing. Only once during those formative years was Jay exposed to blatant anti-Semitism: a swastika was etched in lime on their front lawn. He found himself more angry than fearful.

The Rosenbaums were a respected family within the Jewish community—the only community that really mattered. Not only was Nathan a rabbi; he was a *successful* rabbi. Nathan Rosenbaum had expanded the congregation to almost six hundred families. But there were other, less tangible reasons the Rosenbaums were held in esteem. Nathan Rosenbaum was known as a man who was not afraid to call out for a certain idealism, a purpose in life. Although the right job, the right college, the right clothes and car, a big home, a home in the right suburb, the right neighborhood *within* that suburb, a patio, an enclosed patio, were all symbols eagerly sought by this generation of Jews—both to prove themselves against the prevailing American standard and to distance themselves from their immigrant parents—Rabbi Rosenbaum constantly reminded his congregants that there was a higher mission than merely earning a good living. When the movie *Goodbye Columbus* was released, many of his congregants were scandalized at the portrayal of such venal Jews. Nathan Rosenbaum loved the film. It put a mirror to the Jews of Long Island; those who looked away angrily, he maintained, had been afraid of seeing themselves.

Young Jay agreed with his father that too many Jews, in their drive for upward mobility, were doomed to empty lives. It wasn't enough to be a doctor or lawyer; it was necessary—and more important—to live by the highest Jewish standards, and to make the world a better place. It was a point of pride for young Jay to be a part of a family that confronted itself with such high standards. But it was also a burden.

"I was a pretty good little kid, but I didn't *want* to have to behave; I didn't want a kid to stop telling a dirty joke just because I was there." The rabbi was smiling as he said that, a smile around which I could imagine the face of a ten- or eleven-year-old boy, wanting so badly to fit in with his buddies. We were sitting across from each other at the vegetarian Indian restaurant, in one of our series of what became to be known as the "Annapurna talks."

"It embarrassed me being singled out as somehow different. Anything I said about our family life would always get into the congregational grapevine; I learned to be careful. Being a rabbi's son and living so publicly formed a very private side to me. I was sure I would never go into the rabbinate. I needed to have a part of me where no one could intrude."

Until the seventh or eighth grade, Jay was basically a respectful child, and a somewhat rigid Jew. By ninth and tenth grade, something was changing. He began to make fun of his yeshiva teachers; Rabbi Jacob Heisler was a special target. Pale, unathletic, Old World, Rabbi Heisler was exactly the kind of Jew Jay Rosenbaum did not want to be. Jay wrote songs and passed them out to his schoolmates, satirizing Rabbi Heisler's idiosyncracies, mimicking his Yiddish accent.

Jay's rebellion came to full blossom when he arrived at Jewish Theological Seminary to pursue a non-rabbinic undergraduate degree. "I started wondering—what was me and what was my parents?" Jay Rosenbaum had lived an extremely sheltered life, and he wanted to see what there was beyond the boundaries his family had imposed—and which he had willingly accepted. Instead of confirming in young Jay Rosenbaum the life-enriching elements of Judaism, JTS actually pushed him farther away from the beliefs that had formed him.

"It was all about dispassionate study and nothing about faith. Heschel, whose *God in Search of Man* and *Man in Search of God* I'd read in high school—those books profoundly influenced me—was saying that Judaism was not a set of rules you had to discipline yourself to believe, something you had to compress yourself into. It was an irresistible presence, inviting you. And even Heschel's title had struck me; God was searching for *me*, searching for me, as it's said in the Book of Job, 'like a lion.' You could run from God, but you couldn't hide. I liked the idea of being pursued. At that time, Heschel was renowned on the outside, a hero to me, but at JTS he wasn't considered academically rigorous enough. He was laughed at.

"JTS prided itself on teaching Torah as it would be taught at Harvard. What they were serving up as theological education was a desiccated, lifeless body of facts. People were humiliated in class if they even uttered something like 'I feel.' 'You feel! Who in the hell cares what you feel! What do you think? And what can you prove of what you think you think?' Prayer? Observance? Forget it. Not part of the curriculum. JTS wanted scholars, not practicing Jews. 'Rabbi' was no longer the highest approbation; it was 'doctor,' and the better the school your Ph.D. came from, the more respected you were."

Into this atmosphere of purposeful academic pursuit and flimsy Jewish observance, another breeze began to blow. It was 1968; revolution was in the air. Everything was up for grabs—beliefs, authority, standards. And one day, after an especially dry morning's classes, Jay Rosenbaum walked. He strode boldly down Broadway, from JTS at 122d Street, to Take Home Foods at 114th, and marched up to the crowded counter. He ordered a ham and cheese sandwich, along with a container of milk. Then he marched out and sat down on a bench to the first *traife* meal of his life. He didn't like the taste of pork much, but the exhilaration he felt made up for it. And if it was only coincidental that he had eaten this meal on the Broadway median, it was nonetheless symbolic of where he would be for the next five years—in the middle, between one world and another.

From nonkosher food, to taking the subway on *Shabbat*, to dating gentile girls, Jay Rosenbaum moved easily on—like many college students of the time—to casual sex and to experimenting with drugs. There no longer seemed a compelling reason to live as a Jew, so he put his *kippah* aside, dropped out of JTS, and enrolled at New York University, finally going on to earn a master's degree in special education at Rutgers. He wanted to get lost in the secular culture of New York; he loved the anonymity. Finally, nobody was watching the small-town rabbi's son. The sixties generation became his religious community. His shoulder-length hair was swept back into a ponytail; his beard grew shaggy and reached his chest. When he spent a kibbutz year in Israel, it was as a totally secular Jew.

Turned off by the congregational Jews of the New York area— whose synagogues and temples he saw as little more than urban country clubs—Jay stayed away from weekly worship for years. More for a sense of community than anything else, he eventually started to attend a *havurah* at the West Side Minyan. The *havurot* were the Jewish counterparts of the Catholic folk masses and experimental Protestant liturgies that appealed to the alienated young people of the time. (Oddly enough, Alan Mintz, one of the founders of the *havurah* movement, had been a member of Worcester's Congregation Beth Israel in his youth.)

Jay found he began to look forward to Saturday mornings at the *havurah*, where a group of young Jews, without a rabbi present, sat around on the floor and read the Torah, spending almost as much time discussing as worshiping. He was taken with the group members' deep commitment both to Judaism and to pursuing an inquiry that he felt was sorely lacking in mainstream, congregational Jews.

During those five years, Jay Rosenbaum had no thought of ever seeing JTS again, but in 1975, against his own best instincts, he found himself applying to the rabbinical school. The *havurah* had reawakened his interest in Jewish studies but confirmed in him the utter banality of the life of the congregational rabbi. He was in good company at JTS. Most of his classmates were torn by ambivalence, and few wanted to be congregational rabbis—certainly not the kind of rabbis they knew, who catered to the monied members of the congregation, skirted sensitive issues in their weekly sermons, and lived their isolated, *halakic* life in the midst of legions of uninvolved, uninterested Jews. As part of his fieldwork, and much to his dismay, he was assigned to function as a student rabbi in Cranford, New Jersey.

"This is what I escaped from in North Bellmore. Judaism in Cranford was pareve, neither milk nor meat; it had no edge to it. I didn't see this for my life. I was idealistic. I wanted to deal with issues of faith and morality, and all they were worried about were their High Holiday seats. But then I found out I really liked the contact I had with people's day-to-day problems. I got off my high horse. Compromises—life is a series of compromises. I could see what a struggle it was for people to be good, to live as Jews in Cranford, New Jersey."

While Jay was still in the seminary, his father was diagnosed as having lymphoma. The disease spread quickly; before he died, in 1978, he admonished his son not to follow his example should be become a congregational rabbi. With Jay at his bedside, Nathan Rosenbaum sobbed. He had taken care of his congregants, he had done his best with his kids. But one person had gotten the short end of the stick. There simply had not been enough left over for his wife. There, he had failed. Jay Rosenbaum vowed on his father's deathbed that should he ever have a congregation—which was very unlikely—it would never happen to him. He would keep his priorities straight. His wife, his family would come first.

Soon, graduation was facing Jay Rosenbaum and his classmates at JTS. Although it was de rigueur to sniff at synagogues in wealthy suburbs, Jay found some of the most vocal protesters seeking positions at exactly those places. He held on, looking for "something in Jewish education," but "something" didn't materialize, so in August, months after most of his classmates had found their first assignments, he half-heartedly interviewed for a job at Ahavath Israel in Ewing, near Trenton. He was one of thirty-five applicants and—much to his surprise, and even more to his consternation—he was hired. He was paid $25,000, an average salary for a first congregation of that size.

Except for a few years in the secular wilderness, Jay Rosenbaum—the firstborn and only son of his father—had been reared, schooled, trained, and pointed toward the life of a Judaic prince. It was now time to live out that destiny.

Young Rabbi Rosenbaum went forth, hoping to bring *havurah* vitality to New Jersey, but, faced with a congregation of 150 predominantly older families, he soon knew that it wouldn't work. At first he was dismayed by the stony faces he faced from the pulpit, the lackluster quality of life-cycle events for which he had so carefully prepared. But then his Jewish training and his father's Madison Avenue spark coalesced. He created innovative, religiously based events, such as a *Suk-*

kah Hop, which included a progressive dinner, with meals served under *sukkot* in congregants' backyards. He started Torah dialogues, visited homes, created programs for everyone from toddlers to shut-ins, and made sure that the *Trenton Times* had pictures and copy on Ahavath Israel events. Soon, it was considered a "hot" synagogue, and young couples started to join.

"While neither of us were exactly nuts about New Jersey, it was a wonderful time for me and for Janine," he told me. "She loved being the *rebbetzin;* she taught in a religious school. We had met in the JTS cafeteria when she was attending a Yiddish course, and she loved Judaism as much as I did. We both wanted to live it, breathe it, spread it. Janine gave willingly; nothing was expected of her—the people were so happy to have this young, eager couple in their midst, anything we did was considered great. I have never been loved by a group of people the way I was loved there. We didn't have any children, so we had an enormous amount of freedom. We could give everything to the synagogue."

I visited with Janine one day to talk with her about the life of a *rebbetzin* and happened to mention how full and happy the years at Ahavath Israel must have been. Sitting at her kitchen table, she looked down at the coffee cake she had offered me. When she looked up, her eyes had narrowed, as if she were squinting into the sun. I thought it was the pain in her arms.

"Jay is a more even-tempered, more self-contained person than I am," she said, talking in a lower tone than usual, which I took as a measure of restraint. "He could be a rabbi on the moon and it wouldn't bother him. I *hated* New Jersey. There was an unpolished quality to the people of that congregation; there were no couples that we wanted to be friends with. We lived in the rabbi's house, which was right next to the synagogue; people were in and out of there at all hours. No respect for our privacy, none. I even had a dream one night that they were crawling in through these tiny living-room windows—they could get to us anywhere!

"Jay didn't want to be an assistant someplace, and so Ahavath Israel seemed like a reasonable enough place to start. And he was great there; he gave it his all. Jay and I were still dating when he took that congregation and, believe me, it was a shock to not just be visiting there, but to be a part of that life. Jay was at meetings—this being before we had children—and I was walking around in the malls in the evenings. But I did it; I did it all. It was Jay's work and it was my job to stand with him. I smiled, and I doubt if anyone knew how unhappy I was. But when we drove away from that place, I never looked back."

When Jay Rosenbaum announced he would be moving on from Ahavath Israel, he was sought by attractive congregations in Mission Viejo and San Diego, California. Despite the California possibilities, his real desire was to move to a large Jewish community near a city, New York or Boston. Such assignments are coveted, and the rabbi in place will often stay as long as possible, so when the Rabbinical Assembly informed him that Beth Israel in Worcester was looking for a rabbi, it appeared a reasonable compromise. After all, Worcester was a midsize city near Boston, and Beth Israel was not known as a "rabbi-eating" congregation. It professed to take Judaism seriously and it was looking for an energetic young rabbi to waken it from a somnolence that had become increasingly evident in the past few years. Their rabbi was a wonderful man, a Holocaust survivor, but the synagogue was moribund; young couples were leaving, the average age continued to rise, *Shabbat* attendance was painfully low.

Jay Rosenbaum traveled north to find out how seriously Beth Israel was about renewing itself. He had served out his basic training in an out-of-the-way synagogue and had made it come to life. His wife had tasted the first bitter fruits that befall a rabbi's wife. He was ready for a greater challenge; Janine was more than ready for the move.

Back in his office, the troubling echoes of Joel Kaufman's visit had been dispersed by a string of phone calls. The rabbi's buzzer sounded once more. He picked up the phone warily.

"Finally!" he exclaimed. " 'Leonid Feldman, you can come to Worcester!' Thanks, Sue. Good move. Good decision. Thanks for seeing it through. You'll see; it'll be worth it."

The rabbi scrawled a note to call the other Worcester rabbis and then hurried down the corridor to attend to what he considers one of the most important parts of his job—the education of his day-school children.

It was more than formal religious education he wanted to provide for these young Jews; he wanted to impress upon them the idea that their rabbi was a human being, someone accessible, not some distant, forbidding patriarch. It was thus his custom to hold an "Ask the Rabbi" session with each class in the school, which goes from kindergarten through sixth grade.

The rabbi continued out the back door of the synagogue and climbed the steps outside a trailer, one of the three portable classrooms necessitated by a surge in enrollment a few years back. He entered the third-grade classroom with a huge smile on his face.

"Benjamin; Binyamin." The children introduced themselves by both their English and Hebrew names. Such amenities attended to, they took their lists of questions from their desks.

"How many synagogues are there in Worcester?"

"What makes them different?"

"What actually goes on in a synagogue?"

"What do you do?"

"Is your job difficult?"

"Why does a synagogue have dues?"

"How much are the dues?"

"What is this money spent for?"

"Why does it cost so much?"

They seemed as serious as their parents might have been at a synagogue meeting, closely questioning this man who was both in charge of their immortal souls—a tough area to quantify—as well as quite mortal buildings and a portion of their checkbooks. The rabbi answered their inquisitorial vigor with a generous smile, which he was still wearing as the session ended and he headed for the back door of the main building. "They'll make perfect congregants," he commented as he made his way back toward his office.

By offering himself as the willing target of the children in these classroom visits, Rabbi Rosenbaum hoped the fire of Judaism would somehow, some way, be enkindled. When Joel Kaufman called upon him to institute strategic planning, the rabbi considered it still another way to fan the glowing—possibly dying—embers of congregational life. Neither was especially easy for Jay Rosenbaum; he would prefer to preach and teach, unvarnished, the truths and goodness of Judaism. But the day has long passed for such naïveté. He learned that early in life in his own home, a rabbi's home; it has been reinforced in his years as a rabbi. Jay Rosenbaum knew well the requirements of his job, and he was willing to make the necessary sacrifices—and compromises. He will be as modern, as secular, as ordinary as he needs to be in order to allow his people to see that they, too, are pursued by a lion.

8

In the years after World War II, fragmentary evidence and occasional eyewitness accounts of the plight of Soviet Jews began to reach the West. Each successive year brought more reports of Jews being singled out in an already repressive country for systematic harassment, imprisonment, even execution. The memories of the Holocaust were still fresh in the minds of the world's Jews, yet the closed and forbidding Russian monolith seemed to frustrate any efforts to help Soviet Jews.

But it was becoming increasingly clear that in order to weave the cloth of communism, Soviet leaders were rending the fabric of Jewish life. All religions were considered enemies of the state, but Judaism was especially suspect, as it was so integral not only to a religious life, but to the Jews' community life as well. Jewish law did not resonate with Lenin's or Stalin's law; Jewish spirituality had no place in an idealized, totalitarian state. A Jew was always a Jew, and a Soviet citizen only by accident of birth. Millions of Jews—whose roots went deep into the Russian soil—had to be neutralized if communism were to triumph.

American Jews were well aware that had their own forebears not left Russia and Eastern Europe—most of them around the turn of the century—they, their children and grandchildren could have been the subjects of such cruel repression. American Jews were horrified by the abuses of fellow Jews—and they were ashamed at their own inaction. Russia had been a cradle of emigration, and if Jewish roots were there, the branches transplanted to America flourished in an embarrassing amount of both freedom and wealth.

By the 1970s, the abuses were so widespread—names of dissidents and refuseniks like Andrei Sakharov and Yelena Bonner, Anatoly Sharansky, and others were becoming well known—that the issue could no longer be avoided. Under the aegis of quiet diplomacy and then with such dramatic campaigns as Operation Exodus, an effort on a scale never before attempted was launched to extricate Jews from their oppressors.

After the 400,000 Russian Jews who went directly to Israel, the United States received the next greatest number, and American Jews readily raised hundreds of millions of dollars for them through heart-wrenching campaigns. Some 250,000 Russian Jews were eventually sent to American cities selected by virtue of the presence of sufficient critical masses of Jews to assist the new arrivals in their transition to a new life.

But when these Russian Jews arrived in cities across America—cities like Worcester, which welcomed its first Soviet Jew in 1978—American Jews were astounded to find that these persecuted brethren were hardly what they had expected. They were well educated, had actually lived pretty well—at least materially—in the Soviet Union, and expected to attain a middle-class standard of living quickly in America. And they were only peripherally—if at all—interested in their Jewishness.

Jewish social service agencies, which over more than a hundred years had helped millions of Jewish immigrants to adjust to life in America, found these citizens of a Socialist state actually *expected* services—even *demanded* them. Confronted with this new kind of irreligious immigrant, American synagogues and temples struggled for ways to stake their claim to the Russians' spirituality before their souls were completely co-opted by secular American culture. But how to reach Jews who had no Jewish identity, Jews who lacked the rich, religious foundation and culture into which earlier immigrant generations had been born? Assimilation of Jews into mainstream American life had taken decades; these Russians would be part of American life in a matter of a few years. It was clear to the rabbis that if they did not make some inroads, the Soviet Jews would quietly be added to the ever-growing number of unaffiliated American Jews.

In Worcester, Rabbi Rosenbaum's innovative approach—his weekly sessions of "News, Views, and Schmooze"—had been rich forays into Jewish history and lore, but so far they had drawn only four or five Russians on good days, one or two more typically. The sparse turnout was, of course, of concern to him, but the rabbi was convinced that the usual ploys—invitations to a synagogue service, handing out a Hanukkah menorah, Passover essentials, a *siddur* or other book of prayer—while they were far less labor-intensive, simply did not work. More than once he had characterized this work with the Russians as "paying my dues," showing them that his was not a fleeting interest, a cursory gesture.

But as the rabbi had gone about paying those dues, he had been careful to keep the cost to himself. For this was his shadow, non-dues-paying congregation, one that his dues-paying congregation wants him to serve, just as long as it does not take away from the time he devotes to them.

The Rabbi Feldman talk was an important next step in his plan to bring these immigrants into the Worcester Jewish community. A successful launch by Feldman, followed by a constant building through the four workshops (now billed as "Living Joyously as a Jew"), would culminate triumphantly—the rabbi hoped—in the gala wedding in May for twenty or more couples. His own congregation will be gratified. A new group of Jews would be successfully initiated. He hoped that many of them would acknowledge the support of Beth Israel by joining it.

So, as the January Sunday of Rabbi Feldman's visit arrived, Rabbi Rosenbaum's mood was a mixture of anticipation and anxiety. (It did not help his *tsouris* that he had inadvertently chosen Super Bowl Sunday, at exactly the time the game would begin, as the time for the talk.)

Quite by coincidence, and perhaps serendipity, I happened to be in Palm Beach in the days before the talk and stopped in to talk with Rabbi Feldman before we each traveled north to Worcester. A tall, handsome man with sleepy Slavic looks, he is rabbi of Temple Emanu-El, a stunning white stucco edifice hard by Worth Avenue, the exclusive shopping area of Palm Beach. It is a rather prestigious post for a 1987 graduate of Jewish Theological Seminary (as well as much better paying than Beth Israel in Worcester, currently served by a rabbi with seven years more seniority). But, as the only native-born Russian now serving as a Conservative rabbi, a former Red Legionnaire, and erstwhile believer in and teacher of Scientific Atheism—who then found God and Judaism—Rabbi Feldman was quite a catch for any congregation.

His Sunday school class over, Rabbi Feldman closed his study door and began to tell me of these ubiquitous "Russian Jews" about whom so much is heard (the numbers emigrating, the camps they were sent to, the length of time they have waited for an exit visa) but so little is really known.

"The American Jewish community has done a wonderful job in getting them settled—materially," he began. "Five years after they arrive, Soviet Jews achieve an average American income. Okay for that. But, American Jews don't understand that as for their religious beliefs, the Russians are not starting from zero, religiously speaking. They start from minus zero—they were told that only fools believed in religion. And the American Jewish community has done very, very poorly making them Jews again. Why? Because they preach to them, using words like 'God' and 'Torah.' 'God' was a buzzword that only the stupid person in the Soviet Union would use, a word attributed to naive Americans. Guaranteed to get a laugh. And what is this Torah?

"On the other hand, Russian Jews were the elite; their kids know Faulkner, Dreiser, Shakespeare, Maupassant by the sixth grade. Because socialism is what it is, they learned to hate and to cheat the establishment; they were afraid of organization. They resisted joining anything; it could only get them in trouble. So why should they join a synagogue here? But, they had good jobs, important jobs in the best Russian institutes; they were proud of their three-room apartments, and maybe a tiny dacha. They come to America and get a used sofa and they are embarrassed; American Jews wonder why they aren't falling over themselves in their gratitude. They feel infantilized by Americans. What they need is a buddy; they want to know that Judaism is fun. Now tell me what American is ready to be a buddy? And how many are having fun being Jews? They say it's wonderful to be a Jew, but they don't *show* it."

In the Beth Israel auditorium that evening, some two hundred chairs had been set up for the talk. When Rabbi Rosenbaum arrived with Rabbi Feldman at seven-fifteen, only four people were present, all members of his own congregation. By seven-thirty, some seventy of the chairs were occupied, sixty of them by Russians—less than Rabbi Rosenbaum had hoped for, yet enough not to be an embarrassment. Most of the Russian men were bareheaded; the regular congregants, true to habit, had placed *kippot* upon their heads when they entered the building. The Russians were an eclectic group, differentiated most distinctly by the signals that betray how long they had been in the United States. Those who had come years before—Bertha and Yefim Levin, the Katz family, and Eva Honig—looked completely American in their stylish attire. Eva, a lithe, attractive, dark-haired woman in her late thirties—married to John Honig, a wealthy garment manufacturer—wore a tailored silk blouse, straight black skirt, and fashionable patent-leather pumps. By contrast, most recent male immigrants were wearing shoes of a mysterious slate gray color not often seen in American stores; the women favored bright lipstick and dresses in faint pastels, held together by bulky, poorly sewn seams.

After Rabbi Rosenbaum's brief introduction, Rabbi Feldman began his talk—for the most part in Russian, lapsing occasionally into English to keep the handful of English-speaking congregants roughly apprised of the areas he was covering. He is a dynamic speaker, given to pacing in front of the lectern, his arms shooting into the air to punctuate his points. His rambling talk, delivered without notes and peppered with American jargon, was an impassioned cry for adopting a Jewish way of life. "We have choices, always choices to make. Either there is a God or an Eichmann. Gestapo or God? Stalin or God? Either there is a God or there is a Politburo. We all have been through that.

For me, I believe there is a God. So what do we do about this guy, this God? As Jews, we have a system of laws, *mitzvot*, because we all need training, reminders that we must be good. Because without God's laws, man makes laws, and sometimes those laws tell us to send someone to the gas chamber, someone to the gulag.

"More laws; we Jews are good on the laws. Why the laws of *kashrut*? Three times a day—and even for a snack!—we are reminded that three and a half thousand years ago, when the world was a jungle and people were cannibals, God said, 'People, you must stop killing, but because you will not, I will make it difficult to kill an animal; you must kill it in the least painful way.' *Kashrut* teaches us a powerful lesson: that a common cheeseburger—mixing the milk of life and meat that is dead—is wrong, improper, unholy. Even after having a nice, juicy hamburger, you must wait three hours before having that cup of coffee with cream. What a powerful lesson about life and death.

"*Mitzvot*—practices, exercises so that we can make the world a better place. But you are not doing all this alone; that is the beautiful thing. It would be too hard to do alone. You, and you and you and you"—he pointed to individuals in the audience—"can join the Jewish team, the Jewish club. Whether you know it or not, you are united to all Jews, all over the world. Hey, were there demonstrations for Soviet Pentecostals? No. Only for Soviet Jews. You were never forgotten even when you could not understand what it was to be a Jew. We are a religion, a nation, a team. God's ball club. And you can fight with God, scream at God, but don't ignore God. Please. That hurts Him more than any angry words you could say. You are the future of Judaism in America. The thousands of Soviet Jews who are in Israel, they are the future of Israel—will they become religious or remain secular? And you have that choice: deal with God or ignore Him. I hope you will choose to deal with Him."

After his hour-long talk, Feldman answered questions, both from behind the lectern and near the refreshment table, questions ranging from his personal belief in the Messiah to what exactly was meant by "the chosen people," and how an all-knowing God could allow the Holocaust. The questions and comments—and their somewhat caustic tone—were more those of customary doubters than the newly enfranchised religious. Nonetheless, Rabbi Rosenbaum seemed pleased by Feldman's spirited talk and the equally spirited give-and-take.

The rabbi and his congregants might not reach the Western Wall in Jerusalem this year, but the march toward the east lawn of Beth Israel in Worcester had been launched—with fewer Russians than the rabbi had hoped for, but a credible legion nonetheless.

The rabbi had listened attentively to Rabbi Feldman during their time together during his short stay in Worcester and his overnight at the Rosenbaums' home. He liked Feldman's public admonition for the Russians to deal with God—somehow—and not to ignore Him. It echoed his own words. They were members of the "Jewish team." The rabbi liked that. He was beginning to understand the Russian mentality better, how to approach them. He wanted to know more.

The following week, even though his office work and sermon preparation were behind schedule, the rabbi was not about to pass up the midday talk at the Jewish Federation. He saw it as still another opportunity to learn more about the temperament of his shadow congregation.

Jeff Lipkind, a United Jewish Appeal regional coordinator, was touring the Northeast with two recent Jewish immigrants to Israel—Izabella Tkach-Musikantski from Baku, Azerbaijan, and Tigabu Simon from Ethiopia—as part of a program called "Thank You, America." The tour was designed to express—graphically, dramatically, and personally—the gratitude of two representative foreign Jews to the Jews of America for the many millions of dollars raised for Operation Exodus for the Russians and Operations Moses and Solomon for the Ethiopians.

Mr. Simon was the first speaker. He is fifty-one years old, with the serene face and measured voice of a man at home with himself. A teacher from Gondar, a rural village in the northeast, he calmly told his Worcester audience of some forty people of his harrowing escape. With rebel soldiers five kilometers from the capital of Addis Ababa, he and others of the educated classes at the top of the rebels' hit list were huddled around the Israeli embassy. Finally the word came: get to the airport. He was one of some fifteen hundred people jammed into an El Al Boeing 747 that had been stripped of all furnishings. Gunfire sounded in the distance. The overweight plane lumbered down the runway and, with little pavement left, was airborne. Within thirty-six hours, Tigabu Simon and fourteen thousand other Ethiopian Jews were airlifted out of harm's way. Although his story brimmed with dangerous exploits, he did not dwell on them. Instead, he spent far more time telling of his sentiments upon landing in Israel: "For at last I was home. One day in Israel and then I could have died," he said, his eyes gleaming.

Mr. Simon, at the urging of a questioner, told what it was like to be a Jew in rural Ethiopia, where there has been no real contact with the larger Jewish world for perhaps two thousand years. In fact, Ethiopians are considered by some to be one of the ten lost tribes who were dispersed after the Assyrian conquest in the eighth century B.C.E. His village had no running water or toilets, no electricity, and certainly no Jewish schools, yet the Jews lived in their own community, kept a variation of *kashrut,* would not eat at a non-Jewish home, observed *Shabbat* strictly, and passed down the Bible stories orally from generation to generation—a manifestation of prerabbinic Judaism. Even when Emperor Haile Selassie demanded conversion to Christianity, they resisted, and many of them were turned into *falasha,* landless peasants.

"It was our prayer and our dream to set foot in *Eretz Yisrael* . . . ," Mr. Simon said, his normally quiet tone solemn at the sound of the words, "the Holy Land."

Although they were traveling as a group, the second speaker was late for her remarks, having gone out to shop at Spag's, the legendary Worcester discount store. Mrs. Tkach-Musikantski arrived, breathless, with only ten minutes left of the allotted hour. A chunky woman with coarse, bleached hair and dressed in a dark lavender suit, she related—with not a little bitterness—that her sister, a doctor, and her husband, a textile engineer, were now relegated to making slippers in an Israeli factory. She had had a comfortable life in Baku; now she lived like a peasant. They came with little or no Jewish education or knowledge; yes, she answered a question, they are surrounded by Jewish history, and Jews, in Israel. "I cannot put history in my stomach," she said in broken English.

Jeff Lipkind shifted uneasily in his chair, finding the papers before him extraordinarily interesting. He had asked her to be candid and told her that American audiences didn't expect only sweetness and light, but it was obvious that this portion of his road show was proving to be counterproductive.

Mrs. Tkach-Musikantski bore on with her list of complaints: housing was pathetically inadequate; she had been commanded to learn a new language—Hebrew—without which there was no chance of advancement. Yes, Azerbaijanis were being thrown from windows by ethnic Armenians; yes, Jews were especially targeted; and yes, she and her family had been rescued. But for what? she asked her audience, in seeming retaliation for their questions. Earlier refugees from the Soviet Union had gotten good apartments, she said; she and her family were jammed into a mobile home, which broiled in the sun and froze at night. Her son took a sausage and cheese sandwich to school and was ridiculed. Many Russians talked of returning home. She was one of them.

The flame of Judaism, undiminished by hundreds of years of neglect and waves of persecution in rural Africa, burned on in Tigabu Simon. A mere handful of decades under Soviet communism had been a far more effective means of quenching the flame. Izabella Tkach-Musikantski was a vivid reminder that if Jay Rosenbaum expected thanks for his work with his second congregation, he would have to wait a long time. "Thank you, America" indeed.

After Rabbi Feldman's talk, Rabbi Rosenbaum was sure that the momentum he had been struggling so hard to achieve with the Russians was finally a reality. He was confident that the sixty Russians who attended would spread the word. But then, a few weeks later, the heavily promoted and superbly organized first session of "Living Joyously as a Jew" enticed a mere twenty-five Russians to Beth Israel to learn about the feast of Purim. (More than that many Worcester Jews had been involved in the program's planning and execution.) Outwardly, the rabbi was his usual optimistic self. "It'll build," he told the disappointed volunteers, adding, "I'm just getting to understand the Russian mentality myself." That night, he had trouble falling asleep, trying to figure out what had gone wrong, how he could make the next session better—and more attractive to the Russians.

The continuing frustration with the Russians aside, there were occasional rays of light for the rabbi as Worcester was plunged deeper into the winter months. A child was born to Adam and Lynne Winter, and the young couple made good on their promise, entering their son into a covenant with God in a *Brit Milah,* which the rabbi could not attend because of a funeral that morning. After a second meeting with Joel Kaufman—whose original list had opened with "Goal: Increase membership by one hundred families in one year"—the two had agreed upon a proposal that unequivocally stated, "Our primary goal as a congregation is always to strengthen the knowledge, understanding, and commitment of all our members to Judaism and the Jewish people." And, finally, there had been movement on the nursery-school front. With meticulous diplomacy, the rabbi has gotten Fran Smith to agree tentatively to let Karen Rosen join her next fall on the nursery-school staff, not as a codirector—as the rabbi had requested—but with the decidedly subordinate title of assistant director. The rabbi still hoped that after a year of this relationship, Karen would be able to take over. He had not told Fran Smith of his plan, but hoped that, with this gentle nudge, she would retire and allow Karen to revivify the nursery.

It is not difficult for a rabbi to get wrapped up in the day-to-day requirements of his job, the constant nurturing and hand-holding he must do, the life-cycle events he must attend and services he must perform—and to forget his true dreams for his congregation. This year Rabbi Rosenbaum's fondest dream was the congregation trip to Israel, a trip that would engender new life among his people. But, for now, Jay Rosenbaum had concluded that his dream was fading.

The number of confirmed travelers remained steady at eleven. If Rabbi Rosenbaum found the Russian mentality difficult to penetrate, the mentality of his congregants—which he thought he had fathomed in his six years at Beth Israel—baffled him completely. He could understand that the bad economic times might hold some back, and the issue of how older congregants and the younger ones with children would get along was certainly a reasonable concern. But then word reached him through the synagogue grapevine that there was still another issue. People were leery the trip might be "too religious." Would they have to observe *Shabbos*? Eat kosher? Would they live in constant fear of the rabbi discovering they were less than observant? If they were going to spend three thousand dollars for a two-week summer vacation, would they also in essence be purchasing the services of a religious watchdog?

This line of resistance hurt Rabbi Rosenbaum, and hurt deeply. He *wanted* the trip to be a religious experience—but not repressively so. He had spent six years at Beth Israel trying to convince people that guilt-driven Judaism was dead, trying to offer them a joyous, fulfilling alternative for lives that many of them openly confessed needed a dimension outside work, success, family. When this newest rumor reached the rabbi, he was so discouraged that for a moment he seriously considered calling the trip off then and there and refunding the few deposits he had received.

But, just as he knew that reasons for not making the trip were being discussed in the homes of his congregants, Jay Rosenbaum was equally aware that there were doubts about the trip even within his own home. Although he had publicly maintained his unequivocal desire to go to Israel with his family, privately he knew that the issue was far more complicated than that. The trip would present difficulties for the Rosenbaums as well, difficulties unknown to Beth Israel's congregants.

Janine's chronically painful tendon inflammation had shown no improvement. She was wearing her arm braces constantly. The thought of two weeks in Israel, attending to two small children, ages six and three—with her husband acting as the trip's guide and spiritual leader, and hardly at leisure to help—never had been her idea of a summer vacation. But it went deeper than that.

Although the congregants might have been intrusive during Janine's early life as a *rebbetzin* in New Jersey, she had had another life: her own career as a teacher in a local Jewish day school. There were no children to look after, and she had had more time to spend with her husband, alone. Their Mondays off were often luxuriously lazy days. They might not rise until noon. They might go off and see two movies in the afternoon.

But during her six years at Beth Israel, Janine's attitude toward Jay's work and her role had shifted dramatically. The Rosenbaums had come to Beth Israel when David was ten months old. Two years later, Shoshanah was born. Suddenly, Janine found that her life was more circumscribed—not only by the demands of two small children, but by the entirely separate, and sometimes more complex, demands placed on the *rebbetzin* by a larger, more prestigious synagogue.

Escape into the New Jersey hinterlands was no longer an option. In Worcester, every Jew knew every other Jew, if not by name, by face. While there may have been more Jewish community life, Janine felt she had no private life in Worcester; every time she left the house, it seemed, she would run into a congregant, whereupon conversation quickly and inevitably turned to the synagogue. If she and the rabbi went to a movie where congregants were present, it was guaranteed that faces would turn their way when a suggestive scene flashed on the screen. She felt constantly watched—to the point that she had begun to do her food shopping at the local Big D supermarket at ten o'clock at night.

She had gained forty pounds in the six years at Beth Israel. Eating, she admitted, was frequently her respite, and often her only sure satisfaction.

"Sometimes the congregation acts as if they own both of us," she told me one morning at her kitchen table, "like we both were under contract. I'm not looked upon as a person with my own views, my own needs. I am the rabbi's wife, and I should be doing everything I can to make his life easier so he can put in still more hours at the synagogue. And the bigger the congregation, the less time a rabbi has for his family. It's a strange life, and you learn to be wary. You think you have a friend, and then something you told her in utter confidence comes back to haunt you. I get the criticisms for whatever goes wrong, and I get none of the strokes Jay gets after a wonderful eulogy or a great bar mitzvah. I was and am *shomer Shabbos*. But it's not religion any-more. I'm not proud to say that the bickering, the demands, sometimes the meanness of this congregation, have bled religion right out of me.

"Why would I want to go to Israel with these people? I see them every day. I want to be away, where nobody knows me, where I can be myself for a while."

As Jay's responsibilities at Beth Israel grew and his time at home diminished, the Rosenbaums had many talks—some calm, some heated—about their future. Janine said she would back Jay if he wanted to switch careers: "Do anything, be a garbageman!" she shouted one night; anything, so that she could have more time with her husband. If Jay gave the word that he was ready to move to Israel, she would begin packing immediately. It was a wonderful idea, he would say; their children would be brought up in a totally Jewish envi-ronment, and their family could pursue an even more intensely Jewish life. But what would he do there? There were but a handful of Con-servative synagogues in Israel, a country that has shown little toler-ance for any expression of Judaism other than Orthodoxy. Janine did not care what her husband would do. To live in Israel would be enough for her, regardless of his job.

As for the rabbi's dream—a congregational trip to Israel—this was not her dream. She wanted to do what she did every summer: have her husband exclusively to herself and spend as much time as possible at her parents' home in Seattle, three thousand miles from Worcester, and a world away from Beth Israel.

Her husband's work might be fulfilling him, but in her life there was a gaping hole, one that she had come to realize might never be filled as long as Jay Rosenbaum was about the work toward which he had been pointed in his formative years, and to which he was de-voting his adult life.

*   *   *

"Rip shit! I am positively rip shit!" The rabbi was standing behind his desk as I entered one morning, after knocking. He leaned upon the desk, his hands spread out over a copy of the Torah, several commentaries, and the first few pages of what would be his next *Shabbos* sermon. Even as the rabbi cursed—the first time I had heard him do so—there was a wan smile on his face, a signal that the situation was as ludicrous as it was irritating.

"The Sisterhood won't come up with the seventy-five bucks—a hundred bucks?—it'll cost to bring Tatiana and her family from Washington for the bat mitzvah. Beth Israel Sisterhood with plenty of money; I thought they'd be pleased to do this. That's why I asked them. A little Russian girl. What an opportunity! This one I can't believe!"

Into the rabbi's carefully coordinated campaign to bring the Russian Jews into Beth Israel's orbit, a small, unexpected bonus—a *mitzvah,* he would say—had been rendered. One of the rabbi's young congregants, Erin Goldstein, had been linked two years before to Tatiana Gorodetsky, a Leningrad girl of the same age, as each approached her bat mitzvah. It was part of a national program sponsored by Action for Soviet Jewry in which Erin and her family, active members of Beth Israel, had agreed to participate, both to underscore the plight of Soviet Jews—the program's intent—and also to initiate Erin into the adult responsibilities of Judaism. By chance, Tatiana—whose father, a physicist, had been denied permission to emigrate on security grounds—had recently been allowed to leave, together with the rest of her family. Her bat mitzvah would be celebrated in America. Beth Israel had enthusiastically promoted the "twinning" program as a way to involve their youngsters with the Soviet Jews, as a way to make a bar or bat mitzvah more than the largely social event it was for so many families. Rabbi Rosenbaum could not understand why the Sisterhood would not write a modest check to support what the organization would surely point to as a worthwhile cause—and also one highlighting a young Jewish woman.

Some might call it religious *hondeling,* but Rabbi Rosenbaum finds himself doing just that, and more often than he cares to admit. He reached for the telephone. Whom could he ask for the money to bring Tatiana to Worcester? Sam Cooper, the minyanaire and retired car wash owner? Sam always said yes. Bennie Hillman's son? Maybe Carlton Palley, the candy magnate? The heat of the moment passed; his hand slowly drew back from the handset. He did not want to ask these men for a pittance, when he might have to call upon them with a more serious and substantial request. There was a small amount remaining in the rabbi's discretionary fund; a perfect use.

He scanned the list of things he *had* to accomplish that day. His finger traced down the column. At the bottom of the list was the notation "Combined trip?"

Earlier in the week, at the monthly meeting of the ecumenical clergy group he attends, Rabbi Rosenbaum had heard that a Worcester minister was organizing a tour to Israel that summer. If they combined their groups in a single trip, it would be another example of the inspired ecumenism for which Rabbi Rosenbaum was noted. A telephone call could set the wheels in motion. Unfortunately, a joint delegation would dilute the primary intent of the trip. It would no longer be the total Jewish experience he had envisioned. It was not a phone call he wanted to make, and he had been putting it off.

The following *Shabbos*, as the Torah was read, Erin Goldstein and Tatiana Gorodetsky stood shoulder to shoulder on the Beth Israel *bimah*, linked as Jewish young women by age, paired by an ingenious program, but knowing no more about each other than could be gleaned in the few hours since Tatiana had arrived the day before. Tatiana, her straw blond hair cascading over her shoulders, was dressed in a starched white cotton blouse and dark skirt; Erin, her black curly hair equally long, was a study in color-coordinated lavender, shoes to earrings. As is the custom for the bat mitzvah, the girls read from the Haftarah, which on that *Shabbat* was a passage from I Kings about Hiram's excellent burnished brass vessels for the temple. Erin—a regular synagogue-goer and star pupil in Hebrew school—read her Hebrew flawlessly from the parchment scroll before her. Tatiana—denied the basics of Jewish life and education—read from a sheet of paper, placed over the scroll, on which the Hebrew had been phoneticized.

Vladimir and Marina Gorodetsky looked on proudly, as did Tatiana's grandmother—who carried the wonderful Old Testament name of Hanna—and her sister, Maria. Nearby were the Goldsteins, Kathy and Eliot, and their other children—Ian, older than Erin, and then the younger siblings, Aran, Lauren, and Kevin. Ian, Erin, Aran, Lauren, and Kevin? What kind of names are these for this observant, involved Jewish family?

Raised in an Irish Catholic home, Kathy Conway at one time thought of becoming a nun. Then she met Eliot Goldstein, and her life took her in a direction she never could have predicted. Now, the Goldsteins are one of the pillars of Beth Israel—and perhaps a source for some optimism about Jewish intermarriage.

"In Eliot, I saw Judaism not in a book, but in action," Kathy Goldstein told me later. She at first gives the impression of a certain primness (nunlike, perhaps) but she easily breaks into girlish giggles, often at her own expense. "What did I know about Judaism? Virtually nothing, formally. But this man was different, this man really did try to make the world a better place. He accepts people with such great charity—and it was obvious to me Judaism had made him this way. I found this enormously attractive; this was the kind of man I wanted to spend my life with. And as I thought about what being a Jew would mean, I found myself saying that Catholicism and Judaism have so much in common, I could live like this, I could do this. One event really formed our Judaism: it was a bar mitzvah and it was so hideously overdone, with an ice sculpture of the young boy and all! We didn't want to live out Judaism that way. Judaism—I'd have to add, Conservative Judaism—is so wonderful for its openness to new ideas, introspection, and even disagreement—this is not the Baltimore Catechism, my bible!—and yet it has the closed, dogmatic part that gives you a discipline about your life. Like today, a perfect day—almost.

"I had asked Jay if my parents couldn't have some small part of the service up on the *bimah*. They're not Jews; he wouldn't allow it. Of course, that hurt my feelings, and I wished this guy would loosen up a bit. But I respect him so much; he stands for what he believes in, even when he knows not everybody is going to be happy with his decision. It's going to pay out for him, I know it. Oh, the names? Goldstein has such a sharp sound to it; the Irish names like Erin and Ian soften it. And, after all, they *are* half Irish."

In Rabbi Rosenbaum's sermon, the day's Torah text from Exodus on the exacting standards for the temple sanctuary provided a springboard for a consideration about excellence in life. There was no better time than at a bat mitzvah, the rabbi proclaimed, looking first at Tatiana and then at Erin, to talk about excellence, Jewish excellence. Near the end of the service he gathered the two young women on either side of him at the lectern.

"One hundred years ago, a river of Jewish history in Russia was split into two streams," he said, his arms extended behind them. "Some stayed, while many poor, persecuted Jews left for America. Many of our grandparents were among them. Today, before us, we see a miracle as those two streams are reunited in Erin and Tatiana. Erin, who could grow up and take her freedom for granted; Tatiana, who lived under a system that would not allow her to be a Jew. They stand together today, young Jewish women about to take up their responsibilities in their communities. The commitment shining in their eyes today must be our commitment, too."

Yes, the two streams had come back together, but what a roiling confluence it was proving to be. From the left tributary flow these brave Russians, who have suffered for a heritage about which they have only the haziest notion. These Russians who were trained to idolize communism, who now are faced with the capitalistic possibilities and excesses of America. All the while, Judaism—this morning, in the person of Jay Rosenbaum—bids them to another pursuit, with more lasting rewards. From the right tributary come the people of Beth Israel, the Russians' supposed role models for a new life, yet people equally leery of following the path the rabbi marks out for them on such days as this.

"Commitment; I'm always talking about commitment," the

rabbi told me when he reflected back on that morning. "Forget a commitment to a totally Jewish life. Forget a commitment to observe *Shabbat*. Forget keeping a kosher home. Why can't I get a handful of people to commit to this darned trip to Israel? What's wrong? Is it me?"

9

Just ahead of him in the dingy, poorly lit corridor of 5-West, Howie Fixler recognized a familiar profile emerging from a patient's room. It was eight o'clock at St. Vincent's Hospital in Worcester, and the medical floor was bustling with doctors like himself making their morning rounds, nurses and aides about their own morning routines. Charlie Mills was walking, fast as usual, toward a room farther down the hall. Howie, whose stride is more leisurely, even when he is in a hurry, decided he could wait no longer. He lengthened his stride and headed straight for Charlie.

Although they are both internists who work for Fallon Community Health Plan, a large health maintenance organization, Howie had not seen Charlie lately. While this might not have been the best time to talk, Howie couldn't hold it in anymore. At first he had been irritated when he heard about the trip to Israel Charlie had organized. As the rabbi's own trip failed to attract enough people, that irritation gradually turned to anger. Howie Fixler was not a man who was angered easily, but he realized that his dream of going to Israel in the company not only of his family, but his fellow congregants, was in jeopardy.

"Hey, Charlie, can I talk to you for a minute?" he called out.

"Sure, Howie, sure," Charlie said, looking down at his patient list. The lack of a response from Howie eventually caused Charlie to look over the top of the list and into the eyes of his much shorter associate. Howie's eyes were fixed on Charlie, waiting for his full attention.

"I'm probably out of place on this, Charlie, but I've got to get it out," Howie finally said. "I'm not real good at letting bad feelings build up. It's about the synagogue trip to Israel. And your trip. They're in competition, Charlie, and our group isn't going to make it. The rabbi isn't going to make it."

"I don't want that to happen; you know that," Charlie quickly shot back. "I told Jay. I asked him if there were any hard feelings."

"And he said no, right?"

"Right."

"Well, there are. I'm getting calls. People are shopping around. Charlie's trip? The rabbi's trip?"

"I'm being cast as the spoiler, right? If the congregation's trip doesn't come off, people are going to be mad as hell at me, right? It's not that, Howie. We thought about this long before Jay announced his idea. I'm not in competition. We just want to go and have a good time with our kids. Simple as that."

Howie Fixler stared back. His round, dark glasses encircled eyes that remained locked on Charlie Mills, reinforcing the concern his words had just forwarded.

Both physicians are active members of Congregation Beth Israel, but their paths to both medicine and this level of Judaic commitment could not have been more different. Charlie had been a brilliant student, a Harvard undergraduate who was easily accepted into, then breezed through, medical school. For Howie, it was a struggle; he was on the waiting list for medical school and was accepted only by sheer luck. Then it was a struggle to get through. Each saw medicine as a calling, an honorable vocation. Each has found that being a doctor has not brought him the fulfillment he thought it would bring. Each wants something more in his life.

Charlie's father is an Episcopal priest, so his was a strongly religious upbringing. But, during his Harvard days, Charlie became aware of a quiet reverence in his Jewish friends that he found enormously appealing. When he met Rhonda, it was easy to make the decision to convert. While he is an active member of his *havurah* at Beth Israel, and the Millses keep a kosher home, synagogue services as well as synagogue intrigues enervate him. This is not the Judaism he converted for. In his heart, Charlie wants to move to Israel, to live a completely and intensely Jewish life, without an American overlay.

Howie was born Jewish, was bar mitzvah, but the shallow roots formed in the soil of a marginally observant family quickly withered in his teenage years. With his marriage to Jody and the rearing of their two children, Howie had found himself drawn—propelled, even—back to Judaism as an organizing principle, an ethic, for his life. The Fixlers do not keep a kosher home, but Howie has taken on the chairmanship of the education committee at Beth Israel, a time-consuming and often frustrating and thankless job. The couple were attending Sabbath services more and more regularly; Charlie was there perhaps once a month.

The corridor in 5-West was, for an instant, quiet and empty of people. Charlie Mills, for once, was also quiet.

"Jody and I've been planning this trip for years and now we can finally afford it, Charlie," Howie said. "But I don't want to just go as a tourist."

"I don't either, Howie," Charlie returned, his voice now lower and more measured. "I love Judaism, you know that," he said, his boyish ardor quickly overwhelming the attempt to be serious with Howie Fixler. "This isn't just a vacation—Israel's a real important place in my life, real important."

"There's another dimension. And Jay could give it; we both know that. Charlie, the bottom line is that you're taking people away and he's not going to be able to get enough people together and go himself. It's not right to ask the rabbi to pay. He's going to be doing something for us. Sorry, but that's where it comes out."

"Let me think about it," Charlie said, turning to continue his rounds. A few steps away, he turned back to Howie. "By the way, thanks for telling me."

Ben and Lillian Silverman smiled graciously at the rabbi. The rabbi smiled graciously in return. Ben represented number twelve; Lillian, thirteen.

The three of them stood together a few paces from the *Oneg* table after *Shabbat* services that week, talking about the trip to Israel. The Silvermans, an older retired couple, had finally signed on, but this made only thirteen, just half the number needed. While the rabbi's face—and his recitation of the various places on the Kenes Tours itinerary—conveyed an excitement about the trip, it was an excitement he had to consciously conjure up. The Silvermans were lovely people, solid members, but the prospect of leading a group composed largely of senior citizens was discouraging. He had conceived the trip as an intergenerational affair, a time when older and younger members of Beth Israel could bond together during two highly charged weeks in Israel. Upon their return, they would kindle the fire of communitarian spirit, inspiring stricter Judaic observance and general spiritual growth throughout the congregation. But without a significant group of younger people along, Rabbi Rosenbaum knew there was no chance of this happening. Couples like the Silvermans were already observant, comfortable with their religious practice; they had inhabited this house for a long time, knew its creaky floors and its stout roof and were happy to abide therein. But they were not the kind of people to inspire others to change.

The rabbi had by this time made one key decision about the trip. He would not be joining the group going with the Protestant minister. And, as an unseasonably bitter winter began to loosen its grip on Worcester, and temperatures began not only to reach but actually linger in the thirties, he was preparing himself reluctantly to notify the eleven—and these two new recruits—that the trip was not to be.

He might have done so had not he and Charlie Mills found themselves suddenly and embarrassingly face-to-face at *Oneg* that February morning.

"*Shabbat shalom*, Rabbi," Charlie blurted out, somewhat more animatedly than might be expected for so conventional a greeting.

"*Shabbat shalom*, Charlie," the rabbi replied, in a decidedly more appropriate tone.

The two men stood there, transfixed in an awkward silence.

Charlie, munching on a piece of pound cake, finally broke the silence. "We're looking into Tower Airlines for the Israel tickets, Jay; supposed to be the best fares around. Why don't you do that? Think you could save a bundle. How's your group coming along?"

The rabbi looked past Charlie—something of a rarity in itself for a man whose gaze was usually direct—and then allowed, without inflection, "It doesn't look too good for this year."

Someone to the left of the rabbi called his name, and Rabbi Rosenbaum offered a weak smile to Charlie—a look that asked if he might be excused. Although they had not worked to avoid each other in the preceding months, there had been a certain discomfort between the two men, which on this morning at Beth Israel was palpable.

"Ah, Jay?" In its newfound composure, Charlie's voice carried a request that the rabbi not move on to the next congregant just yet.

"Yes, Charlie?" the rabbi replied, the tone of Dr. Mills's voice causing him to refocus on his face.

Charlie reached down for another piece of pound cake and nervously plunged it into his mouth. "You know, Jay, we should link up over in Israel; we could do a lot of things together."

The sound emitting from the rabbi's mouth was decidedly non-committal.

Charlie stopped chewing and looked squarely at the rabbi. "What would it take for us to go together?" he asked bluntly.

Some of the younger children grabbed at the rabbi's hands. Temporarily distracted, he turned first to them, then quickly back to address Charlie's unanswered question. For a moment he studied his face.

"Serious?"

"Serious."

"Let's talk," the rabbi said quietly. "But it has to be soon; time's running out on this thing."

"Tuesday?"

"Tuesday. You set the time."

And so, two other rivers, diverted at their source some months ago, surged to be rejoined at Beth Israel. Two rivers, each the weaker for the lack of the other, pushed at the barrier that separated them—in this case, a formidable bulwark of suspicion of the young by the elderly, elderly by the young. Howie Fixler had spoken the unspeakable, and Charlie Mills had answered. And, after all was said and done, all the rabbi's good intentions and able work had nothing to do with this propitious moment. A tentative agreement in principle had been reached, but the actual wording had to be settled upon. And made agreeable to both sides.

"I've done some checking on this already, Jay." Charlie Mills laid sheets of paper scrawled with numbers on the rabbi's desk the following Tuesday. "I've looked at your numbers; your travel agent can get the trip two hundred and fifty bucks cheaper than mine. The itineraries aren't much different; we can work that out, combine them. The Ramada Inn we booked is five star, swimming pool, great for the kids from our group. It looks like a win-win situation." Charlie, a tall, trim, but muscular man, is an animated talker, whose words spill out of his mouth in enthusiastic bursts.

"What about *Shabbos?*" the rabbi inquired.

"*Shabbos,*" Charlie replied, his voice dropping lower. "Yes, *Shabbos,* of course. We'll have two of them."

"The Ramada Inn is on the outskirts of Jerusalem, Charlie. People can't walk a mile and a half to *shul* on *Shabbos.*"

"But the Ramada is a great hotel, good price, five star."

The rabbi swiveled in his chair. He peered back over his shoulder to the snow-covered playground equipment just outside his window. The remaining snow was a mottled gray color in the faint light of the cloudy winter's day.

"Charlie, this is a synagogue trip, a congregational mission. This is not a trip to Club Med. Being able to walk to *shul* is very important."

"Jay, Jay, now wait a minute," Charlie replied quickly, as if he had to stop the rabbi from saying anything more. His next comments were direct. "I don't want to spook my families with too much religion. It boils down to that; simple."

"This is a BI trip."

"I know that, I know that, but we don't have to *bill* it as a BI trip. These people want a loose confederation, like the Soviets are trying to work out. They don't want to have to do the whole *Shabbos*. They don't want to feel they're ducking out on the rabbi. That'll blow the thing out of the water, guaranteed."

"Love Israel, but don't be too Jewish, right? A microcosm of the Jewish people. Have I said that before?" By now, the rabbi was smiling at his oft-used words, but he also seemed to be gently pleading for Charlie to show him a way to an honorable solution.

"No, no, we can do all that, everything, but just don't rub people's noses in it. Don't put the BI stamp on it."

This was not an offer of negotiation; this was a call for abrogation.

"But that's the *whole idea!*" the rabbi fired back, his voice growing louder. The look on his face had elements of both pleasure and exasperation, somewhat like that of a parent dealing with a balky but treasured child.

"We can work around it, work around it," Charlie said, pushing his itinerary across the desk. "Let's deal with the trip and these things will fall into place."

"Is the issue *Shabbos*? Or is there more to it than that?"

"Jay, these families care enough about Israel to go, but they want to have a good time with their kids. They don't want to pay eight or ten thousand bucks to go and feel bad. They don't want to go to second-class hotels. When you sell a car to a person, it has to sound exactly right. We have to make this trip sound exactly right."

It was not that Jay Rosenbaum, an ad man's son, did not know the virtues of proper packaging. He just wanted to make sure the product was still intact.

"Look, Charlie, I'm not going to be peeking in people's rooms to see if they're observing *Shabbos*; no head counts. But we have to be within walking distance of a synagogue. Are these people afraid of being part of a Jewish community for two weeks?"

"We can work it out; let's look at this. Tiberias, right, we're doing that; Yad Vashem, the kids shouldn't do that . . ." Charlie pushed ahead, confident that the deal was at that crucial point where acting as if it were already a reality might indeed make it so.

"Maybe this can be the new model of a congregational trip," the rabbi said slowly, as though the thought was forming itself as the words were coming out of his mouth. "Jointly led, rabbi and layperson." His voice, still laced with uncertainty, seemed to convey that he was straining to discover a path to an honorable compromise.

"People buy the car because it's red; this is about emotion. Masada, the rabbinic tunnels . . . it's all here."

"Religion is perceived as a burden; am I right, Charlie? Well, it *is* a burden. *Ol malchut shamayim*—the yoke of the kingdom of heaven. You're a marathon runner; you can't do that and never practice."

"Hey, you don't have to convince me. I just want us all to go. Together."

The rabbi leaned back in his chair. "Together." He let out an audible breath. "I'd given it up for this year. But, maybe. Just maybe. Charlie, I feel the enthusiasm coming back."

"The Dead Sea, Tel Aviv, Haifa—it's all here, Jay."

"Yes, I guess so."

"My rabbi!" Charlie said, impelling his hand across the desk to grasp and shake that of Jay Rosenbaum.

From the deserts of the ancient Middle East to the shady streets of Worcester, Massachusetts, clericalism has always been a contentious and divisive concept within Judaism. As he tried to convince a broadly diverse group of people to travel with him to Israel, Jay Rosenbaum was just the latest in a long line of men who believed themselves called to proclaim the message of God, yet found themselves confronted with the shouts and murmurs of those disinclined to hear.

In its earliest days, it was the biblical high priests who by privilege of birth served as intermediaries between humans and God; then came the prophets, claiming direct inspiration from God. Finally, the rabbis began to emerge in the first century as teachers and interpreters of the law. The rabbi's authority was not divinely granted; rather, it was earned through his intimate familiarity with Jewish law, both code and custom. But he did not have exclusive access to God, as had the high priests and prophets before him. During the early rabbinic period, a body of teachings and practices was codified, establishing that each person could directly approach God. Groups of ordinary Jews could conduct services from morning *minyan* to *Shabbos* and the major holidays, and perform all the rituals that marked birth, marriage, and death. Each person, in essence, was a high priest. Thus, throughout its history, Judaism has taken a somewhat contradictory approach to the rabbinate, at once revering the role of the rabbi, while suspicious that the keeper of so much knowledge might use it to bludgeon people into compliance with the law.

Through the centuries, one aspect of the role of the rabbi has not changed: he teaches and promulgates the law he has spent years studying. As a corollary, he serves as a living proof that this law has validity. In addition to being a scholar who *knows* the law, he must show through his life the goodness of that law.

When the waves of Jews landed on American shores around the turn of the century, many felt they were escaping—not only from the repression of anti-Semitic monarchs and countrymen, but from the repression of the rabbis who often ruled the ghettoes of Eastern Europe with impunity. Heady at the whiff of freedom, the newly minted American Jew was not about to fall under the same dictatorship. As a result, American rabbis like Jay Rosenbaum find themselves caught in a vexing conundrum. Their congregants—and even unaffiliated Jews—consistently express pride in their Jewish heritage and a love for its traditions. They would not think of being married outside a synagogue; they want their children to achieve bar or bat mitzvah; the thought of a son or daughter marrying a gentile is troubling. And yet, they are, for the most part, middle- and upper-middle-class Americans accustomed to "hiring out," to paying for services rendered—even, if needed, services of the spirit. They are not opposed to paying, but they want the service provided at their convenience. They also want their spirituality enfolded in a convivial setting, with friends and acquaintances of *their* choosing, not the disorderly *mishpocha*, the extended family that Judaism calls upon its adherents to form.

Of course, being on call, at the whim or pleasure of the people, is not the way most rabbis—including Jay Rosenbaum—wish to be treated. At one of our talks, the rabbi went deep into Jewish history to explicate the present situation he was facing on the Israel trip.

"It goes all the way back to Moses, all these delights and pains of Jewish leadership," he said midway through a luscious and varied offering at the Annapurna; on this day, it was all carrot dishes. "Moses says to God, 'I can't do this, kill me.' No, God won't allow that. So Moses goes ahead and intercedes for the Jewish people, loving them; meanwhile, they're driving him up a wall. But God listens to Moses and gives him the word. Moses passes it down. His own brother and sister say he has too much power. 'What gives *you* the right to tell us what to do!'

"There is a consumer orientation today in synagogues; synagogues are looked on as a service organization, something to make the congregants happy. They are like guests at a smorgasbord. 'Let me have a little of this ritual and a little of that practice. Oh, no, I don't have any taste for that observance at all. Oh, that person? No, I don't want to sit next to them. Not my type; not my style.' They want what they want, when they want it—and God forbid it be inconvenient.

"I'd like to see the synagogue as a place that draws people into service, where you have to make some sacrifices for the greater good— not just looking for what the synagogue gives to you. The familiar challenge: ask not what your synagogue can do for you; ask what you can do for Jewish life.

"So, here we are with the Israel trip. It's looking better, but it's still up in the air. And every one of those people—in both groups— would say they love Israel, they love being Jews. But I'm raising the stakes beyond this kind of surface infatuation. I want you to travel to-gether; I want you to work together. I want you to return and make this Congregation Beth Israel a real, living, breathing Jewish community. That's a different ball game entirely."

A constant and nagging challenge preoccupies Rabbi Rosenbaum's waking moments and working days, then haunts his mind on too many nights. How is he to transmit the beauties of Judaism that inflame his own heart? There is also the more practical and immediate question: how to make Judaism appealing? How can he entice these finicky, picky eaters to come to the table and sample the fare? How can he encourage them to return again and again, until they discover that this is indeed good, good for them, and good for their families. It is food for their minds and for their souls, a nourishment that will sustain them on life's journey.

One approach the rabbi has tried in years past was about to be tried again at Beth Israel—a crash course, Judaism by immersion, if only for a day. "*Shabbos* in *Shul*" invites those who are willing to spend an entire Saturday, from morning service to *Havdalah*, at the synagogue. If *Shabbos* is a precursor of heaven, "*Shabbos* in *Shul*" should be a precursor of the Saturdays of the future—once his group of congregants had returned from Israel and begun the renewal he had been working so hard to launch.

The day was a mild one, for February, and yet as the rabbi opened the *Shabbos*-morning service, he was aware that even temperate weather—for Worcester at least—had not thawed his congregants' resistance. In fact, attendance was slightly down at the morning service. Perhaps some who regularly attend had not wanted to suffer the embarrassment of leaving the enclosure at noon.

The rabbi's morning sermon proved to be another fascinating mixture of the ancient and the current, dealing with the signs taken to signal the imminent arrival of the *mashiach*. The rabbi invoked the words of yearning from the Torah, then leapt centuries forward to recent floods, the eruption of Mount Pinatubo, the collapse of the Soviet Union, and the belief of many Lubavitchers that people need look no further for the messiah than to their beloved *rebbe*.

From the sanctuary, the rabbi moved to the chapel for his after-lunch talk in which he related the inspiring words of Tigabu Simon and explored the seeming miracle of the Ethiopian Jews—for two millennia robbed of contact with any other branches of Judaism—and dramatically underscored that time and time again in Judaism there were examples "that something was at work that cannot be logically explained." It was the hand of God, the rabbi argued, constantly at work—that was the only explanation.

Yet even with this rich fare, and Rabbi Rosenbaum's beaming face encouraging his people throughout the day, something was missing in this day of carefully orchestrated *Shabbos* observance and Jewish community life.

There were numerous children's activities—for those of nursery age and on up to the handful of teenagers who had been prevailed upon to attend—but the games and projects didn't seem to capture the attention of many of the children; most wandered the synagogue halls, looking up at the clocks or down at their own wristwatches. The afternoon session of Israeli dancing deteriorated into a listless, spiritless walk-through. Somehow the day anticipated and cherished by *shtetl* Jews was little more than a burden to be endured for these Worcesterites who had sacrificed their customary weekend fare for this day of grudging observance.

Even the weather seemed to follow the mood within Congregation Beth Israel. Clouds gathered by early afternoon, the temperature plummeted. As the sun set in the slate gray winter sky and *Shabbos* came to an end, Rabbi Rosenbaum bravely led his listless band through *Havdalah,* then bid them good-bye, the smile still stubbornly fixed on his face.

Undaunted by the tepid participation of his people the preceding Saturday—such days are and must be quickly forgotten if a rabbi's work is to go on—Rabbi Rosenbaum threw open the door of the synagogue library the next Tuesday afternoon at four o'clock, ready to address yet another group targeted for conversion.

He was greeted by a spitball—not thrown *at* him, but certainly not withheld *because* of him—and the din of seven fidgety twelve-year-olds, brought to study at their rabbi's feet after a seven-hour day at their respective public and private schools. There were three girls and four boys—all the boys wearing the trademark of the occasional Jew, disposable *kippot*—in the class. The rabbi set his Midrash on a table, the sign that class was in session. He smiled, nodding at them, as if their chatter were applause for his entrance. A deep breath, his chest caving in his jacket, served as still another silent sign that he was ready to begin. The children went on with their own animated conversations; Brad and Eddie continued their barrage of spitballs.

For a year prior to their bar or bat mitzvah, the youngsters are required to attend this weekly class. As the rabbi knows well, for some it is tolerated only because their parents insist. But for others—while they surely would be reluctant to admit it—it is an important stretch of road on their own spiritual journey. This is the time in a young life when the sense of service to others slowly reveals itself as not merely servitude but as a source of a strange and deep satisfaction. This is the age when the quest for an authentic hero or heroine takes even deeper root in a maturing and increasingly conscious mind. Such young adolescents, tossed about on their individual hormonal seas, yearn not so much for a safe harbor as for a great and brave journey to prove themselves worthy of adulthood.

The rabbi knows that these sessions offer him his only sustained contact with these young people crossing the seas, uncharted for them, between full parental supervision and what is recognized by Jewish tradition as the age of maturity. And he knows equally well that the parents who have joined the synagogue precisely because they want at least the veneer of Judaic life do not wish to be embarrassed by their progeny on his or her day in the limelight, the *Shabbos* on or near the child's thirteenth birthday. It is a combination, Jay Rosenbaum admits, of rabbinic teaching and force-feeding.

Yet it is his abiding hope that some of those for whom this is no more than Judaic window dressing will find that spark, that insight somewhere in his words or in God's words, that will cause them to take their religion seriously. Or perhaps it will be the quiet presence of the young boy or girl sitting next to them that will be the source of inspiration. The rabbi's fondest dream is that they will take their newfound belief back home and become the force that brings their entire family to a properly observant life.

"The two-page handout on the Tower of Babel I gave you last

week—let's review that," the rabbi said brightly, pointing to one of the boys to begin.

"Uh . . . the Jews were building a tower . . . uh . . ."

"Jews?" the rabbi interjected. "There were no Jews yet."

"Uh, the people . . ."

Brad pushed his *kippah* over his forehead, looking like Maurice Chevalier saucily positioning his straw boater before a song.

"Brad! Now, why did they build it?"

"To reach heaven. Make a name for themselves. See God." The answers were volunteered by others.

"Well, there's nothing wrong with all that—why would God be angry?"

Silence.

"Let's consult the Midrash, and when we do, we find . . ."

The young students shifted their obviously heavy heads from one upturned palm to the other.

". . . that the workers on the tower were poorly fed and had to work long hours. The builders cared more about bricks and mortar than they did about people. Brad! Stop that. Move your seat, please."

Brad obeyed exactly and, with a grin, devilish by any religion's standards, noisily scraped his chair along the floor. He is a handsome boy with mahogany hair, and there was a sense he was acting out another play on the only stage at hand.

"But the builders wanted to be well known, popular. Now what do teenagers do today to make themselves popular—things that are not necessarily good for them?"

"Drugs. Smoking. Drinking." The responses came quickly, but were offered with little interest.

"Priorities, it's all about priorities; what is important to them. Now, on the back of the handout, I want you to write down five things that are most important in your life, what you value." The rabbi moved toward Brad, who had by now turned his back and was leaning his chair against the table.

"Brad, I want you to be serious about this," he whispered, leaning over the boy.

"I'm listening, I'm listening to every word!" Brad responded, suddenly wheeling around and feigning deep interest.

While the other children contemplated the words they would commit to paper, Brad quickly made his list and loudly slammed down his pen.

"Okay, outside, Brad."

"With my chair?"

"Leave the chair here." The rabbi's voice was suddenly bled of the enthusiasm with which he had entered the room. His pale blue eyes appeared as two dull, lifeless dots set upon the horizon of his lower lids.

"Good grades, education, get far in my life, friends, family," one girl read from her list once Brad had left, his final statement a slammed door signed by an "oops" grin on his face through the glass.

"Money, more money, and even more money" was Eddie's focused but abbreviated list.

"Family, friends, peace, education—and I couldn't think of a fifth one," admitted one of the girls. "Maybe my dog."

"Religion" only made one list, in fourth place.

"Now, if you were building the tower, that would be at the top of your list, wouldn't it? And today? Maybe being successful—yes, Eddie, rich—"

"If you have enough money you can buy anything," Eddie volunteered helpfully, weighing in perhaps as not a very promising spiritualist, but a pragmatic young soul nonetheless.

"—rich, but if being rich is the most important thing in your life, that's wrong. If a doctor only cares about his work, or a businessman only cares about his business, he'll surely neglect his family. What about a country? If it oppresses people to gain its own goals? See, the Tower of Babel story isn't just about building a tower. It teaches a lot of things. Now write down five things you value most about America. And five things you value most about the Jewish people."

Hands listlessly reached for pens.

"Okay, that's for homework. See you next week."

Within seconds, Rabbi Rosenbaum was left with a line of

crooked chairs. On the table were two of the handouts he had so care-fully prepared. Out in front of the synagogue, cars that had awaited the young students pulled away after this contact with Jewish life and streamed back into the secular world of Worcester. Brad, although he was the first one out and had been waiting the longest time, was still waiting for his ride to come.

Rabbi Rosenbaum walked slowly across the vestibule that leads to the sanctuary. It was not his easy, shoulders-thrown-back stride of the morning, when the day is open, possible, and still before him, but a more shuffling gait. He was not exactly stooped over—the weight of the day had not been that great—but his shoulders seemed to have pivoted closer together, as if to protect his heart. In the overhead fluo-rescent light, I saw lines around his eyes I had not noticed before; he suddenly looked like a much older man.

Seeing the lights on in the administrative office, the rabbi stopped in to see if he had any phone messages. Peggy St. John was still there; she had stayed late to finish some work.

"By the way, Dr. Mills called with the numbers," she said to him.

"Yes?" the rabbi asked tentatively.

"With theirs and ours"—she hesitated tantalizingly, realizing the weight of the rest of her sentence—"a total of thirty-one. More than enough to make the trip."

"*Mazel tov!*" he shouted to this bedrock Congregationalist. A smile had reclaimed the rabbi's face. "We're on our way. A double *mazel tov!*"

IO

"Charlie, look. Do you want me to put a disclaimer at the top of the new itinerary? 'Note: This is *not* a BI trip.' "

"Jay, Jay, by June . . ."

Although both Charlie Mills and Rabbi Rosenbaum were mindful not to repeat actual words from their previous conversation, they were still going over the same areas. Each man carefully approached the philosophical line that divided them, hoping to taunt or persuade the other into stepping over, then drew back onto familiar terrain.

"Better yet, Charlie, how about this: 'Danger! Religious belief and practice may change your life!' "

". . . by June, this won't even be an issue. The group will be a group."

Dr. Charles Mills and Rabbi Jay Rosenbaum stared at each other across the rabbi's desk, a terrain littered with copies of the Midrash, the Torah, a Torah commentary, a few sheets of paper with the next *Shabbos* sermon sketched out, and a half-eaten container of Dannon coffee yogurt. As Charlie leaned forward to emphatically make another point, the rabbi pushed back from the desk, seemingly maintaining a distance so as not to be swept up by the passion of Charlie's arguments.

"The goal, conceptually, is that it *is* a synagogue trip. That's the only reason I organized it. My goal, at least."

"Look, Jay, we all love Israel; we want to go, go with our families, and have a positive experience. But we're not going as soldiers of the Conservative Movement. Why is it so important what we call it, Jay?"

"Because, Charlie, the goal is not to make this a cost-effective vacation. The goal is to take people, as a community, and bring something back to the synagogue."

"They will, they will. Israel turns people on. I've been three times and every time it happens. There'll be a sense of bonding. *Havurah.* You'll see. But people don't want to sign on for a synagogue trip. It sticks in their craw. My group signed on for a couples' trip—they don't want to think about community building."

Their conversation this morning, a few weeks after their first meeting on the combined Israel trip, had actually started well. Charlie said that the five-star Sheraton Plaza near the center of Jerusalem— although it would eat up the airline savings and increase the price by about fifty dollars a person—was acceptable to his group. The hotel, on King George Street, was within blocks of a number of synagogues; that was fine with the rabbi. The overnight in a Bedouin encampment, while personally appealing to both of them, had drawn protests from members of both groups and was not worth the friction: it could be dropped. The Israeli Defense Force installation was declared optional, depending on the military situation; a stop at a swimming oasis in the middle of the desert was added (for the children), as was a speaker on the current political situation (for the adults). A counselor would be hired to ride on the bus and look after the children. The fine print of their itinerary agreed upon, Charlie Mills had again voiced his concern about what to call their hybrid adventure. He had urged the rabbi not to bill it as a BI trip. At this, the rabbi blew up.

"We have to figure out what to call it by the time the two groups get together," the rabbi said a little peevishly. But he had at least come back closer to the desk from his former position, one that had signaled that he would have just as soon been in the courtyard outside his office window as in his office being browbeaten by Charlie Mills, who once again pushed onward.

"Maybe we can just laugh about it and go on to the itinerary."

The hint of a smile tugged at the corners of the rabbi's mouth, trying to disrupt the perfectly straight line formed by his set lips.

"The Charlie and Jay Show?"

The rabbi was doing his best not to smile, but Charlie's boyish enthusiasm was beginning to prevail.

"C'mon, Jay, we'll figure out something to call it. Don't worry. We're going; isn't that the most important thing?"

The intercom buzzer sounded. Peggy St. John reeled off the dispatches. A young Catholic woman, bringing along her reluctant Jewish fiancé—and their year-old child—had arrived to talk about her conversion to Judaism. Marion Freedman had called and asked that the rabbi call back immediately—there was a major hitch in the plans for the Russians' wedding. Another caller had just returned from Florida to receive the dunning letter on dues. "Furious" was Peggy's appraisal of his tone.

"Okay, okay; what other matters came up with your group?" The rabbi was speaking to Charlie as he jotted notes to himself about the calls.

"On the kibbutz visit in the north: the Aframes were worried about the dangers up there. Those Katyusha rockets can go the distance; that's right up by the Lebanese border. And the Cutlers are a little skittish. Now, they're going to go; I'm sure of that—Mark goes every year, sometimes more." (Dr. Mark Cutler, although a member of the Reform Temple Emanuel, had signed on because he wanted to take his wife and young daughter on this trip. Dr. Cutler, a psychiatrist, is one of Worcester's most influential and visible Jews, and currently the president of the Jewish Federation.) "But I don't want to spook them with the wrong tone."

"This isn't a Federation trip, I hope he knows that. We're not going so we can come back and raise money for Israel. This is different."

"That's exactly why Cutler's going, Jay; he knows the nationalistic stuff; he wants the religious part. But I don't want to rub in this community-building part. Soldiers of the Conservative Movement, march on . . ."

The rabbi's face, which had begun to relax, tightened again.

"The Charlie and Jay Show, remember," the physician said, adding a somewhat goofy grin for emphasis. "Let's get the groups together and you'll see; this stuff will melt away."

Charlie rose to leave and the rabbi prepared to go out and meet the woman and her prospective husband, who, the rabbi has already ascertained, seems quite pleased that her conversion to Judaism will take a minimum of a year. At the door, and in a more serious tone, Charlie mentioned a story that had appeared in the morning newspaper. A Palestinian from the West Bank had stabbed four Jewish settlers; two were dead. It was just the latest incidence of the random street violence that sporadically erupts in Israel. The West Bank and Gaza Strip had been sealed off again.

Rabbi Rosenbaum put his arm over Charlie's shoulder. Finally, he could manifest a full smile. "After what I've been through on this, it would take another Gulf War to keep me home. This year in—can we say it, Charlie?—this year in . . ."

"*Jerusalem*, Jay, Jerusalem," Charlie definitively completed the sentence.

Arriving early one afternoon a few weeks later, in mid-March, I knocked on the rabbi's office door; anticipating his "Come in," I stepped inside. I found the rabbi at his desk, his head over a book. In the air was a dull hum, which I quickly realized was emanating from the rabbi. Without looking up, he motioned me to a chair and continued. The hum soon took on texture and form, highs, lows, quickly articulated portions—almost mumbled—and those that were chanted slower and more reverentially. The rabbi was chanting the Megillah, the Book of Esther, which is read, in Hebrew, on the feast of Purim. Purim, perhaps the most mirthful of Jewish holidays, commemorates how the infamous Persian vizier, Haman, tried to exterminate the Jews—and how the Jews, through the wisdom of Esther, the steadfastness of Mordecai, and the support of their God, triumphed over him.

"It's a pattern of musical notes called 'trope,' " the rabbi explained to me as he reached the end of chapter four, with Mordecai in sackcloth and ashes and the Jews fasting for the success of Esther's intervention with the king. "The Torah has its own trope, so does the Haftarah. There are five in all, but the Megillah is the only book that has its own trope, so on Purim we have a entirely different tone. The whole concept of trope is quite remarkable, really. Very smart. When a detail isn't edifying—like the number of bullocks or a lengthy lineage—you move through it quickly. When you reach an important part—say, the Ten Commandments—your voice says you love the text. You embrace it. You can dramatize. And it's a wonderful mnemonic device; the music makes the text easier to remember. The melody is a language in itself; the idea is to have the text become a part of you. You walk down the street and a passage you have heard or sung that bears on the situation pops into your mind. It can happen anywhere; that's the whole idea.

"I remember being in the shower one morning, very upset about a member of my first congregation in New Jersey who was very disrespectful to me. This guy did anything he could to humiliate me, to take me down a peg or two. He wanted to show me he was just as good as me and it was really eating away at me. Then part of the Megillah—about Haman—came to mind, and I realized I was becoming just like Haman. When you get carried away with your ego or honor or position, it's bound to happen. Everybody in the congregation loved me except this guy, but I wanted *him* to love me too. This one guy was doing me in. I was just like Haman demanding that Mordecai bow down and pay him homage. One guy, Mordecai, wouldn't and it drove Haman nuts and eventually undid him. A good lesson for the rabbi."

The rabbi continued the Megillah, retelling how King Achashverosh was so pleased with the sight of Esther, garbed in her queenly robes, that he was ready to grant her up to half his kingdom. The plot thickened once more. The rabbi's eyes moved swiftly along the lines of Hebrew words, tracing right to left. His lips parted just enough to let bursts of soft, nasal tones waft into the quiet, still air of his office. I looked at him, this man I had been walking with these past months. Haman? Jay Rosenbaum?

"I love this stuff," he had told me so often, in good times and in bad, when frustrated and when exhilarated. And indeed he did deeply love the work of a rabbi. But with such a love affair always comes sacrifice, and Jay Rosenbaum, I had certainly seen, was granted no exception. Looking at his crowded appointment book, his many nights of meetings, the nights he worked at home, his limited time with his family, an outsider might compare him to the orthopedic surgeon who feels compelled to mend broken, twisted limbs, to intervene when there is pain or disfigurement. It was no wonder that the ordinary commitments of life pale in comparison to the challenge, the excitement of the work such a person was skilled at performing and felt called to do. The surgeon—and a rabbi like Jay Rosenbaum—made choices, choices that did not necessarily please his family or the ones he loves. But the sense of a calling, of commitment, was so terrifically strong— and the satisfaction at work well done so great—that the sacrifice obviously was worth it.

Jay Rosenbaum knew his wife was distressed that she bore so many of the responsibilities of raising their children and tending to their home, in addition to the many demands made upon her by the synagogue. He also saw that distress turning to unvarnished anger and, eventually, a resigned depression because she saw little hope for change. In essence, Janine Rosenbaum was a corporate widow, but it went even further than that. The corporate widow did not have to face her husband's coworkers each day. But every place Janine went, she was confronted by Worcester Jews who knew something about her husband, and Beth Israel Jews who knew far more.

But there was at least a reward for his sacrifice, and Jay Rosenbaum alluded to it as he rehearsed for Purim night. There was something beyond his fire for Judaism, his deep, religious commitment; there was a little more Haman in him than he might readily admit. In Rabbi Rosenbaum's life, there was a quietly held secret, which some-

time later, he revealed to me. Praise. Approbation. Respect. Love. Jay
Rosenbaum wanted them all.

"People expect a lot of you, but when you deliver for some of
them, they can't love you enough," the rabbi said late one afternoon
when the time seemed right to talk about this delicate subject. " 'My
rabbi,' they say, and they really mean it. Of course that gives me fuel to
go on; without it, who could? But it doesn't last long. Sometimes I
can't get enough of this love a congregation showers on its rabbi. But
in order to earn that love, I feel I always have to have that special
sparkle; I should always be 'on.' And that takes a toll, on me, on my
family. The rabbi isn't supposed to have a bad day. He knows everybody's name, even though he hasn't seen them since last year. He likes
everybody; he's patient all the time. When his best plans turn to dust,
he should still be smiling. I guess I'm hard on myself—after all, I
wouldn't expect that of anyone I have to deal with. And yet I expect it
of myself.

"Sometimes I just want to get up on that *bimah* and say, 'Look
at what I do for you. Stop harassing me!' I just want to scream that
sometimes. Yes, I guess I feel I deserve their love. I've earned it. But for
some I never do enough. I visited them in the hospital five times. But
why didn't I come the sixth time? Their daughter was home from college; why didn't I make a fuss about her when she deigned to come to
services? Why wasn't I at that meeting, the umpteenth one that week?
'Rabbi, what nice work you're doing on early childhood education. But
what about the old people? Forgetting them?' It's endless. I try, but I
can never do enough. I can't satisfy them. And, I guess I can't satisfy
myself."

The intercom buzzer sounded as the last words of the final chapter of
the Megillah passed Rabbi Rosenbaum's lips. He reached into his
lunch bag and pulled out a granola bar, taking a few big bites before
taking the call. It was Rabbi Seth Bernstein, curious about the rumor
going around that a Jewish "campus complex" was being considered in
Worcester, centered around the Jewish Community Center, up Salis-

bury Street. Under this plan, Solomon Schechter Day School would be moved from Beth Israel to the community center.

"You know where I stand on that one," Rabbi Rosenbaum said. "In the old days, the synagogue was at the center of Jewish life. Everything radiated out. Now it's the community center. I think it's better to have kids close to a sanctuary, rather than a swimming pool. Right? Right. You got to fight them every inch or you end up co-opted. I'll fight this one all the way."

The regal Holy Ark and the huge Hebrew letters on the wall behind the *bimah* formed an incongruously staid backdrop to the untidy scene unfolding in the Beth Israel sanctuary. The aisles surged with running figures; the noise level was so high even shouted words traveled no more than a few feet. Peter Pan took off with a swarm of Ninja Turtles; black-suited cowboys and assorted Count Draculas mingled with fairy princesses and furry bunnies. Men cross-dressed as women and women decked themselves out as rouge-cheeked riverboat tarts. It was almost as if the golden calf were soon to be brought out and worshiped. Paganism seemed to have momentarily seized the Jews of Worcester.

The movable wall at the rear of the sanctuary had been thrown back and folding chairs set up in the adjoining social hall to accommodate the overflow, but few of the six or seven hundred people present were seated. If there was ever a time Jay Rosenbaum successfully wedded the modern to the ancient—and made Jews *want* to come to *shul*—it was this night, Purim. For on Purim, he was provided a wonderful tableau. By tradition, this was the day Judaism could poke fun at itself and children and adults alike could forget their usual synagogue demeanor and dress and act as flamboyantly as they wished. During his years at Beth Israel, Jay Rosenbaum had proved himself a master at orchestrating their folly.

In attendance were many of the people who would soon gather together for the first time for the yet-to-be-officially-named trip to Israel. The Millses, Aframes, and Cutlers were there—representing those who had signed up for the young couples' group—as were Murray

Rosenberg and his wife, Freda; Marion Blumberg and Gabriella
Frymer, two older single women; and the Fixlers—representing those
who had wanted a congregational trip from the start. It was much too
noisy for the members of either group to talk with the others about the
trip; in fact, few yet knew who their fellow travelers would be. Instead,
old friends were sought out, as were those Beth Israel members who are
well known in secular Worcester but are rarely seen in synagogue. People such as Larry Abramoff and his wife, Gloria, who run the huge,
ever-expanding Tatnuck Bookseller and have two young sons, and
Stanley Baker's brother, Norman, who has a large, successful used-car
business and was here with his grandchildren. In the synagogue, they
could be approached simply as Jews—and not as some of the most successful and admired businesspeople in Worcester.

On the stage, a man with a stringy, false black beard, sunglasses, a huge earring, gaudy Hawaiian shirt, and floppy hat called
into the microphone for quiet. Jay Rosenbaum—whose costume had
evolved over the months to this—moved about the *bimah* not with the
gliding walk of the reverent rabbi, but with the cocky, pelvic strides of
a rock star. He and Nu? Yids on the Block—made up of five singers,
two of whom also played acoustic guitar and electronic keyboard—
were soon blasting out their message, alternating the group's own
newly minted lyrics and the rabbi's reading of the ancient Book of Esther. Whether or not the cadence of his trope was accurate, whether or
not the congregants would remember certain portions in the shower or
on the street, the rabbi put on an impressive performance. Whisking
through long sections, holding the name of Haman with disgust in his
voice as hoots and rattles registered audience sentiment, mouthing Esther's lines in a squeaky falsetto, Rabbi Rosenbaum was the consum-
mate chameleon. And, when Mordecai's words were delivered, the
rabbi did so with the authority of Charlton Heston's Moses.

The melodies were from songs of the 1960s and '70s, when the
thirtysomething Nu? Yids were coming of age as febrile teenagers. One
rap song was gamely attempted, pandering to contemporaneity. An-
chored by Betsy Bergman, a belting rocker with a Mama Cass voice,
the Nu? Yids harmonized to the tune of "Jamaica Farewell":

Oh, I'm sad to say I'm in a very bad way,
Haman wants to kill the Jews today.
My heart is down, my head is turning around
I must convince Achashverosh to keep the Jews safe and sound.

And, instead of "Thank God I'm a Country Boy," it was "Thank God, I'm a Jewish boy" whose "Jewish life never did me no harm, praying every day with *tefillin* on my arm."

But the line of the night was crooned as part of the chorus of the Shirelles' classic "It's in His Kiss." Nu? Yids wailed that it wasn't Mordecai's Talmudic mind or "acts so kind," not "the way he eats . . . not mixing milk with meat" that distinguished him.

This year at Beth Israel, Mordecai was hailed both for his characteristic Jewish physiology and obvious sexual prowess:

Oh, ya, it's in his bris.
That's where it is, oh, oh, oh.

A lyricist, uncredited on the printed program, had thought of the line. "Go on, Jay, use it!" Janine implored late one night as they sat on the couch, thinking up lyrics.

It's in his bris . . . Oh, ya, it's in his bris.

Howls of approval greeted the line each time it was sung.

As costumed children continued to stream up and down the aisles, elderly members of the congregation—in suits and best dresses—sat, heads reverently bent, considering the words of the Book of Esther. Some followed the text on a scroll encased in a plastic holder, others in the more standard pamphlets. Finally, the last words of Esther were uttered, the last song sung, and Nu? Yids bowed before a standing, thundering ovation. A sparkling, fun-filled evening at Beth Israel, a two-and-a-half hour serving of a most appealing and easily digestible religion had come to a triumphant end.

Nu? Yids mingled with the crowd (and graciously signed a few autographs) as people began to leave; the children especially crowded around their rabbi, whom they usually see as a commanding liturgical presence on the *bimah* or as their knowledgeable teacher in classes. One young girl offered her appraisal of the rabbi's funky outfit. "Cool, dude. You ought to dress like this all the time!" she baited him.

The rabbi stroked his beard petulantly in reply. Later, he would tell me, "There are times you have to be a bit of a salesman in this rabbi business. But I believe in the product. If I get people in through the back door, I still get them in. Humor, the best thing to knock down defenses. Purim is a user-friendly night."

For families like the Fixlers, Aframes, and Millses—representative of the more active synagogue members—Purim night was just another in a line of Jewish holidays and *Shabbat* services that bring them to this sanctuary. Larry Abramoff, the bookstore owner, might be representative of a vastly larger number, for whom Purim marks one of the few times of the year they come to Beth Israel. I was interested in this vantage point on synagogue life.

"My two sons like to come for Purim and so I'm here with them," Larry told me as we talked one day in his small, cluttered office at Tatnuck Bookseller, where his desk occupies far less room than the many boxes of books and other items sold in the store that have laid siege to the space. "I had to go to Hebrew school five days a week when I was a kid, so I don't jam it down my kids' throats. They go to Hebrew school, yes, but they know they can skip once in a while, too. Gloria and I call it a 'mental health day away from Hebrew school.' My Judaism? Where is it? It centers around food, around the table where my family is gathered for a Jewish holiday, where we do what Jews have been doing for five thousand years. Ethics? I never think about it, but I guess it's there. My father was in the wholesale meat business and if you said you liked his shirt, he'd give it to you and probably his pants too. *Tzedaka*—charity; my Judaism must be behind that. I try. I'm active in Massachusetts Audubon; I'm heading up the fund-raising for the Worcester Boy's and Girl's Clubs. Should I do more religious stuff? Probably. Do I want my kids to marry Jewish? I would prefer it, but if they find somebody who's not Jewish, they still have my blessings. I want to be happy in life; I want them to be happy. Jewishly happy? Just happy happy."

Soon, the parking lots, the streets adjacent to the synagogue and the circular driveway in front—all of which had been jammed with cars—were cleared. Jay Rosenbaum, with David just about asleep in his arms, Shoshanah already dozing in her stroller, and Janine carrying the black beard over her arm, headed for the Ford Taurus and their trip home. The rabbi had just staged the best-attended community-wide Worcester Jewish event of the year. Again.

The trip to Israel, after months of struggle—and not a little bit of luck—was finally a reality. And while the rabbi was not about to give in to Charlie Mills's overtures to homogenize its purpose, neither was he foolish enough to antagonize the young couples by blatantly putting the Beth Israel stamp on it. As he had learned in his twelve years in the rabbinate, the best path from point A to point B—while perhaps not the shortest, easiest, or least time-consuming—is sometimes to go via point C. Actually, Rabbi Rosenbaum had a point C and D, and possibly E, in mind: two or even three meetings, in which he would allow the two groups to get acquainted and then tactfully begin to underscore the religious dimension of the trip.

Israel was now two and a half months away, but before Rabbi Rosenbaum could think much about a pilgrimage to the Holy Land, he first had to address another event on which he had already expended a great deal of time: not a going forth, but a gathering in. The wedding of the Russian Jews was to take place on a Thursday evening in little over a month. Not a working day in the past weeks had passed when he had not tended to some aspect of the wedding and dinner. Marion Freedman was now one of his regular callers as she addressed the many details. Her husband, the cantor, complained that they rarely had a chance to talk—if she was not tending to their three children, she was tending to the Russian wedding.

And so, on an appointed evening in April, Rabbi Rosenbaum bolted his dinner, played a quick game of checkers with David, and read Shoshanah a story. Janine had sat at the table with her family that evening, but she hadn't eaten any of the vegetable lasagna she had made. The entire day before, she had been in Boston, seeing another hand specialist. He had prescribed a new medication for her pain. She quickly had the prescription filled, but found, like the others before it, that it nauseated her terribly. She had been throwing up all day and had called her husband twice. The rabbi wanted at least to give her some personal attention, but between hospital calls and the seven o'clock meeting, he had only an hour.

This was an extraordinarily important night. All the procedural details and religious requirements were to be ironed out; more important, it was the only occasion the rabbis would have to talk to the couples they were to marry. And, while the wedding provided a wonderful pretext for the Hadassah dinner, the religious joining of these men and women was the focal point of the evening—the rabbi had to keep reminding himself of that as more immediate, but less important details thrust themselves into his life. And beyond the desire to get a sense of the couples they would be marrying, the rabbis had to confront a more basic—and sensitive—area of Jewish law: were all the men and women actually Jews? There was serious doubt about one couple, and as standardized synagogue records were hardly available for people who could not be public about their Jewishness, there was no easy way to find out. Rabbi Rosenbaum had assigned this couple, the Casdins, to himself.

In addition to Rabbi Rosenbaum, another Conservative rabbi would be officiating—Joshua Gutoff, from nearby Leominster—and five Reform rabbis: Joseph Klein, who is retired; Debra Hachen, an associate in Westborough, as well as the three local Reform rabbis, Simon and Gershon from Temple Emanuel and Bernstein from Temple Sinai. For the moment, the number had settled down to fourteen; fourteen couples had indicated their desire to be married, and each of the seven rabbis would marry two couples, one couple at a time.

Shortly after seven, Rabbi Rosenbaum, seated behind his desk, addressed Rabbis Klein, Gutoff, Bernstein, and Simon (Rabbis Gershon and Hachen couldn't attend and said they would see their couples at another time), who found themselves crowded together on the side of the desk usually reserved for congregants. "There might be fifteen couples or there might be twelve, so the word is 'flex-i-ble.' " Rabbi Rosenbaum drew out the word for emphasis. "One couple is getting cold feet, the Jewishness of at least one of them is in doubt. And for all of them, this is pretty strange, especially for those who have been married for a long time. So all plans are subject to change. On the spot! Not your typical Jewish wedding, folks." He grinned broadly. "We want to make this meaningful for them. And we have to keep on a schedule or the whole thing falls apart. You get fifteen minutes per couple to make it meaningful, so make every minute count."

There is a fair-weather plan and a rainy-weather plan, and Rabbi Rosenbaum detailed each from the signing of the *ketubah* to the reception and the Hadassah dinner. If a normal wedding might send the mother of the bride into paroxysms of anxiety, the bonding of fourteen couples was a deployment requiring both the skill and the bravery of a rabbinic Moshe Dayan. Twenty-eight witnesses, seven cantors, seven translators, fourteen rings, fourteen *ketubot* with all the needed information, fourteen glasses to break, seven *huppot*, or canopies, proper spacing indoors and out to allow for guests to gather around, an accordionist to lead the couples, the Hadassah dinner for over two hundred people, Israeli dancing—as well as the television and newspaper coverage to assure this good work did not go unnoticed.

"Now"—the rabbi took a deep breath—"I know there are some differences between us . . ." Thus, the warning that uncharted waters were being entered.

"He must be talking about those Reform guys; me, I'm Orthodox," Rabbi Simon said sotto voce, a look of mock alarm on his face.

"I *know* how Orthodox you are, Jim—differences, but we have a big and wonderful task in front of us. Let's try to do the best we can."

One of the key differences could prove pivotal for the questionable couple: in Reform Judaism, patrilineal as well as matrilineal descent is recognized in determining whether a person is Jewish; in Conservative Judaism, only matrilineal descent is acknowledged. It was a symbol of the attempts at unity within at least these branches of Judaism that Conservative and Reform rabbis were seated in the same room and would perform side by side on the wedding night. The Orthodox, of course, would not be a part of any such dilution of their belief.

"So, please find out if their parents are Jewish—one generation, that's back far enough. I just hope we don't have to tell anybody it's no go."

An old Jewish adage maintains that if there is a gathering where two people claim to be rabbis, and there is no extended debate about whatever is being discussed, there is probably only one rabbi present. And so, true to form, with five certified rabbis in this office, points of both Talmudic and civil law came under spirited debate. What kind of documentation on their Jewishness was acceptable? On their civil marriage? Any of them divorced? And, if so, by any rare chance had they first been married Jewishly? Had they obtained a *get*? If the rabbis are marrying them Jewishly, are they also marrying them civilly? Rabbi Bernstein maintained an absolute yes; they were acting as officers of the Commonwealth of Massachusetts. Rabbi Simon, who is a nonpracticing lawyer, said unequivocally no.

Rabbi Gutoff, the youngest rabbi present—a sandy-haired man with a most serious face but a well-honed sense of irony—volunteered that the Commonwealth of Massachusetts would not rise or fall by what happened on the east lawn of Beth Israel; regardless, "if they're married already, its irrelevant to the state. I hate to say it, but the governor won't be there to check on us." Their discussion was not so much the bickering of religious legalists as it was a friendly but spirited table tennis game of ideas, with the deftest forehand prevailing—and the loser just waiting for the next serve.

By eight o'clock, some fifteen minutes late, the rabbis emerged from the office, ready to meet their couples. The rabbis stopped short in the hallway, confronted by five men.

A look of utter bewilderment spread across Rabbi Rosenbaum's face.

"The wives?" he asked, looking down the hallway.

The men, none of whom understood much English, looked at him blankly. "Shopping," David Shpitalnik said.

"Sh . . . shopping?" the rabbi sputtered.

"Oh, sick," offered Eva Honig, who was there to translate. "All sick."

"Sick," the rabbi repeated, flatly.

The evening's plan called for the rabbis to meet one of their couples before a group orientation session at eight-fifteen and the other couple after. Rabbi Rosenbaum smiled, although a bit more thinly than usual, and led Valery Casdin into the chapel for their premarital conference.

Mr. Casdin, a slight man with a shock of wiry brown hair that rose to a startling peak in front of the disposable *kippah* he had obtained in the Beth Israel vestibule, had had a small luggage manufacturing business in Vilnius, Lithuania. His wife, Larisa, has a master's degree in computer science and was an accountant before coming to America. They arrived in Worcester with their one child in August, some eight months before.

As he haltingly related his life story to the rabbi, it was obvious that Mr. Casdin's life in Vilnius was far more comfortable than his life thus far in Worcester. Neither he nor his wife had yet been able to find work. They have a small apartment and receive public assistance, for which all legal immigrants are eligible. It was a humiliation to him. Casdin told of his luggage business, which employed sixteen people, with a mixture of pride and reservation. "It what you do in Vilnius," he said, "you try make money. Rubles, many rubles. Nothing else to do. In America, different."

The rabbi saw an opening. "It makes sense when you're starting over again, to get married again. As a Jew. Before God. Tell me something about what you know about Judaism."

Casdin allowed that for the past seven or eight years he had read extensively about Jewish history—which was a dangerous practice, given the government's antipathy toward both Jews and religion—but knew next to nothing about Jewish tradition. "When I come to *Shabbos* service, I understand little."

"You're not alone. Most American Jews don't either. They know Hebrew letters, but they don't understand the words."

Casdin, a youthful-looking but quite serious man, crinkled his eyes as a preamble to a smile. "On holiday, you have fifty grams vodka, you drink toast; that is holiday. It was forbidden."

The rabbi tactfully asked about his parents, whom Valery said were Jewish. "And Larisa, did she have the same Jewish background?" Mr. Casdin nodded. The basics taken care of, the rabbi leaned back in his chair, a sign that business matters had been concluded and that a different kind of conversation could ensue. "Now, tell me what this means to you."

"This difficult question," Mr. Casdin said carefully. "I send my boy to Yeshiva"—he attends the small school operated by the ultra-Orthodox Lubavitchers—"so he can learn. It is start for him. But, wedding? For me? I think it make distance between my family and Judaism a little less. I lose connection with my people. But this, this start. For me. For wife. Feeling of Judaism like drop in time of darkness. Small. But still there."

The rabbi brightened at such a direct statement. "The feeling of Jewishness is there in every Jew, even in time of darkness. Yes, a drop in the darkness"—he reiterated the mixed metaphor—"I like that. For those of us born with so much, with freedom, we are humbled. We take a lot for granted. You are our cousins, finally reunited. Something strong unites us, even when we are apart."

"Yes. Jew is Jew."

"Yes, Valery, a Jew *is* a Jew."

The other members of the early group and those of the later group—including some wives—began to filter into the chapel for the orientation session. Soon they were scattered about the first half-dozen rows. They sat, somewhat impassively, couples in their early thirties to mid-sixties, few of them speaking to their mates. They had been married a minimum of eight years; the oldest of them, forty years. They were hardly the nervous to-be-weds that clergy must usually deal with, and the normal concerns of caterer and florist and honeymoon could be set aside. Taken together, they represented well over a hundred years of married life, married life that had seen hunger and persecution and imprisonment; married life that required the conniving, the cajoling, the compromising needed to get their children an education, to secure and keep a good job, to stay on the right side of authorities looking for any opportunity to penalize them. Theirs have been lives in which openly being a Jew, talking about things Jewish, or observing Jewish holidays were distinct and potentially dangerous liabilities.

As the rabbi droned on through some of the details of the ceremony—fair-weather plan, foul-weather plan; two couples to a *huppah*, one at a time; goblets, accordion, seating arrangements at the banquet—what had begun as a group feeling of stolid patience seemed to deteriorate into manifest ennui. Bertha Levin had the look of a woman sitting through a story she'd heard many times before and never liked anyhow. Many of the Russians studied their hands, or the walls; few were looking at Rabbi Rosenbaum. The rabbi, usually a man who senses whether or not he has his audience, began to talk faster. He seemed to lose them even more.

Finally, with the extensive logistics covered and a limited amount of time left, the rabbi moved on. This was also a "teaching moment" and, even as distant as his audience now seemed to be, Rabbi Rosenbaum would rarely—if ever—have the attention of so many Russians at one time. "The word for marriage in Hebrew is *kiddushin*, which means 'holiness.' If the purpose of Judaism is to build the ideal society in the world, then we have to begin with the basic building block of society. The Jewish marriage is a laboratory of ethics, sharing, treating another person with dignity. If we can't succeed with two people, then everything else is a waste of time. You already know what married life is about"—a statement greeted by assorted chuckles and snorts. "But now there is a chance to start fresh. And you men will agree to the terms of the *ketubah*." He held one aloft. "The words are two thousand years old. A wonderful document you will give to your wife. In it, you will promise to support her emotionally and materially. If you want to divorce her, you must think again. It is a document that wisely protects the woman, by putting a two-hundred *zuzim* lien on the man's property. Today, this is symbolic, but in ancient days, a goat cost two *zuzim*, so this was quite an amount of money and assured the woman would be taken care of."

At the end of his treatise, the rabbi asked for questions. There were two, both from men. "Is there protection for husband?" and "How many goats I get if wife divorce me?"

It was classic Russian humor by people who, in order to maintain their personal identity and sense of worth in a society devoted to undermining them, continually needed to maintain a stoic indifference, regarding even the most serious moments of life cynically—or at a minimum, with a sense of dark humor. The rabbi joined in their rising laughter.

"Don't worry, you good Jewish men won't do these fine ladies wrong!" The rabbi by now had to shout over the pandemonium.

As they rose to leave this session, the Russian language once more became the common currency. Bertha Levin placed one of her thick-fingered hands on Rabbi Rosenbaum's arm. "Don't be in such a worry," she said. "It all work out."

"What was wrong about it?"
"It was like . . . like cheating."
"How do you think they felt about it?"
"Scared."
"And you were doing it for fun?"
No response.
"For fun, right?"
"No, it was actually to make money."
"To make money." The rabbi's voice was low.
"The money, yeah."

A few days after the meeting with the Russians, the rabbi was sitting in a classroom at the opposite end of the synagogue from the chapel. The rabbi's knees extended above the top of the low table, but he had not wanted to talk looking down on the two sixth-grade boys before him. He wanted them to be equals, at least in height, for this confrontation. The room was again quiet. When dealing with the young, the rabbi had learned, silence was a most effective tool, and he was allowing it to work.

"Explain it to me again, please," the rabbi said finally.

The boys looked at each other, neither eager to speak. Finally one of them, the taller of the two, a handsome, dark-haired boy, was ready.

"Well, we'd give these second graders a gumball, like we were just giving them something. Then we'd say, 'That'll be two bucks.' If they tried to give it back, we wouldn't take it. 'Two bucks or I'll tell the principal,' we'd say. 'I'll tell your parents.' "

"Anything else?"

They looked down in unison.

"Was there any threat of physical violence? You, sixth graders, standing over second graders?"

Silence.

"Was there?"

"Sort of."

"This happened in Hebrew school? Just the opposite of what you are learning. What do we learn? Be honest with money. Be honest in business. In our religion we are kind to the weaker, the smaller. Our people know pretty well what it is to be pushed around. Don't you think?"

They nodded. Someone walked by in the hallway and, like indicted criminals who did not want their faces to appear on a television report or on the pages of a newspaper, the boys turned away, shielding their faces in their hands.

"I'm not angry with you. I'm hurt. Our people are hurt. This is not what being a Jew stands for. There will always be someone smaller, someone weaker. You can do this all your life or . . ."

The boys awaited the completion of the sentence. Their eyes rose slowly to meet his.

"Or you won't. Today I'm giving you an assignment. A one-page paper on what the word *ethics* means to you. And another assignment. The next time you see somebody smaller or weaker being pushed around by somebody bigger and stronger, I want you to help them. Understood?"

Silence.

"Are we finished? Can we go?"

The rabbi rose from his uncomfortable chair and shook hands with each of them. Outside in the circular driveway, two cars were waiting—and perhaps a stiffer penalty than they had just received.

How easy—how much fun—was a Judaism that could be packaged for two hours' consumption on a Purim night. How difficult it was to have Judaism infuse the lives of his people, both the reluctant Israel pilgrims and these minor-league bullies. Jay Rosenbaum—son of a rabbi, son of an advertising man—knew the difference between an impulse buyer and a faithful customer.

II

Until quite recently, American Jews went about their religious practices with a pronounced insularity. Their Judaism might consist of daily or occasional observances, but whatever its frequency of acknowledgment, it was a religion central to their lives and deeply felt. Yet, contrarily, practicing Jews often sensed that many Americans considered them little better than pagans, acting out strange, ancient rituals. Gentiles neither understood nor seemed inclined to learn about a religion that to them appeared frozen in time. Jewish tradition, services, and holidays were alien to a dominantly Christian nation; they seemed out of sync chronologically, theologically, even emotionally.

Within their own synagogue communities and homes across America—surely different in circumstance from the European ghetto days, yet similar in the ease of familiarity—Jews could gather to perform their rituals, eat their special foods, and simply relish being Jewish. Hebrew or Yiddish spoken on those occasions was a badge of honor, not an invitation to derision, as it would have been in the world outside. No one would criticize them for being different, and the specter of anti-Semitism was safely on the other side of the door. It was considered better to worship and celebrate apart, to maintain a wary, fortress mentality. And why not? After all, it could always be argued, what had the Jews experienced at the hands of gentiles in years and ages past? History offered little comfort.

With the rabbis of Jay Rosenbaum's generation, this outlook changed radically. Now, Jews want the non-Jewish world to understand them, their worship, and their theology. Of course, the roots of this new openness can be traced to the ecumenism begun a few decades ago, but there is another agenda as well. If Jews and Jewish practice are known and explained, the Jew becomes less of an exotic— and possibly less a target for thoughtless hate.

And so the presence of Rabbi Rosenbaum at noon on a Monday (another day off preempted) at the First Congregational Church in Boylston, some ten miles from Worcester, served as but another example of his efforts to bridge religious differences. There, in the fellowship hall—with its glistening linoleum floors, cathedral ceiling, and rich paneled walls—neat rows of tables with disposable paper coverings stood in readiness: a typical church-supper setting. But instead of the ubiquitous casseroles and gelatin salads with suspended pieces of fruit, there were plates containing horseradish and *haroset*, a lamb shank-bone, and cups filled with kosher wine. Huge flats of matzoh overwhelmed proper-sized paper dinner plates.

While the atmosphere within this church hall was most open and welcoming, Jews just a few miles away—and within the past week—had experienced other expressions of sentiment toward them. Swastikas were found one morning on dormitory walls at Clark University in Worcester. Clark has a large number of Jewish students and periodically serves as a sounding-board for the anti-Jewish sentiments of some of its students, as well as for some of the marginalized young people of the poor Main South neighborhood where Clark is located. Within the same month, Jewish tombstones in a cemetery in the town of Everett had been overturned, broken, and defaced with swastikas and other profanities. Small but persistent reminders of modern-day anti-Semitism are all too readily at hand.

Rabbi Rosenbaum and the pastor of First Congregational, Reverend Charles Ford, have had members of their youth groups visit one another's places of worship and have jointly hosted a few combined adult functions, but by far the most anticipated and successful event has been the annual "Model Seder," which the rabbi inaugurated three years ago.

The rabbi entered the fellowship hall and, as clergy of every stripe are wont to do, his eyes did a quick count. This year, there were well over eighty people in attendance, the best turnout yet. "I play better on the road than in my home ballpark," he confided to Rev. Ford.

"Once you do a seder, you know it; the ritual is straightforward; there are books to help you," Rabbi Rosenbaum said early in his presentation to the group, which consisted of far more women than men, ranging in age from late twenties to some in their seventies. "But the reason Jews repeat the seder year after year is because our lives are constantly changing, the world is constantly changing; we need to apply the age-old lessons to what is happening today. So the seder is not the repetition of some outdated, quaint custom, like pulling out some picture album and remembering how things used to be. If Jews only know how to do a seder perfectly, if we know it only intellectually, we are missing the point. The point is to live it."

The rabbi intoned some of the Hebrew prayers, explained them briefly, and then performed an abbreviated version of each of the fourteen steps of the seder. The Protestant brethren of First Congregational proved to be most willing and interested participants. Their responses to the prayers were crisp and loud; at the rabbi's gentle prods, they passed the various foods with military-school alacrity. Not all that long ago, such a gathering would have been considered heretical for either side: Protestants acknowledging a ritual led by a man who did not believe in the human manifestation of God that was at the foundation of their faith; a Jew sitting at table with Christians who proclaimed what he believed to be but the backdrop to their fuller belief.

Reverend Ford asked if there were any questions. The first was about the Passover practice of ridding the house of all yeast-bearing foods, or *hametz*. "A perfect example of old ways teaching us today," he exclaimed. "Spring cleaning means one thing, and this is a special kind of spring cleaning. What does yeast do? It puffs things up, makes them rise, be bigger than what they were before. We, too, need to periodically do some internal housecleaning, getting rid of the things that puff us up. And what better time than spring, with the dead of winter behind and new life emerging all around us.

"The matzoh?" he said, picking up on a comment about the matzoh being like Communion wafers. "It's more than just bread without yeast, quickly taken along because the Israelites didn't have time to have their bread rise before their escape from Egypt. More than the manna in the desert. Look at it," the rabbi said, holding a piece in the air. "Thin, pressed down. Symbolic of the Jewish people in those days, under the heel of the pharaoh, and look how God delivered them. We have many Russian Jews coming into Worcester these days; they are living matzoh. We, ourselves, in our lives are pressed down—by economic problems, poor health, difficult relationships, all sorts of failures. The matzoh reminds us and encourages us to eat this food and know that God will deliver us.

"The Messiah" Ah *mashiach!* Somehow I think we have some differences of opinion on that one." The rabbi smiled broadly toward the last table and his questioner, whose stern look and long preamble underscored a fundamentalist orientation. "And where do the gentiles fit in because we are called the chosen people? No, my friend, everybody will not have to be Jewish when the *mashiach* comes. But I hope you'll leave some room for us when you get to heaven."

A warm round of applause dovetailed into the laughter, leaving the fundamentalist with a stony look and his hand in the air, ready for the next interrogatory.

Reverend Ford leaned over and whispered in the rabbi's ear, "Jay, I could take you anyplace."

In a little over an hour, Rabbi Rosenbaum had successfully delineated a path to their salvation—as well as his own. His message: all men and women are slaves to something, but only in God can they expect to find their true freedom. The Exodus story—while a venerable cornerstone of Judaic belief, it is not often invoked in Christian services—had provided the context. This group of eighty mainline Protestants had been taken into their distant past, given symbolic tears to drink and smashed bread to eat. They had been asked to reflect with this man, a throwback to the Old Testament, upon writings many of them believed had been resoundingly superceded by the New Testament. Yet the rabbi had neither pandered to their beliefs nor compromised his own.

As the rabbi was about to leave, a woman blocked his way. He smiled. She did not.

"I didn't understand how much we owe to you . . . you people," she said quickly. Embarrassed by her candor, she wheeled quickly about, then disappeared into the kitchen.

It was now Thursday of the same week, the second night of Passover in the Jewish world, and twenty-two mismatched chairs were set before an eclectic assortment of end tables, card tables, and a single dining-room table forming a rather bumpy U crowded into the basement recreation room of the Rosenbaums' house on Longworth Street. The luxury of space and the well-intentioned, but nonetheless show-and-tell quality of the First Congregational Church had been traded for the intimacy of a real *mishpocha* and the intensity of an undiluted Jewish observance. But, in the Rosenbaum house, it was not without its cost.

The thorough housecleaning and removal of all *hametz,* as well as the extensive, careful shopping (foods must not contain fermented grain and must be certified kosher for Passover) had exacerbated the inflammation that afflicts Janine's hands. The actual cooking of the seder meal, which had begun several days before, certainly hadn't helped. There had been another flare-up—sudden, but not entirely unexpected—just before the guests began to arrive. Janine admits she customarily becomes, as she puts it, "stressed out" just before a major function like this. Were the radish roses perfect? Was every place setting complete? More paprika to add some color to the fish? That wrinkle where two tables met unevenly; couldn't it be smoothed out? Jay Rosenbaum, in one of his rare expressions of anger, told his wife that they were *never* again having a seder at home.

But when Janine opened the door to greet her guests, it was with a warm smile and a huge hug, waving off any compliments for the elegant table she had set, for the feast of baked haddock, vegetables,

kugel, mock chicken soup, and homemade gefilte fish she had prepared.

"Nothing. Nothing. Come in. Come in!"

The invited included some of the Rosenbaums' closer friends,
like Cantor Freedman and his family; some marginal members of the
congregation, like Linda and Steve Rubenstein; some nonmembers,
like neighbors Ed and Barbara Leyden, who are nominally Reform; and
a couple for whom this would be their first real seder—Simon and Zina
Mats. While it might be considered prestigious or politic to be invited
to the rabbi's for a seder meal, this is not the case at all. Actually, the
rabbi tries to find out who would not normally have family coming or
family to go to for Passover. The seder guest list, properly drawn, is
supposed to be a study in compassion, not status.

Passover celebrates God's freeing the Jews from slavery in
Egypt, this emancipation following the ten plagues that were visited
on the Egyptians, the last of which was the killing of the firstborn son
in every family. The Hebrews were instructed to mark the lintels of
their doors with lamb's blood, so that the angel of death would "pass
over" their house. Passover also marks the beginning of Jewish nationhood; this year in Worcester, just after the Beth Israel congregational
trip to Israel had finally been assured, the holiday had an even deeper
significance for Rabbi Rosenbaum.

Passover is by far the most widely observed Jewish holiday, and
even those Jews who have not set foot inside a synagogue or done anything overtly religious all year will somehow host or find a place to
share a seder meal. Notwithstanding its deep emotional pull, the modern-day enactment of the Exodus story in the homes of American Jews
has often turned into an exercise in convenience rather than the careful remembrance of a rich tradition. The essentials are not the issue,
and are usually all present: *karpas,* parsley or any green herb as a sign of
spring; bitter herbs, usually horseradish, to recall the bitterness of the
Israelites' suffering during their bondage; *haroset,* a thick paste of
ground apples and walnuts, representing the mortar the Jews used as
slaves to build Egyptian cities; salt water, for the tears shed in misery; a
lamb's shankbone, to represent the Pascal sacrifice; an egg, symbol of

mourning; the wine of gladness at the release from Egyptian captivity; and unleavened bread, matzoh, both because the Jews left in such a hurry their bread had no time to rise, and to remember the "poor bread" they were given as slaves in Egypt.

But despite the symbols, the Passover ceremony in many Jews' homes has become a faded replica of the Passovers of their youths. Even with microwaves and precooked staples, the assumed pressures of children with television-skewed short attention spans and the fatigue of two wage-earning adults mitigates against the completion of the entire seder (or "order of service")—the full retelling of the Exodus story, the recitation of the many prayers and singing of songs, and a leisurely meal to allow both food and words to digest. Usually. But decidedly not so in the Rosenbaum house.

At each of the twenty-two places sat a copy of the Haggadah—the Rabbinical Assembly's version, entitled *Feast of Freedom*, which is one of the more than two thousand versions written since the saga of the Exodus was first put into a discrete form and published near the end of the fifteenth century. Some parts of the Haggadah are from the Torah, other sections date from the Middle Ages, but this ingenious compilation, consisting of fourteen steps—from *Kadesh*, the first blessing of the wine, to *Nirtzah*, the closing prayer—splendidly fulfills the Torah's command that the Jews' liberation from Egyptian slavery be told from generation to generation. So popular is the Passover celebration that for many Jews, the Haggadah is more familiar to them than the Torah itself.

"And now we begin," Rabbi Rosenbaum said, extending his arms to embrace his guests. "Why is this night different from all other nights?"

"On all other nights, we eat either bread or matzoh," the children readily volunteered, in one voice. "On this night only matzoh."

He stood there, ramrod straight, suddenly a giant in the low-ceilinged recreation room. This may have been my imagination, but his eyes seemed to take the dull fluorescent ceiling light and increase its weak candlepower a hundredfold. "Yes, indeed; yes!" the rabbi said, repeating the famous line in Hebrew.

The Passover meal is a celebration of a triumph; in their wisdom, the ancient rabbis wanted to assure that it was implanted at a young age. As a result, Passover is not the occasion for a lecture but rather a Judeo-Socratic dialogue that takes a people from under the pharaoh's heel, and by God's power—and their sometimes wavering, sometimes towering faith—out of Egypt, across the Red Sea, through forty years in the desert, to the land "flowing with milk and honey."

"On all other nights, we eat bread and matzoh; why tonight do we eat only matzoh?"

"Our forefathers had to leave in a hurry and so . . ."

"What does the shankbone of a lamb remind us of?"

"The Passover sacrifice; a lamb was slaughtered and the blood smeared on . . ."

"Parsley?"

"Spring. Rebirth. Renewal."

David Rosenbaum and Josh Leyden displayed a prodigious grasp of Jewish history. With great relish and meticulous care, the rabbi easily alternated between dialogue with the children and certain embellishments to bring ancient truths to bear on events of the recent past. As each of God's miracles was retold, the *"Dayeinu"* was sung. *"Dayeinu"* means "It would be sufficient": each and every manifestation of God's power and kindness would be sufficient to show Him as worthy of their praise and allegiance.

"It is fresh each year," the rabbi said, a glass of Manischewitz in his hand, focusing on Simon and Zina. "You have left the captivity of Russia, as Moses left Egypt, to be free and free to worship God. But we are all captives, each year in a different way; and we all must break the chains that confine us. Perhaps it is our pride, our ambition, our laziness. Conformity; we are asked to go along with what is in fashion, what's hip. 'Give up your way of thinking! It's old-fashioned, out of date. Get with it!' But we know that these patterns of living are ultimately destructive for us as Jews. And so we must leave that captivity in every generation; each person must once again be free."

It was now past ten o'clock and the children had abandoned the table to play games or generally chase one another up and down the stairs that led to the Rosenbaums' living room. But the rabbi was anything but finished. It was not the wine, which he had only sipped—although he constantly filled the huge goblet before him to overflowing, to express God's abundance—that was inflaming his heart.

"This year, the Passover means even more. The ultimate goal of the Exodus was to receive the Torah and carry it into the Promised Land to build a Jewish civilization. We sit in Worcester, but we all know that our expression as Jews is only complete in one place. That place is Israel. There, Judaism is not confined to a ritual life; there *everything* is Jewish. As you know, with some members of our congregation we will soon be going there. Not as tourists, but as pilgrims. Let us sing the final song, and let us sing it loudly and with pride."

The words of "*L'Shana Ha'ba'ah Be'Yerushalayim*" floated over a table now littered with fragments of the meal and stained with wine. Jay Rosenbaum's voice rose above all others. "Next Year in Jerusalem."

Once the last guest had left, Janine did some perfunctory cleaning up as Jay readied the children for bed. When Janine came in to say goodnight to David, she plopped down heavily on his bed. It had been an exhausting day, following an exhausting week.

"Mom," David said as he pulled his covers up over his shoulders, "this is the best day of my life. Ever."

"Me too, David, me too."

"I know I get nuts leading up to it, but having those people around the table, eating food I prepared—that gives me enormous satisfaction; I get so warm inside," Janine told me later when we talked about the evening. "If anything kills me about my damn arms it's that I can't do more of it. Russians at the table, neighbors, people from the *shul*. They all get to know each other. It's a reminder that we were once strangers and now we're not; we're unified by this experience of thousands of years ago that has been repeated and repeated and repeated. This is what kids remember when they grow up. It's what I love about Judaism.

"Now is this religious?" She was smiling mischievously. "Jay and I have some pretty heated discussions about this because I keep on telling him that you can be an ethnic Jew without really being religious. Guess what? He won't buy that! But, yes, way down deep, I feel religious about it. I do."

A generous assortment of food was once again set out for the sustenance and enjoyment of the *mishpocha*, but this time, the group was gathered in the comfortable living room of Charlie and Rhonda Mills's home, about a mile up Salisbury Street from the synagogue. Wonderful nut-filled pastries and cookies from Widoff's Bakery, bowls of dried fruit and nuts, as well as hot and cold drinks, covered a good portion of the counter separating the kitchen (which is kosher) from the living room. The food was both ample and appealing, but not the center of attention that it was at a seder, where every item has symbolic weight. And this was a *mishpocha* brought together not to celebrate an ancient tradition from a faraway land, but to hold a conclave to see if they had the fortitude to forge a new covenant at Congregation Beth Israel in Worcester, Massachusetts. It was the first meeting of the combined young couples' group and those who had signed up for the rabbi's congregational trip. Only twelve people were present; the group now numbered twenty-nine, the Hardings* having dropped out. After years of squabbling, they had decided to divorce instead.

". . . the Sheraton Plaza?"

". . . does it have a pool? Outdoor or in?"

". . . about the Bedouin encampment . . ."

". . . that is *crazy*; it's not a good idea for the kids, and as for me . . ."

". . . we thought it would be an adventure. . . . Okay, okay; what about . . ."

A somewhat hapless smile was frozen on Jay Rosenbaum's face as he looked about him. The rabbi had asked for questions about the itinerary; he expected them to be dispatched quickly, so that he might begin to talk about the deeper significance of the trip. He had misjudged.

". . . what exactly does this mean, 'Shabbos' at leisure'? Could you be a little more specific about what that . . ."

". . . passports . . ."

". . . getting to the airport . . ."

". . . leave the luggage at the hotel when we go north? We'll have to pack and unpack a hundred times . . ."

". . . deposit? What if I decide . . . ?"

The rabbi was somewhat surprised to find that many of the questions—and complaints—came not from the anticipated source, the older synagogue members, whose suspected irascibility had caused the younger couples to form their own group last year. Instead, the questions came from the younger travelers themselves. They scrutinized the itinerary as a team of accountants might study the balance sheet of a takeover target, and they were not shy about exercising their line-item vetoes. Meanwhile, the Silvermans sat in amused detachment on the couch, oblivious to the tense back-and-forth going on about them, laughing at their own private jokes and occasionally landing a friendly punch or nudge.

The food went largely untouched; the rabbi did not fare as well. I had gotten to know him well enough to sense, as the close questioning wore on into a second hour, that he was exercising extraordinary restraint—and that he had all but abandoned this evening as a chance to talk about the kind of trip to Israel *he* envisioned.

"I mean, who do these people think I am, their tour guide?" he complained to me later. "I've just got to be patient. At least the older folks and the young couples didn't seem to be butting heads. That's important. I've got to keep focusing on what's going right. After all, we're *going*. They'll come around. I know it. I hope so. The next meeting, we'll focus on the real meaning of the trip and what Israel means to them; that'll get it off this kind of stuff."

The food on the counter at the Millses' home was just as ample a few weeks later. And just as untouched. About an hour after the meeting had started, the look on Jay Rosenbaum's face was the same too. Nineteen people were gathered in the Millses' living room, and Rabbi Rosenbaum was being called on to practice still more patience.

". . . and before the state of Israel was founded, Jews had an inferiority complex . . ."

". . . they said that Jews wouldn't fight . . ."

". . . well, we showed 'em . . ."

". . . I was called a dirty Jew, a chicken . . ."

". . . how many wars?; four, five; we won 'em all . . ."

". . . just make sure those children don't hold us back, I'm not paying . . ."

". . . Israel proves we can't be pushed around; we can stand tall . . ."

". . . Israel needs our support . . ."

". . . I just love the people over there; they're so brave . . ."

All of the other young couples—Mark and Sandy Cutler, Steve and Denise Sosnoff, the Fixlers, Carl and Debbie Aframe—were there in addition to the Millses. Two older couples—Murray and Freda Rosenberg and Ben and Lillian Silverman—were present, as were the older single women, Marion Blumberg, Gabriella Frymer, and Rose Goldstein, as well as Dr. Maxwell Gould, a retired physician. The rabbi had planned this second meeting with care, to avoid having it deteriorate into incidentals. Rather than opening with questions, he had begun by asking for reports from the members who had volunteered to do some research. The rabbi was hopeful that the reports on such subjects as the Sadducees and Pharisees, Qumran and Masada—while somewhat prosaic—would set the tone for a different consideration of the trip to Israel.

"So why go to Israel? What does Israel mean to you?" he had quickly asked, only to receive a string of predominantly hypernationalistic responses. It wasn't the direction he had been hoping for. In fact, nothing about the trip was going the way he had wanted.

The people sitting before him had little idea of what was happening behind the scenes concerning their trip. Channy Greenberg had been receiving telephone calls almost daily from either Dr. Mills or Rabbi Rosenbaum, who, in turn, had received a flurry of calls from the people who said they were going. The itinerary and accommodations had been in a constant state of flux; she had done seven different pricings for the trip and changed virtually every stop at least once. Instead of a night in the Bedouin encampment, the group would stay at the Nirvana Hotel on the Dead Sea—not the desert of their forefathers for these pilgrims, but the Nirvana of the tourists. The irony was not lost on the rabbi. And, when the Nirvana was finally decided upon, it was one of those times when he wondered if all the work was worth it. And now this. More of this.

"I guess for me," the rabbi began, after everyone in the room had had their say, "being a Jew can't be expressed fully except in Israel. I'm not a minority there; every act that you do is a Jewish act. I need to see . . ." He needed to see the places told about in Scripture, walk where the prophets walked. But this, his standard speech—which I had heard him deliver at the first organizational meeting, and many times since—was sadly lacking the fire of November, the urgency of purpose with which he had tried to convince people to come along. Jay Rosenbaum wanted to go further with the group tonight, to talk about breaking out of the slavery of a secular life and tasting the liberation of the observant Jewish life—a Passover theme, to be sure—and how the trip to Israel would provide the inspiration for such a dramatic exodus. But this was not the right climate to air such ambitions, as he well knew. Instead, he asked if *they* had anything further to say.

"Tell me more about your feelings. Is Israel more than just a refuge, more than just a militarily strong country?" the rabbi inquired. It sounded more like a plea than a question.

Heads nodded vigorously in assent. Of course Israel was more than that. But no one volunteered how or why.

"Next time we get together, maybe we can talk about what we expect to happen there. Okay? Thanks for coming."

Rabbi Rosenbaum helped himself to one of the many leftover pastries on the counter. People were talking to him, and he too nodded in assent. But the look on his face was the one that would drive Janine to shout "Jay, do you hear what I'm saying!"

* * *

"What do I have to do?" he later asked me. "I don't want us to go over there just to be cheerleaders for the state of Israel. It's the typical American outlook. Israel has turned into a spectator sport; every Jew loves to buy tickets so they can watch and vicariously feel like part of the action. But they don't want to get out onto the field. These people look at Israel as if it were isolated from Jewish history. That until Israel, Jewish history was some kind of burden they had to live with, that we were all schlumps. And the state of Israel was the first thing we did right. Israel is a replacement for religion for American Jews. Don't they see that the more you appreciate and understand what happened going back to Abraham, the greater appreciation you can have for Israel today? Nationalism and religion: we are impoverished by the split. Can't I get them to see you can have both? How do I have to say this?

"One more meeting. We're going to have one more meeting. We've got to. Don't these people get it?"

"Thanks for coming," the rabbi absentmindedly repeated as the guests gathered their coats and began to leave. He seemed to be studying their faces as they passed before him for the last time that evening, as if to plumb what was going on in their minds, what he might say to inspire them, what he might do to make them a true *mishpocha*, ready to endure the sacrifices any extended family must make for one another. The rabbi might have been disappointed with their somewhat shallow responses, but there was more that each of them could have said, I was to find. Perhaps Carl Aframe, the *Shabbat* regular; Ben Silverman, one of the older travelers; and Steve Sosnoff, a marginal member, might provide some insights.

"It's hard for me to talk about it openly," Carl would tell me. "I never think it comes out right, so I just keep my mouth shut about it. Or, I stay on the surface. They look at me and see Carl Aframe, the fast-talking lawyer; words come easy for him. There's another Carl Aframe they don't know. He's the guy who wants his daughter Ruthie—who's about to have her bat mitzvah—to have the same abiding emotional commitment to Israel that he has. Israel *and* Judaism are burning inside me. I want my wife and kids to feel the same way. I want to sense the presence of God in Israel. Now, how can you say that to a group of BI people? And in front of a rabbi?"

And so, even for the openly religious Carl Aframe, his faith is both a more private issue than might be expected of such a readily expressive man and far deeper than his fellow congregants at Beth Israel might expect. Yet he is loath to talk about it with the very person charged with the care of his soul.

"I'm glad it just isn't a group of us older folks going," Ben Silverman said. "I think it's great that kids are going along. Kids allow you to show compassion. We adopted our younger son, Richard, at age five; he was an abandoned child and behind in his physical and mental development. Thank God, we were able to raise him to a normal life. The kids will add spice to the trip. Look, they're Jews, too!"

Ben Silverman, straightforward, uncomplicated, hewing to the faith of his youth, showing a father's compassion and a Jew's passion for a trip he sees as a natural expression of the man that he is.

"I'm totally confused about Judaism, I always have been," Steve Sosnoff told me. "But somehow it's got me. My parents were pretty lax Reform Jews, and I went to Hebrew school five days a week at the Orthodox synagogue. Why? I honestly don't know, but I did it. Something was driving me. Now's the right time for this trip. For one thing, I finally got the money together. And also my daughter is close to bat mitzvah. And for me, I'm going through some major changes in my life. Is this a trip about God and religious Judaism, or just something about a people, the only people I have, the only people that I'm close to? There is a God, I know that. But is it a God that tells me I have to be in *shul* every Saturday? That I don't know. I'm usually at a soccer game on Saturday. This trip? I want to go with my family and have a nice time. And frankly, I would have preferred to go just as a couples' group. We just have more in common. Did you hear all the infighting? Geez!"

And Steve Sosnoff might speak as Everyman—overwhelmed

by the complexities of his life, unsure if Judaism can provide *the* answer, although sure that it supplies *some* guidelines for the modern
day.

Rabbi Rosenbaum must lead them all, knowing so much about
them externally, their inner lives often remaining a mystery.

12

The Rabbinical Assembly, the national organization of Conservative Movement rabbis, usually holds its annual convention in May at The Concord hotel at Kiamesha Lake, some one hundred miles north of New York. The Concord, a legendary Jewish resort in what was once called the "borscht belt"—because of the many Jewish resorts that once dotted the region—is chosen not only for its nostalgic significance, but also because it is the only place large enough to house the rabbis and their spouses and readily able to serve kosher meals. The convention is at once a massive college reunion—as virtually every American rabbi in the Conservative Movement is a graduate of Jewish Theological Seminary—and a grand ingathering of men (and now, more and more, women)—who labor in disparate vineyards all year long, with little contact with one another.

The meeting has its professional side—with the predictable plethora of lectures and workshops—but there is a personal side that is equally, or even more appealing to those who attend. The RA, as it is called, provides a time to trade tips on everything from religious education to fund-raising, to subtly compare job performance, perhaps poke around for a new assignment, find out who's making what for salary, and generally to be able to commiserate with other front-line troops on the state of their respective congregations, the state of Judaism in America. It is, in short, the rabbis' only opportunity to kvetch, without fear of reprisal, about the difficulty of the work they do the rest of the year. Rabbis' wives also find a sympathetic and understanding community in one another's company. What might be bottled up in congregational life is uncorked at the convention each year.

Rabbi Rosenbaum looks forward to attending the convention. It is a time for intellectual stimulation, some personal vindication, and a mini-vacation for him and Janine; there are no telephone calls, and meals are someone else's responsibility. But this year, Rabbi Rosenbaum found himself shuffling the convention reservation from pile to pile. As he had grumbled about his own congregation's tepid and tardy response to the proposed Israel trip, he admitted that he, too, was procrastinating. His many "plates in the air"—especially the staggering logistics of the Russian wedding and the innumerable details of the Israel trip—not only filled each working day, but spilled over into the next. It seemed that just as he finished one project, something else came up.

Gilya Kaufman, one of the Russians, had been diagnosed with an extremely virulent strain of prostate cancer. Yael Cohen, a faithful minyanaire, required emergency bypass surgery. His wife had had the same operation and never recovered. A longtime member came in and announced he was leaving his wife for another woman, who was also married. A few days later, he was back in Rabbi Rosenbaum's office to say he was returning home; his new love had contracted cold feet. Standard separations and divorces the rabbi has handled, but this was a new and confusing twist. On the nursery-school front, it appeared that Fran Smith was stonewalling Karen Rosen as her associate for the coming year. "I'm so happy that you're going to be part of *my* school," Fran told Karen in a tone that left no doubt who was in charge and who would remain so. This tender shoot of transition had to be nurtured carefully in the days ahead.

Finally, two weeks before the convention, Rabbi Rosenbaum looked at the day's crowded schedule on his calendar—and ahead to the days he had penciled in for the time at The Concord—and decided he simply didn't have the time to go.

I had looked forward to accompanying the rabbi to the convention, as much to see the face of Conservative Judaism as to see and talk with other rabbis, and to put Rabbi Rosenbaum in the context of his peers. So I decided to go by myself.

* * *

The Concord, the site for this yearly meeting, could serve as a potent symbol of the state of American Judaism. The Concord's lawns are still well tended, the meals are served in legendary excess, the assembly rooms have grand names such as The Columns, Cordillion, and Athenian, but The Concord is now but an oasis in a once blooming Jewish paradise. The famous Grossinger's has closed, and such landmarks as the Nevele and Brown's barely stay open. The bungalow communities that used to provide summer escape for the urban Jews of New York City are ramshackle reminders (except for those taken over by thriving ultra-Orthodox groups) that such simple, ethnically intense vacations are no longer in favor.

The Judaism that built the borscht belt is dead, the impulse that caused Jews to live—and to vacation—together has been attenuated by an American culture that provides many other outlets for spirituality and other places to vacation. The Concord might be a nice place to visit these days—for kitsch or for old times' sake—but few want to stay for any length of time, or come regularly. Much the same can be said about synagogues across America. Each provides but one option among many, and it is an option exercised at the will and whim of American Jews, and no longer a customary act.

And yet, the Rabbinical Assembly, for the few days it is convened at The Concord, is as communal a Jewish undertaking as even the rabbis themselves are wont to experience during the year. It is at once a grand bazaar and the place to wrestle Talmudically with the intricacies and vagaries of Judaism. It is a place to discuss issues both current and esoteric and to set policy—policy that, in the finest anarchic tradition of nonhierarchical religious belief, any rabbi is free to ignore. It is a time to gather in all tribes and wanderers, teachers and prophets, scribes and chieftains: the clerical *mishpocha* living in the diaspora of their various congregations, classrooms, and offices. The scholarly, the secular, those for whom the flame still burns bright and others for whom it is all but extinguished, the liberal and the Orthodox, yeshiva-trained and the newly aware, the Yiddish-speaking and those with the latest contemporary slang—all are here in their contentious complexity. It is a noisy and serious time, both venal and divine, unforgiving and compassionate: it is totally, thoroughly, unashamedly, uncompromisingly Jewish.

En route to the meeting rooms, I walked from The Concord lobby past booths offering *kippot* from Ethiopia; stained-glass *mezuzot*, menorahs, and other artifacts; Judaic pottery and jewelry; *tefillin* (with demonstrations at 9:30 A.M. and 1:30 P.M. on how they are made); books and audiovisual educational materials; and a Hasidic *sofer*, who inscribes and repairs Torahs, mends their mantles, Ark covers, and other religious paraphernalia. Yearly one-stop shopping for the rabbis has always been a key feature of the convention.

Sprinkled among the booths and displays were the tables of various tour agencies, offering their many versions of congregational trips to Israel. (Include Paris? Venice?) At the Kenes booth, wearing that wonderful, infectious smile that she had brought to Worcester the past November, I found Channy Greenberg.

She told me proudly that she has been in the Israel tour business for over twenty years. She has arranged travel, accommodations, and touring for tens of thousands of American Jews. She has handled trips of a dozen people from poor Orthodox *shuls*; she has transported, without a hitch, Zubin Mehta and the entire New York Philharmonic.

When I mentioned the Beth Israel trip, her smile became fixed, the freeze frame of a professional—not unlike Rabbi Rosenbaum—who knew when not to allow inner emotions to show.

"A lot of changes, I think," I offered.

"Yes," she replied.

"That many?"

"More than any group I've ever taken to Israel." The smile relaxed. The secret was out.

The theme for this year's convention was "Revitalizing *Kehillot* in the Nineties: The Rabbinic Role." *Kehillot*, communities, were at the forefront of the planners' minds when they wrote in the convention brochure, "Our intention is to concentrate upon the remarkable variety of successes which are attributable to our RA membership at the local level." But as I listened both to the major addresses and to snippets of conversation in the halls and at meals, another picture of this massive and mainstream movement in American Judaism was being presented. In his presidential address, Rabbi Irwin Groner detailed the great spiritual hunger among Jews in America, while acknowledging that most are not turning to Judaism to satisfy it. "Intermarriage and alienation are so high—we can say with the Bible—that our hope has been cut off. For whom do we labor?" Some American Jews are rejecting materialism and are searching for a moral foundation for their lives, but again, as Rabbi Groner lamented, they are not finding it in Judaism.

One speaker told of "rescuing Jewish souls" with a startling urgency, as if Complacency were another nation—like Ethiopia or Syria or the old Soviet Union—inhospitable to Jews. Various approaches to "outreach" and "inreach" were critiqued, and new strategies were formulated. The sessions had the feeling of a group of salesmen preparing a unified pitch, or of senior military officers planning an assault.

"Our worst fears are being confirmed," one speaker pronounced gravely. "Anti-Semitism? Forget it. We are talking about alienation and assimilation. We are talking about the very survival of Judaism in our open, American society. While Jews are secure, Judaism is not."

Presentations were made before hundreds of rabbis in the grand ballrooms of The Concord, where heavy curtains on the windows and on the stage give the feeling of protection, security, dignity, timelessness, and plenty of time to consider the issues at hand. And there were smaller groups meeting in smaller rooms, with blinds open to the sun, windows open to the brisk winds of change. In talk after talk, discussion after discussion, the statistics presented offered persistent reminders. Intermarriage was at record levels; the number of Jews affiliated with synagogues was dropping every year; the number of contributors to Jewish causes continued to shrink. The premise of *A Certain People*—the title of Charles Silberman's acclaimed book on American Jews, which, while acknowledging contemporary Judaism's many problems, saw a renaissance afoot and unlimited possibilities in prospect—was categorically refuted as naïve. There was no light at the end of this tunnel. The Conservative Movement was at a crossroads.

The Conservative Movement was drifting, proud of its past, but unsure of its present and even more confused about its future.

"The facts are at best sobering; at worst they are alarming," intoned Rabbi David Gordis, sounding as if he were standing over a fallen comrade, laid in pine box and dressed in a burial shroud, and not a legion of inspired soldiers fully able to turn the tide of battle. "No longer are we talking about a helpless population who are victims of external forces. People give to Holocaust memorials and to the defense of Israel, but they continue not to flee, but simply to drift away, from Judaism."

But even as this daunting assessment of Conservative Judaism was being presented, the more than five hundred rabbis attending were constantly offered infusions of encouragement ("*Mitzvot:* Actualizing Our Partnership with God"; "Spiritual Resources for Healing"; "Making God Smile: Some Ways to Play with Leading the *Davening*"; "Letting a Fresh Wind Blow Through Your Synagogue") and were stirred to rethink both the ancient ("Sephardic Jews Come of Age: How Golden Was It?") and look deeply into the present ("The Quarrel: Can You Love Someone Whose Views You Hate?").

Using as an example the movie *Field of Dreams* and the baseball diamond fashioned out of a cornfield—so that Shoeless Joe Jackson and the 1919 Chicago Black Sox players would return—Rabbi Lawrence Kushner exhorted, "If we build it, they will come." His voice low, he evoked the final scene, with hundreds of car lights weaving along the roads, headed toward the diamond. "They are out there, driving around, looking, searching for *something* to build their lives around," he whispered huskily into the microphone. "Your job is not about making sound business decisions and having an ever-increasing annual budget. You must follow your dream." He went on, asserting that if the rabbis unashamedly shine their own beacon from the vantage point of their individual congregations and communities, people will come.

As examined in the presentations and discussions in the various workshops, I found that the beacon these days had two distinct beams, with two different wattages. One was that of the rabbi as teacher, wise counsel, and program coordinator. The other was that of the rabbi as—simply—a person. This, for the Rabbinical Assembly, appeared to be a breakthrough realization.

While the Jewish Theological Seminary surely wanted its rabbis to represent what was best and most exemplary about Judaism, they educated their men (women were admitted only after 1985) to be Talmudic and biblical scholars, able to do textural analysis and critical scholarship. They were to be conversant with Jewish history, Jewish philosophy, and Hebrew literature and *halakha*. The rabbi was to *know*, to speak with surety and authority in this land of negotiation, compromise, and equivocation. "Take off your shoes, the place where you are standing is holy ground," a new rabbinical student was told upon arriving at JTS.

Now, in sessions like that of Rabbi William Lebeau, today's rabbis were told that sharing their own doubts, revealing their own parched throats and aching feet, was good—both for them and for their congregants. "The message of the rabbi is not the seminary, but himself or herself, each person's individual spiritual struggle," Rabbi Lebeau told his attentive group of twenty-five. "It is not enough to say we find beauty in Judaic traditions, but—like our people—we must also admit how difficult it is to hold on to them. Tell your people when God felt closest to you, when He was farthest away. Don't be like the old rabbi who told me, 'I have a folder on "doubt"; it's bulging. Would I ever preach on it? Of course not!' "

The heightened sensitivity training of the 1970s—the admittance by people of faith that they were equally people of doubt—had finally arrived in 1990s Conservative Judaism. As I sat through Rabbi Lebeau's session, I found myself wondering what Rabbi Rosenbaum might have said about all this. He was not a man to share much of himself with his congregants, in person or from the pulpit.

As I wandered from workshop to meal to conversation to speech, I began to distinguish three distinct generations of rabbis in the Conservative Movement. The older men, now in their fifties and sixties, came from the era when Jewishness was old-fashioned, exotic—and, for the most part, segregated from mainstream America. A good number had Orthodox parents, many of them Eastern European immigrants, who gave American Judaism its unique flavor, steeping their children in Old World Judaism. But as Rabbi Groner had noted in his address, the era of ethnicity was over for American Judaism; it was now about religion—take it or leave it. But how was that to be translated into reality without ethnic underpinnings and ethnic neighborhoods, the very feeling of being Jewish that, while it could be cause for being shunned and excluded, was a visceral part of their generation's lives?

Then there was the middle generation of rabbis—the men of Jay Rosenbaum's age—whose families may have had one foot in ethnic European Judaism and the other firmly planted on American soil, a past shaped by the cobblestone *shtetl* streets, a present proclaimed by well-manicured suburban lawns. This generation, children of the 1960s and 1970s, were tossed about by religious and political anarchy, yet somehow regained their bearings to make the counter-countercultural choice of the clerical and observant life.

A good number of the younger men and women who are Conservative rabbis represented still another, and quite distinct, generation. Instead of having their Jewishness inculcated by a European grandmother or grandfather and reinforced by constant contact with other Jewish kids in their neighborhood or synagogue, many had to learn about their Jewishness at JTS. Their parents—proud, progressive practitioners of the New Permissiveness—vowed to raise open-minded children and eschewed administering the stiff doses of Judaism they had felt forced to swallow. They raised a largely irreligious brood.

Rabbi Joshua Gutoff—whom I had met at the rehearsal for the Russian couples' wedding—was one of this younger group and might speak for many of the rabbis of his generation. "All of us hear how much people love Judaism, its traditions, its history, its unchangeableness," he said as we sat elbow to elbow in the bar off the hotel lobby. It was a lonely place even at happy hour, with hundreds of abstemious rabbis in residence at The Concord. "Judaism is behind a wall of glass to most Jews, hermetically sealed—and that's just the way they want it. Still in sight, but basically out of reach. In its fixedness, it is irrelevant. And, as it is unchanging, people rationalize that they don't have to think about it. That's the attitude the rabbi confronts from the majority of congregants today. You sometimes wonder why you are doing this. Are you a ritual high priest? Are you just oiling the gears of a bar and bat mitzvah mill to make grandparents feel good?"

Rabbi Murray Levine, one of the older rabbis, who serves a congregation in the Boston suburb of Framingham (and whose wife, Malka, happens to teach in Beth Israel's Solomon Schechter Day School in Worcester) just smiled at my questions. "It's a long life, and Judaism demands more than anyone can possibly do. Your congregation wants to see progress, wants to measure progress, but if as a rabbi you try to do that, you're kidding yourself. It's far deeper and more profound than numbers of this or that. And on top of everything, the rabbi is supposed to be the perfect person, the one with all the knowledge on any question. Constant progress and perfection. That's a tall order, no?"

And there was a rabbi at the convention, an air force chaplain, nearing the end of his military career, who burst into tears before the audience at a fairly large seminar. "I just don't know if I mattered at all," he sobbed.

In my conversations with rabbis and their wives, I was constantly swept into rich and heated discussions dealing with everything from contract renewals to congregational trips to Israel to the life of a rabbinic spouse. When the subject of contract renewals came up, it was almost as if we were talking about the performance and payment of professional athletes, not men and women of God. The Rabbinical Assembly had recently sent out a bulletin advising rabbis to keep a log of their accomplishments to present at contract time. A growing number of rabbis were hiring lawyers to negotiate with the synagogue boards. "Why not?" one rabbi asked me, at once taken and embarrassed by the thought. "All the people on the board are businessmen, bankers, lawyers. They know how to negotiate. You don't. And there you are, *kippah* in hand, supposedly happy for anything they might deign to give you. Hire the best lawyer you can find and stay out of it."

The mention of congregational trips to Israel drew responses that ranged from an open guffaw, to eye-rolling incredulity, to a few soft sighs of reverie. A good number of the rabbis declared flatly that they simply would not risk organizing—much less joining—such a trip. Others told horror stories of unpleasable congregants for whom they were expected to be rabbi, tour guide, personal assistant, and wet nurse. A small number admitted the trip was the high point of their careers.

One morning I sat at breakfast with Malka Levine. We had a difficult time keeping our conversation on track as waiters conveyed food to our table. To say "present" or "offer" would do a disservice to the single-minded Concord staff; while "throw" might be more accurate, it could not carry the weight of the plates that landed resoundingly on our table, laden with heaps of lox and cream cheese and whitefish and bagels. Finally, the assault of calories and cholesterol over, Malka and I talked in depth, uninterrupted, about the previous day's session she had attended, which had been devoted to rabbinic spouses. "The pain in that room," she said, shaking her head. She is an attractive woman of certain years, with a tone in her voice at once sympathetic and understanding of human woes, yet light-hearted enough to show she has discovered it is pointless to wallow in each day's measure of them. "I just couldn't believe it. These were mostly middle-aged and younger rabbis' wives. Skirt too short, kids act up in *shul*, 'My dear, we didn't see you at the Sisterhood breakfast; don't you *care?*' They just haven't learned to let all this stuff go in one ear and out the other. And to wear a smile all the time."

In Rabbi Debbie Cantor's session, "Is This the Person I Married: Reconciling Your View of Your Spouse with the Congregational View of the Rabbi," it was clear that most women did not know what they were signing on for when they married a rabbi or rabbinical student. "I don't expect to be treated like a wife—I gave that up years ago," confessed a woman in her late twenties. "I beg him to treat me just like a member of the congregation." Another woman agreed: "Who is my rabbi? This guy I'm married to? Come on! The *rebbetzin* is the rabbi's rabbi. Who does the *rebbetzin* have? She should join another congregation." The thirty or so women at the session—there was a single male spouse, in addition to Rabbi Cantor's, but he knitted quietly—agreed yes, it was terribly hard to live with a man so revered by the congregation, a man whose job it was to live the righteous life and speak with justice, wisdom, and charity on the *bimah* as well as in the frozen-food aisle at the supermarket. "We're in the middle of a big argument, the phone rings, and all of a sudden he has this sweet voice," one wife noted. "He hangs up and we go right back to the argument. I could kill him!"

Another spouse, this one married only a few years, recalled a conversation she had just had with her mother. "My father was a doctor; he was never home, always tired. My mother said, 'Under no circumstances marry a doctor.' So my mother looks at me last month and says, 'You drip, you married a *poor* doctor! And another thing, I didn't have to socialize with his patients. You do! If your father didn't like patients, he dropped them. Try dropping dues-paying members of your congregation!' "

Near the end of the session, acknowledging the hectic and pressure-filled work week of rabbinic couples, I asked if they found renewal on *Shabbos*. This was something that Rabbi Rosenbaum constantly stressed to his congregation, trying to convince them to embrace this holy day each week.

My answer was a chorus of howls. "He leaves at eight-thirty, gets home at three, goes back to *shul* at five. So this is holy time? This is a time to unwind?"

As I walked out into the hallway after that meeting, with the rabbinic spouses in my wake still stewing, and yet energized by this opportunity to be validated in the presence of their peers, I had a whole new appreciation for Janine Rosenbaum.

After hearing of all the agonies of Jewish clerical life, when I attended morning *minyan* in the huge meeting room called The Columns, I witnessed a wonderful sight. Fresh-faced rabbis wearing brand new *tefillin* prayed beside older men with their leather boxes and straps dark and shiny with age and perspiration; *kippot* sat atop balding heads and women's coifs. There were heads of blond hair and black; beards and clean-shaven chins and cheeks; well-fitted suits and baggy trousers; designer ties and those spotted with the residue of many meals. If there was a stereotype of the rabbi's physical appearance, it would be quickly refuted here. Two hundred people chanting, singing, praying, with friends and foes all about them in splendid profusion, divided by politics and theology and temperament, but here unified by ancient words spoken by and about their God, handed down through generations of equally fractious and stiff-necked people. They bobbed up on the balls of their feet as they said their *Kedushah* ("Holy, holy, holy"), reaching up toward heaven so that they might be that much closer to God. They *shukeled*, swaying forward and back, bending reverentially at the waist. Their voices were clear and strong, resonating through the halls.

And even as the ungodly large portions of Concord food were served to their tables meal after meal, the rabbis were asked, meal after meal, to contribute to the Mazon fund, so that the hungry would also be fed. Always, the attempt to be better; no ordinary conventioneers, these.

As I was about to leave The Concord, I saw a familiar face, out on a veranda, turned toward the sun. Rabbi Neil Gillman, his body almost completely horizontal on the row of small chairs he had assembled, was taking a break from the afternoon's tribulations, revelations, and deliberations. He is a professor of Jewish philosophy at Jewish Theological Seminary, a short, somewhat squat man with a gently rounded potbelly and a face that combines the flinty eyes of a frontline Sinai war veteran with the fatigue of a modern-day Moses, tired of wandering in the wilderness with the feckless band he is supposed to lead. It was Rabbi Gillman, along with a small group of faculty, who led a movement back to stricter Jewish observance at JTS, toward a greater accent on spirituality and personal piety rather than on abstract scholarship. Although a little young for it, Rabbi Gillman is considered somewhat of the éminence grise at JTS, wise and outspoken about Conservative Judaism.

"Orthodox Judaism is what it is, Reform was created by congregations; the Conservative Movement was basically created by the seminary, JTS," he began when I asked him for his thoughts on the state of his branch of Judaism. "And the seminary decided that all these pants makers and shopkeepers had to be told exactly what they had to do and what they had to believe. So for a hundred years, we infantilized the laity. It's all *our* fault." His eyes were now closed to the sun. He continued. "We told these immigrants coming over from Eastern Europe that the rabbi had the truth, that they were stupid oxen. And then the world changed. Laypeople got a good education, they turned into important *machers,* and now the rabbi is in the hot seat. When rabbis hire lawyers to negotiate their contracts, what kind of relationship is that? Does it sound adversarial? You bet it is.

"Conservative Judaism got very satisfied with itself, very satisfied with all the fine buildings we had the money to construct, but along the way, God got locked out of the synagogue. We were proud to have dinner dances, and people came; God wasn't invited. We never taught them that God listens when they pray. Now we want to reintroduce God to them and we find we're offering something nobody wants. And rabbis come back to me all the time and say, 'Why didn't you prepare us for what was out there?' Why do we have a toll-free eight-hundred-number hotline for rabbis with problems? Why do we have rabbis' wives hating the work their husband has to do?"

By his tone, Rabbi Gillman implied he wanted to impart an answer; I waited. The view from the veranda was most appealing—lush grass, well-tended trees and bushes, a few casually strolling guests. It was difficult to believe that just beyond The Concord's grounds was a rural wasteland, once a Jewish haven. Recent years had not been kind to Jewishness—both here in the Catskills and, Rabbi Gillman was maintaining, in America at large.

"Look, for a hundred years, JTS was a great graduate school; it was not a seminary. Most of the men at this convention were prepared to be great teachers, but they didn't learn anything about dealing with people. Only after they got out did they find out about God—yes,

God!—about spirituality, morality, sexuality, intimacy, loneliness, prayer. And so they are pissed. They feel JTS sold them down the river.

"So they're out there every Saturday morning preaching about anti-Semitism and Soviet Jewry, politics, ethics, and psychiatry and they think they're the perfectly modern rabbi. It's not enough. Again, they never were taught the basics—that when they pray, God listens. People want to hear that, know that, believe that. They don't preach that we observe *Shabbos* because God commanded it; but that's the truth, and people want the truth.

"People . . ." He hesitated once more, his eyes closing as he again turned his face full to the warming sun, as if he were a solar battery in need of restorative energy. "People want to hear about God in this individualistic, selfish century. They want to hear about a transcendant God, a Jewish community that really means something, that really works. You'd think the synagogue would be a haven in this crazy society. It isn't; something's missing. We're still talking about budgets and contracts, performance reports and board meetings.

"The Orthodox have community, the Reform go to the mall and don't worry about it. We're in the middle—a good place, a tough place. And the Conservative Movement did a remarkable thing, marrying the best of tradition and the best of what needed to change. Tradition and change. Our motto. But, internally, we stopped growing. And our rabbis are out there, feeling very lonely and isolated, wondering what to do next."

I mentioned that I have been spending time with Rabbi Rosenbaum and had been impressed by his work at Beth Israel. "His father, Nate; ah, there was a rabbi," he said, smiling with the memory. "He was a rabbi before he was a rabbi, came out of a congregation to go to school. Gentle, lovely, gracious. Admired by the other students."

His son, Jay?

"Jay, Jay," he said, tapping his lower lip with his index finger. "Didn't leave much of an impression. What I remember of him was that he was slightly depressed, removed, quiet. Never expected great things of him."

I was taken aback by Rabbi Gillman's unflinching appraisal. I told him in more detail of the Israel trip the rabbi had finally cobbled together. I told him of a regional rabbis' meeting I had attended a few weeks before in Natick, a Boston suburb, where Rabbi Rosenbaum was little less than a star, telling about the many programs he had started for children and young families and showing a dazzling tape of the Purim performance by Nu? Yids on the Block.

"Israel," Rabbi Gillman said, even more fatigue creeping into his voice. "So Jay wants to take them to Israel to find their Jewishness. Good luck, Jay Rosenbaum." Rabbi Gillman turned from the sun and looked squarely at me. "Don't tell me about Purim. Tell me about what families do on *Shabbos,* tell me how many *shomer Shabbos* families he has. Don't tell me about taking them to Israel. Tell me about what happens to their lives when they get back to America. Tell me that."

13

The late afternoon of May 21 descended on Worcester like a soft cloudless dream; not so much as a hint of rain was in the air. The east lawn of Congregation Beth Israel was a shade of deep, lush emerald made possible only at this time of the year by the perfidious moisture of spring and the still slanting rays of the sun. Cardboard signs, designating where the Russian couples would be married, had been arrayed with tactical precision. God appeared to be smiling down on Rabbi Rosenbaum and Jamesbury Drive.

A television reporter and cameraman from New England Cable News pulled up in the driveway; a picture of one of the couples had already appeared in the day's *Worcester Telegram & Gazette*. Inside the synagogue hall, tables were festively decorated with centerpieces of tiny pink asters and white mums. Rabbi Rosenbaum, in his best blue marrying suit, was ready with thoughts for the two couples he would join, Jewishly, in marriage, and a silent prayer that the whole business would come off as scheduled. Plan A was on.

As guests began to arrive and drift leisurely into the sanctuary, I found the rabbi in the library just off the vestibule. There, out of sight, was a scene of barely restrained pandemonium. Witnesses, rabbis, grooms, and cantors dodged and darted among the tables that held the *ketubot,* ready for signing. Where was the other witness for the Reytblats? Have the Fastovskys arrived? Which cantor? Rabbi Rosenbaum, can I . . . ? Rabbi Rosenbaum, have you . . . ?

Rabbi Joseph Klein, retired from Temple Emanuel and now in his late seventies, had failed to meet with his couple, the Shpitalniks, and presented a blank look, and an equally blank *ketubah,* to Rabbi Rosenbaum. The rabbi, after a moment of stunned hesitation, set off to find a translator, but Rabbi Klein grandly waved him off. Being of the generation where Yiddish was still a normal part of a young Jew's growing up, whether in America or Russia, Rabbi Klein and David Shpitalnik quickly researched and mapped out a family tree in that venerable tongue. The printed program listed ten couples; three other couples had dropped out, for reasons both known and unknown to the rabbi. In addition, Boris and Marina Voronin, who had arrived in America just two weeks before, had been included only a few days ago by Debra Hachen, one of the presiding rabbis. The accordionist was sick, so the rabbi quickly collared someone else to lead the couples to and from the east lawn.

Cantor Freedman stood off to the side, staring at the wall. Between conducting traffic and checking the completeness of the *ketubot,* Rabbi Rosenbaum finally had a chance to make his way through the melee to the cantor. The problem was a private crisis, affecting only the two of them, and the rabbi wanted to keep it that way.

"Steve, I think it's lousy, too." The rabbi's voice was both compassionate and low.

"Jay, I just can't believe this!" the cantor exploded, his rage so intense he appeared on the verge of tears.

"It's shortsighted as hell; I think they'll realize that."

"Yeh, right. I'm out of there. And here's my wife, killing herself to make this thing happen tonight. I put in more hours than I get paid for . . . shit!"

The rabbi put a hand on the cantor's shoulder. At their last meeting, the Solomon Schechter board of directors, in order to close a budget gap, decided to phase out the 15 percent tuition discount given to children of the cantor and the rabbi. Marion, the cantor's wife, was now pregnant with their fourth child. Even with the discount, affording Schechter had been tough for the Freedmans on his salary of $49,000 a year. Now, it was an impossibility.

"If they want my kids in public school, they got it," he said bitterly, moving out from beneath the rabbi's extended hand.

"Thanks for understanding."

The cantor turned back to the rabbi, smoldering. "Yeah, understanding. Let's get on with this thing."

The Russian men in place near or before the *ketubot* about to be signed by the witnesses had taken on a different air from that with which they had presented themselves to the rabbis a few weeks before. Although there was a swirl of strangers about them, they knew they were the center of attention, the reason for everyone else to be here. Their hands clasped in front of them, the Russians awaited their moment with a quiet confidence.

All the *ketubot* finally in order, and all aggravations momentarily relegated to the back of his mind, Rabbi Rosenbaum stood in the midst of the Russian grooms and their witnesses. "Before you, you have a contract, a *ketubah*, in which you will soon agree to provide care and sustenance to your wife," he said in a booming, official voice. "It is a contract between a man and a woman. We all know that the Torah details another contract, the contract between God and the Jewish people." At this, his voice changed remarkably, taking on a tone that embraced rather than proclaimed. This was no longer an audience, but travelers at the beginning of a road he was encouraging them to follow. "Ah, the Torah! Even when the Torah was confiscated by the Soviet leaders, you clung to your belief in God—your contract—and you believed that some day you could live again as Jews, that you and your loved one could some day be joined as a family under God. This," he said decisively, "is that day. This is a moment of triumph for you, and for us. We have been separated too long. We don't have to wait anymore. Please sign."

As attention focused on the men and the ancient tradition of contracting for the welfare of their wives with the *ketubot*, the women, as tradition would have it, were relegated to the periphery. They had been crowded into the bridal room—designed for a single bride and a gaggle of nervous aunts, a mother, and some giggling friends, and not a regiment of brides-to-be—making last-minute adjustments to look beautiful, if not exactly virginal. They were not sick, they were not shopping, and they fully intended to present themselves in not too many minutes to lay claim to the men in the library.

The Beth Israel sanctuary was about half full—250 people had come for the wedding and most had tickets for the dinner afterward—when the brides filed up the main aisle and were seated on the *bimah* for the *bedecken* ceremony. Veils were draped over the brides' faces, a gesture of modesty dating back to Rebecca's marriage to Isaac, as the prayer from the Book of Genesis was pronounced: "You are our sister; may you become the mother of myriads of our people." While the more usual scene would be that of a single bride in this position—her countenance and demeanor conveying to the audience something of her inner self as well as her promise as a Jewish wife—these eleven women provided quite a rich tableau of matrimonial variety. On one hand, there was Bertha Levin, married at the height of communism's power, some thirty-seven years before, to Yefim. On the other, Marina Voronin, who six months before had taken Boris as her husband in the eyes of a crumbling state. Bertha, in a close-fitting, white beaded dress, weathered and thickened by life and three children; Marina, a mere slip of a girl, a study in a creamy taffeta. But on this balmy Worcester evening, they were both brides—each with a certain kind of innocence that such an event bequeaths, which no number of years can diminish. Each stood beneath the words of God boldly emblazoned on the wall behind them, ready to pledge a new married life, both to a man, and before that God.

The grooms, in single file, were soon led down the aisle (was there just a bit of swagger in their walk?) to join and claim their partners on the *bimah*. After thunderous applause from the audience, the couples proceeded toward the east lawn, *huppah* carriers in their wake, walking together now toward their own shared life journey. Was it the overwhelming presence of love, or the last-minute jitters that caused the Russians to suddenly look so serious?

Under the cover and protection of a finely embroidered *tallit*, Rabbi Rosenbaum gazed proudly upon Boris and Aviva Salnikov, the first of the two couples he would join in Jewish marriage. Boris, with his trimmed beard and high cheekbones, bore a striking resemblance to Abraham Lincoln. He stared straight ahead. His wife, dressed in a wispy light peach dress, looked up at him as if he were even more famous. "The Jews were wandering many years in the wilderness before they reached their goal," the rabbi addressed them. "And when they reached the Promised Land, God said, 'I remember the love you showed Me in your youth and your wandering.' These Jews had a special place in God's heart. You, too, Boris and Aviva, were wandering, never knowing when you could leave the Soviet Union. And so this day, you can look back and know that you—like the Israelites—had God with you in the wilderness. God remained faithful to you. But you, *you* were also faithful to Him. God is grateful for your wonderful example. We are grateful."

The Salnikovs stood off to the side of the *huppah* as Rabbi Rosenbaum then joined Valery and Larisa Casdin in marriage. Two glasses, wrapped in towels, were placed on the ground. In unison, the two grooms crushed the glasses, signifying that even on a day filled with great happiness, the destruction of Zion was to be remembered and grieved.

A final chorus of "*mazel tov*"s and a wave of applause drifted across the broad expanse of grass, and the eleven couples, with huge grins now replacing the somewhat apprehensive looks of a half hour before, promenaded back into the synagogue hall so that the Hadassah dinner—at forty-four dollars a plate—might proceed.

As the guests found their seats, Marion Freedman confided to the rabbi that what they were witnessing was both a splendid event as well as a financial disaster. Because of the many free meals for the newlyweds, their children, visiting rabbis and cantors, instead of the usual ten or twelve thousand dollars' profit—which was sent each year to the Hadassah Medical Center in Jerusalem—this year barely three thousand dollars would be realized.

Bertha Levin, hesitating in the vestibule near where Rabbi Rosenbaum was standing with Marion, took her Yefim's arm and pulled him toward the rabbi. Yefim was dressed in an elegant fawn-colored suit, perhaps not exactly what a Worcester man of his age might have chosen, but a splendid, well-fitting garment nonetheless. Bertha squeezed her husband's arm to her ample breast. "Rabbi Rosenbaum, this . . . this is happiest day of my life," she said, beaming.

As the Levins moved on to the dinner, Marion moved to follow them. The rabbi took her arm, holding her back. "Marion," he whispered, "this year, I think we've made more than money."

After months of preparation and pitfalls, Rabbi Jay Rosenbaum had successfully brought the Jews of Bobruysk and Odessa and Vilnius westward to the *huppah* in Worcester. He had stayed the course, even when the poor attendance at "News, Views, and Schmooze" and the tepid reception to "Living Joyously as a Jew" made him wonder if he wasn't just fooling himself. His persistence had paid off; the Russians had found that he was not just another American Jew with a generous initial offering who wanted little more to do with them afterward.

The Russian couples finally married Jewishly could not afford to take time for a honeymoon, even after such a momentous evening. And neither could Jay Rosenbaum enjoy a respite; he had to get right back to the business of being a rabbi—and *business* it was that he had to attend to. The board of directors had criticized Richard Sobel, Beth Israel's executive director, for not being aggressive enough in collecting dues. Sobel, in turn, had been driven to desperation—as manifested by a letter in the May congregational newsletter. Utilizing a language familiar to many of the synagogue's professionals, Sobel wrote, "The diagnosis for this past year is a weak heartbeat from a poor flow of the congregation's lifeblood—MONEY. . . . Yes we do call, but only when you are behind in payments, just as the phone company would or the credit card company . . . in fact they would not call. They would write you a letter telling you that your service has been cut . . . canceled. . . . Compared to other synagogues, we are way below average. We cannot continue. . . ."

Of course, this was not a tack Jay Rosenbaum would have taken, but because of his distaste for financial matters, he had granted Sobel free rein in going about his sometimes onerous task as bill collector. The adage in synagogue dues collecting goes "If you remind them, they will complain." The rabbi anticipated—then received—irate telephone calls as well as snide remarks, in person, alluding to the synagogue's insatiable lust for money.

As May slipped into June, Jay Rosenbaum desperately wanted to begin—personally, and with members of the group—to allow minds to clear for the experience of Israel. The best he could do was just get through a fraction of his daily list of appointments, meetings, and activities. What little time he could cadge from his schedule was spent on the banal: shopping for children's clothes, obtaining passports.

There were innumerable loose ends to tie up at the synagogue before the trip. One of the major ongoing projects was preparation of the master plan addressing Beth Israel's key problems. Membership, fund-raising, early childhood development, and youth activities—each merited a section in a document, hammered out over a period of months with Joel Kaufman. As they finally came to an agreement on the text, two areas were, thankfully, already being addressed. Karen Rosen would come in next school year to be Fran Smith's assistant director in the nursery—and with any luck would become the director the following year. Because of Karen's involvement and personal appeal, five new parents had already signed up their children. And Robyn Kravitz, a Beth Israel member and recent college graduate, had agreed to energize the activities of post–bar and –bat mitzvah teenagers. But neither the rabbi nor Dr. Kaufman had been able to convince anyone to take the lead in the crucial areas of membership or fundraising. With summer approaching, the rabbi found himself forced to put over the launching of membership and fund-raising drives until fall.

But beyond the problems of the synagogue, there were still other problems at home.

Janine's wrists and arms were hurting more than ever. Medication that had given her some relief in the past was no longer effective. The latest anti-inflammatory drug made her violently ill. It was Janine who bore the greatest responsibility for handling the details and logistics of the Rosenbaums' trip to Israel, in addition to having a six-year-old and three-year-old to tend to and a husband who was rarely home. She was often testy and irritable as the departure date drew near. Still, she agreed with her husband that a final get-together of the Israel group was essential—and that it had to be a social event. And, as it was his idea, it would be held at their home. The group was to leave on June 24, so the evening of June 17 was set for a covered-dish dinner. Food, the age-old pretext for content, would provide a last opportunity to consider why, indeed, the group was going.

Although Janine might not cherish all the obligations that befall her as Beth Israel's *rebbetzin*, once she committed herself to a task, she committed herself fully. The evening was quickly cast as a *"Kumsitz* Kick-off" (*"kumsitz"* is derived from "come, sit" and is now a popular Israeli word for a campfire singalong). In order to occupy the children while the adults talked (in a crucial strategic move, the Rosenbaums had thought it wise to come up with some way to assure the older members that the youngsters would not be a problem on the trip), each of them would make a collage on a map of Israel and then go on a scavenger hunt to find answers to questions pertaining to life in Israel. The Rosenbaum home was a beehive of activity in preparation for the evening, and their own preparations for the trip were even further forestalled. A trip to the Brookline section of Boston was required to get such items as Israel stickers, travel brochures, and (what would a campfire be without them?) kosher marshmallows. Because Janine's hands could no longer wield scissors, late in the evenings Jay cut out eleven Israel maps from construction paper. Janine dug out a group of Israel posters. As an added touch, folksinger David Strebnik agreed to lead the group in Israeli songs around the campfire.

In the midst of these crowded weeks, the rabbi hoped for the occasional *mitzvah* that would fuel him onward. But such moments seemed to elude him. When a delegation of Russian Jews made an appointment to see him, the rabbi braced himself. People coming in groups to see him usually did not bode well. And a group led by the formidable Bertha Levin was even more ominous. Something with the wedding? Jobs? Housing? What would it be? Bertha Levin, Eva Honig, Simon Mats, and the Salnikovs solemnly filed into his office one afternoon—a tad late for their appointment—and sat down. They peered at one another hesitantly, each waiting for someone else to speak.

"We don't quite know how to say this . . ." Eva Honig said, looking up from her folded hands to the rabbi.

"Yes? Go ahead," the rabbi replied calmly. The issue of dues? Somebody from Hadassah had said something critical about how little money the wedding raised? More complaints from congregants about the Russians' lack of gratitude and reluctance to join the synagogue?

"As we all prepared for the wedding, we . . . well . . . we realized how little we know about Judaism. We are ashamed how little we know. And we want to learn more. Can you help us, Rabbi?"

The look on Rabbi Rosenbaum's face was a mixture of incredulity and exceeding happiness, the look of a man who had just traced his finger across the numbers of the daily lottery in his newspaper, matching them one by one with the ticket clutched in his trembling hand.

"Yes, yes, of course. We can do that. What specifically are you interested in?"

"Everything," Simon Mats said. "Everything."

"Yes, everything," the rabbi replied. "We'll have speakers, a whole course. We'll start a special course in the fall. And maybe a *havurah*? There are enough of you. Yes, of course. Of course!"

If the wedding—a public acclamation of their Jewishness—marked a turning point in Rabbi Rosenbaum's ministry to the Russians, this was something else. This was a *cri de coeur* that resonated deeply within the rabbi's own heart.

In the days immediately before the Beth Israel congregational mission was due to leave Worcester, a chain of violent incidents erupted in Israel. A fifteen-year-old girl was brutally killed on the streets of Jerusalem by a knife-wielding Palestinian. A rabbi was hacked to death near the West Bank, with the result that the West Bank and Gaza Strip were sealed off for days. Subsequent Palestinian protests were put down by riot police; dozens more were injured in the fighting. After swimming from Aqaba in Jordan, terrorists came ashore near the seaside resort of Eilat and murdered a sentry, before being killed themselves. Rabbi Rosenbaum anticipated calls—or outright cancella-tions—from those who might be getting cold feet. He asked Charlie Mills whether he had gotten any calls. The rabbi was relieved; the an-swer was no.

The trip was still on.

Commanding views of the Western Wall and Masada, rich pastiches of architectural details, a teeming marketplace, the Orthodox at prayer, and close-ups of faces—displaying the rich diversity of Jews in Israel—looked down from the off-white painted walls of the Rosen-baums' basement recreation room onto a rather ordinary group of mid-dle-class Worcester residents. It was June 17, the carefully planned "*Kumsitz* Kick-off." The adults, chatting among themselves, ranged in age from their mid-thirties into the early seventies; the children, from three-year-old Shoshanah Rosenbaum to several preteens who per-sisted in leaving the sliding glass door open, thereby bidding flies and mosquitoes to join the gathering. Soon, Janine organized the children into the phase-one activity, and the Israel maps were covered with cutout pictures, stickers, and stamps. A resource packet was ready for each family to peruse, offering insights on subjects from the Second Temple and the Israeli elections to jet lag. Also handed out were the tickets, the updated (and hopefully final) itinerary, a Kenes Tours travel bag, and a pocket-sized *siddur*.

The meal, by design, was Israeli through and through, except for two distinctly Eastern European kugels that Janine had made late in the afternoon, when her customary preparty anxiety convinced her that there would not be enough food. There were platters of falafel, tabbouleh, baba ghanouj, hummus, a huge green salad, and pita bread. The children wolfed down their portions and were quickly whisked outside to begin their scavenger hunt.

In a corner, Rabbi Rosenbaum took a seat and balanced a paper plate on his knees. He had not yet gotten around to eating, al-though most of his guests were by now half done. For a moment, he was finally not part of any conversation. He looked out over his pil-grims near their hour of departure. It was not difficult to see with what pride and affection he regarded them. His thoughts at that moment, he later confided, had to do with the complexion—and complexity—of the group.

"I was just thinking what a diverse bunch they were, a group with jagged edges," he would say. "For the most part, these are Jews in formation. Some, like Murray Rosenberg, the Silvermans, the single women—they come from the old school. But the young couples—the Fixlers, the Sosnoffs—they are just beginning to learn what Judaism is. Howie wants more; he could go all the way some day. And Carl Aframe? I've got to draw him into the inner circle; he's ready. Charlie Mills? Doesn't attend *Shabbos* often enough and he drives, but he's really into Judaism. Steve Sosnoff? Just putting his toe in the water; leery. Jagged edges—yes, and that's good.

"Every one of them is going to be changed. Maybe not in an apparent way, but I know it will happen. For the older ones, I just want *nachas*, good feelings. This may be the last time many of them go to Israel. For the younger ones, I want the stakes to be raised, the heat turned up, the comfort level tested. Yes, and my comfort level needs to be tested, too. But I'm not telling them that.

"So often, I think I come across as Dr. No in the congregation. 'You can't do that; you shouldn't eat that; you can't act that way.' I sure didn't feel that way that night. I wanted to say yes."

People talked about being in a rut, the rabbi went on, and sometimes even he wondered if he wasn't repeating his father's life. He loved rabbinic life, but it took so much out of him and away from his family. Was he going to look back twenty years from now and wonder if he'd been fair to them? And, even with all his effort, he did not have a Jewish community to relate to. How could he keep going without some kind of core group that really took it seriously, really observed the holidays, *Shabbos?* What would happen to his kids when they were teenagers, without a peer group that wanted an intensely Jewish life? He probably should be in Newton or Brookline, where there was an observant community, he concluded.

"Look, if I really put my family first, I wouldn't be a rabbi. I hate to admit that, but it's true. And, really, if I had the courage, I'd be living in Israel. That's where I'd be."

At the moment, sitting in reverie, his meal still untouched, Jay Rosenbaum *was* in Israel. He had just arrived from the airport, observed *Shabbos* in Jerusalem, and was speeding north from Jerusalem, through the Jezreel Valley and farther into the Galilee, and just about to swing east toward the Golan Heights.

Before he could go much farther, a question stopped him cold.

"Should we exchange currency at the airport or wait to get to a bank? Maybe at the hotel?"

The rabbi removed his finger from the map of Israel, where he had been tracing the itinerary.

"They allow smoking on the flight! Rabbi, couldn't we get a nonsmoking flight?"

And—yet again—he was closely questioned about the exact meaning of *"Shabbos* at leisure" as listed in their itinerary.

The smile never wavered on the rabbi's face. "You may do as you want, but for many of you, this might be the first time you will be exposed to a traditional *Shabbat.* I would try to milk it; forgo modern conveniences, see the relatives on another day. Give it a chance. Now, on the Golan we will visit . . ."

With the children back in the room after their scavenger hunt around the neighborhood for answers to questions Janine had taken from the *Jewish Kids' Catalogue,* the rabbi tested the depth of their knowledge. "Who serves in the Israeli military?" ("Everyone," they answered proudly.) "What is the main ingredient of falafel?" ("Chickpeas.") He quickly moved on from the secular. "Why is *Shabbos* in Israel different from *Shabbos* in America?" (In Israel everything shuts down; in America, nothing shuts down.) "Are all Jews in Israel religious Jews?" (A moment of silence. "Naw.")

Izzy Lubarsky, one of the minyanaires who had retired from the clothing business, had gotten together four large suitcases of shirts, trousers, and sweaters that he wanted transported—without paying the prohibitive tariff—to Rebbetzin Kapach, a legendary one-woman social service agency in Israel who would then distribute them to the needy. The goods were apportioned out to be tucked inconspicuously into the Worcester travelers' suitcases.

Such trifling illegalities attended to, the rabbi was ready for his final request. "Let's try something," he said, passing out blank pieces of paper and envelopes. Each person was to put down what they hoped would happen on the trip. The children were all outside now; their voices echoed from the outermost limits of the Rosenbaums' quarter-acre lot. For the first time that evening, the room was silent as the adults began to write.

The thoughts they wrote down would be a mixture of wishes for a safe and happy trip, for a deepening of their love for and knowledge of Judaism, for a wonderful family experience. While these sentiments would be kept secret from one another, there were, I would find, still other secrets that could not be committed to paper or uttered aloud.

"This rabbi, he should loosen up; I hope he's not this intense on the trip. That's what I was thinking," Murray Rosenberg bluntly told me. "Israel? I was there fifteen years ago. I have relatives who were pioneers; I want to check on them. Israel? It's where civilization began. What more do you have to say? Let's just get there. What's all this hoopla with what we want to find and all that. And what we have to *feel*. This feeling business has gone too far."

"It's a funny time in my life, but I guess it's the right time to go," said Steve Sosnoff. "We just sold the family business—we make orthopedic appliances—and I have the money. But I'm wondering about my own future. I've got a contract for a few years and then, at the age of forty-one, who knows? I might be unemployed. So, as usual, I'm totally confused. Everybody on this trip seems to know more about Israel than I do. I'm the guy who'll have his nose in the travel book to find out what's going on. Maybe this is my midlife crisis coming on. But Judaism has always been there in my life. It's my identity. I guess I'm looking for something to hold on to. I just hope everybody gets along."

"I have another agenda, no doubt about it," said Charlie Mills. "I want to live in Israel; I want my family to live in Israel. I'm always trying to figure out some way to spend some years there; maybe this trip will make that happen. I fell in love with Israel on my first trip. Now I'm more sober about it and its realities. But the Israelis are so resilient in the face of incredible odds. They are brusque, but they have a unique charm that endears them to those of us in the Diaspora. I just want to be with them; anything, just to be with them."

As dusk settled and the travelers' final task was accomplished, the group meandered down to the cul-de-sac at the end of Longworth Street. There, they gathered around a pile of logs and kindling foraged from the Rosenbaums' garage and the thin sward of forest that weaves between the various developments and house lots. David Strebnik— who in his last incarnation was the lead guitarist for Nu? Yids on the Block—strummed softly on his guitar, playing such well-known Israeli songs as *"Erev Shel Shoshanim,"* a love song about walking out into fragrant Israeli fields, and *"Erev Ba,"* heralding the descent of a lovely evening. When Janine finally arrived, after some cursory picking up of paper plates and cups, she saw that the kids had brought along only a single bag of marshmallows for roasting over what was now a blazing fire. She hurried back to the house for another bag, just to be sure they didn't run out. Both she and Jay are expert readers of group dynamics, and she sensed that their fellow travelers—the evening's business transacted—would soon be leaving.

With two more bags of marshmallows cradled in her arms, she rushed through her front door. In her haste, she missed the front step and turned her ankle. Initially, she continued down the sidewalk at a brisk pace, but by the time she reached the end of the street, she was limping badly. One of the older women inquired, but Janine said it was nothing.

After twenty minutes of song and marshmallows, the group began to leave. In another hour, Janine had cleaned the house and the children were in bed. "Not good," she said to Jay as she sat on the edge of the bed, pulling off her sock. Her ankle was bluish and already badly swollen.

* * *

A few days later, on the last *Shabbos* before the trip, Janine sat at the end of a back row in the sanctuary of Congregation Beth Israel, her leg, wrapped in an elastic bandage, propped on the armrest in front of her. On the *bimah* her husband—readily admitting his lack of gardening expertise—told of the seedlings he had planted a few days before in a tiny plot he had cleared in their small backyard. "Those plants, to me, are symbolic of the hope of growth, real growth, in my life and the lives of you who will, this week, be in Jerusalem." He savored the words. "Not *next year*. This *week*. This week in Jerusalem!"

The remaining days blurred for the Rosenbaums, with Janine limping about the house in an inflatable brace Howie Fixler recommended, packing for all of them. A sudden trip to New York City, although for an occasion of celebration, further complicated the rabbi's life; his sister asked him to officiate at the *Brit Milah* of her newborn son, Jacob, at Young Israel, a modern Orthodox synagogue in Jamaica Estates. In the last hours before the trip he had worked so hard to realize, Rabbi Rosenbaum was doing his best to tend to both personal and congregational needs with his usual good humor and patience.

Indeed, as he reviewed his "Rabbi's Message: Looking Back, Looking Ahead" column in the June issue of the congregation's monthly newsletter, it had been a good year. The list of accomplishments was satisfying—including the miracle of the Russian wedding and the realization of the once-hopeless Israel trip; the joy of Purim and a Judaicly intense Yom HaShoah. His congregants had helped to serve meals to the homeless at the Mustard Seed, a Worcester soup kitchen affiliated with the Catholic Worker movement. The Beth Israel Religious School Mitzvah Marathon had children leading their parents in a *motzi* before meals and detailing what they as American Jews would tell the president of the United States. But, for Rabbi Rosenbaum, it was not enough.

Glancing up from the newsletter on his desk, he made his assessment. "All this is good stuff. But we're not yet striving for something greater. What? What is my dream? Here it is: if Congregation Beth Israel in Worcester, Massachusetts, ever became a truly observant community—just this *one* synagogue—it would change the face of Conservative Judaism in this country. And that's what we have to aim for—what I have to aim for. Nothing less."

At the end of his column, the rabbi had been generous in his praise for his office staff, the various board and committee members, and all the volunteers. He accorded a special thanks to his congregation president, Manouch Darvish, for "his hard work, ever-present support, and fair judgment."

And so, when Dr. Darvish, the dentist, paid a visit to the rabbi on the eve of the trip, Rabbi Rosenbaum greeted him warmly at the office door.

"About ready, eh, Jay?" Dr. Darvish began once they were seated, the door closed. Dr. Darvish is a trim man of medium height, meticulously groomed, with sharp, dark features pointing to his Iranian heritage. Pleasantries completed, Dr. Darvish moved on to the purpose of his visit.

"Jay, I hope you aren't thinking of a full vacation this year. Are you?"

"Vacation?" the rabbi replied somewhat incredulously, his eyes widening.

"Yes, Jay, vacation," Dr. Darvish said calmly in return. "You know, you're going to be away a lot this summer, and what with our financial problems, some of the board were wondering . . . ."

"Yes, Manouch, I *am* planning on my vacation. I don't exactly consider taking twenty-five members of the congregation to Israel a vacation." The rabbi hesitated, but Dr. Darvish said nothing more.

Finally, the rabbi spoke again. "I work six days a week, sixty hours a week. Sometimes more. What do people want from me?"

"Just think about it, Jay."

"I don't need to think about it," the rabbi snapped. "Is there anything *else* before I go?"

14

Israel, to Jews around the world, is both holy object and graven image. It is a loving father and incorrigible brother; a beam of religious integrity and the harsh light of hate and retribution; a precursor of universal Judaic observance and a bellwether of blatant secularity; a holy land of milk, honey, and bloodshed.

The state of Israel was created by a United Nations mandate after World War II as a global gesture of conscience, a partial recompense for the horror of the Holocaust. It was to be a homeland for Jews scattered by the Diaspora, a place to which they could return at will or in need, a guarantee that such mass and selective slaughter would never again be visited upon the Jewish people.

But seen from a strictly Jewish perspective, the roots of the claim to Israel have nothing to do with mass slaughter, emigration, or the edicts of an organization then but a few years old. Fundamentally, the Jews' claim comes not from any worldly source, but from the belief that this land had been promised to them by God. The land of Israel was God's part of a bargain made first with Abraham and his wandering tribe 3,500 years earlier and recorded in the Book of Genesis: if they, this chosen tribe, would worship Him and keep His laws, God, in turn, would provide them with a place uniquely theirs. According to Scripture, Israel was to be both a haven and a showcase through which the Jews could evangelize all the nations. This elemental understanding of the Jews' connectedness to this tiny, barren, inhospitable land was echoed in Israel's Proclamation of Independence in 1948: "The Land of Israel was the birthplace of the Jewish people. . . . Here they wrote and gave the Bible to the world."

But, strangely, the God who inspired that Bible, and made a covenant for the promised land, did not appear in the proclamation.

The founding of Israel was not only a matter of contention between Jews and the Arabs of Palestine; Jews did not even agree among themselves as to what this new state should be. Among Israel's founders, a dominant role was played by secular Jews from Europe, many of them Zionists who saw the Jewish people not as a religious entity but as an ethnic reality. These pioneers would not allow the mention of a supreme being whom they refused to honor; after all, if He did exist, He had terribly abandoned them during the Holocaust. At the same time, religious Jews, who believed their God had delivered them over the centuries and was now with them at the dawn of a new era, would not allow the nation's life to begin without Him. A compromise term—"Rock of Israel"—was agreed upon by secular and religious Jews, an ambiguity each faction could imbue with its own meaning, reflecting the tension between Judaism and Jewishness with which Israel would have to contend.

The creation of Israel was a heady and heroic time. Hours after Israel declared itself independent on May 14, 1948, six Arab nations attacked. Former guerrillas with names like Begin, Dayan, Rabin, and Shamir—who would later put aside their weapons to govern the state of Israel—became officers in a young army and fought to return the Promised Land to the chosen people after nearly fourteen centuries of exile. Miraculously, the new Israelites withstood this onslaught, emerging victorious twenty months later—much to their surprise, and the world's as well.

Centuries-old enmities and competing claims to this land did not, of course, go away. There would be almost continuous armed strife, and occasionally all-out war. In 1956, Israel—with the connivance of the French and British—invaded the Sinai Peninsula, then occupied by Egypt, and forced a truce. When the truce collapsed in 1967, Israel stood alone and decimated its Arab foes in just six days, a time span so remarkably short it would come to name the war. The Golan Heights, Gaza Strip, and the Sinai were taken, as well as the

West Bank of the Jordan River. Jerusalem was finally reunited. In 1973, on the feast of Yom Kippur, a surprise attack by the forces of Egypt, Syria, and Iraq almost overwhelmed the Israelis, but after heavy initial losses, Israel recouped and triumphed. Jews around the world looked with pride upon their own who had fiercely established, then bravely preserved, a homeland.

Over the years since independence, two million Jews from some seventy countries—those dispossessed by Hitler or living under repressive regimes from Russia to Ethiopia, Yemen, and Iraq—poured into Israel. Humiliated, second-class citizens in their countries of birth, they came to a place where Jewishness was treasured, not despised.

For the largest group of Jews who remained, willingly, in the Diaspora—those of America—Israel provided an ideal arrangement. They could be staunchly Jewish in their advocacy and support of Israel, reverential to its holy places, adamant about its territorial integrity, eager to visit, ever willing to send their young for a (temporary) experience on a kibbutz—and at the same time continue assimilating into mainstream American life. They could, and did, give unstintingly to preserve a homeland history had long denied them, while sinking their roots ever deeper into American soil. Without the Jews of America, who were by far the wealthiest Jews in the world, Israel would probably not exist today. In one outstanding year—1948, the year of independence—the United Jewish Appeal raised $178 million for Israel. It was four times what was given to the Red Cross that year by all Americans. Since then, tens of billions of dollars have come from American Jews in outright gifts and through the purchase of Israel Bonds. Israel additionally now receives $3 billion a year in foreign aid from the United States government.

But the relationship between the Jews of Israel and the Jews of America has been fraught with tension—and sometimes animosity. American Jews send their eighteen-year-olds off to college; Israeli Jews send them to the Lebanese border, or to patrol the Golan Heights. Yes, the Jews of America support with their checkbooks, but the Jews of Israel have to live in varying states of military alert. Not infrequently, in ways both strong and subtle, the message of Israelis to their American cousins has been a bitter one: if you want to be a real Jew, come live in this place you claim to love so dearly.

The Jews of America, while being stalwart backers of Israel, are far more selective and tepid about their adherence to the dictates and practices of Judaism. They can be as religious as they wish, when they wish to be, attend only High Holy Day services (the "three-day-a-year Jews"), and still be considered—and consider themselves—totally Jewish. In essence, they can be both full-time and part-time Jews. For the majority of Jews in Israel, who are not religious, this is an impossibility.

Even though Israel remains conflicted about its destiny as a "light unto the nations"—just as his congregants remain conflicted about their lives as religious Jews in America—Rabbi Rosenbaum wanted his small group to experience a place where the debate between secular and religious Jewishness was confronted head on, in the open, every day. Simultaneously exposed to a totally Jewish way of life while daily being refreshed at the headwaters of their faith, they would see—he *knew*—that they must change their lives. They would be transformed, convinced of the utter necessity of religious Judaism, and determined to revivify the Worcester congregation by leading the life of observant Jews. It was a grand plan.

And if this bold bid, rendered in the seventh year of his rabbinate at Congregation Beth Israel, were not answered? If his congregants were not open to such a transformation, were not about to join him and his family in the creation of an observant community? The rabbi himself would have to sort out for himself if the pareve Judaism of Beth Israel was substantial enough food to carry him through the years ahead.

When a bright yellow school bus lurched to a stop in front of Congregation Beth Israel at eight o'clock on a Wednesday morning in late June, it was met with incredulity—then anger. Since the bus had no storage space beneath, the luggage of the twenty-three adults and twelve children had to be piled onto or stuffed between the seats of the last four rows. The children eagerly scrambled aboard, laughing and quickly forming their own coalition at the rear of the bus. They were followed by the grown-ups, few of whom were as jolly. Janine Rosenbaum, still wearing her inflatable ankle brace, was the last aboard. She grimaced as she raised the sore leg, resting her heel on a steel crossbar. With luggage taking up a quarter of the space, there were just enough seats. Seemingly unaffected by the grumbling going on about him at this rather modest means of conveyance, Rabbi Rosenbaum, dressed in white T-shirt and jeans, asked the driver to hesitate for a few minutes so that he might lead the group in a prayer of departure. "May it be Your will, Lord our God and God of our ancestors, to guide us in peace . . . to lead us to our desired destination. . . . Save us from every enemy and disaster on the way. . . . Praised are You, Lord, who hears our prayer."

The driver started the engine and the Congregation Beth Israel trip was at last under way. Out of the seclusion of Jamesbury Drive the bus traveled onto Salisbury Street, past the great Protestant and Catholic churches of central Worcester, and finally onto Route 290, the road that would speed the travelers to the Massachusetts Turnpike—ironically, the road that in midcentury speeded the demise of the neighborhood and synagogues beloved by the first Jews of Worcester.

It was a gorgeous, sunny June day, and the smell of freshly mown grass along the Mass Pike wafted into the bus. Conversations hurdled two or three seats, bounced across the aisle, and incorporated anywhere from two to six people—and sometimes only a single person, suddenly cut off by the shifting tides of interest and greater volume. I was seated next to Charlie Mills during the hour-and-a-quarter ride to Logan International Airport in Boston, and I found him uncharacteristically pensive.

"Not a good start," he confided, speaking in a low tone. "Did you see what happened back there? I couldn't believe it! I sure hope we did the right thing—and that we're still talking to each other in two weeks. The Israelis already look at American Jews as fat cats, complainers, unsatisfiable children—day-trippers who love to boast about

Israel and all the UJA money they've contributed, who think the Israelis should get down on their knees and thank them. But the Israeli thinks, Where are these Americans when the shelling starts? When the first SCUD comes in? At home hiding behind their checkbook, that's where they are. Perfect example of what I'm talking about just happened minutes ago. 'What's the difference?' the Israeli would say. 'The bus'll get you where you want to go.' Did you hear all that bitching back there? I just hope we don't come across as the unpleasable, ugly Americans. Let's hope this thing holds together. Where's a prayer for that?" he said, flashing his infectious grin as he feigned a motion to grab his *siddur* from his Kenes Tours carry-on bag.

After a one o'clock feeder flight to Montreal, we boarded an El Al Boeing 747 bound for Ben-Gurion Airport. Immediately we were given a taste of the Jewish experience the rabbi promised. On board were a good number of Hasidim, wearing broad-brimmed black felt hats, their curled *peyos* twirled about their ears. Their silent wives were wearing head kerchiefs or the hallmark knitted caps. A noisy group of older teenagers, sponsored by the Young Zionist League of Canada, paraded through the aisles wearing T-shirts on which Rabbi Yehuda Halevi's famous words were emblazoned in Hebrew: "My heart is in the East, while I am in the West." Israeli couples were speaking to each other in Hebrew, perhaps reflecting on their visit to relatives in the States. But the average passenger was, if anything, almost nondescript: the American Jew, twenty-odd of whom, on this particular flight, were from Worcester, Massachusetts.

Before takeoff, it was difficult for the flight attendants to convince everyone to take their seats. As the message was repeated once more over the public-address system, the rabbi was summoned to the back of the plane where one of the members of his group, Gabriella Frymer, was refusing to give up the seat she had commandeered from one of the Young Zionists. She had inadvertently been assigned a seat in the smoking section, where she had no intention of sitting.

"You in charge of this group?" inquired one observer, his voice conveying a kind of lighthearted empathy.

"No, no," the rabbi said, thinking the reference was to the

Young Zionists, who were talking animatedly and blocking the aisle. The rabbi motioned toward Gaby—an immovable mass with arms folded in front of her, completely oblivious to a pleading flight attendant—and others of the Worcester group. "These are mine."

The man surveyed Gaby's defiant face and then turned with a compassionate look to the rabbi. "Oh, my goodness; you *are* in for trouble," he said.

Finally, with the Worcester delegation in their assigned seats and Gaby firmly ensconced in the nonsmoking section, El Al flight 203 took off, banked to the right, and headed east.

The delegation from Worcester broke down roughly into two groups— which at first had basically been the dividing line between those traveling with the rabbi and those Charlie Mills had signed up. The first group was composed largely of older congregants; the second group was for the most part in their thirties or early forties, traveling with their children. The travelers' expectations for the trip also fell into the same rough categories.

The first group included two elderly couples from Beth Israel— Murray and Freda Rosenberg and Benjamin and Lillian Silverman— and four older adults—Marion Blumberg, Gabriella Frymer, Rose Goldstein, and Dr. Maxwell Gould, who is a member of Temple Emanuel, a Reform synagogue. Except for Marion and Rose, who are friends, none knew the others especially well. Jody Fixler's parents, Eli and Marian Freeman, from Utica, New York, had also joined the trip, along with Mrs. Frymer's daughter-in-law, Anne, and her eleven-year-old granddaughter, Rebecca, from Lexington, near Boston.

Virtually all of the elderly Beth Israel travelers have relatives who perished in the Holocaust, and they have watched for over forty years as Israel struggled to become a nation. For them, being able to make the trip is itself a badge of honor, a recognition that Jews finally have a safe haven from the world's hates, a haven they have proved strong enough to defend. Most of them were born into working-class, immigrant, and therefore Orthodox families, and eventually embraced Conservative Judaism as a way of preserving what they felt was best in the tradition, while acknowledging both the peculiarities and the openness of American life. But they are thoroughly Jewish and married Jewish partners. Many of them have been active in Jewish organizations: Lillian Silverman was once president of the Beth Israel Sisterhood; others, like Murray Rosenberg, who attends morning *minyan* faithfully, are among the most loyal attenders at *shul*.

For them, the trip is one of reaffirmation.

They are content and sure within Judaism. Yet, they are concerned that their children—whom they see instinctively in the younger couples on the trip—are not as attentive to their faith, nor as bonded to the timeless values of the Jewish people. Some have even married outside Judaism and do not practice at all.

In the second group there are five couples, in addition to the rabbi and his wife: Debbie and Carl Aframe; Jody and Howie Fixler; Rhonda and Charlie Mills; Sandy and Mark Cutler; and Denise and Steve Sosnoff. Sandy Cutler teaches in the Worcester public schools, Rhonda at Schechter; the other women do not hold jobs outside their homes.

For the younger couples, the trip to Israel is one of continuing—though halting—discovery.

Virtually all of them have turned away from Judaism at one time in their lives (Charlie Mills and Debbie Aframe are converts) and, at their own pace, are finding exactly what place this religion will have in their lives. Simply choosing to come on this trip shows they care about Judaism—for while it has significant appeal, Israel is not exactly a vacation spot of choice. Whatever their present level of commitment, the young couples are all enormously concerned that their children not simply slip under the encroaching waves of secular American culture without the buoyancy of a stout religious bark to keep their faith from drowning entirely.

The level of religious commitment of these younger couples varies widely. Both Charlie Mills and Carl Aframe have been members of a *havurah* for years; Howie Fixler joined one more recently. Carl is a regular at *Shabbat* services, sometimes with his wife; Charlie and Rhonda come less frequently. The Fixlers—fueled primarily by

Howie's interest—have experienced a recent upsurge in religious observance and have been attending services more regularly, but do not
keep a kosher home, which the Millses and Aframes do. Mark Cutler,
a member of Temple Emanuel, is the current president of the Worcester Jewish Federation; although he has made many United Jewish Appeal–sponsored trips to Israel, he does not keep a kosher home and
attends weekly services infrequently. Steve and Denise Sosnoff were
raised in perhaps the least observant Jewish homes, yet they send their
children to Hebrew school at Beth Israel, as do the Fixlers. The Mills,
Aframe, and Cutler children attend the Solomon Schechter Day
School at the synagogue.

       None of the couples are especially close to any of the others
socially. Charlie and Mark Cutler—a busy psychiatrist who works as
many or more hours than the two internists—share a passion for running and will sometimes compete in races together. While Charlie and
Howie are both internists, each has a small sphere of friends that does
not include the other. The Aframes are perhaps the most social couple
but are not close friends with the others. The Sosnoffs live in Paxton, a
bedroom community not far from Worcester, and have made a life for
themselves there.

       The Aframes have two children on the trip, Ruth, twelve, and
Julia, nine. The Cutlers' two sons are at camp; only their youngest,
Michelle, nine, is along. The Fixlers' Daniel, ten, and Leah, eight; the
Millses' Aliza, nine, and Talia, five; the Sosnoffs' Jodi, twelve, and
Richard, eight; and, of course, David and Shoshanah Rosenbaum, now
seven and four respectively, round out the group.

       For the children, this is a trip of adventure and perhaps some
education—at least to the extent that their parents will allow the first
and not force-feed the second.

       The varying levels of observance and commitment among the
travelers is just another way in which these pilgrims are a microcosm of
the American Jewish experience. And none of them—contrary to
what the rabbi might hope for—has admitted to be going to Israel
open to the idea of conversion, or any radical life-style change. They
are going to have a good time and to drink in Jewish history; they are,

if anything, going to enhance and fine-tune the comfort level of their faith.

As we flew east, a light supper was served; nightfall descended at an accelerated pace. It was difficult to imagine how anyone could still be punctually observant, given the speed with which the time zones slipped by, but as the light outside the cabin windows faded, a group of Hasidic men negotiated their way past the beer-drinking young Canadians and the other passengers clustered in the aisles. They gathered in a wide spot in the aisle near one of the doors. Without saying anything to one another, some members of the Beth Israel group joined them: Murray Rosenberg, Howie Fixler, Carl Aframe, Mark Cutler, and Rabbi Rosenbaum. Facing what appeared to be north (not east, toward Jerusalem, as is typical of the observance), the men were soon intoning night prayer, their heads bobbing toward a brightly lit EXIT sign, unconcerned with whatever else might be going on about them.

For those who fly El Al to and from Israel, this is a quite normal occurrence; to the first-timer, it was a most extraordinary addition to the usual in-flight routine. And it was, again, a microcosm of the larger Jewish experience. Murray, wearing a baseball cap, shared his *siddur* with an acne-riddled yeshiva boy in a broad-brimmed felt hat. The rabbi stood shoulder to shoulder with a Hasid of approximately the same age whose beard nearly reached his belt. Dozens of generations and countless migrations have divided them, but here, at 39,000 feet, on a journey of thousands of miles that would take but a few hours, they were united—Jews going to their spiritual home together.

An hour later the cabin lights were turned off, and as best they could, the passengers on El Al flight 203 tried to get some rest.

15

For the principal airport in a country that has enemies crowded around—sometimes two deep—Ben-Gurion had a sleepy, pastoral look about it in the morning mist that Thursday in June. From the air, as El Al flight 203 made a long, lazy loop before beginning its final approach, neither an overt military presence nor any substantial fortifications were in evidence. A few military transports, with camouflage paint, were parked off to the side, much the same as National Guard aircraft might be parked at any American airport. Between the runways of Ben-Gurion, where many American airports have assiduously cultivated grass, there were neat rows of knee-high cotton plants.

A substantial breakfast had been served to the passengers, most of whom were groggy from whatever sleep they had been able to snatch in the preceding ten hours. As we neared the ground, necks craned to get a view. Finally, the wheels touched down on the runway. There was thunderous applause, a tradition still observed upon first making contact with the Holy Land.

Disembarking into the brilliant morning sunlight, the Beth Israel congregants were directed to a bus, a shuttle to the terminal. For the first time, the young parents in the Worcester group were noticeably preoccupied with keeping their children close about them. Jody Fixler had an alarmed and wary look on her face. One hand was clamped firmly on Daniel, the other on Leah (Howie had wandered off). As the older couples stepped off the plane and walked across the tarmac, I could sense there was still another quality about them; it was certainly not fear. At first, it might have been ascribed to age or the withering heat, or to the natural confusion of an airport arrival in a foreign land. But the true cause was far deeper. Lillian Silverman smiled serenely as she later expressed it.

"My heart was just pounding," she said. "Just to think, I was setting foot in the land of my ancestors. Jacob, Moses, Abraham, and me. All of us walking on the same ground. I just couldn't believe it. How lucky I was. Lucky to be alive and have my health; lucky to be a Jew. Lucky to see the day when any Jew, any time, had a place they could call their own. Thank God, thank God for it all!"

Ben Silverman, at seventy-three a year younger than his wife of forty-eight years, echoed Lillian's thoughts.

"I could see it on Lil's face. How well do I know her? How can you explain this feeling you get? It's overpowering. Thousands of years ago, my people walked on this soil. And now me, Ben Silverman, of Worcester, Massachusetts. Lil had to convince me to come when we were here twenty years ago. Now, this time, she didn't have to do any convincing. This is my home. My soul's home. Look, I love the United States, and if it's a choice between the U.S. and Israel, it's the U.S. for me. But this is different. I live in the U.S. I *belong* here."

Howie Fixler's somewhat distracted demeanor—an additional cause for his wife's alarm (would she have to look after *him* as well as her children?)—was an outward manifestation of inner sentiments. "I just felt suspended in time; there was no before, no after," he told me later. "Here it was, *Israel, the* place, and yet when I looked around at the scenery at this airport, which looked no different from so many airports, there was nothing to support the deep emotions that were going through me. It kind of paralyzed me."

Awaiting the Worcester group within the terminal was a Kenes Tours representative, who then led them outside to a bus with a RABBI ROSENBAUM sign prominently displayed in its front window. Our guide, David Leshnick, introduced himself; he was suntanned and given to a wide, but somewhat fixed, grin. Despite his thinning hair, he presented a quite youthful air. On our way out of the airport, we passed a lone soldier, his elbow resting on the barrel of an Uzi slung casually over his shoulder, standing in the shade of a guard post. With

Tel Aviv and the Mediterranean behind us, we headed east on Route 1. Toward Jerusalem.

What was immediately striking about the terrain of this bitterly contested land was its stark, relentless barrenness. Dun-colored rocky soil studded with huge boulders stretched to an irregular horizon. The color changed with surgical precision where irrigation had wrested life from this parched soil; startling fields of wheat, patches of corn and sunflowers, orchards, orange groves, and vineyards rose up, almost miragelike, out of the morning haze. Still more varieties of vegetables and other crops could be seen in the valleys and on the flatlands, where enclaves of low-slung red-tiled homes and small stands of trees marked the older villages. Clusters of seemingly alien townhouses, preferred in the newer settlements, have been appended to hillsides, giving a strangely lush suburban flavor to what was once—and still is—desert.

A short distance from the airport the bus pulled off the highway for a stop at the tank museum at Latrun. The children, finally liberated after some eighteen hours in airplanes and terminals, scampered about the captured Russian-built tanks of Syria and Jordan. There was also a line of battle-scarred (but freshly painted) machines of the triumphant Israelis, many of which had been pieced together from captured enemy tanks. David advised the group that his stories would often have two layers—one of ancient biblical history, the other of the modern-day building of the state of Israel—but sometimes more. "Whatever rock you see here, turn it over and you have a story," he said authoritatively.

Latrun was a perfect way to begin the trip, he told the group, as the Ayalon Valley where we were standing has, since antiquity, been the gateway to Jerusalem. Here was both the scene of the first major battle for the ancient Promised Land—with Joshua and, later, Judah and the Maccabees marching along the road we had just turned off—and the corridor through which Israeli soldiers bitterly fought the Jordanians on their way to reclaim Jerusalem in 1967. This particular corridor of history also had an interesting middle layer: for a few of the intervening years, Latrun had been a British taggert fort, with Yitzhak

Shamir as one of its many guests. "And when the British pulled out, they turned over all their taggert forts to the Arabs," he said, somewhat flatly, hands on hips as he stood before a memorial wall upon which were inscribed the names of the tank corps' dead. "So if you had any doubt whose side the English were on in forty-eight, you can put that doubt behind you."

After a disquisition by David on the bravery of the intrepid Israeli tank corps and the wretched incompetence of the Arabs—setting a tone that soon became familiar—we traveled on. Except for an occasional abandoned bunker, a battered tank, or a piece of field artillery, left in place as a reminder to friend and foe alike, the roadside attractions were limited.

The temperature quickly climbed into the low nineties. About an hour later—it was not yet noon—we arrived in a parking area, disembarked from our air-conditioned bus with its tinted glass, and stepped into the glaring sunlight and stifling heat. Although we could not see the reason for stopping here, a short walk to the promontory revealed the answer.

Jews down through the ages most often traveled to Jerusalem at Passover, *Shavuot*, and *Sukkot*—holidays around which the history of the Jewish people revolves. Passover marks the birth of Judaism, *Shavuot* the giving of the Torah, and *Sukkot* the forty years of wandering in the wilderness. And here where we now stood, at the Tayelet, pilgrims would pause on their long journey—usually made by foot—to relive those signal events in their long history and look down upon Jerusalem, giving thanks to God for being able to gaze upon the Holy City. And they would pray that the temple their ancestors built, and which their enemies destroyed, would someday be rebuilt.

The pilgrims from Worcester had been whisked across the Atlantic in a jet and then conveyed to this point by a sleek, fast bus. But, after walking the few yards to the guardrail, they fell into a silence as old as Judaism itself. Before them was a sprawling, breathtaking panorama. In the near foreground, as the land dropped away, Bedouin herdsmen watched over a flock of sheep on a hillside that appeared bereft of vegetation. As the vista opened up, there were clusters of homes and apartment buildings, which started in the flatter crevices of the valleys and grew up the hillsides, almost as if propelled by moisture they had absorbed. Solar panels glistened in the sun. Crude roadways had been cut into the higher reaches of the hills and appeared as poorly healed scars of a lighter-colored soil. In the distance the land rose again; once the eye fixed on the golden Dome of the Rock, it was possible to make out through the light haze the outline of the Old City, as well as the Jerusalem that has sprawled far beyond its ancient walls. As a backdrop, there were the three famed mounts—Mount Moriah, Mount Scopus, and the Mount of Olives. Strict zoning requires all buildings to be constructed of the indigenous limestone dolomite— tan in color, but golden when struck by the rising or setting sun—and to be no taller than four stories, the height of the tallest buildings in the Old City. As a result, there was a distinct uniformity to the city. The only conquests over these rigid rules have been won by a few apartment buildings and the major hotels, in the distance off to the left, which dominate an otherwise modest skyline. The largest of these hotels was our destination: the Sheraton Plaza, a massive rectangular structure.

The group from Worcester stood quietly in the blistering mid-morning heat, and David, who made *aliyah* ten years ago from New York, appeared before us, hands again on his hips. We could not see his eyes behind his dark aviator sunglasses.

"There are six million Jews in America, many of whom don't even know what being Jewish is about. Half of them are intermarrying. There are five and a half million Jews in Israel. Intermarriage isn't even considered. We *know* we are Jews; by making *aliyah*, we have made a statement of our Jewishness. We have come home. *Aliyah* is our lifeblood; without Jews who care enough about Israel to live here, we cannot go on. If any of you are serious about being Jews, this is the place you should be. That may sound categorical, but it's the truth." He hesitated so that his stiff dose of medicine might at least be swallowed, if not yet absorbed. "So when your kids marry non-Jews, remember David Leshnick said, Get to Israel. The Jews of Israel are soon going to overtake you in numbers; soon there will be more Jews here than in any place on earth, including the United States.

"We have many problems. The absorption of the *olim* who come from Russia and Ethiopia is one. We have problems with your wonderful government, which held back on the loan guarantees we needed to build housing for the *olim*. We have problems with your military, which didn't knock out Saddam Hussein the way we could have in the Gulf War. We have problems with so-called peace agreements because the Arabs have never kept their word. *Never*. Hopefully, in the days ahead you'll see firsthand what Israel is about—for those of you here for the first time, for those who have been here many times, it is a country changing constantly, a country that we are very proud of. The rabbi has asked to lead you in prayer."

From the looks on their faces—most of which were directed at their shoes, instead of at the panorama before them—it appeared the Worcester group was a bit taken aback by such chastening. But they said nothing in return.

As Rabbi Rosenbaum would tell me later, he found David's introduction to Israel—regardless of its inappropriate and somewhat stridently irreligious tone—to be overstated and out-of-date. Such a "righteous Israel" posture no longer carried much credence in America, he felt. "He didn't have to sell us on Israel; we're sold," he told me. "And everybody knows the days of 'Israel right or wrong' are over; we can be critical of Israel and still love her." The rabbi knew he would not be in agreement with David's politics, but he had been impressed with the guide's sure grasp of ancient history; the nearly continuous monologue on the bus from the airport proved his knowledge beyond doubt. Although it was certainly not the kind of tone he had hoped for, the rabbi decided to keep his counsel. He inhaled deeply and opened his *siddur*.

The sun was by now almost directly overhead, not the time of day for Jerusalem to take on its golden hue. But as the rabbi looked up from the *siddur* and over the pilgrims he had brought so far to stand in this place, his face radiated an internal incandescence.

"Praised are You, Lord our God, King of the universe, for granting us life, for sustaining us and for helping us to reach this day. . . ." The rabbi intoned the traditional *Shehecheyanu*, a prayer said when something is done the first time or for the first time in a long time. His formal prayers finished, but his prayer book still open in his hands, Rabbi Rosenbaum continued with his own thoughts. "I cannot believe we're standing here. But we are. We talked about this trip. For months we talked. And, for a long while it looked like it wasn't going to happen. But it has. What strikes me as I look down on Jerusalem for the first time in over twenty years," he said, turning to his right and the sweeping view before them, "is that Israel is not a museum, something preserved. Look at all the new housing, new buildings; this is a living place. Just the way it should be. Not a place to visit and admire, but a place to live in. Years ago, when the people were building the first temple, then the second, God was with them. Today, we no longer have animal sacrifice, so a great temple is not what our people are building. They are building a nation—and God is with us again. And we all realize this is not just a physical rebuilding. It is also the spiritual rebuilding of Jewish life. For them. For us." He closed his *siddur*. "Let's go see it."

That transcendent look with which Jay Rosenbaum beheld both the beloved city and his modest band of travelers remained on his face even as we were swallowed up in the heavy traffic, greeted by a chorus of bellowing car horns. The bus slowly made its way toward our hotel.

The Sheraton Plaza was even more imposing close up than it had appeared from the Tayelet, but there seemed to be something constricted and closed about the exterior design. Later, one of the hotel staff explained to me that narrow windows and stingy balconies make the building more resistant to artillery, mortar, and rifle fire. Inside, the lobby was spacious and extravagantly gilded; among the hotel's many amenities, every floor had its own bomb shelter. After checking in, the Rosenbaums—like most of the group—took an afternoon nap. The itinerary called for "balance of the day at leisure," a necessary concession, even here in the Promised Land, to allow visitors to convalesce from the trip and prepare for the days ahead.

In the late afternoon, with Shoshanah in a stroller and Janine limping a few steps behind, the Rosenbaum family slowly navigated the ten blocks to Ben Yehuda Street. Ben Yehuda is the spine of a pedestrian mall, teeming with stores and restaurants—*the* place in Jerusalem to shop, eat, or simply stroll. In our few hours in Israel, I had listened as members of the group remarked to one another—and to me, the only non-Jew in their midst—about the special feeling a Jew feels being here, but it was on this outing to Ben Yehuda that it finally hit me.

Here, side by side on the crowded street, were soldiers with assault rifles slung over their shoulders and *kippot* on their heads, sauntering as young warriors do; the ultra-Orthodox, wearing gray-and-white-striped long coats, rushing through the throngs, adhering to the Talmudic admonition never to waste time. There were American teenagers with Jim Morrison T-shirts and young female Israeli soldiers with gorgeously hennaed hair, perfect makeup, and ill-fitting khaki shirts and trousers. A West Bank settler shoved his way through a crowd of laughing young French kids; both the tip of his holster and the fringe of his *tsitsit* hung below the bottom of his jacket. His wife, wearing a fashionable patterned silk blouse, followed in his considerable wake. There were Russian Jews, Ethiopian Jews, Jews from Toronto and Mamaroneck and Des Moines. Here, unlike anywhere else on earth, you are assumed to be a Jew—and you can be any kind of Jew you want to be. There is no outside world to acknowledge, render homage to, or fear. A young, proud country; a venerable, tested religion; a rich history. Suddenly, overwhelmingly, I felt the intoxication of the place.

The Rosenbaums and I had a wonderful kosher vegetarian meal—fresh-made pasta, pizza with an extraordinarily thin crust, and a superb lasagna—at a restaurant with the internationally accepted name of Mamma Mia's. Although still suffering from jet lag, the rabbi was absolutely buoyant. "I was worried about how the young families and the older couples would do, but I think everybody is getting along very, very well," he told Janine and me, although from Janine's look it seemed she had already heard this at least a few times from him. "Everybody needs a good night's sleep; we've got a great itinerary in front of us. Charlie, David, and I decided to cancel our visit to Mea Shearim to watch them bake challah for *Shabbos*." (The schedule had called for a 9:45 P.M. trip to the Hasidic neighborhood to see the making of the braided bread.) "But things are going great. Just great!"

The bliss of the rabbi's first evening in Jerusalem ended abruptly when we arrived back at the lobby of the Sheraton Plaza. Seated on a group of soft leatherette chairs were Murray and Freda Rosenberg, Gaby Frymer, the Silvermans, and Marion Blumberg. They were outraged, Murray fumed, that the challah trip had been canceled. His wife was also angry that the tour guide hadn't suggested some nearby restaurants for dinner. "I have paid a lot of money for this trip," Gaby scolded in her thick German accent. The rabbi said nothing in reply. Murray persisted: "You promised the kids weren't going to get in the way and here we are, the first night and it's canceled. And that stop at the tank museum; that wasn't on the itinerary; we should have been taken right to the hotel. That was just for the kids. Tanks!"

The Rosenbaums appeared stunned by the continuing verbal onslaught. Janine turned her back to the group, and the look on her face—which only I could see—changed from an eye-rolling incredulity to a hard glare of anger. But when she finally turned to confront her husband's congregants, she was wearing a tired smile. She hobbled over to the group and plopped down in their midst, in essence rendering a peace offering by her presence. David and Shoshanah, ready for bed but obviously used to such detours of placation, stood by silently. The rabbi explained that the hotel rooms could not be occupied before noon, there were many restaurants within walking distance—also, the hotel served food—and that the challah-baking trip would have required the group to walk back to the hotel, returning after eleven o'clock. With the full schedule planned for the next day, it seemed wise to bypass it.

Amazingly, his explanation to the grumblers was entirely without rancor or even impatience. It was not unlike the tone of voice he employed when a tired, fussy Shoshanah insisted on staying up past her bedtime and he had to list the reasons why she could not.

The travelers were not about to be pacified. Gaby rose out of her seat and, sternly exhaling her continuing displeasure, headed for the elevator. The rest of her cohorts followed, single file.

In rooms scattered about the hotel, the others of the Worcester group prepared for a night's rest. The rooms were well appointed and clean, but, for a family with children, crowded. Rollaway beds staged their own occupation of the limited floor space, an occupation the guests know would have to endure in the days ahead.

16

"The path we'll be taking this morning is generally the path Is-raeli Defense Forces took as they fought their way, in hand-to-hand combat, to reclaim the Western Wall in 1967. Before you is the Zion Gate; you will see many bullet and mortar holes in the stones, from over the decades. Our friends the British had closed this area off to the Israelis, as it was held by our even dearer friends, the Jordanians. And so it was the scene of many battles as the Haganah—the Israeli underground—smuggled young Jewish soldiers and weapons into the Jewish Quarter of the Old City.

"On your left, the Dormition Abbey, the spot where Mary is supposed to have entered into eternal sleep," David added, with a pass-ing nod to another, much younger, religious narrative. "We're going to see a lot of stuff this morning, go back deep into Jewish history and yet see what's happening in Jerusalem today. Let's stay together. And hey, remember gang, *savlanut*." He proffered his boyish grin.

The group from Worcester wound its way through the baffle of the Zion Gate, barely wide enough for a car, a safety measure con-structed centuries before so that chariots and bulwarks could not easily be foisted upon the inhabitants of the Old City. Coming out of the shade and quiet of the massive gate, they were immediately thrust into teeming Habab Street, which divides the Armenian and Jewish quar-ters. A few feet in front of them a donkey cart rattled by, led by an Arab wearing a burnoose and smoking a filtered cigarette; a Toyota delivery van screeched to a stop to let man and beast pass, but only by inches. Washed clothes fluttered from rococo balconies. History and polyester shirts were on ready display.

"Hot!"

"Where's the water?"

"These stones; I'm going to break an ankle."

The Worcester group gingerly trod the cobblestone street, shooting cautious looks to right and left, not unlike, I imagined, the Israeli soldiers who warily stalked this route not too many years before.

"Where is he; I can't see the guide."

"What's this over here; isn't he going to tell us about anything?"

"How much farther?"

David Leshnick, at no time more than ten yards away from any member of the group—although those ten yards might have contained a dozen inhabitants of the quarter, beasts of burden, hand-pulled carts, heaps of garbage, and a car or truck—was grinning even more widely behind his aviator sunglasses. The rabbi, walking alongside him, wore a somewhat more forced smile.

"Been doing this for six years now, hundreds of groups," David told the rabbi in a stage whisper obviously intended for those with ears to hear. "Maybe the kvetching starts on day three or four. Never heard stuff like this on the first day before. A record!" he chuckled. "Where did you get *this* bunch from?"

Another forced smile.

When the rabbi and David had assembled the group in the Sheraton lobby less than an hour before, they had been greeted by a chorus of complaints. The canceled trip to the challah bakery, the food, the size of the hotel rooms were but the opening volleys. Freda Rosenberg's face was frozen in displeasure; Gaby Frymer's arms were crossed in front of her in stern protest. Carl Aframe held one hand to his back and described a fitful night in a crowded room, where anyone en route to the bathroom had to crawl over the bodies of the other family members. He was trying to be funny. No one laughed.

Trying to infuse a better spirit into this, their first full day in Israel, the rabbi in response had offered *"Savlanut"*—"Be patient"—

the popular Hebrew word that has become a mantra in a country that has faced war and privation, as well as regular shortages of food, water, electricity, and gasoline.

"Yeah, patient," members of his group retorted with unabated irritation.

An hour later, patience seemingly not foremost on anyone's mind, we continued to make our way through the narrow streets of the Old City, where merchants were just hanging out their array of souvenirs and reputed antiquities. Undaunted, David went on with his commentary, exposing the group to generous servings of history and breathtaking views, such as the Mount of Olives, where burial sites crowd together so that those interred can be in proximity to the place where the *mashiach* is first supposed to appear. "Look around you at the Old City; we had to rebuild it, almost from scratch. Look for yourself, the new stones match the old. Here, we believe in the past as much as we believe in the present," he said, somewhat arrogantly, as if he were speaking to a group of visiting Rotarians.

Indeed, we could see as we made our way past buildings and through narrow alleyways, the Israeli government and individual initiative have together done an incredible job recreating the Old City, using newly hewn blocks of limestone dolomite to build old-looking new structures.

Our venue this morning was to be the Jewish Quarter, where high priests and Levites lived three thousand years ago, close by the temple that was finally built so that the God who had brought the Israelites into their land flowing with milk and honey could be worshiped properly. Our guide through the quarter was to be Fran Alpert—a tiny, sprightly, fast-talking Chicagoan, who with her husband and children made *aliyah* fifteen years ago and subsequently founded a tour company, Archaeological Seminars.

Even as members of the group dropped heavily into seats in the cool reprieve of her small, cavelike lecture hall a few steps off Shonei Halakhot, she began. "Tired? Right? Hot? Right? Brain overloaded? Right? 'Vacation; this is a vacation?' you're saying to yourself. Listen, when you come to Israel, it's not a vacation, it's an endurance contest.

Do you win, or does the rabbi and your guide win? Okay, I'm going to further overload you. But to understand your heritage, the Bible, you've got to know some of this stuff. Don't feel bad; nobody remembers dates. People, places, events . . . ready? 'If I forget thee, O Jerusalem, let my hand wither.' I'm here to remind you. Let's go!"

As a series of slides flashed across a screen, Mrs. Alpert blasted off on her timeline through six thousand years of history.

"Forget the Chalcolithic Age—4000 B.C.E.—metal tools, ceremonial objects. Cut to a thousand years later. Beginning of conversations with God; God speaks to Abraham; the Age of the Patriarchs is upon us—1900 to 1750 B.C.E. in the Canaanite Era. God tells Abraham to 'go to a land where I will make you a mighty nation.' Sarah, Isaac, Rebecca, Rachel, Leah, and Isaiah. Famine. Jews are taken to Egypt, made slaves; 'Where is our God?' Moses leads the people out of Egypt; law given at Sinai; wandering in desert for forty years. Tribe crosses the Jordan and the name changes from Hebrews to Israelites. Hurray! Joshua conquers Promised Land—we're now at 1200 B.C.E."

Mrs. Alpert appeared not to require the normal intake of oxygen. Her breathless treatise swirled on. "The period of the judges; Saul, David, and Solomon finally gets the temple built—it's 930 B.C.E. Jerusalem is a major city. Solomon dies, country divided; people still had pagan gods; offended God. Twelve tribes not closely knit, ten northern tribes form Kingdom of Israel; two in the south, Kingdom of Judah. Quiet time, but Assyrians are getting stronger; they sweep down, conquer all of Israel. Babylonians are next, destroy Jerusalem and the temple in 586 B.C.E.; Jews exiled 'by the waters of Babylon,' remember? No temple in Babylon, so Jews begin to gather in meeting places to read five books of Torah; synagogues soon to follow. Persia conquers Babylon, Jews come back, rebuild temple with Ezra in 515 B.C.E. Romans come to power—what do they care about these Jews?—so Jews invite Romans to protect them."

Not only did there appear to be no time to take a breath—Fran Alpert's words often ran together, fusing into huge historical hunks. "AssimilationSadduceesPhariseesEssenesDeadSeaScrollsRemember? It's now the time of Christ. Sects, tension, great revolt against the Romans. Enough of these Jews; Second Temple destroyed in 70, now in the Common Era. Three years later, Masada. Dispersion of the Jews, Rome, Turkey, slaves, traders. Romans stay on in Jerusalem. Bar-Kochba revolts against Romans in 132; crushed. Hadrian levels Jerusalem, makes it a pagan city. Romans converted to Christianity, make Jerusalem a Christian city, churches, shrines go up. The years 324 to 640. Talmud completed about this time. Moslems rise up, conquer Jerusalem—640 to 1099. Dome of the Rock built. Crusaders get on their horses to rescue the Holy Sepulcher; no Jewish population at all in Jerusalem.

"Saladin conquers, then the Mamelukes, the Turks and Brits, and in 1948, for the first time in two thousand years, we have a modern Jewish state whose birthday we just celebrated on May fourteenth. Are there any questions?"

Applause instead for her virtuoso performance.

After this whirlwind four-minute verbal excursion, we continued through the Jewish Quarter with Mrs. Alpert. We found that the entire Old City covers but a square mile; 25,000 people live within its walls. The Jewish Quarter, roughly a quarter-mile area, is home to 5,500 people—almost all Jews—who worship at sixteen *minyanim*. Laying aside the difficulties of living so close to the Muslim, Armenian, and Christian quarters—all of which are primarily Muslim, and each of which is home to many Palestinians—there is an uneasy alliance within the Jewish Quarter itself between the Orthodox, who have many *yeshivot* here, and the thousands upon thousands of visitors who wander through its streets to glimpse its history, see some of the archeological digs, and generally witness modern-day *shtetl* life. Jews like David and Fran would be considered *traife*, unclean, by the Orthodox, who see theirs as not just the authentic, but the *only* Jewish life.

We had a chance to glimpse that tension—Jew to Jew—as we waited behind a group of noisy American teenagers on a Young Israel tour in front of the entrance to the Herodian mansions. Two boys in designer T-shirts started wrestling playfully. "Go, go, go, *go!*" their friends urged them. The longer the teenagers waited, the louder they became.

Suddenly, a bottle crashed to the street in their midst, some ten crowded yards in front of us. It was immediately obvious that the bottle had been dropped from a window in the Yeshivat Hakotel, built above the excavation, as a response to the teens' rowdy behavior. It quickly turned into a scene of confusion (some of our group were momentarily lost in the crowd) and alarm (would more bottles be dropped on their group and ours?). A burly Orthodox man, his snub-nosed .38-caliber pistol in view under his jacket open to the hot morning air, jumped into his battered car, which had rock-proof screens over the windows, gunned the engine, and blasted on his horn for the street to clear in front of him. There was no room to move, no place of easy shelter. Momentarily stunned and wide-eyed, members of the Worcester group alternated startled looks upward to the open—and now threatening—window above us and back to street level, to the tiny woman who had brought us to this place.

Saying nothing, Fran Alpert deftly shuffled the group into the small waiting room for the Herodian mansions. As we waited our turn to descend the stairs into the dig, she shrugged at a question about the tension and danger of living in Jerusalem. "Look, my husband and I had everything in Oak Park; a great house, a good business. But what did it all add up to?" she said, not with any tone of sanctimony, but rather with the certain pragmatism of a good decision made. "We were marginal Jews, wanted to do more about it, but just couldn't seem to make it work in the U.S. So, we bagged it all, sold our house, brought over our youngest kids, and here we are. Sure, it's crowded, there are problems, but instead of living in a suburb, I live in a *shtetl*." Her face was beaming at the thought. "Somehow it works; I love it. I go to the end of my street and—believe me, this is *not* Oak Park—I see the Western Wall. What's better than that?" she said warmly. "Okay, let's go visit the Cohens. We're expected."

The historical site, which had just opened to the public earlier in the year, was discovered when an excavation for a sewer line—part of the rebuilding of Jerusalem—unearthed what archaeologists would later decide was the home of the temple's chief high priest. As these were *Kohanim*—descendants of the priestly order who performed temple rites—Fran Alpert personalized the owners as "Mr. and Mrs. Cohen." She explained how Jews throughout history made accommodations to the prevailing culture while maintaining their own unique practices. "For instance, the Cohens had three *mikvaot,* so they could purify themselves before entering the temple," Mrs. Alpert said, pointing out narrow steps leading to a small cisternlike room. "But because Mrs. Cohen, certainly an upper-class lady, wanted at once both to keep her Jewishness *and* to appear as contemporary as all the other girls on the block, she also had ornate tile mosaics on her floors." She extended a hand toward a reconstructed section of the mosaic, large enough to indicate the pattern within. "She was modern, but she was still Jewish, so there are no images of humans in the mosaic, which pagan Romans would have but which the Second Commandment forbids."

In a display case nearby she pointed out the oil lamps used for temple worship and also pagan idols: clay phallic symbols, figures of animals and children. "So folks," Mrs. Alpert continued, "the Jews who lived here gave homage to God and let Him take care of war and peace and all the major issues, but when it came to what sex their child would be or how many chickens would be hatched, they went back to the old, safe pagan ways. You are Americanized in Worcester; in Oak Park, I was Americanized. The pressure was on right here, in this house. Mrs. Cohen—wife of a high priest, forget a mere rabbi!—was being Canaanized right here in Jerusalem."

A contemplative mood seemed to settle upon our group. A red-blooded American soccer game for their children on a *Shabbos* morning instead of hours spent giving homage to God? The tantalizing specialty of the house in one of Worcester's fine Chinese restaurants— moo shu pork or a zesty shrimp dish? The right house in the right neighborhood with the right schools instead of the house that puts them within walking distance of the synagogue? Those gifts—small as they were—at Christmas; a holly wreath? Who in the group was not taking stock of how "Worcesterized" they might be? And whether it mattered.

Our trip through the Jewish Quarter of the Old City wound

through the Cardo, the ancient main street of the Romans, and up onto a rooftop to get a sense of space—or lack of it. A few feet below us were remnants of an ancient roadway built by the Romans (which now looked like little more than a section of paved drainage ditch); at eye level sprouted a forest of TV antennas. Mrs. Alpert bid us good-bye, and David was once again in charge of our destiny. As we began to anticipate, along with his very knowledgeable treatises on distant and recent history, we would also receive (or be subjected to) his personal commentary, praising everything Israeli and denigrating everything not. "Look around you; this city did not look like this in 1967. When Jordan occupied the Jewish Quarter, they lived like pigs, throwing garbage in the streets. When Arabs occupied the Mount of Olives, out of respect for the Jews, they used centuries-old tombstones for their latrine covers. When we got the Old City back, seventy percent of the housing was uninhabitable. So much for our wonderful neighbors. And we're supposed to live with these people. Okay, let's go."

To this, Rabbi Rosenbaum added nothing. I could see that his face was uncharacteristically bled of emotion. If he was feeling something, he was not about to reveal it. As I had come to know the ways of the rabbi, I realized that he is not a man to fail to make his likes and dislikes known, but he is always conscious of the timing, the setting for such honesty. He has learned in his years in the rabbinate that the well-intended but poorly framed remark loses the impact it could have had if rendered at exactly the right moment. Opinions voiced too frequently are in danger of becoming a drone, of being ignored.

The rabbi took his son David's hand and proceeded down still another narrow walkway, through a series of open and closed courtyards and small squares and finally to a long covered stairway. At the top, an Israeli soldier halted us. His Uzi was slung over his back to leave his hands free. He searched our bags and eyed any baggy clothing, of which there was precious little on this sweltering morning. He motioned us, one by one, down the stairs.

If Jerusalem has a Jewish epicenter, we had reached it.

It was here that Abraham lay Isaac on a stone, ready to sacrifice his only son to God; here that the first covenant, or *Brit Milah*, was

sealed. Here it was that the First Temple was built, the culmination of
over five hundred years of wandering and yearning. Here the ark of the
covenant was finally given a proper home and the sacrifice dictated by
God could finally be rendered. And five hundred years after the First
Temple was destroyed, the Second Temple rose on this spot. It too
would be desecrated and reduced to rubble. All that is left is a single
wall. The Western Wall.

Access to the wall—which is actually part of a retaining wall
that surrounded the Second Temple, and not a temple wall itself—had
been basically denied the Jews for centuries, causing grief throughout
the Jewish world. For it was to the Western Wall that Jews came to
mourn the destruction of this holy place—thus giving it another
name, the Wailing Wall—and to pray for the rebuilding of the temple,
of Jerusalem, and, in essence, of their identity as a single people, living
in a single place. So when Israeli soldiers fought their way through the
streets of the Old City in 1967 and were finally able to blow the *shofar*
at the wall, it was the realization of a nineteen-hundred-year-old
dream, the end of Jewish suffering and persecution, the dawning of a
new era. It marked one of the most significant, moving moments in
Jewish history.

At the bottom of the stairs, another man attempted to halt us
once more, waving his arms. He gestured toward the legs of the women
in our group who were wearing shorts. At David's somewhat irate
questioning, he readily admitted that he was not religious himself, but
that he had been hired by the Orthodox who maintain *yeshivot* overlooking the wall and who have designated themselves its guardian.
Quite simply, this was his job; he asked for no payment from the group.
Once the women accepted the wraparounds he pressed upon them—
and covered their shoulders if they were wearing sleeveless blouses—
we continued toward the wall.

The gently sloping cobblestone approach to the wall was teeming with people: clusters of tour groups, fast-walking black hats, casual
tourists bent over their guidebooks, and plenty of soldiers, their arms
resting on assault rifles straddled in front of them. Above us, outlined
against a cloudless blue sky, the golden sphere of the Dome of the

Rock, Islam's second holiest shrine, glistened brilliantly in the noon-day sun.

At this time of day, the wall was in partial shadow. The varying textures of its mammoth three- and four-foot-high stones—some bland and smooth, some craggy and pitted, with deep crevices—seemed to present a pastiche of Judaism. Some are ancient stones, weathered by hundreds of years of wind and rain, the objects of derision and targets of spittle and human waste when others held this ground. Some stones are newly converted to this purpose, easily laid in place by modern mechanical devices and as yet untested by the ravages of time. Their smooth faces pressed boldly outward, gleaming with a texture and hue their older siblings lost centuries ago. Darkened spots blotched the wall from its midpoint on up, appearing as the blackened reminders of mortar or artillery shells. Closer examination revealed them to be patches of vegetation, which had miraculously taken root in the arid, forbidding wall.

It is often said that Jews come not to pray *to* the wall, but *through* the wall. They come to pray to the God they have sought and escaped from, honored and abandoned through their millennia of history. But perhaps the wall also provides a reflection of them as well—a rough-hewn mirror, showing the Jewish people in all their diversity, a study in unity out of discord.

The group from Worcester was quickly absorbed into the crowd. A chain-link fence separates the area where men pray from that allotted to the women, and each went their assigned way. Some approached in pairs, most individually; none at a hurried pace. A few steps taken, a pause. It was as if each level of experience had to be absorbed before going farther. Twelve-year-old Ruth Aframe, a normally chatty girl, broke off from the children's group. She slowly approached the wall, alone, her mother watching from a distance; her father, on the other side of the chain-link fence, paused. Ruth, now within a few yards of the wall, squinted up at its top, lost in the brilliance of the sun. She slowly extended a hand and tenderly touched the stones worn smooth by other pilgrims' contact.

Howie and Daniel Fixler, each with the fine *kippah* he wears each time he enters their Worcester synagogue—*kippot* that will never be regarded the same way after this day—approached the wall, not bound as father and son, not men of different ages and different heights (although, strangely—is it the slant of the ground?—they appear of almost equal stature), but as two male Jews who have come to pray together. They stood quietly before the wall. Their hands reached out to touch it.

Marion Blumberg and Denise Sosnoff, standing at the wall together, are separated by a generation, a tumultuous period in American history and Jewish life. Both came from Orthodox homes, yet there the similarity ended. Marion was a *Shabbat* regular, while Denise's Judaism was a far more tentative part of her suburban life. But now, with her two children growing, it loomed larger. The Sosnoffs' home life had little Jewish content. When Denise asked her daughter, Jodi, if she would marry Jewish, Jodi told her it really didn't matter. Marion's only child, twenty-one-year-old Joseph, is dating a Jewish girl; she would have it no other way.

Marion Blumberg took a piece of paper from her purse and wrote "Ma Pa *Bubbe Zayde.*" She folded it carefully and stuffed it between two of the huge stones. She stepped back. And she prayed.

"The wind will blow that away, I know it," she later told me, "but *I was there*. It's a miracle, really. My parents never had much, raised six kids; we lived in a tenement. They were lucky to get to a movie, forget about Israel. I don't have much either, lived in my share of tenements, too. I'm probably on the low end at Beth Israel economically, but who cares? I can't buy Israel Bonds, but I pay my synagogue dues. I saved three thousand dollars, and I made it. It's a once-in-a-lifetime experience for me. I'll never be able to afford it again. But I just know my parents must be so proud of me that I made it here. It's just like being in movie for me, a wonderful Jewish movie."

Denise Sosnoff bowed her head, shaded by the massive wall. Her slip of paper was already in place, one massive stone over from Marion's.

" 'You always wanted to get here, Dad, but you never did,' " were her thoughts, she later told me. " 'You probably won't, either.' He has cancer of the colon and he's eighty years old. He had an office-supply business and he worked so hard. I was standing there for him. As for me? I love Judaism, but I'm not doing much about it. Maybe I was praying that I would. I don't know."

Ben Silverman, wearing one of the oddly shaped cardboard *kippot* made available to men who brought no head covering, kissed the wall and bowed his head to pray. Lillian was on the women's side. Neither had planned it this way, but each brought one of their two children in their thoughts to hold up to God's presence.

"I was crying," Lillian told me, "just thinking that my oldest son, Harvey—he's a doctor *and* an agnostic—will never come here, that his children would never see this. My grandchildren will not be raised Jewish. Years of Jewish tradition down through the ages ends with me. Believe me, I was crying."

Ben had their other son in mind, he told me, the boy who couldn't speak when they adopted him at five, the boy who was considered mentally retarded through much of his early schooling. "I believe in prayer. The last time I was at the wall, twenty-two years ago, I prayed for the child of one of the women who worked in my pharmacy, had some kind of intestinal problem. It worked! When I got back, the child was cured. Now this time, I was praying for my Richard. He's overweight and he's clumsy and he loses jobs, but I love that boy so much. I just want him to be okay, have a good life. That's all."

Rabbi Rosenbaum and his David inclined their foreheads to touch the wall—as if to rest after a voyage of many miles, many days. Each closed his eyes.

Later reflecting on this poignant experience, the rabbi smiled. "How strange, I was thinking. How strange we should come to worship and pray at a wall built by Herod, one of the greatest builders and lousiest Jews of all time. Jewish history! Contradictions! Then I prayed for David, standing right next to me. He's so sincere. 'I want you to be connected to this, David,' I said. 'We are connected to each other and to God. Never forget that, my son.'"

When the group gathered at the appointed spot a half hour later, the members were uncommonly silent. Conversations trailed off as heads kept turning back to the wall, trying to somehow take it in, to understand its meaning. When David the guide began to speak about our next stop, eyes turned to him, now uncommonly clear, even glassy.

Suddenly, in the distance over David's shoulder, high on the Mount, massive wooden gates were thrown open. A huge throng burst through the opening and streamed down from the Dome of the Rock. Was this a mirage? In an instant, the sweet reverie of the moment was swept aside and another emotion took over—somewhere between apprehension and low-grade panic. No one in the group uttered a sound.

Down they surged, men in burnooses and sport shirts, women in ornately decorated long gowns and modern dresses. Hundreds of Arabs, soon thousands, a seemingly endless, constantly replenishing tide. Was it our imagination, or were they walking ever faster, almost at a run? Was this human river growing wider, overflowing the stone steps of the pathway?

If the Western Wall is sacred to the Jews, so the Dome of the Rock is precious to Muslims, for this is where Muhammad is believed to have ascended to heaven. The thousands spilling down the pathway had spent their morning (it was a Friday, the Muslim equivalent of the Sabbath) fasting and praying at the El Aqsa Mosque in strict observance of their creed. As is so typical in Jerusalem, worshipers of God—a God who, with perhaps a certain mirthful deviousness, continually tests the limits of human cooperation—had made it mandatory that two peoples with ages-old cultural, political, and theological differences should have to worship within a stone's throw of each other. There are times when that unit of measure takes on an all-too-literal dimension.

At David's bidding, we waited in the shade of the guard post near the gate as the Muslims streamed through. The guards, who were wearing bulletproof vests, had left their shelter and stood in a line, fingers poised near the triggers of their automatic rifles. We, in Western dress, cameras dangling at our chests, were regarded with indifferent looks and sometimes heated stares by these other worshipers. Suddenly, Muslims were in profusion; Jews were few, the minority once more. It is not wise to interrupt the flow, David advised us. People have been knifed for doing just that.

It was after one o'clock by the time we returned to the safety of our bus. The rabbi took the microphone and asked for volunteers to shop for various items so that tomorrow the group might have a midday *Shabbos* picnic together. As the trip had developed in his mind over the preceding months, he had envisioned a wonderful outing, an example of the peace, companionship, and community that *Shabbos* offers to those who live by its spirit; a precursor, as Jewish law and practice have maintained, of life in heaven (and perhaps, the rabbi thought, in Worcester).

Gazes that fixed with great interest on anything outside the bus, or within it—except for him—greeted his request. A deadening silence ensued.

"Someone can get the bread, someone the cheese. Fruit; yes, fruit. Wine? Whatever you'd like. An outdoor feast. Yes? Volunteers?"

But instead of signing on as eager partners in his dream, some of the couples with children admitted they had other plans. He persisted. Another request sounded over the bus's speakers. We were by now traveling slowly along Jaffa Road, which was clogged with cars and shoppers, as time was short before *Shabbos* in Jerusalem would begin. Shops would be closing by midafternoon and not opening again until Sunday. The bus lurched to a stop across from one of the entrances to Mahane Yehuda, the huge outdoor market area. As the bus was blocking cars behind us, we had to disembark quickly. None of the group had responded to the rabbi's call for *Shabbos* fraternity. "So, each person can get what they need," he said, somewhat flatly, as he was hustled off the bus.

For a moment, Rabbi Rosenbaum stood motionless on the curbstone; he looked stunned, as if he had been struck. His people, a "microcosm of the Jewish experience in Worcester," were not about to forestall personal preferences for what their rabbi had presented as a communal opportunity. Janine grabbed his arm; the group was already across Jaffa Road.

Mahane Yehuda is usually crowded, but on a Friday the wide
aisles between stands displaying a vast array of fruits and vegetables,
falafel, and other ready-to-eat foods are almost impassable. Within
minutes our legion was hopelessly dispersed, some members lost. As
David tried to reassemble his scattered flock, he heard the laments
of two dissonant choruses: those who were ready to stand and eat of
the cornucopia of foods offered al fresco, and those, equally famished, who must, it seemed, sit down. Additionally, there were those
like the Millses and Cutlers, old hands in Jerusalem, who now
wanted to be released from the group to wander where they might;
those who were angry that there was no time for souvenir shopping;
and a good number who fumed that bringing them into this may-
hem was the rabbi's worst idea yet. After a shrug from David, the
Worcester group broke down roughly by age, the families with children generally going their own way, as the rabbi, his family, the
Fixlers, and the older congregants tried the doors of a few restaurants, only to find them already closed. Finally locating an open restaurant, blocks away from the crush, they sat down for a two o'clock
lunch.

As they waited and finally ordered, the *Shabbos* clock was tick-
ing. Shops continued to close. They bolted the meal and were soon
back on the street so that those who wished might buy food for tomorrow.

As the day's heat yielded to a gentle evening breeze, the long-awaited
Shabbat in Jerusalem was finally at hand. Just after six o'clock, the
rabbi and perhaps a third of his group crossed King George Street to
the Jerusalem Great Synagogue for *Kabbalat Shabbat*, the service that
ushers in the twenty-four-hour observance. As the synagogue is an Orthodox *shul*, the women were consigned to the balcony. The service,
entirely in Hebrew, was enhanced by an impressive choir but overwhelmed by a cantor, more of the performance than congregation-par-
ticipation school and not to Rabbi Rosenbaum's taste. While the
Orthodox worshipers bobbed up jerkily to *daven*, or pray, almost lung-
ing over, bending at the waist in their *shukeling*, Rabbi Rosenbaum's

movements were rhythmic and smooth, exactly how he would pray in Worcester. It was almost dark when we emerged; King George Street, usually a bustling thoroughfare, was strangely quiet, except for an occasional taxi.

Across the street, in the hotel, provisions for *Shabbat* observance were in place: hundreds of candles that had been lit by individuals flickered on a huge table on the lower level outside the dining area; two elevators were programmed to open on either odd or even floors, so the *shomerei Shabbat* could avail themselves of this conveyance without having to press the desired button. Meals had been arranged and paid for in advance so that no money need be handled or checks signed. A small private room was ours for the *Shabbat* meal; wherever they had wandered since the Mahane Yehuda dispersion, all the Worcester delegation had somehow found their way here.

Rabbi Rosenbaum greeted the first *Shabbat* in Jerusalem with a *Kiddush* cup brimming with wine, with prayer, and with songs—songs sung in the rather ordinary function room of a Sheraton hotel, yet in a location unlike any in the world. "Build up Jerusalem, the holy city, in our time. Praised are you, Lord, who in His mercy rebuilds Jerusalem . . . good to us all, whose goodness is constant throughout all time. . . . May the Merciful bless the state of Israel, the dawn of our redemption." The rabbi's voice was uncommonly strong and sure, resounding from an acoustical-tiled ceiling and institutional gold damask curtains designed to absorb, not enhance, the human voice.

I had known Rabbi Rosenbaum for almost a year now and had come to take his pleasant and smiling demeanor for granted. But it was not a normal smile I saw on his face just then; something far more than mere earthly pleasure or rabbinic veneer was at work. Contrary and stiff-necked as they may be, a cross-section of his tribe was with him, from the youngest to the eldest, the most observant to the lax. He had successfully rounded them up in their own Canaans and convinced them to follow him on a pilgrimage. He was now in the place where— and at the hour when—God demanded His due.

The rabbi's prayers completed, he sat in their midst, a mighty Moses who had proclaimed God's wonder, not the ordinary rabbi of the afternoon, pleading over a bus's public-address system for cheese and fruit and bread.

The waiters tonight were Arabs, who exhibited both a certain nervousness as well as a practiced eagerness to please. This is considered a good, if limited, job for them, as some of the hotel's *Shabbos goyim*, performing work that Jews avoid on this day. The meal, like all the food at this hotel, was kosher; it began with gefilte fish, worked its way through main course choices of chicken, veal, or a vegetarian platter, and ended with a nondairy ice cream. The meal at an end, the rabbi rose and extended his hands, palms up. "So here we are! I'm sure so many things are flooding through your minds it's hard to keep anything straight. Maybe I can ask the simple question, again. What does it mean to be here, here in Jerusalem, today, right now?"

For Murray, who proclaimed himself "a labor man in America, and a Labor man here," and Carl Aframe, who just as solidly backs the Likud party, the rabbi's question quickly produced a spirited political volley.

"Only chance for peace is with Labor."

"Likud is tough; just like they have to be. Only thing that works with the Palestinians."

"C'mon," Murray said incredulously, his eyes widening, "you'll be at war forever!"

"It's not going away; been like this for thousands of years and it is not going to change," Carl retorted, his fist slamming down on the tablecloth, the judge's verdict thus rendered.

The spirited debate on the chances for Israeli-Arab rapprochement could have been construed as strictly political debate—and the evening's discussion, once again, did not proceed along lines the rabbi might have hoped for. But it did not escape the rabbi's attention that the words "moral" and "morality" (and "immorality") were also part of the debate, and that the issue of Israel's being held to tougher, higher standards than any other country in the world was hotly contested. Most of the Beth Israel group ended up agreeing that such expectations were grossly unfair. "Why us?" they asked.

It was a start, Rabbi Rosenbaum assured himself.

* * *

Shortly after eight the next morning, the rabbi stood in the lobby, his hands crossed in front of him. He was alone. He eyed the elevator doors as they opened once more. The automatic elevators—busy on their appointed rounds even now—most often yielded no one, and when there was someone within, the face was not a familiar one. The night before, at the conclusion of the dinner and prayers, the rabbi had invited his people to accompany him for some "synagogue hopping" to sample the rich offerings within walking distance of the hotel. Having such access was one of the reasons this hotel had been chosen in the first place. Finally, the elevator produced someone he knew. With a shrug of resignation the rabbi departed, the only fellow worshiper being Mark Cutler, a Reform Jew and not even a member of his congregation.

At Yeshurun, the Orthodox synagogue, they were joined an hour later by Murray Rosenberg and Charlie Mills. Upon arriving for the conclusion of the service at the synagogue within the Center for Conservative Judaism, the rabbi was pleased to see that the Fixlers, Sosnoffs, and Silvermans were among the worshipers. As we walked the short distance back to the hotel, someone noted the absence of a rabbi at the Orthodox service, even though there was a bar mitzvah.

"A bit of a problem *and* a point of pride here," the rabbi replied. "Israelis are pretty pragmatic people. Services are looked on as an obligation—something the observant Jew must do. And they're very well handled by laypeople. Nothing wrong with that service, was there? Their Hebrew is flawless; they use it every day. But, to my mind," he said, slowing his pace to make the best eye contact a man in the midst of a dozen or so people could accomplish, "they're missing something." His voice dropped to a slightly lower pitch, shifting out of what was evolving into an exhortative tone to one more conversational and appropriate to a sidewalk stroll. "The idea of making your entire life holy is missing. Not that we rabbis, not that we know everything—you would agree, no?—but the role of the rabbi as teacher, interpreter, counselor is missing. I don't want to sound judgmental about this, but there is an Israeli sense of getting the job done and then going on with the rest of your life. The rabbi isn't looked to as somebody with something to say about social issues, about *life*, like we"—he hesitated, sensing he was again beginning to preach—"at least try to do in America."

"Jews have problems here too, Rabbi?" someone said, affecting a comical Yiddish accent.

"Be sure of that. We have ours, they have theirs," the rabbi responded.

"Ben! Hurry up, you'll get lost," Lillian Silverman called back to her husband, who had fallen behind the group and was looking somewhat absentmindedly around him. "Ben!"

"I hear you, Lil," he said, pointing at his hearing aid. But he turned back, intent on completing his observation—and his thought.

"It was so wonderful, just to walk the street on *Shabbat*," he told me later, with absolute recall of the moment. "Look at them. Men walk to synagogue wearing their *tallitot*; look, that one with a nice suit and *tsitsit*. They are so proud. Maybe they do this in Crown Heights, where there is a heavy Jewish population, but on a regular downtown street? In America, there seems to be the feeling that we shouldn't flaunt our Jewishness too openly. This is just wonderful. How great to be a Jew here."

At two o'clock, those who accepted the rabbi's invitation for a *Shabbos* picnic set out for Independence Park, a ten-acre greensward in the midst of Jerusalem, located just behind the hotel. For a while, the group wandered about, searching out shade and a place where the few children—David and Shoshanah Rosenbaum and Daniel and Leah Fixler—could play. Eventually a shaded area was found, but not the playground Janine thought was nearby. The picnic site ended up being a bleak expanse of bare dirt and pebbles, bounded by a short expanse of what appeared to be raised curbstones.

As small, wrinkled waxed bags were opened and their contents removed, the meal was revealed to be as humble as the surroundings: challah; some once-flaky cheese turnovers, now limp and bare from their exodus out of Mahane Yehuda; watermelon and plums; and some bitter Israeli wine, for which no one, after sampling, seemed to have much taste. In addition to the Rosenbaums and Fixlers, the Silvermans had joined the rather small experimental community of *shomer Shabbat* pilgrims, as had two of the elderly singles, Marion Blumberg and Max Gould. Dr. Gould, who had already earned a reputation for his abrupt outspokenness, looked up from his somewhat barren paper plate and said loudly with unbridled exasperation, "Hey, why didn't somebody bring a salami?"

Why, indeed. It was not the ample *Shabbat* noonday meal the rabbi had envisioned.

Rabbi Rosenbaum smiled weakly in reply and tore off another piece of challah. Janine kept her own counsel. The conversations among people seemingly unsure of why they were here in the first place started and ended fitfully. I found my mind drifting away from this rather spiritless adventure, wondering what the many absent congregants were doing, in observance (or defiance) of the Sabbath. Eventually, for some inexplicable reason, I thought of Moses. Moses, leading his people out of bondage, promising them a better, fuller life with God, but having to take care of all the logistics of life along the way. Poor Moses. What did he say when they complained that they would have preferred a more varied cuisine than the manna sent by a merciful God to keep them alive? How did he respond when the chosen people wished God had been more selective in His choosing and provided more interesting companions for their sojourn?

There, seated on an outcropping of rock (albeit one fashioned by modern machinery), sat Rabbi Jay Rosenbaum, the modern-day stand-in for the beleaguered patriarch. For once, I did not have to ask what was going through his mind. It was written plainly on his face.

The Sabbath is demarcated by candle lighting—both at its beginning, with *kabbalat Shabbat* to welcome and sanctify the special day, and at its end, at sundown on Saturday, with *Havdalah,* a celebration to launch the observant Jew into the week. Two other elements are necessary for *Havdalah:* wine and fragrant spices. All three, plus some small paper cups, were in Rabbi Rosenbaum's backpack as the Worces-

ter group, once again swelled to full strength, walked onto the cobblestones before the Western Wall as the last glow of the sun outlined the
yeshivot behind us.

Havdalah for the Orthodox Jews of Jerusalem is a major weekly
event at the wall; tonight, their yeshiva students came across the approach, arms linked, shuffling their feet in rhythm to the *nigun*, a repe-
titious melody without words. Their muffled echoes drifted across the
cobblestones. Ultra-Orthodox walked about in splendid profusion, in
beaver hats and black felt hats, in striped long coats of gray and white
cotton and coats of lush silk that resemble smoking jackets. Some wore
simple black suits; *tsitsit* dangled everywhere. The wall itself was already crowded with still other varieties of the Orthodox, *shukeling* in
prayer, as well as a smaller number of conventional Jews in Western
attire.

Rabbi Jay Rosenbaum, in T-shirt, tan shorts, and a finely embroidered brown Ethiopian *kippah*, assembled his people about him in
two facing semicircles, men on one side, women on the other, so as not
to raise the ire of the Orthodox who regularly break up anything
resembling a mixed-sex service. He had observed an undrawn line, the
extension of the chain-link fence that separated men from women at
the wall. We were as close as mixed groups could get to the wall, near
the barriers that separate those praying at the wall from those who
might want nothing more than to observe, as many men and women
about us were doing.

With a few words underscoring the significance of this *Havdalah* in the Holy City, the rabbi began in Hebrew the verse that translates as "Behold, God is my deliverance; I am confident and unafraid."
His voice grew deeper, more resonant in the open air. His words
drifted out over the heads and shoulders of hundreds upon hundreds
of Jews. His prayers and theirs soon mingled in the night air, a rich
offering of accents from many lands, all of them sent winging toward
the revered wall. "The Lord is my strength, my might, my deliverance. . . ." And the group from Worcester responded, "Grant us the
blessings of light, of gladness and of honor which the miracle of deliv-

erance brought to our ancestors. I lift the cup of deliverance and call upon the Lord."

The rabbi lifted his tiny paper cup of wine, filled to overflowing to symbolize that, with God on their side, Jews need not be concerned for material needs, for everything they require will be provided them. "We lit two separate candles to begin *Shabbos*, and now this candle, with wicks intertwined, shows that God and man are unified by this day," the rabbi said. The noise about us, with the talk of tourists competing with the cacophony of voices at the wall, caused members of our group to draw nearer. The rabbi continued, in a somewhat louder voice, "We have been refreshed by *Shabbos* rest and by *Shabbos* prayers and now we have the opportunity to bring its holiness into the six days before us. Six days—together—in the Holy Land!" A ripple of wind washed over us, but David Rosenbaum, shielded by the ingathering of children about him, admirably kept the *Havdalah* candle alight. A bottle containing sticks of cinnamon was passed from hand to hand, the traditional refreshment at Sabbath's end to vivify a person for the week ahead.

The people of Worcester inhaled deeply, taking in the fragrance of the spice and the warm Jerusalem night air. *Havdalah* completed, they turned to leave. Tears streamed down Janine's face. Steve Sosnoff and Charlie Mills stood fixed, staring at the wall.

"My mind was a blur," Steve would recall. "I was *outside*; I was praying. It was disorienting; I had a little trouble walking."

Even after Steve had turned to join the group, Charlie Mills continued to stare at the wall. A pragmatic physician, schooled in the scientific method and trained to keep his emotions in check, he would recall that reason had abandoned him that night. He felt he was having a vision. The wall was talking to him.

"Don't worship me. Build it," were the words he heard.

The "it"—he knew well—was Israel.

17

Whether it was the invigoration of *Shabbos* in Jerusalem, the vicissitudes of renal biology, an internal clock confused by a leap of seven time zones, or simply the clarion call of inspiration, Rabbi Jay Rosenbaum awoke with a start at three o'clock the next morning. He sat bolt upright in bed, his mind perfectly lucid and a single word on his lips.

"Feeling!" he blurted out in an uncharacteristically loud voice—so loud that people having breakfast at nearby tables in the Sheraton Plaza dining room looked our way. "Feeling!" he repeated to me, recalling his nocturnal revelation. "What I want most for our people on this trip is feeling, not fact. Yes, I want them to learn Jewish history and know events and places and people, and when we read the Torah, and mention the Galilee or the Assyrians, they'll have some background." For a moment I wondered if the rabbi had not contracted a virus from Fran Alpert; the pace of his breathless monologue resembled that of our Jewish Quarter guide. "But what I want more for them is to *feel* what it has been like to be a Jew down through the years. I want them to feel the pressures that Jews have always had to deal with. To somehow sense that the tug of the world has always been there. It's so easy to look back and admire the ancient Jews, but then to keep them at a safe distance, on a shelf to be admired." The rabbi had tried to slow his pace, but his normal control mechanisms weren't functioning. " 'Not a part of my life,' they probably would say. But these are all part of our extended family. I can't get that house of the *Kohanim* out of my mind. Temple oil lamps and pagan idols. Cultures clashing; which will win?

"And along with feeling . . ." He hesitated, smiling impishly over his plate laden with a sampling of tofu, granola, yogurt, and fresh fruit from the plentiful breakfast buffet. "I want them not to be so sure of what they *do* know, or what they will hear and see—I want them to know the complexity, the ambiguities of Jewish life. Yes, there is history to learn, but *what* history?"

As we ate our breakfast together and the rabbi relived some of the highlights of the trip thus far, he mentioned nothing about what had seemed to me to be chronic grumbling during these early days. I couldn't resist asking what effect it had had on him.

"If I listened to that," he responded with some incredulity, "I'd go nuts. I'd go into another line of work. I just don't hear it. These are Jews; they love to argue. These are American consumers; they want their money's worth. They expect service. But this is Israel." He closed his eyes, savoring a thought that seemed to be whisking through his mind. "Israel will make its impact on them. Wait and see. Feeling!"

As we lingered over coffee, Carl Aframe wandered by, a breakfast plate piled high in his hands, and on his face, a huge, pleased grin. "Jay, *Shabbos* yesterday; totally amazing!"

"I'm glad you liked it," the rabbi said, his tone asking for specifics.

"I woke up yesterday morning." Carl hesitated, momentarily overcome with the splendor of his thought.

"Yes?"

"And I realized that Carl Aframe . . ."

"Yes?"

". . . type-A personality Carl Aframe could do absolutely nothing all day. What a wonderful feeling!"

"Oh."

While their *Shabbos* path may have diverged—the Aframes had visited with a gathering of his cousins in the German Colony section of Jerusalem—Carl, too, had spent a restless night. But what he had lost in sleep, he had gained in contemplation. When he met up with us over breakfast, his discovery was still too fresh—too foolish, really—to fully divulge to anyone. Later, he tried it out on me.

"Of course it was more than what I said about *Shabbos*, but are you going to blurt out to the rabbi over your orange juice?" he said. " 'I'm hooked, Rabbi. I want to live here, Rabbi.' They'd put me away if I said that. 'Oh, there goes Aframe again.' But what I felt at the wall won't let go of me. What I felt all *Shabbat*. I was in Israel in seventy-three alone and then in seventy-four with Debbie; I was so damn idealistic about Israel then, but I didn't do anything about it. I went back and made it in Worcester; nice house, best suits; my kids are in private school. I showed 'em what Abe Aframe's kid could do. But for what?

"I have a law practice in Worcester. I do not have a purpose in Worcester. Everybody has a purpose here. My cousins, Karen and Peter from Connecticut, they're here, teaching English. They have a real purpose in life. My old idealism of twenty years ago has become a real idealism. The country has changed and so have I. You don't have to be an Orthodox Jew, like you have to be in the States, to live a fully Jewish life here. I can see it now. Clearly! They've got to need insolvency lawyers here, don't they? I'm good at what I do. I can figure out a bankruptcy case in fifteen minutes. I want to get back here, bad. I've got to be careful how I position this so I don't scare the hell out of my family."

It was Sunday, a working day for a country that closes down on Saturday, and the afternoon's schedule called for a visit to the Knesset, Israel's parliament. But with Yitzhak Rabin and his cabinet ministers deep in meetings and security tight, we found the building closed to visitors. Instead, David took us to the huge outdoor bronze menorah across Kaplan Street on which are depicted the signal events and personages of Jewish history—Moses receiving the Ten Commandments; Hillel, standing on one leg (his famous summary of the moral life, "What is hateful to you, do not do to others," was succinctly uttered in this position); the Warsaw ghetto uprising are but some of them—but, as David proffered, it was a sweeping and decidedly secular history of a people. God was relegated to a minor, supporting role.

Rabbi Rosenbaum looked at David and then back to the menorah. Again, he turned to David, studying his tanned face. Even after his apocalyptic revelation of the night before, it was apparent that the rabbi was not about to say anything before the time was right. Silently, he joined the others and boarded the bus.

Our next stop was perhaps the most emotionally charged of many a Jew's visit to Israel. For at Yad Vashem, it is remembered that the six million who died in the most systematic and cruelly efficient slaughter of human beings in history died simply because they were Jews. As for the travelers from Worcester, the decision to come here— or not—was not made lightly. Young Daniel Fixler and Janine Rosenbaum were illustrative of what went into those individual decisions.

Howie Fixler had wondered if, at ten, Daniel was old enough to come. He knew eight-year-old Leah was definitely too young, but he wanted Daniel to see the Holocaust museum as a sort of modern-day corollary to the Jewish education he was receiving at Congregation Beth Israel. But he did not push it. Then, standing shoulder to shoulder with his son at the Western Wall, Howie had had a whole new sense of this person standing beside him. Daniel too was a Jewish man; Daniel too was an inheritor of the beauty and the pain of Judaism. Daniel—with such a powerful biblical name—would have to carry his religious beliefs and traditions into a world that would constantly and subtly work to co-opt him—as it for many years had co-opted himself. When Howie and Jody casually mentioned at breakfast what was on the day's itinerary, Daniel answered the unasked question.

"I want to see it, Dad," he said, looking at his father straight on.

Janine Rosenbaum had the exact opposite sentiment. She had no reason to see Yad Vashem.

She had lived in a Holocaust museum for all the years she spent with her parents, who had lost their entire families to the death camps. It was not that her parents told her of the horrors of those days; they rarely mentioned them. But Janine would hear them walking about at night, restless, unable to sleep, and she knew the demons of those days stalked them. There was no extended family such as her other Jewish friends had, no grandparents, uncles, or aunts; only two cousins had survived, and they lived in Israel. At Passover seders, her mother or father might begin a sentence, "In camp . . ." and then their eyes would glaze over and they would sit there, unable to continue. Janine would never herself go to summer camp—she wanted nothing to do with a place that was confined and where she was away from her parents.

One of the few reminders of the Holocaust was a picture book her parents kept on a high shelf and forbade her to look at. One day she did. One photograph that etched itself in her brain was that of a Nazi soldier holding a scrawny Jewish baby by its neck, as if it were no more than a chicken about to be slaughtered. She ran to the bathroom and threw up.

Janine Rosenbaum did not need to see any more such pictures at Yad Vashem.

Those from Worcester who had chosen to come to Yad Vashem on this Sunday morning walked from the bus toward the museum, protected from the searing sun by the spreading branches of the carob trees that mark the Avenue of the Righteous. David pointed out that at one time Israel had hoped to have a forest of trees planted, one for each of the gentiles who helped the Jews during those years of horror. By now, we could almost anticipate the tone—if not the exact content—of his next statement. "We couldn't find enough gentiles," he said, motioning with a quick toss of his hand, to this shady lane where several hundred trees grow, each with a nameplate at its base (one is dedicated to the now-famous Oskar Schindler). The rabbi nodded and followed the silent group. Howie Fixler laid his hand on his son's shoulder, as if to get his pulse. Daniel squinted at the sunlight coming through the trees and continued to walk toward the museum.

Some of the pictures and artifacts, arranged chronologically from the rise of Nazism to the liberation of the death camps, are by now well known because of the many exhibits that have traveled throughout America, as well as the extensive literature on the Holocaust. But the cumulative effect within the darkened museum is something few are prepared for. Walking through a labyrinth formed by high dividers, the visitor is confronted at every turn by increasingly ominous documentation. Anti-Semitic posters articulate in bold print what would soon be carried out by brute force. In photographs, well-dressed Jews with top hats, starched collars, women in fine dresses, children who look dressed for *shul,* are herded into trucks to begin a journey toward death. A tattered yellow Star of David that all Jews were forced to wear had been stitched hastily to a sleeve, a placation that was not to work. In another photograph, Nazi officers survey their human chattel, their faces a mixture of marvel and arrogance at the efficiency of it all. A boy, with a startled look in his eye, is pushed along by a rifle-bearing Nazi.

Daniel Fixler, about the same age as that boy—a boy dressed in a fine cloth coat, billed cap, and freshly shined shoes—stared at the picture. Could the streets of Worcester turn so ugly for him, a young Jew? Could faces look on him with so much hate? Could men in uniforms—men in authority, to whom his parents have taught him to give respect—ever treat *him* like this? Being a Jew was a source of pride for him; he loved wearing his fine silk *kippah.* Could such a sign of his Jewishness ever mark him for death?

Of the older Worcester travelers, virtually all could name relatives who are numbered among those six million. But only one of them was actually in Germany to witness the Nazis' rise to power. Gabriella Frymer was living in Frankfurt in September of 1938 when Kristallnacht shattered not only windows of synagogues and Jewish shops, but the tenuous hope that this menace might miraculously pass. She was able to escape the next year at the age of twenty-five; her mother and younger brother and sister, as well as many relatives, would die in death camps.

As members of the Worcester group were dispersed among others who had come to Yad Vashem that day, reemerging to whisper to one another about a particularly haunting photo or display, Gaby walked on, seemingly alone. When their paths converged, fellow Beth Israel congregants cast quick glances her way, to see what she was looking at, to gauge her reaction. But no one approached her, either to comfort or to question.

Eyes squeezed tightly in futile attempts to forestall what few can control. They walked on. Hankies daubed at tears, were placed back in pocket or purse, only to be quickly withdrawn for further use. Finally, most of the group arrived in the section on the death camps. Skeletons, both the dead and the living, gaped out at them. Gaby stood transfixed before a picture of the gas ovens. As she remained there for painful seconds, a member of the group made a move toward her. Before a word could be proffered, Gaby turned angrily.

"And don't say I was lucky to get out. Just don't say it!" Her eyes were blazing in an anger to which even her tears could not give relief.

There was an added silence upon the silence of this hall of agony.

The group from Worcester emerged from the dark building into the sunlight. No one was speaking; they seemed to be moving in slow motion, as if weights were attached to their feet. Coming briskly down the path was another group, freshly emerged from their tour bus. The group from Worcester looked up at them, knowing something they did not yet know, carrying an indelible mark that the newcomers as yet did not have. Steve Sosnoff took Denise's hand. He looked back over his shoulder toward the building. He had decided not to bring the children; he had been wrong.

In the past few days, the group from Worcester had been exposed to a crash course in some of the most intense moments of Jewish history, both ancient and modern. The tour architects from Kenes must have anticipated that a reprieve would be needed about then, and a more conventional—and perhaps more easily digestible—type of touring was now in store. The itinerary called for the group to leave Jerusalem on Monday and spend four days on the road, traveling as far north as the Syrian and Lebanese borders, west to Haifa on the Mediterranean, and east to the Golan Heights. It would be a mix of the ancient and modern, of recreation and Judaic education. The group was scheduled to see the restored Talmudic village at Katzrin, the mountain fortress of Masada, and the extraordinary ruins of a Roman town at Bet She'an. Also, we would visit one of the earliest synagogues at Meirot, an Israeli Defense Force base three miles from the Jordanian border, and a destroyed Syrian bunker on the Golan. The Sea of Galilee and the Dead Sea; rafting on the Jordan River; a swim at the lush oasis at Gan Hashlos-ha; camel rides in the desert; and a visit to (of all anomalies) a Jewish dude ranch were planned.

Our stop in Haifa included a visit to the Bahai Shrine and the lush Persian Gardens surrounding it, in which a wedding was taking place. During our visit to the kibbutz at Hanaton—the only one run by the small Conservative Movement in Israel—we learned that getting people to live on a kibbutz was a considerably harder sell these days. The once-idealized life of the kibbutznik is not as popular now that Israel offers modern conveniences unthinkable in its early days as a state. The Zionist-socialist dream of living in common, apportioning to each according to need, while drawing upon individual talents, has been eclipsed by the lure of capitalistic business opportunities and the possibility of a private home or apartment.

Traveling farther north and west, and especially after we passed Capernaum, we were repeatedly reminded that this is a country basically in a constant state of war. In Jerusalem, we had grown used to seeing many soldiers on the streets, armed and unarmed. But on the well-maintained highways in this section of the country, we began to see convoys of truck-borne field artillery, armored personnel carriers, and supply vehicles. Soldiers were everywhere. Strangely, though, Israel's constant military preparedness had a rather homespun quality to it. It is a commuter's conflict. Soldiers hitchhike and ride public buses to their assigned posts in this land where war can easily be waged an hour or two from home.

By afternoon's end we arrived at the banks of the Jordan, strapped on life preservers, and prepared to climb into huge rubber inner tubes for a ride down the famed river.

For all its mythic significance, the Jordan—at this point at least—is a narrow, very muddy, and polluted river, being the final repository of the runoff of huge doses of fertilizers and other chemicals used to make the desert bloom so abundantly. Some of our number—Freda Rosenberg and Gaby Frymer among them—took one look at the river and the proposed means of conveyance and went no farther, but the rest of the adults and all of the children except for Shoshanah were soon off on the gently moving river. It proved to be a rather surrealistic ride. Open spots in the thick brush along the bank alternately yielded views of bucolic fields and small villages and then, startlingly, imposing portable steel bridges that could be stretched across in a few minutes for the rapid deployment of Israeli Defense Force tanks and vehicles.

The arms of Murray Rosenberg, the eldest rafter, slowed and then went limp after about fifteen minutes into what was to be an hour-and-a-half trip downstream. For a while he hitched on to the rabbi's rubber raft; just as the rabbi flagged, Charlie Mills came to the rescue. Charlie had paddled vigorously ahead, passing all of us, and had reached the end point. He then paddled back, upriver and against the mild current, amazingly rejoining us when we had gone no farther than the midpoint. He ferried Murray the rest of the way.

We emerged from the river, wondering if the dank smell of the drying water on our bodies would produce anything more lasting and ominous than the mild rash incurred by some of our number. But the response to our odoriferous immersion in the venerable Jordan was more of laughter—tinged with a certain resignation that nothing is as it seems in Israel—than complaint. After showers at the tourist kibbutz at Ayelet Hashachar in the Galilee (not only crops are tended in community, but also tourists) we climbed back aboard the bus for our dinner outing.

It was the strangest of strange evenings. We arrived a half hour later at Baba Yona Ranch to see a handful of rawboned horses and a few head of cattle munching on coarse hay within corrals that looked as out of place on the bleak desert landscape as did the lush orchards and fields we had first encountered near the airport. Skewers of vegetables and marinated meat sizzled over a barbecue pit. The texture of the meat was vaguely familiar, as was its taste, but as the group hungrily munched away after a full day's activities, the mystery remained unsolved. Finally someone with an enlightened palate pronounced, "Turkey." Indeed, barbecued turkey. The Israelis have found that turkey provides an efficient source of protein—considering the ratio of pounds of grain used as feed to pounds of meat produced—and innovative uses of the bird have been promoted.

The owner of Baba Yona is an inventive fellow, an Israeli who heard about dude ranches in America and, as he was looking for a business to launch, said why not a Jewish dude ranch? The Worcester group seemed his only customers that night, but this didn't preclude anything less than a full evening's entertainment. A duo playing electric accordion and keyboard serenaded us during dinner with an impressive selection of American and Israeli songs. We drank Cokes and ice-cold Maccabee beer and sang along to that old standby, *"Erev Shel Shoshanim,"* and other Israeli favorites. Then the duo struck up a different beat, more in keeping with the mini–theme park we were visiting. Shoshanah's grand twirls and Gaby's hand clapping provided the incentive for the rest of the group to get onto to the floor for square dancing. Nine-year-old Aliza Mills needed little encouragement, later on, to take the microphone and end the evening demonstrating the gifts of a budding *chanteuse*.

Barbecued turkey and a polluted holy river. As I went over my notes in my room at the kibbutz that night, I realized I hadn't heard a single complaint all day. And there had been laughter. A lot of it. The people of Beth Israel—even with Murray's abruptness, Charlie Mills's sometimes annoying hyperactivity, Freda Rosenberg's rather dour disposition, and the short attention spans of the preteens—actually seemed to be having a good time with one another.

I found myself jotting down something to the effect that while religious belief may provide inspiration for the soul, community activities were the real unifier. There was nothing overtly religious about this day in Israel, and yet the spirits of the group from Worcester had never been higher. Today, being Jews together in Israel had been simply fun.

As Carl Aframe would later tell me, "That night at the dude ranch marked the turning point in the trip for me. The barriers broke down. Diversity—instead of being a drawback or reason for contention—became a highlight."

Just before seven the next morning, Rabbi Rosenbaum quietly

closed the door of his room at Ayelet Hashachar and began the short walk through the courtyard that separates the two rows of cinder-block buildings of this modest resort complex. The automatic sprinklers had just turned off. The rabbi further slowed his already leisurely pace. Then he stopped. There was something about the quality of the light that morning, a quality he had not noticed before in Israel. The grass sparkled around him, crystalline with moisture. The poppies, anemones, cyclamen, daisies, and roses were brilliant explosions of yellow and scarlet, fuchsia, and purple in the pure, early morning light. The sunlight streamed through the palm fronds, casting sheer curtains of light that at once concealed and enhanced the stunning array of plant life.

Something was different this morning in Israel. The rabbi continued on toward the parking lot, alone.

When he arrived on the edge of the parking lot, he was surprised to find that—unlike the poor turnout for his morning of "synagogue hopping" just a few days before—most members of his group had heeded his call to rise early and leave for this excursion. Even after a late night, even before breakfast was served, they had come. They got into the six jeeps standing by and started on their way. Soon the vehicles left the paved roads and began the ascent into the Naftalle Range. The hardpan, rocky roads, rutted by the infrequent but torrential rains, tossed them from side to side; dust rose from the jeeps' wheels, quickly coating both vehicles and riders with a layer of fine dirt. Finally, we reached the summit at Meirot, where the sweeping vista of barren mountains and valleys dotted with sparse vegetation spread out before us.

"After the destruction of the Second Temple in 70 C.E.," David began when the group had gathered around him, "a new period in Jewish history was about to unfold. The Jews had gone to the temple three times a year and brought animals to be sacrificed. The high priest sacrificed them, and that was that. But when the temple was destroyed and the Jews dispersed, what could they do? Centers of learning grew up wherever groups of Jews settled, where the Torah could be read and discussed. Rabbis came into being as teachers, and meetinghouses—

batei knesset—were constructed, one of them here at Meirot. These eventually would become houses of prayer. Synagogues." There was a strange intonation in David's voice at this word: not of any open derision, but flat and uninflected; uninterested, as if this were a minor moment in Jewish history, one that could be noted or not.

David nodded to the rabbi, who continued, "People were trying to figure out how to deal with God, how to pay Him homage. This synagogue from 135 c.e.—here where we are standing at Meirot—says more about the Judaism we practice today than the great temples in Jerusalem." His voice was anything but uninterested, brimming with anticipation as if the secrets of this mountaintop would be revealed that very morning, revealed to this very group. "It is during this time that the Talmud and the Mishnah are written. Sacrifice turns to prayer as a way of reaching God, and rabbinic Judaism is codified. I don't know how it registers with you, but it's a fascinating era and really I—" The rabbi stopped short, obviously deciding to offer no more explanation. If he was to allow the emotional weight of the moment to have its impact, he knew he must parcel his words carefully. He retrieved his *tefillin* from their velvet sack and adroitly bound the word of God onto his head and upon his arm. He reverentially kissed the middle of his *tallit* and swirled it about his shoulders. He moved to a spot between two of the taller stubs of pillars that remain.

The outline of the synagogue at Meirot was evident. It had been a rather modest place, perhaps forty by eighty feet. Simple, rounded Doric columns and lintels—almost smooth now after all the centuries—showed both Roman and Greek influences. The huge rectangular blocks that once had borne the weight of the walls provided easy stepping stones for the children, who scampered onto them, using them as a playscape.

The rabbi squinted into the sun, now far above the horizon, a searing white ball in a cloudless pale blue morning sky. He opened his *siddur* to the page for morning prayer.

"Praised are You, Lord our God, King of the Universe who enables His creatures to distinguish between night and day." Rabbi Rosenbaum's words echoed among the bare ruined columns and foun-

dation stones. "Who made me in His image, who made me a Jew . . .
who provides for all my needs, who guides us on our path, who
strengthens the people Israel with courage, who crowns the people Israel with glory, who restores vigor to the weary."

The words that the rabbi had said so many mornings of his life
fused into the chorus of the ages and washed over the small gathering
of his followers on the sun-drenched mountaintop in the Galilee.
Clustered about him were his people, their hands crossed in front of
them. He had shared these prayers with most of the men and some of
the women in the Beth Israel chapel. But now he stood exposed to the
elements amidst the ruins of a building approximately the same size as
that comfortable paneled place with padded seats, a climate-con-
trolled room that knew no season.

The rabbi passed the *siddur* to Sandy Cutler.

"Praised are You, Lord God, King of the Universe who
removes sleep from my eyes. . . . May we feel at home with Your Torah.
. . . Let no evil impulse control us. . . ."

Still another set of waiting hands received the *siddur*.

"We are Your partners, partners to Your covenant, descendants of Your beloved Abraham to whom You made a pledge. . . . It is
our duty to thank You and praise You, to glorify and sanctify Your
name. . . . How good is our portion. . . ."

David was standing off to the side; it was he who was now
alone. His hands were plunged deeply into his pockets, his head down.

The *siddur* was passed again.

"May it be Your will, Lord, our God and God of our ancestors
. . . may we be disciples . . . loving peace and pursuing peace, loving our
fellow creatures and drawing them near to the Torah."

With morning prayer over, the group remained in silence for a
moment. As the silence became uncomfortable, someone—with a nervous laugh—suggested some breakfast. They turned from the ancient
stones toward the jeeps.

The rabbi made no open proclamation of his thoughts about
that morning at Meirot, but later, I would find that he had talked
about it privately with a good number of the group. When I asked him

about this, he was unaware that he had shared his sentiments with so many. It was not, he said, a conscious effort.

"The quiet; the smallness of our group and the vastness of the scenery from that mountaintop," the rabbi said later. "Morning prayer expresses our wonder at the majesty of God's creation—in Worcester, you have to use your imagination. At Meirot, there it was! There we were in the open air at a *bet ha-knesset* where prayers have been offered for almost two thousand years. Spiritually elevated, closer to God. What a powerful, powerful feeling. The prayers we say today were formed in places like Meirot. With groups maybe no bigger than ours. Isn't that an amazing thought?"

Back at the jeeps, Carl Aframe was the first one aboard, urging the others to hurry; he was ready for a big breakfast. Indeed, the group from Worcester may well have been hungry at eight o'clock—and yet surely another appetite had been satisfied.

18

Our bus slowed on its northward journey on Route 90 as it reached the periphery of Qiryat Shemonah. It is here that Route 99 begins and heads abruptly east, toward the Golan Heights. Although there were many conversations in process aboard the bus, Rabbi Rosenbaum, in his customary seat near the front, was uncommonly quiet. His face was expressionless as he peered out the window.

It had grown, he noted.

Qiryat Shemonah is one of the larger towns in northern Israel and not an especially attractive place, filled as it is with rather nondescript dun-colored apartment buildings and low-slung houses that spread up the hillside in the distance. On the streets near where our bus passed were many men and women with pronounced Slavic features—broad faces, high cheekbones, and, when they smiled and waved at us, readily apparent silvery fillings. The preponderance of Russian *olim* in such a place says something immediately to the informed observer. There are only three possibilities: that this a new settlement in need of settlers, a dangerous place, or an undesirable location where Israelis would rather not live.

The vast majority of the buildings seemed hardly new, so the first possibility is unlikely. But, boldly situated on a long finger of land protruding northward—with the Lebanese border five kilometers to the west and the Golan Heights less than twenty kilometers to the east—Qiryat Shemonah qualifies as both dangerous and undesirable.

The rabbi's eyes fixed on a sign alongside the highway, proclaiming that a Holiday Inn was to built there. The sign was rusted with age. We reached Route 99 and turned east.

This morning, I found Rabbi Rosenbaum curtained within another of his deep, reflective moods. With increasing frequency, the shroud of quiet contemplation had been drawn over the rabbi's usually pleasant, smiling face as he mulled over the places visited thus far, the unique atmosphere each had presented, the memorable moments that had resulted—and how he might maximize the experiences for the people of Beth Israel who were traveling with him. There had been many such moments so far, yet there had also been a series of less wonderful moments, which had continued throughout the trip. These, too, were part of his ruminations. Earlier that morning, Sandy Cutler had screamed at their young guide at Ayelet Hashachar that she wanted her daughter to see the kibbutz's cows *now*, even though she had been told that this was not part of a normal tour. This had set off a chorus of disgruntled murmurs among the younger couples to the effect that not enough was being done to engage the interests of their children. Another painful reckoning had occurred when the same couples boycotted the meal at a kosher Chinese restaurant overlooking the Sea of Galilee, refusing to pay the fourteen dollars per person David had said the meal would cost. Indeed, the food had turned out to be barely palatable, and the rabbi had heard the group's suspicions that perhaps David's insistence on that particular restaurant could be explained by an under-the-table consideration from the owners in return for his diligence. Indeed, David himself was becoming the focus of many of the less pleasant moments. There had been growing irritation among the group about David's often denigrating, dismissive comments in response to questions that were certainly well intentioned, no matter how insipid they may have appeared to him. But his suspected *hondeling* was even more irritating. More than one person pointed out that during a stop at the ancient town of Safed, David strongly urged that they shop at a specific store—a store later found to be higher priced than most, if not all, of the others.

Regardless of David's role in all this, the rabbi knew that Janine was livid at the younger couples' refusal to spend fourteen dollars on a dinner with the group, particularly after learning that one of the

Worcester refuseniks had bought a bracelet costing thousands of dollars the same night.

Every time Rabbi Rosenbaum was tempted to believe that his group had finally jelled, that the Worcester pilgrims were finally ready to put individual needs and quirks aside, something had flared up to disrupt the fragile social ecosystem. And now, that morning, by virtue of the fact that Qiryat Shemonah lay en route to the Golan Heights, the rabbi had been unexpectedly, dramatically—and somewhat unwillingly—catapulted into his past.

Jay Rosenbaum had spent the better part of 1972 in Qiryat Shemona as a twenty-two-year-old volunteer with *Sherut La'am*, "Service to the People," a sort of Israeli VISTA program. There was nothing religious—so he assured himself when he signed up for the program—in coming to Israel. In fact, at the time he was continuing his flight from the heavy religious overlay of his youth. Although a drab, unexciting town, Qiryat Shemonah was a wonderful place where Jay could at once be totally Jewish and totally irreligious. Better still, there was an ever-present element of danger; this was Israel's frontier. Just months before he had arrived, Katyusha rockets fired from Lebanon had landed on the town. Alerts were common. The next attack could happen any day. There was the romance of being in a constant state of danger.

And there was a woman.

She was a vibrant, twenty-five-year-old botanist from Kentucky Jay met in a *Sherut La'am* orientation class. Idealistic about the state of Israel and totally uninterested in religion, their affinity was immediate. So was the attraction: they moved into an apartment together, giving all appearances of being married—a necessary ruse for cohabitation in those days. Jay, then planning on a career teaching retarded children, knew something about testing and so was assigned to perform psychological tests on the town's elementary-school youngsters. He performed his work diligently, but there was plenty of time for long hikes in the mountains, for evenings of Israeli dancing, for being in love and for making love—in the privacy of their apartment, or outdoors under the vast skies of a country he loved as much as she did. At year's end, Jay Rosenbaum vowed to come right back, to rejoin her, and to stay.

He would not know it at the time, but at Qiryat Shemonah, Jay Rosenbaum was reaching the outer limits of his escape from Judaism. Once back in New York, he became involved in the West Side Minyan's *havurah*. By the time he was twenty-five, he had returned to the Jewish Theological Seminary and had begun studying for the rabbinate. His life's path took a more circuitous route; once determined to return immediately, he had not come back to Israel until now, twenty years later—as a rabbi, and married to another woman.

As Route 99 climbed out of the basin of the Hula Valley, traffic gradually began to diminish until there was almost none at all. We found we were on a road to nowhere. Route 99 ends at the Syrian border, guarded by both sides and certainly not open. In place of stands of crops, we began to see random outcroppings of barbed wire along the road. Yellow signs emblazoned with a red triangle warned that there were minefields beyond.

"Until you see it for yourself," Channy Greenberg had told the group months before, "try to keep an open mind about the Golan Heights. If you've never seen it, believe me—you simply can't imagine. Just wait till you get there. And remember I said this," she advised, gently wagging a finger, "you'll never think about it, or about Israel, the same way again." As we clambered up the narrow, dusty footpath from the side of the road, passing rock and earthen bunkers reinforced by steel beams, and finally arrived at the crest, Channy Greenberg's admonition proved poignantly true.

We stood before the Syrian command post at Tel Faquar, dug into the hillside. Behind us, over the next set of hills, some fifteen miles away, was the Syrian capital, Damascus. Before us was the fertile Huleh Valley, irrigated by the River Jordan and nicknamed Israel's breadbasket for its abundant agriculture. In the middle distance beyond the irrigated fields, Qiryat Shemonah was clearly visible—and well within artillery range.

A rusting Syrian armored vehicle rested at a disconcerting angle on a steep embankment. It was not hard to visualize how shells could be launched with devastating effect from this elevated vantage point—and how difficult it would be for ground troops to take such a fortress without suffering enormous casualties.

"Now I see what they mean," Steve Sosnoff said as he stood on the promontory. Normally a smiling, good-natured man, there was now a serious look on his face. His hand was resting on a crudely fashioned Star of David welded to an overturned helmet, a memorial to the Israeli soldiers who died capturing this outpost in 1967, and then defending it in the 1973 Yom Kippur War.

But for the most part, members of the group said nothing, quiet as they had been in the holiest of holy places in Jerusalem, and at the memorial to the Holocaust dead. They gazed down from this barren knob in the rolling hills, down onto the precious, fragile homeland of their ancient faith. Who among them stood there proudly as conquerors, sure of their place, sure of their right to be there? And who were the questioning seekers, looking down on the desert wasteland of their own spiritual lives? Now that they had attained this high ground, what should they do with it?

Our next stop was the partially restored Talmudic village at Katzrin—one of the many centers of learning that were established by the Jews fleeing Jerusalem after the destruction of the Second Temple. We gathered for a group picture, with the ruins of the local synagogue as a backdrop. At Bet She'an we strolled the newly excavated streets of an ancient Roman city and sat on the flat stone seats of the amphitheater as David explained the town's history. This time his venom was directed at the Romans, "who forced Jewish mothers and sons to fornicate in public view, so they could have some entertainment on a Sunday afternoon. Fathers were forced to fight their sons to the death. Remember all this when we get to Masada. I think you'll realize why the Jews there chose suicide rather than live under the Romans."

The next day, as we lumbered our way generally south, toward the Dead Sea, we visited an Israeli Defense Force tank base five kilometers from the Jordanian border. We were somewhat amazed to find a group of Americans there, dressed in Israeli army fatigues, doing groundskeeping work. They schedule their vacations to do this, volunteering for reservist duty each summer. If there is a war, they fight it; if not, weeds need to be pulled and flowers planted in the parched earth. Even at this remote outpost, the desert will bloom.

We were escorted around the base by a young IDF journalist, who was also a stringer for some Dutch publications. He served as our interpreter while the young tank platoon commander gave a short talk in Hebrew about his unit. The commander, a short, sinewy, and muscular man in his early twenties, with a deep, desert tan and hair cut so short his scalp glistened through, spoke of the competence of his three four-man tank units without arrogance, but with the quiet confidence of a battle-tested veteran. He was a career army man, he said, and while this was a relatively quiet area, he and his men stand ready to fight—and if necessary, die—to protect their country. His voice was somewhat flat and unemotional, as though he were telling us about a new hydraulic system for his tanks, or an advanced computer program that would speed up logistics support.

When he asked for questions, members of the Worcester group inquired about the difficulties of maintaining readiness in such a remote place, about negotiations with the Palestinians, base amenities, and leave policy.

The rabbi stood for his interrogatory. "In the States, we hear about the philosophy the army tries to instill in its soldiers. We hear that the concept from the Book of Deuteronomy—*tohar ha-neshek*, "purity of armaments"—are discussed during your training. I just wonder how that works in a practical way when you're at war?"

The commander looked off to the side, out the window, as the rabbi's words were translated. He was not especially religious himself, he answered in a single sentence, and looked back to the audience for the next question.

But no one spoke. The silence in the room was broken by a vehicle starting up on the street outside the briefing room where we were sitting.

"I think the lieutenant is a bit modest; I don't think he would want to say it directly," the translator finally said. *"Tohar ha-neshek* is not something soldiers talk about very much in their daily lives. The enemy must be watched; we can never relax and let our guard down. But I think you will find on this small base that the men and women under his command know that *tohar ha-neshek* is a target they must shoot for. Sometimes the target is hit, sometimes it is missed. Of course we must win at battle—that is first," he said decisively. "But if we are bullies or we use our guns and our tanks improperly, we have lost something."

He translated what he had said back to the tank commander, who shrugged noncommittally.

At the commander's bidding, and much to the delight of the children, one of his crews climbed into a tank. The vehicle rumbled off to give us a battlefield demonstration, complete with cannon fire, machine-gun strafing, and smoke screens. As the youthful tank corpsmen emerged from their vehicle, they welcomed the children aboard for a photo opportunity atop the tank.

Outside the base, and as we made our way farther south, we noticed tiny Arab and Bedouin settlements scattered through the bleak valleys and canyons. In contrast to the smallest Israeli villages—which appeared tidy, solid, and well tended, even here in the dangerous northern tier of Israel, along the eastern border with Syria and Jordan—the Arab and Bedouin settlements were largely squalid encampments. Rusting hulks of old buses served as homes, as did tents of burlap and filthy, wind-whipped plastic sheeting. Infants, often wearing no more than a grimy T-shirt, waved to us. Two children, wearing ragged shorts, stood before a group of a half-dozen mud and stucco huts with corrugated metal roofs. It was as good as housing got for the non-Jewish desert people we had seen.

And so, when we arrived at the plush Hotel Nirvana on the shore of the Dead Sea and were reminded that this was the night for our Bedouin-style dinner, some of the Worcester group hardly appeared enthusiastic. But they were pleased that they had made their sentiments known in Worcester months before about not extending an al fresco dinner into a full-fledged encampment. Regardless of what surprises dinner itself might hold, the night would find them at the lush, air-conditioned Nirvana, not on the rock-hard ground beneath a Bedouin tent.

We arrived at the desert outpost at Kfar Hanokdim just as the sun was disappearing behind the high mountains that rose above this saucer of flat, barren land near the Dead Sea. It is at this time of day that the desert gives up its last hot breath and a gentle cooling breeze washes over the land. As we disembarked from the bus, we were confronted by a rather inviting refreshment stand, with adjoining picnic tables, covered with a permanent awning. To our right was a huge tent, cobbled together from sheets of varying shades of a gray material, its sides heaving in response to the evening breeze. At the opening of the tent, two large flaps seemed to wave in welcome, bidding us to enter. Protecting the top of the tent were huge palm fronds.

It was certainly larger than any of the Bedouin tents we had seen in those wretched encampments, but similar in appearance, so some members of the group approached it warily. Once inside, they were happily surprised to find that the tent had been most comfortably appointed with covered foam mattresses, provided for our reclining. Hajai, our Israeli host and the owner of the place, detailed the rudiments of Bedouin hospitality, while an emaciated, chain-smoking Bedouin, who was probably in his mid-twenties but looked older, roasted coffee beans over an open fire. He then prepared coffee, sweetening it liberally with sugar, and passed around small cups of the thick, strong drink, a sort of desert espresso. He then quite adroitly baked an enormous pita on an inverted metal dome over the fire and, when it was finished, simply sailed it across the fire. It landed squarely in Marion Blumberg's lap. As if she did this every evening at dinner, Marion tore off a generous piece and passed it along. Huge platters of hummus and vegetables were brought to us and briskly passed. Forks were made available, but the human hand seemed a much better implement for eating in a reclining position and was almost universally employed. By the time roasted lamb and turkey—that Israeli staple—were served in the gentle light of propane lanterns, the Worcester group appeared to be every bit a desert people—eating with their hands, talking volubly about that day's trek.

After our Bedouin feast, we were ushered out a few hundred yards beyond the tent, where a half-dozen donkeys were lashed together on a long rope. Six camels sat on their haunches, lazily chewing their cud, eyeing the advance of a potential annoyance. Their smell reached us before we reached them, and some of the women screwed up their noses in protest. But everyone clambered on, assisted by another stick-thin Bedouin. A short distance into the desert we dismounted and traded animals for the return trip. A final soft drink or beer, and we headed for the bus.

So what kind of experience had this oft-debated evening eventually provided the group from Beth Israel? A sad-eyed young Bedouin, sitting cross-legged before his fire, exhibiting hospitality on command; lush appointments and too much food. An eager host who packaged a hermetically sealed slice of desert life for day-tripper consumption; the mangy, flea-infested camels and donkeys taking the brave adventurers a quarter-mile into the darkening desert. Judging by their comments on the trip back to Nirvana, our "desert experience," while enjoyable, seemed a bit contrived to a good number of the group. But for Rabbi Rosenbaum, who again fell silent on the noisy bus trip back to the hotel, it had been a quite different experience altogether.

"You could say there was something staged about it, but I forgot about that right away," he later told me. "We were in a tent, we were eating on the ground. I had the sense of a desert people and what it must have been like for them, cooking food, pitching a tent, making sure they had water in such a barren place. King David wanted to build God a temple and God said no, the tent is just fine. God didn't need to dwell in a fancy place; the tent was good enough for Him. I kept thinking about all our beautiful synagogues! All God wants is a tent, as long as He is there and His people are gathered around Him. And He *was* there that night; I felt that deeply. Deeply.

"That night reclaimed a big piece of our history for me. We were desert people, shepherds, nomads; we could pick up our tent and move and take not only our belongings, but our history with us. And out there in the desert, you are far more dependent on God. A lot more than when you're sitting in a posh dining room at the Sheraton Plaza. We try to escape this or try to shield ourselves from the harshness, but we are still a wandering people, we are still nomads. We still carry our history wherever we go, still so dependent on God.

"And if that camel ride was strange for me, how was it for Moses? This city boy, an Egyptian prince raised in a palace—he was a part of the popular culture of his time. Moses had to learn to be a shepherd before he could rescue his people from Egypt, because he needed to establish his roots. That ride provided a wonderful leap of the imagination for me. The Bible came alive out there! I'll never, never forget it."

By the time Rabbi Rosenbaum put his children to bed that night, he was exhausted. But he found himself equally exhilarated. In the darkness of their well-appointed and spacious room at the Nirvana, when he and Janine finally had a few minutes to talk, the rabbi relived, in hushed whispers, both the Bedouin outing and two other experiences within the past forty-eight hours that had etched themselves in his brain. The first was morning prayer at Meirot, and he told his wife once again of the strength, the majesty he felt standing with his people amidst those ancient stones. He had never before in his life quite felt that way saying those familiar prayers; he had never felt so certain of the power, the sureness of the faith that was such an integral part of his life. The second experience, he then told her, was the mere passing through Qiryat Shemonah and the rush of memories that overwhelmed him, reminding him of his unfulfilled dream of someday coming back to live in Israel for good. He said nothing, of course, of the young botanist.

By that time, Janine had begun to doze off. The rabbi was still wide awake and, much to his own surprise, he turned to his wife, laying beside him, and blurted out, "Why can't we live in Israel? What's standing in our way? Why can't we make *aliyah?*"

These startling questions quickly brought Janine to full consciousness. "We *could*, Jay; we could do it! Why not?"

A rush of reason quickly followed in the wake of the rabbi's emotional outburst. "But what would I do; what could I do here? How would I earn a living?"

"I don't care," Janine replied, beginning to cry. "I just want to come here and live. This is where we should be—Israel. Not Worcester, Massachusetts."

"*Shabbat*; we could really live like . . ."

". . . home, Jay, it could really be a home for us."

The rabbi suddenly became silent.

"Jay?"

"There's a big day tomorrow—Masada. Let's just sleep on it, honey." His wife soon fell asleep, but too much was coursing through the rabbi's mind for him to rest.

"*Aliyah*, it's always been there," he would later tell me. "But why did I say all that to Janine? I know how she feels about it. I guess I was testing my own feelings. I don't know; I just don't know.

"It's an easy way out of the American dilemma. In a way it's safe; I know my kids would grow up and marry Jewish. I've always said it and I still believe every Jew's true home is Israel. But I don't fit into an easy slot here; I'd have to start my life over again. I would be a nomad; I would be picking up my tent and setting it down in a new place. Yet it would be the ultimate Jewish experience.

"So, what stands in my way? Inconvenience and cowardice. Simple as that.

"As this trip evolved, I realized I was, in essence, asking these people who were with me to make the equivalent of *aliyah*, to become *shomer Shabbos*. I am asking them to overturn their lives. They—me—we're not prepared to do that, to overturn our lives. *Aliyah* is something I believe in. But I'm not acting on it. I just can't. Not yet, anyhow. But when will be the right time? Ever?"

Restless, the rabbi finally went to the window. Outside, the huge pool area was flooded with light; chaise longues and tables, their umbrellas folded for the night, sat in neat rows, ready for the next day's enjoyment. Beyond the fence surrounding this lush resort hotel lay the Dead Sea. Huge chunks of salt floated at the surface of the brackish water.

Moses had lived in luxury, insulated from the demands of this harsh land and the trials of its people. Eventually he had found that he could no longer stand his distance—he had to join his people and return to his own desert roots before he could truly fulfill his destiny. So too, centuries later, Jay Rosenbaum, a rabbi from Worcester, had been confronted—at the Disneyland-like Bedouin encampment at Kfar Hanokdim—with his own need to return to the source of Judaism if he was to live fully as a Jew.

19

Shortly after eight the next morning, as the group from Worcester waited their turn to board the cable car at Masada, the temperature had already soared into the breath-arresting nineties. There was little shade on the cable-car platform. An air-conditioned tourist shop beckoned nearby, but it and other amenities of the twentieth century would soon have to be left behind in order to begin a journey into the first century. On this holy mountaintop, all must stand as equals: none are offered escape, no immunity, no preferential treatment. In the distance, on the Snake Path that winds up the mountain—a massive, flat-topped volcanic outcropping rising above unremittingly barren desert—someone pointed out unusual activity. We blinked into the brilliant morning sun, squeezing the perspiration from our eyes that was already blurring our vision. At first, it appeared as nothing more than a colony of beige ants following an irregular crevice on the mountainside. On closer examination, we could make out that it was a single-file line of uniformed soldiers. They were not just marching in this astounding heat; they were running.

As we began our ascent, David explained with unvarnished pride that the soldiers had also run *up* the mountain the night before. At the completion of their basic training, all Israeli conscripts—with a rifle in one hand and a Bible in the other—recite an oath, pledging that "Masada will not fall a second time." Some commanders bring their units to the top of Masada to reinforce both the moment and the oath at a nighttime ceremony before a huge bonfire.

Once we reached the top, David began the story of Masada,

carved from the rock by Alexander Jannaeus and rebuilt by the Jewish King Herod in 35 B.C.E. It was to be an impregnable mountaintop fortress in the middle of the desert, a safe retreat should his subjects revolt or a powerful enemy appear. But it is not for Herod's efforts that Masada is so well known. Masada is immortalized in Jewish history because of the 967 zealots who, taking their last stand at the end of the Jewish revolt against the rule of Rome, committed mass suicide rather than be taken captive by the Romans who had laid siege to the fortress for two years. After Jerusalem, Masada is the most popular destination for Jewish visitors to Israel. It is venerated as a powerful symbol of Jewish survival.

David reviewed the horrors of Jewish slavery under the Romans and the obscene public spectacles of the amphitheaters to underscore why the people on Masada acted as they did. But this morning the guide's voice had a noticeably different quality. Unlike his other historical forays, David's five-minute opening treatise on Masada gradually unfolded as perhaps the most poignant and emotive of his extemporaneous soliloquies. "On Masada, those men and women said, 'We would rather die—die at our own hand—than be subject to people like that.' It is the message of Israel then. It is the message of Israel today. This mountaintop is soaked with our blood. This land is soaked with our blood, generations of blood. *Our* blood." His voice started to crack. "In Israel, we fight for something we believe in. It comes down to this: if nothing's worth dying for, then nothing's worth living for."

The wind on the mountaintop whispered along the stubby remains of once-stout walls, sending tiny swirls of dust to rise up and dance in the open spaces where marketplaces and courtyards once stood. Our group was uncommonly silent. No questions, no comments were forthcoming. Twice I saw the rabbi look at David as if he were about to speak, but he did not. Finally, one by one, we moved on, to look in on a New Jersey boy's bar mitzvah amidst the ruins of the oldest known synagogue in the world, to run hands along the rough stones, to peer down at the faint but unmistakable outline of the Roman encampments hard by the mountain's base.

I would later find that there was a subtext to both David's talk and the rabbi's self-imposed silence. This was not a moment of David's that the rabbi wanted to diminish in any way whatsoever, even though his own historical sense—as well as his current emotions—had brought him to other conclusions. Like most people the rabbi encountered in his work, David Leshnick presented one person on the surface (in David's case, cockily competent and somewhat arrogant), and another man within, one not so handily put together. After traveling together for a week, the rabbi had discovered that other man two evenings before at Ayelet Hashachar.

For once free of the constraints imposed on each of them by the rest of the group, they sat off in a corner of the lobby at the kibbutz resort and found themselves in an increasingly heated discussion about David's blatantly secular approach to Jewish history. After one of the rabbi's probing questions, the guide—in midsentence of his retort—had stopped short. His veneer of confidence suddenly dissolved; his face turned painfully sad. For once, he had nothing cynical, dismissive, or clever to say. He then confided to the rabbi that his life was in tatters when he came to Israel over ten years ago. He was out of a job, broke, his marriage a failure. *Aliyah* and Israel had given him the cause in life that had eluded him in the United States. Israel had little to do with Judaism for him; it had everything to do with giving his life meaning. He was a part of something far bigger than himself; he was a building block, not unlike those many anonymous stones in the Western Wall, or in the structures here on Masada. He had been an ordinary—and by American standards, unsuccessful—man. Here, he mattered.

Israel had indeed proved to be his promised land. He had remarried and had a child. He had never felt so fulfilled in all his life.

Once we descended from Masada on the cable car and were back aboard the bus, sufficient time had elapsed to make the rabbi's words not rejoinder, but commentary. He took the microphone in his hand. "I got to thinking about Solomon and Herod as we were walking around up on Masada," his words went out over the bus's public-address system. I noted a tone of pensiveness in his voice just then, as if he were not yet sure of exactly what he would say next. "Two great

Jewish kings, powerful rulers, great builders for sure. But were they great Jews? Not really. Herod was a real beast; building was more important than people. Solomon had a slew of pagan wives. The zealots at Masada were very brave, but they also slaughtered anybody who didn't go along with their view of Judaism.

"As we look out at this land Israel that surrounds us, we have to always remember it cuts two ways." His voice now seemed more sure, his cadence more regular; his pauses began to be for dramatic effect, and not in the hope that his thoughts would have time to jell. "God gave it to us as a sacred trust, but we have to keep our part of the bargain. It's not given in perpetuity; it's given to us in order for Jews to have a place to set an example for the world, a place to live a life of sanctity. A tough job, yes. But it's *our* job.

"So what happens when people stray from Judaism? Regardless of how Jewish they say they are, or how accomplished or powerful or wealthy they are, if they don't live the observant life and they leave the Torah behind, finding it inconvenient or irrelevant to their lives—sorry to report, folks, but they ultimately fail. It's the same thing that leads to the downfall of the Jewish people time and time again in history. They are driven into still another exile, somehow, someplace.

"We have just stood on Masada; we have been to Yad Vashem. It's confusing. When to fight, when not to fight, how to fight: these are different for each generation. What do you do about the popular culture, the pressures of the day, the enemy of the day—and there will always be one. Yochanan ben Zakkai in 70 C.E. knew that it was suicide to fight the Romans, so he asked to be allowed to establish just one yeshiva so that the teaching of the Torah could go on, even under those horrible circumstances. He was condemned as a traitor. But where are the Romans today? And where is the Torah? To die on Masada or to find a way? Jews throughout history were persecuted—and they always found a way to make a compromise, give up this, buy their freedom. Then came the Holocaust, and accommodation—which had worked for two thousand years—was exactly wrong. So modern Zionism says 'never again' to the Holocaust. 'We take our heroes from Masada. No accommodation!' Sure, we can take a lesson from Masada—a powerful lesson—but it can't be applied in every situation. You just can't say 'never again' and think you're the perfect Jew. Jewish life, Jewish choices always have been complex and always will be. The way for one historical period is not the way for every period.

"For most Jews around the world, no one is oppressing us now. There is no Titus or Vespasian, no Hitler." The rabbi's voice reached lower, to that pensive, more personal register—as if he were now speaking to them individually, in the privacy of his office. There was a wistfulness about him, almost as if he were wishing for a formidable adversary to appear so that he might himself have the opportunity to be tested and proven. "And especially in America, *we* have control over our lives. But what are we going to do with those lives? Maybe we are our own worst enemies. Do we pick and choose what is convenient or comfortable or romantic and discard the rest? Everyone has to answer that for himself, herself." His voice uncharacteristically began to trail off. "And so do I . . ."

Our bus sped along the highway. Signs alongside the road promised wonderful food, comfortable lodgings, and shopping delights just ahead. Beyond the signs, sheep and goats grazed on the arid hills, taking as their sustenance what could not be seen—or even imagined—from this vantage point. After an awkward pause, the rabbi concluded simply, "I just got to thinking up there on Masada; thanks for listening," and sat down. Silence enfolded the pilgrims from Worcester, and they were not about to fight its embrace. We headed farther north, back toward Jerusalem.

We had spent the past four days in a sort of Jewish fairyland, a place of bigger-than-life historical events and people. It was a Jewishness not at all difficult to be proud of. As the bus finally turned west, on our last leg and toward the holy city, many of the passengers dozed off. I flipped through my notepads, trying to sift the important moments from the transitory. I found my mind reaching back farther, to the first meeting for the trip in November in the Beth Israel library, and to the subsequent meetings for those who finally committed themselves. What great pride in Israel, past and present, had been proclaimed, time and time again, as they gathered. But, from the start, the rabbi could barely hear such words. It had never been his purpose to help people polish an amulet of ethnic pride. He was not looking for his people to return merely as cheerleaders for Israel's nationhood, willing supporters for Israel's needs. His expectations for them had always been higher—the highest, really. He wanted the trip to unsettle them, to challenge the comfort level at which they had been living their Judaism—and to force a dramatic life-style change.

Only the weeks and months ahead would show how the days in Israel had affected the other members of the group, but it was obvious that one pilgrim's comfort level had been already breached. Ironically, that pilgrim was Jay Rosenbaum. Israel had disoriented him. The architect of this grand experiment to revivify a midsized Massachusetts synagogue had been drawn into the vortex he had shaped and set in motion. Jay Rosenbaum had found that his outwardly exemplary and observant life—when placed within the larger template of life in the Promised Land—filled but one small corner.

The next morning, Jay and Janine Rosenbaum chatted warmly with their fellow travelers in the Sheraton Plaza's breakfast buffet line. They enthusiastically detailed the day's schedule: a visit to Absalom's Caves to see stalactites and stalagmites, an archaeological dig at Tel Maresha, a tour of the newly reconstructed Callenbarium, and an ancient olive press. They relived, with appropriate chuckles, some of the funnier moments of the trip thus far—the dude ranch ranked high— and seemed most interested in who bought what where and for how much. By looking at them standing there—plates in hand, smiles on their faces, children at their sides—no one could possibly know that these past days in Israel had inexplicably unleashed the pent-up emotions that Jay and Janine Rosenbaum have successfully contained for years.

"My life is good in the United States; that's the problem. I have no major complaints. It's so much tougher here; that's what I was thinking about," the rabbi would tell me later that morning while these thoughts were still fresh in his mind. "My kids would have to do military service. And me? There are plenty of unemployed Conserva-

tive rabbis here already. I know that shouldn't matter; I would be making a statement about Judaism by coming here. And it would send a
powerful message: 'Look, it's important enough to this guy Rosenbaum
that he'd bag a good job, pack up his family, and move over here.' I
know that. When Israel is strong, Judaism is strong.

"There's always the argument I can fall back on: 'Hey, look,
I'm doing my bit for Judaism in Worcester. What if every Conservative
rabbi moved to Israel; what would become of the American Jews?'
Frankly, it just doesn't stack up. I know that if I'm honest with myself,
I know that if every American Jew could go to Israel, they should. This
is really where we belong. The Jewish ideal is to live in a Jewish community. I don't have that in Worcester. I would have it here.

"Worcester. Worcester. I said I had no major problems at Beth
Israel. Then I'm told to take this trip as vacation time. How about that
for gratitude for a job well done?

"But my real problem is, once my rebellious years were over, I
never thought about being anything other than a congregational
rabbi. Then I see how Fran Alpert carved out a new career. I look at
David Leshnick and think maybe, *maybe* there could be a job here as
some kind of a spiritual tour guide. I could offer something with more
Judaic intensity. People who have been here a lot of times and want
the spiritual dimension—I could give them that, couldn't I?

"But let me get a grip. I'd be dishonest if I said that I'm going
back to the States to figure out a way to make *aliyah*. I'm not. But the
wheels are spinning. On the other hand, if I sign another contract at
Beth Israel, maybe they'll give me a sabbatical and I can come for a
year and then . . . I know. I'm rationalizing. I'm not willing to make the
sacrifice; I'm comfortable in America. I'm a coward, really. And it
makes me sad to hear myself say all this. It's such a paradox: if I wanted
to live my life as a truly religious Jew, it probably would mean leaving
the rabbinate.

"As for Janine, she'd do it in a minute. She's more of an Israeli
than I am."

Perhaps. Or perhaps what the woman standing in front of him
at the buffet table—trying to determine what flavor of yogurt Sho-

shanah, a finicky eater, might find appetizing—saw in Israel was as much about ecstasy (albeit a different version) as escape.

"It's not about religion for me, I admit it," Janine forthrightly began our conversation later. "I've been *shomer Shabbat* for a lot of my adult life. But it's not about God. I love those Hebrew prayers—they link my people for thousands of years and I don't want to lose that link. But I don't really pray. I love the traditions. But God? I have a problem with God. Where was this God during the Holocaust? I'm still asking that, after all these years. I should be able to get past that, but I can't. If Jay would make *aliyah*, it's for religious reasons. I just want to live my life with Jews, being a Jew, not living in the fishbowl I live in as a *rebbetzin*. I'm watched in everything I do. If we moved to Israel, I could be a free person again. It's tough to keep *Shabbos* at home; it's a chore. My kids are left out. What happens when they get to be teenagers? Will they be able to withstand the peer pressure?

"I've been crying my way through this trip, both in front of people and by myself; I know it. It's not because my ankle hurts or my arms ache. No, it's because every rock is precious to these people; they've worked so hard to make their country; they've put up with so much. I love that. I'm not for organized religion. I'm more *tachlis*, bottom line. I love Israel and what it stands for. I want to be here. Just let me do it! So I cry a lot here. I can't even do that at home—and believe me, it costs me to just smile and be noncommittal.

"In the end, I feel guilty, yes, perpetually guilty for not living in Israel. I'm not putting my mouth where my money is. Here, life for a Jew has meaning. In Worcester? I don't know if my life has any meaning there."

Another sumptuous breakfast was soon over, and the group from Beth Israel launched off on another day's activities. It was by now Friday, and the second *Shabbat* in Jerusalem was approaching, but Rabbi Rosenbaum was not about to attempt to gather a group for synagogue hopping or to mount a second communal picnic. Instead, the next morning he savored—selfishly—the last *Shabbat* in Israel by attending services at the Center for Conservative Judaism. Rabbi Yousef Green's sermon—in which he announced his retirement—dealt with knowing when to move on in life. As Jay and Janine Rosenbaum—on that Saturday morning just two anonymous congregants in the pews—sifted through the events and emotions of the past days, Rabbi Green's words provided still more seeds for their contemplation.

Our last days in Israel called for a series of visits without which no congregational tour would be complete. For these are the visits to places that the generosity of world Jewry has provided Israel, arranged so that Jews can see where their donations have gone, be properly thanked for them, and be shown that still more help is needed.

At the Mevasseret Zion Absorption Center on the outskirts of Jerusalem, a thousand Ethiopian *olim* were currently being housed, schooled, and acculturated for about six months, before they would be more fully integrated into Israeli life. On our visit there, Zipporah Libben—an American who made *aliyah* and was now active in resettlement work—told how immigration to Israel was unique in all the world. Any Jew, at any time, is guaranteed entry. As we sat in a modest classroom facing lines of shaky Hebrew letters on the blackboard, indicating a recent *olim*'s effort, she pointed out that ingathering embraced those from Worcester as well as those from other outposts—in Ethiopia and Russia, for instance. "Without new *olim*, Israel cannot go on. Come for a visit. Someday," she said warmly, allowing her eyes to wander over the people assembled before her, hoping that her own flame would in turn ignite others, "come to stay. Yes, you and you and you," she pointed to members of the group, who appeared a bit nervous to have been so chosen. "Then *you* will help build this young country. This is not the death of the Holocaust. This is birth; the strength of Israel is in our numbers."

Flanked by some Ethiopian coworkers, she told in graphic detail of the persecution of Ethiopian Jews and the heroic efforts of Operation Solomon. "They came in airplanes, but in reality it was *you*, through your generosity, who brought them here. You were at the airfield. You sustain them as they make the transition to Israeli society.

A million more potential *olim* are waiting in the pipeline. If only we had the money to bring them here, to build housing, to find them jobs . . ." The request was implicit.

Rabbi Rosenbaum chose to make his point audibly, biblically, and directly. He recalled the story of Joseph, whose brother Reuben found him trapped in a pit. At first, Reuben passed by; when he returned, Joseph was gone, sold into slavery. "The job is still not done," the rabbi said. "Many are still in the pit. A million wait to come. We can pass them by or we can take them on our shoulders. That costs. When the Federation comes knocking, remember, this is where your money goes. Help all you can."

Murray Rosenberg, sitting in the first row, his baseball cap tilted slightly, but nonetheless jauntily, over his right eye, readily nodded in agreement. It had been a wonderful trip for the Rosenbergs, full of the *nachas* the rabbi had hoped the older members of the group would experience. He and Freda were able to visit four families of cousins, including Jonas Musel in the kibbutz Bet Zera. Jonas was an Israeli pioneer, having settled here in the 1930s. He was pushing ninety and near death in a semicoma, but Murray and Freda were able to pay a final visit. When they went out to dinner with another set of kibbutznik cousins, Murray savored both the native-grown trout as well as the many men who wore pistols at their belts. And now, occupying a seat in an absorption center he had indirectly helped build, the same seat that an *olim* or a wealthy *macher* might occupy, his heart was swelling with Jewish pride.

"Israel! Civilization started here. All the great religions started here. I feel like I've come home," he enthusiastically told me later that morning. "I looked at those people at the absorption center. Ethiopians, but Jews! The ingathering. I had a part in this. But then we got herded back to the bus. The damn schedule! Why the hell didn't we stay longer, so we could have talked to some of them, see where they live? We never get a chance to schmooze with people. I love him, but this damned rabbi is always moving us along."

A half hour later, at the Hadassah Medical Center, the group was led past floor-to-ceiling engraved marble tablets listing the many major benefactors of this huge hospital complex. There was an almost religious feeling in this hallway, as if holy words had been inscribed here for the pilgrim's benefit. Eyes scanned the long lists to see if a familiar name could be spotted. Congregation Beth Israel in Worcester was certainly not listed in this philanthropic pantheon; nonetheless, the synagogue women's group sends its annual check. At times, it is substantial; this past year, after the Russian wedding, rather modest.

We were eventually led into the hospital synagogue where Marc Chagall's twelve stained-glass windows—depictions of Jacob blessing his sons and Moses blessing the tribes of Israel—are the jewels in the crowned, circular ceiling. Brilliant sunlight broadcast beams of vivid colors onto our upturned faces. Standing in our midst, Janine Rosenbaum had tears streaming shamelessly down her face.

Onto the bus, off the bus. We drove to an expanse of otherwise barren ground near Independence Park and bought tiny tree seedlings to plant, in order to leave some green legacy of our visit. The ground is pathetically dry and rocky, and many of the Worcester group wondered among themselves if their little gift would survive, but no one registered an open complaint.

At the Israel Museum complex, we filed into the Shrine of the Book—a dramatic white structure, shaped like a lid of the urns that were found in caves near Qumran—to see fragments of the Dead Sea Scrolls that the urns had protected for centuries. Regardless of the stunning historical importance of these scraps of aged, brownish parchment, it was obvious that the children were especially played out by our long days and many quick stops. The rabbi cut his own visit short to the Shrine of the Book to take Shoshanah and David to a sandbox in the playground near the refreshment stand.

David looked up from his play, the fair skin on his full, freckled cheeks flushed despite frequent applications of sunblock. "Daddy, why can't we just live here?"

Jay Rosenbaum took a bite from his ice-cream bar and stared at his son. "I know, David, I know," he said, nodding with a somewhat generic agreement.

"*What* do you know?" replied his son, Talmudic enough not to let a nonanswer serve for a legitimate question.

Rabbi Rosenbaum just smiled weakly in return.

20

With the Beth Israel congregational trip drawing to a close, the activities scheduled for the final two days were limited to allow ample time for shopping, packing, and general decompression from what had been, except for *Shabbat,* a forced march through the land. Although much of the news that reaches America about life in Israel centers on random or calculated acts of violence, the group from Worcester had experienced nothing more threatening than a few unwelcoming stares on walks through the Souk and other Arab areas in the Old City—as well as in Mea Shearim, where the ultra-Orthodox live. (There, the pilgrims from Worcester, clad in their comfortable trekking clothes, had come upon a huge banner spanning Hanevi'im Street, reading "Passig With Immodes Dress Is Strickl Fopbidden.") The only assaults suffered had been the self-inflicted ones on pocketbooks and wallets, the result of badly struck bargains or inflated prices at tourist shops. And, of course, an occasional case of intestinal maladjustment manifested itself, but nothing that lingered longer than a few days.

Beyond such transitory difficulties, however, these past two weeks had also unleashed forces sufficient to produce severe emotional whiplash in even the most steady temperament. The people from Worcester had been tended to in luxurious comfort by attentive waiters and hoteliers, slept in air-conditioned rooms, and been whisked from place to place in a bus devoted exclusively to their needs and comfort—only to be starkly confronted with their religious heritage, whether in the form of visits to places central to the drama of Judaism

(the wall, Yad Vashem, and Meirot among them) or with visceral ven-
tures in role playing, such as the Bedouin dinner.

Although Rabbi Rosenbaum had been tactful for the most part
in delivering his ad hoc lectures, there had been the constant implication that this place or that experience should mean *something more*.
And always the implied question: If you have been moved or touched,
what are you going to do with that inspiration? Or, if you have *not*
been moved, why not? The people from Beth Israel had been invited
time and again by their rabbi to wrestle with God in this land so dear
to Him. If some found it difficult to come to grips with the challenge,
others appeared to have been joyfully overpowered by it. The rabbi
hoped that on their last night together, they might—finally and publicly—present to the group (and perhaps themselves) the tally of the
Israel experience.

Our last evening together had been carefully constructed by
the rabbi, with Channy Greenberg's assistance, to provide the group
with a comfortable setting and ample opportunity—with two weeks of
Israel at an end and a lifetime ahead—to consider these questions and
share their impressions of Israel.

We arrived early on Tuesday evening at the Misadonet Kurdish restaurant, on the outskirts of Jerusalem and en route to the airport
(our flight was to leave at one in the morning). While there was still
sufficient light, we gathered on the high steps of the restaurant for a
group picture. Charlie Mills—ever the clown—lay prostrate on the
ground, looking like he was about to do a push-up. Then we were
seated on the restaurant's patio at a long L-shaped table under a canvas
canopy. Rabbi Rosenbaum seemed pleased with the cozy atmosphere
of the place.

Unfortunately, as with so many of his well-intentioned plans
for the trip, it was soon evident that this one was not working out as he
had hoped. Misadonet Kurdish restaurant proved a less than ideal
place for reflection. Traffic whizzed by on the street, only yards from
where we were sitting, creating a constant din; the children became
restless as the meal took an inordinate amount of time to be served. Jay
Rosenbaum looked at his watch, but otherwise waited patiently for the

meal to be over. At dessert time, waiters brought out still more trays, displaying a vast array of delicacies. Coffee followed. There were conversations—shouted for the most part because of the street noise—going all about him, but Rabbi Rosenbaum quietly sipped on his coffee. He looked out over the gathering, waiting for the right moment. Even when Shoshanah tugged at his sleeve, she had to do it a second, then a third time to get his attention. Her father's mind was wandering over a vast tableau indeed—from the streets of Worcester to those of Israel.

"How many times on this trip have I said it—how many times have these people said it—'Life is good in the States, but it's so hard to be a Jew,' " he told me later. "And look, if I feel this way—and I'm a professional religious man—how is it for these people, ordinary Jews? They are good people, they cared enough about their Jewishness, their families, to come to Israel—and with a rabbi no less! But where is the joy of being a Jew in America? It's such a job there. Here? I could see the joy of being Jewish, all the time. I could see it like I never saw it in Worcester.

"Listen, I know what they go through. When you live in a small Jewish community like Worcester, you live in a diaspora within the Diaspora. Sometimes when I'm walking down the street I'd like to take off my kippah and fling it away, and fade into the woodwork. The separateness I have to live with; it just gets to me sometimes. Life is a lot harder here, but it's so easy to be a Jew.

"But I can't do it. I can't make that step. I'm a logical man; I don't do things impetuously. Aliyah. What a crazy thought, what a wonderful thought. But somewhere in those twenty years since I left here, vowing to come right back and stay, I came to a point where I can't see doing anything different. I found a niche. Yet I wonder, what would have happened if I would have stayed here a second year back then? Who knows? Looking back, I mourn the road not traveled."

The last tray of desserts was finally removed and the rabbi rose to his feet. "Some of you have told me privately of something that specially touched you on this trip," he began, his words growing louder as he saw some of the people at the back straining to hear him. "And I'm sure if the hotel walls had ears, they could tell stories, too." There was a ripple of laughter. "Good stories, happy stories, of course. Complaints? Us?" the rabbi continued, grinning. "Now, let's go around the table; it might be one special thing; it might be a larger feeling. Whatever."

The rabbi looked to his immediate right. "Carl, you're first."

"Me? Because I've been so quiet on this trip, right?" the voluble lawyer replied. Seated next to him, Debbie Aframe fixed an apprehensive look on her husband, waiting to hear what he would say. She is an attractive, trim woman with brown, curly hair. Tonight she appeared pensive, not her usual outgoing self. Equally uncharacteristically, her husband took a long moment to collect his thoughts.

"He would come in a minute," Debbie had told me earlier. "I know it. Whew! The conflict we had this trip. It's so wonderful to be here, to give our kids a totally Jewish experience, but Israel is a real point of tension between us. I could never do this; I could never live here. I'm too mainstream American. This might be right for Carl, but it's very foreign to me."

Finally, Carl was ready. "So many things; where do I start? Just waking up in my hotel room and realizing it's *Shabbat,* and this was Israel where *Shabbat* means something. This wonderful feeling came over me. I had always heard that *Shabbat* was supposed to be a precursor of heaven. Precursor? I felt I was in heaven already. That's what Israel meant to me. . . ." The words Carl Aframe carefully selected to impart to his fellow travelers—as well as to his wife and two children—floated out over the gathering. But, of course, while the members of the group were ready, even eager, to be far more forthcoming about the religious dimension of the trip than they ever could have been in the tortuous organization meetings in Worcester, there were still other thoughts, too personal to share at this, the last supper. Carl's inner thoughts, for instance.

"Debbie converted after we were married seven years," Carl would tell me later. "A Reform rabbi did the ceremony, but none of my family came. That hurt; her reception into the so-called Jewish community. My father's father was a rabbi, but my parents—although they were kosher—were basically nonobservant. But they wouldn't come because I married this *shiksa*. But I want it; I want Judaism. I guess I'm a throwback, but it's real and it's deep. This is the place for me, I just know it now. The States? Look, I was president of B'nai B'rith in Worcester and yes, we'd say our *b'rachot* at breakfast meetings. Maybe somebody would put their hand on their head; not a *kippah* in sight. Beth Israel? I don't feel that congregation is seriously interested in religion. It's a cultural, social thing for them. That just doesn't sustain Judaism for me. By coming to Israel to live, I could do more than talk the talk about being an observant Jew. I could walk the walk. Carl Aframe: a walking contradiction—I know it. What am I going to do?"

Debbie Aframe, whose own transition from Methodism to Judaism had been neither easy nor comfortable, was next to speak at the Kurdish restaurant. "Carl has most of the words for this family," she said, laying her hand tenderly on her husband's shoulder. "All I can say is that it's really easy to be a Jew here. And it's fun!"

When the circle of memories arrived at Steve Sosnoff, he began with a rejoinder. "I wasn't all that religious when I came," he said, and after a brief hesitation continued, "and nothing much has changed. But what I remember is *Havdalah* on the roof of our hotel at the end of the second *Shabbos*. That was a really great feeling; you could pray out in the open and nobody really cared." Ready to sit down, he added an afterthought. "We stumbled a bit at the beginning, but you, Rabbi, and you, Charlie—you two pulled us together. The things we learned and did outnumbered the aggravations one hundred to one." Applause drowned out the street noise. The clapping continued until the rabbi stood and put his hands over his head, acknowledging their praise and begging them to stop.

"Funny, it wasn't the wall or places like that that got to me," Steve would tell me later. "At the wall, you kind of have to be religious and reverent. But there on the roof we were just regular people at a hotel and we had come together to *pray*. That's amazing to me. I couldn't do that in Paxton, Massachusetts. We were just beginning to peak at that supper, it was sad it had to come to an end. Did all those good feelings happen because we had a common cause? A lot of energy was expended just trying to get along, to keep yourself open to what was going on. You could feel it. It certainly wasn't a group outing to Cape Cod! But it leaves me just as confused about my religious beliefs. I'm not going to change my life. Saturdays will still probably find me at a soccer game with my kids instead of in *shul*. But I'll always think about what we did those two weeks in Israel—always."

As Steve sat down, his wife, Denise, told the group she was so charmed by the lilt of Hebrew and ashamed of her scant knowledge of the language that she was vowing then and there to study Hebrew upon her return to Worcester. Rhonda Mills said that the trip had guaranteed that her girls would be coming back for a longer stay during their high-school years. The Aframes, Sosnoffs, and Fixlers would be doing the same. "Everybody had their doubts about how this trip was going to work," Rhonda continued, her eyes passing over the group. She appeared on the verge of tears. "I couldn't imagine better people to go with."

Charlie Mills was next. A man given to a continual jocular manner—tasteless, ill-timed, and inappropriate comments included—Charlie wore a serious look on his face as he pushed back his chair. Such an uncharacteristic demeanor often proved but a prelude to humor, but this was not the case tonight. "When you're a doctor," he said, "people come to you with problems, and they react in different ways. In Israel you see people who aren't burdened by their problems. They taught me an important lesson, something that I'll be taking back to America, about how to deal with what faces me in life. These are remarkable people, the Israelis, and I wanted to come here to be with them. I have, and now sadly I'll be going home, but . . ."

Rhonda Mills took a deep breath and looked up at her husband. Her hands were folded calmly on the table in front of her, belying her nervousness. Would Charlie say what was really on his mind, what they had talked—and argued—about almost from day one of the trip? Actually, Charlie's mind just then was wandering far afield from *aliyah*, which he knew was a subject Rhonda wanted to hear nothing more about.

"It was nice to be along with these people, and the trip worked out remarkably well—and, believe me, I had my misgivings—that's what I was thinking as I stood there," he later told me. "I was happy about that, but sad it was coming to an end. And after that? I was going back to my own spiritual struggle by myself. I guess everybody has to do the same thing.

"I give Jay a lot of credit. There was a lot of tension on the trip, especially early on, and he really made it a wonderful experience for everybody, even with that jerk of a guide we had. But who I really feel for is Janine. If it was work for Jay, for her it was double. You can tell that she just doesn't have this in her heart. I lived in a rectory, I know the difference. My mother bought on. Janine hasn't.

"I would like to say I know Jay better after this trip, but I really don't. Maybe he chose this profession because it's prescribed. He has a preselected role, so it doesn't put a demand on his real personality—whatever that might be. And Charlie Mills? I go back to my little group at BI—because that's the way everybody wants it there, and who am I to fight that? I go back to Worcester and try to figure out a way to get back to Israel. Forever? No, but for a good, long time."

The Rosenbergs and the Silvermans explained that seeing their relatives was their high point. Max Gould begged forgiveness for his occasional grumpiness: "It was because I missed my wife of fifty-two years, who wasn't with me. We're coming back together!" The older members talked of the warm feelings of togetherness within the group and their thankfulness for being able to visit so many places central to their Jewish heritage, offering uniform praise (and not a word of complaint) for the tour architects and for all their traveling companions. Marion Blumberg effused that she was fulfilled the first day, "just getting off the plane and setting foot in the Holy Land; and on top of that, I got a great Israeli tan!" The inner murmurings of Lillian Silverman—sitting there with a huge grin, her normally well-coiffed ash blond hair somewhat wilted by the experience and the lack of the weekly attention of her favorite Worcester hairdresser—might speak to the experience of some of the other seniors.

"How can I say it?" she told me later. "I just had this incredible feeling of pride in being in Israel—and, at the same time, an incredible humility. What a great country; what great people Jews are. How blessed we are. This will probably be Ben's and my last trip, but look, we're healthy; we could walk around. There was nothing we couldn't do with the group. But I was so sad to be leaving. Be sure I'll do my bit for all the Jewish causes when I get home. And I'll keep on praying that being Jewish won't end with me. Someday, somehow, my grand-children will be here."

Janine, fighting back tears, thanked the group for "schlepping my children and helping me out as much as you did."

Mark Cutler, the psychiatrist—a man in the profession of elic-iting feelings, yet not one to readily display his own—looked directly at the rabbi. "I've been on a half-dozen UJA missions," he said, adding emphatically, "this was *not* a UJA trip. Those were about the financial needs of Israel; this was different, this was about the spiritual needs of Jews. Like me. And I'll never forget *Havdalah* at the Western Wall. Never. You, Rabbi Rosenbaum, gave this trip a deeper meaning for my family and myself, and I thank you for that."

The children listed their high moments, which ranged from "praying at that synagogue"—Meirot—to "the great water slide at Sachne," the desert oasis. They liked the donkey and camel rides, but generally found the animals smelly. "I liked just being in a Jewish place," said Michelle Cutler. "On a scale of ten, it was a ten and a half," Ruth Aframe shouted. Aliza Mills drew herself up to her full four feet, six inches. "I had a dream about putting my prayer in the Western Wall," she said, "and now I've really done it. Israel is now part of me and I'm part of it."

Charlie Mills, never a man to cry, nonetheless had to swallow hard because of the lump in his throat.

Because of some shifting that had gone on during the forty-five min-utes it had taken to go around the table, Rabbi Rosenbaum was not the last, but the next to last speaker. "I guess the best part for me was that we became a *mishpocha*, a family. I stand here a bit overwhelmed by the experience. For once, believe it or not, I'm at a loss for words." He gazed about, at those he had gathered, led, and would now see dispersed. His face was gleaming in the pale light. "As for high points, there were so many; I need some distance to sort them out. But don't worry! You'll be hearing about them for months in my sermons."

Howie Fixler, who cannot escape that wonderful little-boy look about him when he has discovered something new, admitted that "what comes out of my mouth is not necessarily what's in my heart." And he said no more.

"We miss you already; we'll feel lonely," the rabbi said, unable to resist a closing word. "We were a microcosm—oh, oh, I say that all the time—well, we *are* a microcosm of the Jewish people; we are a pain in the neck but we love each other. In spite of roadblocks and detours, the ancient Jews somehow made it to the Promised Land—and with God's help, so did we. Now, have a safe journey going back."

The Rosenbaums were not traveling back to the United States with the group. The rabbi's nephew from Newton, Massachusetts, was to have his bar mitzvah at the Western Wall the following Monday morning, and the Rosenbaums would return the day after. And so, with a round of hugs and tears, we boarded the "Rabbi Rosenbaum" bus for the last time. The rabbi, Janine, and their children waved as we headed for Ben-Gurion Airport.

The return flight was an uneventful, quiet flight west through the elongated night. We arrived at Kennedy International Airport shortly before sunrise and were directed to a waiting room for the connecting flight to Boston. An Orthodox Jew, counting only six black-hatted *landsmen* in addition to himself for a morning *minyan*, scanned the room, his eyes requesting three more. Howie and his father-in-law, Eli Freeman, Mark, Murray, and Carl readily joined the seven, as though praying in an airport waiting room was something they did routinely. Below still another Exit sign, the men huddled with *tallitot* covering their shoulders, *tefillin* upon forehead and arm, and *kippot* upon their heads—appurtenances of Jewish ritual that were not in evidence minutes ago, and which would again be lost to public scrutiny once the obligation of this *Shacharit* had been honored.

On board the American Airlines flight to Boston, the chirpy voices and solicitous queries of the flight attendants proved quite a change from their El Al counterparts, for whom terrorists and bombs rank higher on the list of concerns than enough pillows or the right brand of diet soda. Below us we could see the sandy Atlantic coastline, a few forlorn lighthouses, and finally, with the sun glistening off the glassy surface of Boston Harbor, our destination, Logan International Airport. We were soon through customs and found the same small yellow school bus that had delivered us here fourteen days before. It was waiting outside at exactly the right exit, and precisely on time—a welcoming sight to weary transatlantic travelers. No complaints on this leg of the journey were registered about our humble means of conveyance; in fact, a quick collection was taken up to give the driver a tip.

As we lumbered along the Massachusetts Turnpike, there was some scattered conversation on the bus. But, I found, most people were silently looking out the windows, trying to get their bearings as they faced toward Worcester, with Israel now decidedly behind them. Here they were, back in America, their part of America, where plants, trees, even weeds grow lush and effortlessly but where—as they have all said—being a Jew is anything but effortless. The scenery outside the bus windows was so unlike the landscape they had seen for the past two weeks in Israel—Israel of the barren, unforgiving terrain where, despite everything, Jewishness thrives.

The bus exited the Mass Pike at Route 290, passed the regal, white-columned grand churches of downtown Worcester, and turned onto Salisbury Street. In a few minutes, we were at Beth Israel, set back from mainstream American life on Jamesbury Drive.

I had left my car in the rabbi's driveway, and when I went to retrieve it, for some reason I walked into his backyard. There, in the middle of the lawn, was the small patch of a garden he had mentioned in his last *Shabbat* sermon. The tomatoes, peppers, lettuce, and zucchini plants the rabbi had planted on the eve of the Israel trip had thrived during the past two weeks. Obviously not anticipating such astounding growth in what proved to be a fecund season, Rabbi Rosenbaum had placed them much too close together. Still in their adolescence, they were crowding one another, reaching for the sun.

The rabbi would have to learn about such things, I thought. He would have to make allowances for those times when unpromising small plants finally decide to grow.

21

The young customs agent looked up from the declaration form into the eyes of Janine Rosenbaum. "Welcome home," he said, somewhat routinely. She burst into tears.

After this emotional reentry to America the following Tuesday, the Rosenbaums and the other passengers from the El Al flight continued on into JFK's cavernous main international arrivals terminal. A once mighty river of *kippot*—formed as hundreds of El Al passengers made their way from the gate—flowed out into this gulf of Americans and foreign visitors and was quickly assimilated in a throng of thousands. A babel of different tongues drowned out their once distinctive and unified voice.

There were more immediate concerns for the Rosenbaums than being strangers in their homeland. Where to get something to eat? For the last three weeks, kosher food abounded. Now this. The rabbi scanned the offerings of a small cafeteria and picked out boxes of cereal for his family. Welcome home indeed.

The bar mitzvah of their nephew at the Kotel, as the Western Wall is popularly known, had provided still another memorable Israel experience, as had the last evening in Jerusalem. The Rosenbaums had gone to the apartment of Bennie and Suzanne Hefetz, who live not far from Fran Alpert in the Jewish Quarter of the Old City. Suzanne is a Seattle friend of Janine's; Bennie is in the jewelry business. After going to live in Israel and returning to the States a number of times, they finally made *aliyah* seven years ago.

It had been a fantastic evening, where English and Hebrew

mixed as easily as honey in hot tea, an evening where the vagaries of
Israeli life and politics dominated at least one conversation, and sometimes two, simultaneously. The Hefetzes pulled out a photo album;
now they could howl with laughter at the sight of their three-year-old
in a gas mask, a constant companion during the Gulf War, when it was
feared that Iraqi SCUD missiles aimed at Israel carried chemical war-
heads. They described their life as "absolutely wonderful and absolutely exhausting," living as they did with three small children in a
tiny apartment within a walled city where anti-Jewish hatred could
manifest itself at any time, in a young nation that has fought five major
wars in its forty-four-year history and that constantly struggles to
maintain a fragile power balance within the volatile Middle East.

After dinner, the two couples and their children took a stroll.
There, not more than a few minutes from their front door, which
opens onto Shone Halakhot—a cobblestone street first paved centuries before by the Turks—they rounded a corner, climbed a short set of
stairs, and looked down. Before them, brilliantly illuminated at night,
was the Western Wall.

It left the rabbi breathless and served as still another powerful
reminder of what life in Israel could hold. He could not get that sight
out of his mind in the few hours left in Israel. The wall and other images of the trip kept roiling about in his mind as he lapsed in and out of
a fitful sleep on the return flight. Accompanying those majestic memories was the continuing, gnawing thought: *if* he would allow himself
to think seriously about a life in Israel, what could he do there? He had
no good answer.

But this was a theoretical dilemma. When the rabbi returned
to Congregation Beth Israel on that Thursday morning, there was
nothing theoretical at all about what he would do in Worcester, Massachusetts. There was a sermon to prepare for *Shabbat* two days hence;
a full stack of telephone messages to return; sick congregants to visit;
colleagues to thank for filling in for him; a fall schedule to prepare; a
pile of correspondence to answer.

After he completed a phone call at midmorning, Rabbi Rosenbaum sat quietly at his desk for a few moments. From the look on his

face, it was as if he were disoriented and trying to regain his bearings, for what he was doing was at once so familiar and yet so foreign to him now. He swiveled his chair and looked back over his shoulder. There, through his partially opened venetian blinds, was the nursery-school playground. Brightly colored equipment—swings, climbing toys, a tee-ter-totter, a playhouse—were spread about the verdant inner court-yard. The paradox of this American tableau—when set against what he had looked upon just days before through windows in Jerusalem—did not escape him.

The intercom buzzer brusquely ended his reverie. The rabbi in-stinctively reached for the phone. It was Dr. Manouch Darvish, who wanted to see him. Because of his limited time before he was to leave on vacation, the rabbi was trying to schedule only the most urgent of appointments. But when his synagogue president calls, the rabbi, of course, must say yes.

After a welcome back that Rabbi Rosenbaum found noticeably truncated—lasting as it did some twenty seconds—Dr. Darvish said that some members of the board would like to meet privately with him to discuss "some matters of concern."

"Like?"

"This is not me, Jay," Dr. Darvish replied quickly, sensing an uncharacteristic tone of irritation in the rabbi's voice. "Some people are talking and when that happens it's better to get it on the table."

"This whole business of vacation time?"

"That's part of it, but let's get everybody together. We all think you're doing a terrific—"

Rabbi Rosenbaum cut off any further bromides. "I didn't ex-pect fanfare when I came back, but . . ." He held his counsel.

"Tuesday night? Earle Halsband's house?"

A combination of overstimulation, exhaustion, and a profusion of of-fice duties precluded his usual, careful preparation of a *Shabbos* sermon, so when Jay Rosenbaum approached the lectern that Saturday morn-ing, all he had to guide him were three pages of random, scribbled notes. Even if it had been expected that the rabbi would bring back

invaluable insights from the congregational trip to Israel, the expecta-
tion was not sufficient impetus for members of Beth Israel to give up
this balmy July morning to be with him. Scattered about the sanctuary
were fewer than one hundred people—no more and no less than the
average summer turnout. Carl Aframe was present, as was Marion
Blumberg and Murray Rosenberg, *Shabbat* regulars; Freda Rosenberg,
who rarely came for the weekly service, was also there.

The first part of Rabbi Rosenbaum's sermon was largely anec-
dotal. He described the splendor of morning prayer at Meirot and the
beauty of *Havdalah* at the Western Wall, of the Bedouin encampment
and planting a tree to leave a green legacy. He told of the Ethiopian
olim he saw at the absorption center, still in their native garb, and recalled a proud, fully integrated young Ethiopian in army fatigues striding along Ben Yehuda Street in the company of his fellow Jewish
soldiers. Israel was a country with a family feeling, he said with affection, and he told of an elderly man offering to take Shoshanah onto his
lap on a crowded bus. The rabbi had readily agreed, something he
would never think of doing in America.

He talked about the extraordinariness of everyday life in Israel,
where just going out for groceries was a trip into history. And he
pointed out that while living with so much history added meaning to
life, it could also be draining. "In America," the rabbi quoted Bennie
Hefetz, "the ordinary person lives on Oak Street. Here you live on
Nachmanides Street. Everything here has meaning; even your address.
There is no such thing as an 'ordinary' Jew in Israel; it's just impossible.
Everything is personal here. And sometimes it just wears you out.

"Outside the airport on our first day, our guide pointed to a
field," the rabbi went on, now moving through his second page of
notes. "It looked like an ordinary field. But then we were told that it
was the very field where Joshua commanded the sun to stand still.
Every day was like that for us in Israel. Almost every hour had something, and my head is still spinning, trying to sort out what we saw and
learned and felt."

After reciting a list of felicitous moments, of the excitement of
gazing upon the Western Wall, of standing in the house of a temple

high priest and atop Masada, the rabbi hesitated. After delivering hundreds upon hundreds of sermons, he knew when he was rambling and unfocused, when there was no energy behind his words. He drew a deep breath.

"But, there is another Israel, and I have to tell you about that one, too. As wonderful a country that Israel is—and it is—it is certainly not perfect." Rabbi Rosenbaum underscored his point by telling of an incident at Ramat Rachel, the lovely, family-oriented kibbutz south of Jerusalem where he and his family spent their additional week. "I went to the reception desk as *Shabbat* was approaching. I wanted to know where their synagogue was, so I could attend services with members of the kibbutz. The woman behind the desk looked at me a little strangely and handed me a key. I looked down at it, puzzled. 'It's for our synagogue; nobody else asked for it.' There were hundreds of people in that kibbutz. Jews. In Israel. Israel is a source of pride to us all, but if it is only the pride of being a Jewish state, there is something missing. What about its religious future? We worry about our religious future here in America; it is no different over there.

"At times, we didn't think we would have enough people for this trip. And," the rabbi smiled broadly, "even on the trip we had some difficult moments. But I think everyone who went will agree it was a great time. The old, the young—the young taking care of the even younger. We did things that would be classified as religious, and we rafted down the Jordan River—and we went to, of all things, a Jewish dude ranch! And we had a great time there. We were a community. And I hope that sense of community is something we can bring back to you."

When we talked not long after the service, Rabbi Rosenbaum told me that he had found the first *Shabbos* sermon after his return—putting aside his own fatigue and scant preparation—unexpectedly wrenching.

"Standing here, looking out at them, I knew how much I missed Israel already," he said. "A feeling of incredible sadness came over me. Almost a depression. We had had a very special experience together, but I wasn't able to put all the pieces together. It was too fresh in my mind and I couldn't narrow down what had happened. What I wanted to do in that sermon was share my enthusiasm—which I was probably too tired to do—and my warmth for this group. We came so far from that first meeting last year, so far from the complaining that marked the first day.

"Moreover, I had been exposed to something I thought I knew so much about—but I learned so much more about Judaism, about being a Jew, about Israel. They did too. It was worth all the trouble. Now comes the big question: where are we all going from here? Who knows? Who knows?"

The rabbi had one more week in Worcester before he and his family left for their planned three weeks with Janine's parents in Seattle. This was the part of the summer treasured and anticipated by Janine—but strangely, it also has always had a bittersweet quality for her. For three weeks, she would have her husband to herself, without phone calls, meetings, and long days at the office. Their children would have the full-time attention of both parents. But, upon their return, as Janine told me with a note of resignation in her voice, "I lose him." Each year, the Jewish High Holy Days of Rosh Hashanah and Yom Kippur require an enormous amount of work and preparation for sermons that are, for many of the Jews of Beth Israel, the only formal Judaic instruction they will receive all year. The rabbi must make the best use possible of his annual window of opportunity. Also, the beginning of another synagogue year demands a tremendous effort, as day-school and after-school programs begin and the various boards and service groups are revived. New and innovative approaches must be sought, both to entice new people to come to BI and to move peripheral members toward a more intensely Jewish life. The rabbi is looked to as the source of inspiration and energy for it all.

And so, as the rabbi sat down with members of his board of directors on a Tuesday night in mid-July—a week after his return—he was a man between worlds, still savoring the wonderful days in Israel, while anticipating the time in Seattle with his wife and family as well as the promise of the days that lay beyond. Yet he knew he must also be very much present in Worcester. A group of synagogue leaders do not casually ask to see their rabbi privately.

In the rabbi's opinion, the men who had gathered—among them Dr. Darvish, Earle Halsband, David Finegold, and Barry Aframe (Carl's cousin)—were not synagogue troublemakers or unsatisfiable gadflies, but the solid backbone of his congregation. After another abbreviated welcome back, they quickly entreated Rabbi Rosenbaum "not to take this the wrong way." They emphasized that they continued to be more than pleased with his performance on all fronts, but that, again, "some people are talking."

The rabbi sat back in his chair to hear what "some people" were saying.

First was the issue of congregation dues. The men before him had heard that the rabbi was excusing certain people from paying their dues. Such arbitrary benevolence made efforts to extract dues from the recalcitrant more difficult, casting the finance committee as tough and unfeeling, while the rabbi was commonly being portrayed as a "soft touch."

The rabbi explained that yes, he did sometimes advocate for people he knew were having financial difficulties, but that no, he did not categorically allow such dispensations, leaving such matters to the synagogue's executive director and the finance committee.

The second issue the men wanted to discuss concerned a newly arrived Russian couple, Vladimir and Olga Kotlowitz* and their son, Yuri, whom the rabbi had been preparing for his bar mitzvah. The Kotlowitzes had not paid their dues. Without paying dues—at least some token amount—the delegation maintained that they should not receive the services of the synagogue.

"I thought we were trying to make it easy for the Russians to be a part of BI, but let me take a look into it," the rabbi told them. The rabbi had answered their questions concerning these two matters in a calm voice. He knew the main reason for the meeting, and that issue had yet to be raised.

Restating that his performance as their rabbi was absolutely exemplary, and repeating that he should not "take this the wrong way," the men next addressed the issue of the Israel trip. They had not understood it to be a congregational trip. Beth Israel was facing another deficit year and, if anything, the financial condition of the synagogue continued to worsen. The rabbi would be away for a good part of the summer; especially now, his presence was crucial. Could he count the trip to Israel in part or in its entirety as vacation time?

Whatever surface calm with which Jay Rosenbaum had masked his feelings dissolved.

"I thought this was all settled before I left," the rabbi answered, his stare and deadpan intonation conveying a deep-seated anger. "I work six days a week routinely, sometimes seven. I am available twenty-four hours a day when I'm here. Are you telling me that you're not getting your money's worth? Do you know what it takes to put a trip like that together. Do you?" He awaited an answer to the rhetorical questions. "My father was a rabbi for twenty-five years and he never did it. Most rabbis wouldn't think of it! Far from cheating you, you get far more than you pay for. I didn't expect a parade in my honor when I got back, but this really hurts. I'm disappointed more than I can tell you. I expect encouragement for the things I do. Not this."

The men implored him not to misunderstand them; he is a wonderful rabbi, they felt blessed to have him. It was not them, but others who were complaining.

The rabbi would not be deflected by so flimsy an argument. *They* asked for this meeting, he reminded them. *They* were in this living room, not a faceless *them*.

But neither were the members of the delegation about to be deflected. Because of the Israel trip, they persisted, could the rabbi perhaps take five weeks of vacation this year instead of the six called for in his contract?

The rabbi said he would not.

Could the rabbi check with other rabbis to see how other congregations look upon such trips to Israel?

"Gentlemen, if *you* want to check on that, be my guest. I'm not doing it."

*   *   *

By the time the rabbi returned to Worcester from his three weeks in Seattle, the wounds of that meeting had healed—at least on the surface—as they must if his work was to go on. Although the evening at Earle Halsband's home had been one of the most charged and troubling confrontations he had experienced in his six years at Beth Israel, Rabbi Rosenbaum knew well that such incidents are surely the fate of a modern-day rabbi. Perhaps he was rationalizing, he would readily admit, but he believed that he has been treated better at Beth Israel than a good many of his contemporaries in their synagogues. Regardless of a nagging resentment at the close questioning at the hands of the board members that Tuesday, it was now the busiest season of a rabbi's year; congregational life had to go on.

It was the time, once again, for Jews in synagogues around the globe to gather to celebrate the creation of the world with Rosh Hashanah and to begin *Aseret Y'mei Teshuvah,* the ten days of repentance and renewal that would culminate with Yom Kippur and its day-long fast, marking the beginning of the Jewish New Year. According to the Jewish calendar, that world was created over 5750 years ago. At this most holy time, Jews are asked to look deeply into themselves, take stock of their failures, and launch into the new year with renewed, religious resoluteness.

On Yom Kippur morning, in the sanctuary of but one of Judaism's thousands of houses of worship, Rabbi Jay Rosenbaum approached the lectern and cleared his throat. For the past ten days, he had had the kind of attention from his followers that he does not command the rest of the year. The members of Beth Israel had taken days off from the work they perform alongside non-Jews; if they owned their own businesses, they had closed them. Today, they would forgo food. For these past few days, they had been openly and unashamedly Jewish, setting themselves aside and apart from the secular world in which they may pass so anonymously the rest of the year. And now, with the High Holidays once again at an end, the time had come for the rabbi to build upon these days, to impart insights into Judaism that would both sustain the faithful and convert the indifferent. If ever there is a sermon that rabbis prepare with care and present with longing, it is the sermon for Yom Kippur. For Jay Rosenbaum, this year it would be a sermon entitled "Israel: Land of Vision."

Resplendent in his white silken robe and white *kippah*, Rabbi Jay Rosenbaum grasped the lectern firmly and pulled himself to his full height before his people. Some twelve hundred were present, the largest yearly ingathering of Beth Israel members. Many of his congregants were also attired in white, an outward sign of an inward disposition to lead a pure and holy life in the new year, but also a solemn reminder that it is in white that they will be buried. Virtually all the people from his congregation who were on the Israel trip were there.

For this occasion, the rabbi had fashioned a richly detailed and uncommonly personal meditation on *Eretz Yisrael*, calling first on his many years of rabbinic training and service, and then upon those charged days in the Promised Land. Rabbi Rosenbaum launched into his disquisition by underscoring the centrality of the land of Israel in the cycle of Jewish life. "There is barely a page in the *siddur* that does not mention the Land of Israel"—Israel at mealtime, at a wedding, *Brit Milah*, funeral; Israel on *Shabbat* and in daily prayer. "It is overwhelming; can this land measure up to such adoration?" the rabbi pondered. "Is it God's appearance in a land that makes it holy, or the fact that the land is a place where men and women throughout the ages have come to look for God?"

The land of Israel was not stones and fields and desert; instead, the rabbi explained, "like the Torah itself, the deeper meaning always lies within." He told of ancient ruins and the modern Jerusalem homes above them he had visited, of the Nirvana Hotel and nearby Masada, of a kosher Chinese restaurant and the windswept ruins at Meirot. He detailed chance meetings with Jews who survived the Soviet gulags and death camps in Germany; he told of David, the guide, who had escaped from New York. In Israel, they had all found a life they had never experienced before.

"Israel . . . ," the rabbi intoned huskily, the word taking on breadth and depth, a weight like no other word in his sermon. "Israel, the *only* place in the world where the mere fact of setting our foot on the ground we call *kodesh*, holy, raises the moral standards by which we live."

The faces of his congregants—the faces of those with whom he had traveled in Israel—were fixed upon him, waiting to hear what would come next. The few conversations that had sprung up during the sermon had by now withered under the heat of his words. There was no sound within those walls but that coming from the man on the *bimah*. This was not the same Jay Rosenbaum who had been inspired— but still unfocused—soon after his days in Israel. This was certainly another man; it was now almost two months after the trip, and the pieces had begun to come together. His sermon continued as a love song to Israel, soaring, aching, reverential, immediate. It was almost as if he were talking about a love too great to ignore, an affinity he could no longer resist.

"*Eretz Yisrael* calls each Jew to spiritual renewal," he implored as the sermon drew to a close. It was clear that an exhortation was impending. Something must be done with this love and reverence and need for Israel that the rabbi had so passionately presented. A commitment would be sought, a change demanded. "Our ancestors watch over us. We must not let them down." Rabbi Rosenbaum hesitated. His eyes swept over the hundreds of upturned faces.

In the audience, at least two of his fellow travelers awaited his next words with anticipation. Carl Aframe and Charlie Mills hoped against hope that the rabbi might—just might—say what they wanted so desperately to hear. If he did, then they might be able to turn to their wives and their children and say that they, too, were ready to follow his example. If their rabbi was ready to make this sacrifice, why not them? If Jay Rosenbaum was willing to leave behind the comforts of America and the security of a job to make *aliyah* so as to live fully as a Jew in Israel, could they not do the same? They knew how complicated such a choice would be. They thought they knew their rabbi well enough to know that he was an unlikely candidate for such an audacious act.

But might he? The long and dramatic pause at an end, the rabbi went on.

"And so you must go—I must go—to Israel as often as we possibly can. It is not only our hypothetical homeland, it is our one true home. We need to go there as often as we are able. To send every Jewish child to visit. We who have been blessed with good fortune in our land need to support the land of Jewish dreams, to support . . ."

As often as we possibly can.

To visit.

To support.

These words, while spoken with a fervor equal to the earlier parts of his sermon, hung leadenly in the air.

The rabbi continued. Soon his congregants would be approached for the annual Israel Bonds appeal. They must give "with all their might." They were not Soviet *olim* or the woman who walked across the Sinai to reach Israel, but they could assure that these fellow Jews and their children had homes and food and jobs and schooling. His final prayer echoed throughout the sanctuary. "Bring peace to the land and lasting joy to those who dwell within. And let us say, Amen."

"To *those* who dwell within." Not *these* before him.

The people of Congregation Beth Israel filed out of the synagogue, congratulating their rabbi for a sermon they called "brilliant," "inspiring," "wonderful." Their rabbi accepted their compliments warmly.

"Thank you. So good to see you. Thank you."

A few hours later, as the sun completed the day's passage over the skies of Worcester, the twenty-five hours of Yom Kippur and the ten days of the High Holidays neared their end. The final service—the *Ne'ilah*, or "shutting"—evokes the image of the "shutting of the gates." On Yom Kippur, Jewish tradition holds, God decides the fate of every person. So it is that as the conclusion of the *Ne'ilah* approaches, when the *shofar* will be blown for the final time in the High Holidays, Jews pray with a special intensity so that they may be inside the gates of Heaven before those gates are closed.

"*Adonai hu ha-Elohim.*" Rabbi Rosenbaum's voice joined with the voices of the huge gathering before him, repeating the words shouted in praise by another crowd many years before, Israelites standing in awe with Elijah, whose entreaty to God to prove Himself had been proved indeed by a great fire. *"Adonai hu ha-Elohim"*: "The Lord, He [alone] is God." The paean of adoration was repeated a second time, a third—seven times in all.

Yael Cohen's bypass surgery had kept him from performing his traditional duty, but he had been schooling Al Harris for months. Harris raised the huge ram's horn to his lips. A blast of his breath through the twisting, hollow passages sent a flat, plaintive cry heavenward.

"L'Shana Ha'ba'ah Be'Yerushalayim." Rabbi Rosenbaum triumphantly proclaimed those familiar words, spreading his arms exultingly to embrace his congregation. *"L'Shana Ha'ba'ah Be'Yerushalayim."* There was only one place to live fully as a Jew, these venerable words unabashedly affirm. There was only one place where God's plan can be enacted to show the world how to live. Anything less, anywhere else is not enough. *"L'Shana Ha'ba'ah Be'Yerushalayim."*

"Next year in Jerusalem."

But even as these words passed his lips, in his heart the rabbi knew that regardless of the clarion call of the *Ne'ilah* on that sacred night, regardless of God's commandment—the *mitzvah*—that Jews live in the land He has set aside for them, regardless of all Jay Rosenbaum had said about the centrality of Israel in Jewish life, it would not be next year in Jerusalem for him.

No, it would be next year in Worcester.

His congregants walked out into the warm September night, taking with them his words—to do with as best they could in the new year ahead. They did not have to go to Israel to seek their God. And neither did their rabbi. Instead of their person in Israel, they could send a stand-in in the form of a check for Israel Bonds. As Jay Rosenbaum would do.

The High Holidays marked only the beginning of a period of grueling congregational work for Rabbi Rosenbaum. As the days unfolded, it seemed as though the rabbi was trying to prove to his board of directors that he was more than willing to exhaust himself in the service of Congregation Beth Israel. He launched the Russian *havurah* group and set up a new program in which marginal members would share a *Shabbat* meal with an observant family. With Karen Rosen in place as the assistant to Fran Smith in the nursery, he had brokered a fragile alliance, and he did his best to nurture a smooth transition. He taught weekly nursery-school, Hebrew-school, and Hebrew high-school classes. Bar and bat mitzvah instruction was soon back in full swing; newborns were welcomed warmly and the dead laid to rest with dignity and respect. The search was on for someone to spearhead the fund-raising and membership campaigns as part of the strategic plan he and Joel Kaufman had forged the previous spring. Looking ahead to next spring, the rabbi reserved a block of rooms at a Ramada Inn in Rhode Island for the second biennial congregational retreat.

In addition to Rosh Hashanah and Yom Kippur, the two other major holy days of this time of year—*Sukkot* and *Simhat Torah*—were soon upon him. *Sukkot,* when temporary structures are built to commemorate the forty years the Israelites wandered, finding shelter where they could, and *Simhat Torah,* when the completion of yet another reading of the five holy books is joyously celebrated, each required additional sermon preparation and staggering logistical feats.

Shirley Rosenbaum, visiting from New York, fulfilled a Jewish mother stereotype by noting to her daughter-in-law that her Jay appeared to have lost a substantial amount of weight. Janine confirmed that he had been working too much, attending meetings virtually every night and eating poorly. She too was concerned. After two and a half months without a day off, Rabbi Rosenbaum finally, in October, took off a Monday.

It was at about this time that the rabbi learned that Yuri Kotlowitz would not be having his bar mitzvah as scheduled at Beth Israel. During the rabbi's absence in Seattle, and before he could talk to the family, someone from the congregation had told the Russian couple that they would be expected to pay something toward their synagogue dues before their son was bar mitzvah. Incensed, the couple decided instead to have their son's ceremony at the Lubavitcher synagogue, Tifereth Israel, which asked for no payment, token or otherwise.

Fall weather gradually turned cooler in central Massachusetts, and soon the date was at hand that marked a year since Channy Greenberg had stood in the Beth Israel library and presented the possibility of a congregational trip to Israel. Oddly enough—and much to Rabbi Rosenbaum's surprise—she had never called to see how the trip had gone.

A year had passed in the lives of the Worcester men, women, and children who had eventually made that trip, and in the life of its architect, Rabbi Jay Rosenbaum. The rabbi had conceived of the trip as the inauguration of a new kind of congregational life for Beth Israel—communitarian, observant. But this November—with the Israel trip some four months behind them, the memories beginning to fade, and the photographs now put away—found none of the travelers prepared to make the kind of commitment the rabbi had hoped for. None were ready to forgo the travel and pleasures of an American Saturday and become *shomer Shabbos*, to be a part of that critical mass of families the rabbi saw as crucial to the spiritual health of both his synagogue and his family. Of those families who did not keep a kosher home, none had given an indication they wanted to kasher their kitchen.

While it surely was difficult to assess what might have been the deeper impact of the trip on those thirty-five lives at such an early reckoning (and equally impossible to project what it might mean in the future), those fourteen days in Israel had openly affected individual lives and family relationships in disparate ways.

The Sosnoffs—Denise especially—lamenting their rather limited Jewish observance, and remembering the richness and pleasure they experienced as Jews in Israel, had vowed that they and their children would become more intensely involved in the synagogue's youth education and social programs. They did not want Jodi and Richard to lose the precious heritage that they now realized was gradually slipping away. They, the Fixlers, Aframes, and Millses continued to talk about sending or accompanying their children to Israel as they grow into their teens. Denise signed up for a basic Hebrew course.

To varying degrees, the days in Israel had a unifying effect in the homes of all the young couples, bringing children and parents together in an appreciation of their Jewishness after what was uniformly regarded as a wonderful, successful trip. But conversely—reflecting the contradictions that Israel presents to most Jews—those days also brought conflict into some of the same homes.

In Carl Aframe's fashionably appointed law office in downtown Worcester, a single sheet of notepad paper was affixed to the wall with a piece of tape. It bore the phone number of the Israel Bar Association office that provides information for foreigners who wish to join the Israeli bar. Carl decided to keep it displayed there, knowing that posting it at home or talking anymore about his overwhelming desire to make *aliyah* would only further irritate Debbie, who remained categorically opposed to the idea. Carl's increasingly serious proposals to sell everything and move to Israel had precipitated some of the most serious arguments of their marriage.

Heated arguments had also ensued at the Millses' home. Charlie was also talking about *aliyah*—and irritating Rhonda. Charlie, the convert, wanted to live in Israel; his wife, born a Jew, would not hear of it. Carl, born a Jew and ready for *aliyah*; his wife, the convert, resisting. Both men claimed—to each other, whenever they had the chance, but tactfully out of earshot of their wives—that they simply could not live the level of Jewish intensity that they felt in their hearts while living in America, while attending an American synagogue.

Howie Fixler took a middle road, choosing to make his heightened Jewish awareness work for him in Worcester, at Congregation Beth Israel. He made a commitment to spend more time on his work with the education committee at the synagogue, and began attending *Shabbat* services with his family more regularly. While he would be happy to see their home made kosher, his wife Jody saw no modern sense in this ancient practice and would have no part of it.

There was still another couple who found themselves divided on the issue of *aliyah*, a couple for whom the trip was both revelatory and unsettling. But for Jay and Janine Rosenbaum—as for the others who hold the dream of moving to *Eretz Yisrael* in their hearts—such a dream had necessarily to be swept aside as their lives and the exigencies of earning a livelihood pressed on. As Carl Aframe continued his practice as a Worcester bankruptcy lawyer, Charlie Mills as an internist at the Fallon clinic, so did Jay Rosenbaum continue as the rabbi of Congregation Beth Israel.

Rabbi Rosenbaum was in the midst of still another busy year at Beth Israel, the second of a three-year contract. A year before, the rabbi had hoped for a radical transformation in the lives of his people, the disruption of their tepid comfort level of lax observance. Much of his work in the past twelve months—culminating in the trip to Israel—was dedicated to just that end. In the year ahead, he would have to try again. With innovative approaches and proven programs, insightful sermons and inspirational life-cycle events, he would continue to assail that comfort level his congregants seem to stubbornly maintain. As his contract went into its final year, he would be seeking another term at Congregation Beth Israel.

Rabbi Rosenbaum had been starkly confronted with his own ambivalence about making the deeper commitment to Judaism that *aliyah* would represent. Somewhat ironically, the rabbi had found that he, too, did not want to breach his own comfort level as a Jew in America—albeit a high and admirable level indeed. To undertake a life-changing embrace of Judaism—for his fellow travelers to the Holy Land, or for the rabbi himself—would require more than any of them was ready to give. Being the rabbi of a midsize congregation, Jay Rosenbaum had found, was just the right level of Judaic commitment for him. There was too much to lose, too much uncertainty—as well as the wrenching experience of leaving family, friends, and aging parents behind—for him to consider moving to Israel. For the foreseeable future, he, Janine, and their children would live out their Judaism on the sidewalks of Worcester and not the cobblestone streets of Jerusalem.

I could not help but think of Moses once again. Like Moses, the rabbi had led a sheltered and privileged early life. Moses was housed and educated in the pharaoh's palace; Jay Rosenbaum lived in a nurturing Jewish home, was educated in the best Judaic schools, and eventually found a venerated position within the Jewish world.

But unlike the patriarch before him, when faced with the desert experience, Jay Rosenbaum turned away—for the moment, at least. A ride on a camel in the desert was enough; the rabbi will once again climb into his Ford Taurus to make his rounds. He will live in America, on Longworth Street, not on some Israeli street with a mystical name. He will serve a tribe encamped in the Diaspora—a worthy and worthwhile undertaking, to be sure—and look east in prayer toward a land he loves, a land he has been commanded to inhabit but cannot yet find the faith or a need so great to embrace.

Both the rabbi and his people have room to grow in the years ahead. Perhaps this is the gift they have received from their spiritual journey—new prospects for growth and a deeper understanding of how much farther they have to go. For now, faced by their own unique challenges, equipped by their historic tradition, and led by a God who calls each of them by name, the good people of Congregation Beth Israel continue to march in the desert of their latter-day promised land.

How well the people know—and how dramatically the rabbi has learned—how difficult the life of the righteous Jew can be.

Epilogue

M ore than another year has since passed in the lives of both Congregation Beth Israel and Rabbi Jay Rosenbaum. Among his other efforts to bring the message of Judaism to both congregants and to the unaffiliated Jews of the Worcester area, the rabbi had the synagogue newsletter attractively redesigned. Brushing aside any ambiguities and presenting a bright new face, the first issue of *Or Hadash* (*"The New Light"*), in September, answered a headline—"Why BI? Join Us and See!"—with a bold statement of purpose, which read in part:

> Joining Beth Israel means finding Jewish roots. In a time
> and place in modern history where too many options
> often lead to confusion and alienation, Beth Israel offers
> religious tradition, identity and spiritual guidance in a
> warm, caring social environment that nurtures personal
> growth. Not a bad combination for the late 20th century.

At about this time a national study revealed that only one in four Jews attended religious services a minimum of once a month and only one in three (a figure also thought to be considerably inflated) claimed to be affiliated with a synagogue. These figures showed Jews to be the most "unchurched" of Americans. Set against this grim backdrop, Beth Israel's forthright proclamation was all the more bold and, to the casual onlooker, could be handsomely validated by an impressive list of accomplishments in the year since the congregational trip to Israel.

333

Seeking to demonstrate that outreach was not his only goal, Rabbi Rosenbaum emphasized inreach through the *Shabbat* Hosts program. Families like the Fixlers and Millses shared their *Shabbat* meal with more marginal members of the congregation. Rhonda Mills was especially active in this new effort, which paired up some seventy-five families. Once a month, Friday-night *Shabbat* services were tailored to family worship, with a combination of formal service, singing, and religious instruction. An average of eighty to one hundred people attended.

A year-long evening program, spearheaded by Kathy Goldstein and the rabbi and housed at the Sullivan Middle School where Kathy is a teacher, taught English to Russian immigrants. Some forty new Americans began to master the language of their new land with the aid of BI volunteers and the latest in computer-assisted learning tools. With Robyn Kravitz putting substantial time and effort into United Synagogue Youth, the group had a successful year. Additionally, because Beth Israel was considered such fertile ground for Jewish growth, it was one of three synagogues awarded a grant from Avi Chai, a philanthropic foundation, which included Camp Ramah scholarships and money for leadership development and a rabbinic student to work part-time in BI family education.

Sukkot had always been one Jewish holiday at Beth Israel that never seemed to engender much interest, and in the past year Rabbi Rosenbaum had put an enormous effort into a plan to energize this, the Feast of Tabernacles. He had T-shirts and buttons printed with MAKE A LULAV SHAKE and encouraged his people to try a new kind of "shake," combining one branch of palm, three of myrtle, and two of willow with an *etrog,* a citruslike fruit found in the Mideast. As Moses was commanded by God in the Book of Leviticus to combine these elements, as a thanksgiving for the earth, and to live in booths for seven days, so Jay Rosenbaum urged his people to take the *lulav* as well as their food into their homemade shelters and relive the forty years' wandering in the desert when the Israelites lived in booths and tents. In backyards, on patios and decks throughout secular Worcester, over a hundred temporary Judaic shelters boldly bloomed, far exceeding the usual thirty-five or so. It was such a success that Rabbi Rosenbaum sent his materials and game plan to Conservative Movement headquarters in New York, and was informed that a national drive for an enhanced *Sukkot* observ-ance would be mounted, based on his experience.

The Solomon Schechter Day School, notwithstanding its own monetary problems, but looking to higher enrollments in the future and the continuing need for solid Jewish education, announced a $2 million building addition. And, on another monetary front, the people of Beth Israel, after another inspiring Yom Kippur sermon by Rabbi Rosenbaum, generously bought $57,000 in Israel Bonds.

Of course, not all of Rabbi Rosenbaum's many efforts were such unqualified successes. The Russian *havurah* group continued to meet; meanwhile, an indignity had been visited upon many others among these new immigrants. All those Russians who had been brought on as "free members" were mysteriously dropped from the membership list. When the rabbi asked why, he was told that they had not paid their dues. "They are not *supposed* to pay dues!" he exploded, demanding they be reinstated.

The Beth Israel nursery opened in the fall with an increased enrollment. But neither Fran Smith nor Karen Rosen was there to greet them. After spending an uncomfortable year as Fran's assistant, Karen was offered a job as director of early childhood education at the Jewish Community Center. She talked this over with the rabbi, saying she wanted to stay at BI but could wait no longer for Fran, who showed no indication of retiring. Karen took the job. A week later, the rabbi was astounded to receive Fran Smith's resignation. He felt betrayed. For some months, the very existence of the nursery was in jeopardy, but before the school year began, the rabbi found and hired Donna Dankner, an effervescent Jewish educator who lives in nearby West-borough.

Later, still another resignation was tendered. Michael Halzel, the Solomon Schechter Day School headmaster—who had had con-tinuing difficulties dealing with both the Schechter board and the

Beth Israel board, and who had received rather mediocre performance ratings from parents—"decided to pursue opportunities elsewhere." A search was launched for a new headmaster.

And there were some far deeper, fundamental problems at Congregation Beth Israel. The synagogue had been operating at a slight budget deficit for the past few years, and this year a significantly larger deficit loomed. The board of directors finally decided to act, raising the dues from $650 to $950 a year. Predictably, some members simply dropped their synagogue membership. But even before the dues were raised, membership had continued on its gentle, downward slide from the 530 families it had when I began. The number was now 499.

While the rabbi did not oppose raising the dues, he made it clear that other sources of income were needed if the synagogue was to thrive. The various fund-raising schemes—from Big D certificates for use at the local supermarket chain, to Dial-A-Meal precooked kosher meals, to the "mortgage *mitzvah*," in which the synagogue would receive a percentage of the closing costs—had produced little revenue. After some torturous board meetings, during which blame was amply apportioned but no real plan was developed, the board, in essence, turned to the rabbi, saying they would put off slashing the budget for several months if *he* could come up with a financial plan. One especially vocal member was even grumbling that the financial predicament was the rabbi's fault after all; he had not organized the parlor meetings that were supposed to instill a new spirit of generosity among the congregants. The rabbi had difficulty controlling himself when the responsibility for the financial welfare of Beth Israel was tossed back into his lap—especially as he looked around the room at the men and women present who were talking about saving a thousand dollars here and there. Many of them were moderately wealthy, many were successful businesspeople who were as familiar with cash flow and spreadsheets as he was with the Torah and Midrash. He wondered why this, too, was his job. He was never supposed to organize the parlor meetings; it had simply been one of the many ideas he had advanced.

*   *   *

Such were some of the statistical facts, personnel changes, program content, and various anomalies—all easily quantifiable surface components of synagogue life as still another new year was launched. As for movement in the spiritual lives and in the personal growth of Beth Israel congregants—certainly much more difficult to quantify and assess—Rabbi Rosenbaum could see some encouraging signs.

Sheila Trugman and her husband Richard Rudnick had purchased a home on Rollingwood Drive for themselves and their four children. They had done so expressly because the house was within walking distance of the synagogue, obviating a drive to *shul* and bringing them one significant step closer to becoming a *shomer Shabbat* family. Judy Wolfe, who had recently kashered her home, became a *Shabbat* regular. And Mattie Castiel began attending Friday-night services with both her young children. This seed the rabbi had sown at Zachary's *Brit Milah*—and for which he had not held out great promise—had yielded a young but strong sprout.

As for the people who had accompanied him on the Israel trip, the older members—Murray Rosenberg, Marion Blumberg, Rose Goldstein, and the Silvermans—continued their good *Shabbat* attendance. As did Carl Aframe. His bankruptcy business weakened slightly, but this was of little concern to him. The telephone number for the Israeli bar was still taped to his office wall, somewhat yellowed and slightly curled at the edges. He had stopped talking about *aliyah* at home. But the dream was still alive in his heart. He enrolled in an intensive Hebrew course and was speaking passably after his first year. He hoped that in perhaps five years, the time would be right. His daughter Ruth read her Hebrew flawlessly at her bat mitzvah.

Howie Fixler made good on his commitment and worked hard as the head of the school committee; he, Jody, and their children attended *Shabbat* services at least every other week. Charlie Mills, who could find no way to make *aliyah* and preserve a happy home, found himself increasingly restless in Worcester. He was offered a very promising job in Tampa, Florida, but, after a trip to Tampa, he and Rhonda found the Jewish presence there too diffuse and opted to remain within

Worcester's tightly knit community. Mark Cutler's son made his bar mitzvah at Temple Emanuel, the Reform synagogue; afterward, the boy and his friends were transported to Fenway Park and a Boston Red Sox game. This un-*Shabbos* act was shrugged off at Beth Israel and the Cutlers continued to send their children to Beth Israel's day school for their Judaic education.

Steve Sosnoff continued with his work at the orthopedic lab, whose name was changed from the one his father gave it—Worcester Orthopedic Appliance Company—to NovaCare, which the new owners preferred. Even as he faced the end of his own contract and possible unemployment, he received the résumé of an orthopedic technician, who himself was seeking employment. The man was extraordinarily qualified, far more so than the technician Steve now employed. But after the Israel trip, and reflecting on his experiences there, he said, "So, should I just toss my guy out? I can't do that. I try to look at people, not numbers," referring both to the bottom line at the company he once owned and the impressive résumé of a potential new employee. Steve talked about "trying to find something I can hold on to," but that something, for now, was not Jewish practice. Denise began her study of Hebrew, but after having trouble finding time to do the homework, dropped out after the first course. Jodi made her bat mitzvah—and her parents proud with her excellent Haftarah reading and talk.

As for the prayers rendered at the Western Wall, at least Ben Silverman's was answered. His thirty-six-year-old son got a job at a Big D supermarket and was enrolled in a local community college. He hoped eventually to get a degree and be able to work with troubled children.

Rabbi Rosenbaum wanted to keep the enthusiasm for spiritual renewal alive through the retreat he had planned for April. But only six families signed up—he needed a minimum of fifteen—and he was forced to call it off.

On a brighter note, the year just passed yielded a bumper crop of New Englanders who made *aliyah*, some 101 of them, 40 percent more than the year before. The story in Boston's *Jewish Advocate* noted that most of the new *olim* were between twenty and forty years of age and, for the most part, were "between jobs" and ready for a new challenge.

None of the 101 were from Congregation Beth Israel, or the house of its rabbi.

There was a continuing warm feeling among the travelers to Israel; when they would see each other in *shul*—especially in the early months of the year—they would recall a moment or place: the wall, Meirot, the Bedouin encampment, Charlie's Herculean rowing on the Jordan. But as the months trailed on, there were fewer references to the trip, although all of them said they wanted to go again—and would be happy to go with one another. The rabbi confessed that it had taken him a full year to recover from the intensity of the trip.

Janine was asked by Karen Rosen to take part in her daughter Emily's bat mitzvah; she was chosen to be the person who opened the Ark, an honor. At first, Janine resisted. What would she wear? More important, what would she wear that would make her appear thinner? Her arms were hurting—as they relentlessly did—and she was otherwise not in the best state of mind that *Shabbos* morning of the week Emily Rosen turned thirteen. Janine had a long, serious look on her face as she mounted the *bimah* and approached the Ark.

She opened the folding doors. The light fell on the Torahs, bedecked in their ornately embroidered damask covers. Resting atop the fine wooden handles upon which the parchment was rolled, the intricately tooled silver crowns glistened. Janine hesitated, her plastic-sheathed arms poised in midair. She found herself somewhat breathless. *This* is what it's all about, she said to herself. She reached in and lovingly cradled one of the Torahs in her aching arms, and when she turned, she was beaming. And crying.

She was still strong enough to bear the word of God so that others that day might hear it. Board meetings, ugly rumors, her husband's absences, unsatisfiable congregants, the constant haggling over Beth Israel's finances, programs, and their future were, for that magic moment, irrelevant. The vagaries of congregational life, of the observant life, would be visited upon her again, but for that instant she could see that this was the essence of Judaism and—as had been said before and repeated many times—the rest was commentary. She had felt the presence of God.

There was no one within the Beth Israel congregation, at least as far as the rabbi could tell—and this was not something he would question anyone about—who in this year became *shomer Shabbos,* and no one appeared to be making any immediate movement toward *aliyah.* There were, in fact, no dramatic, perceivable life-style changes. It might be concluded that the people of Beth Israel were basically living at their personal religious comfort level, dealing with and sorting out the issues of their individual lives with as much or as little Judaism as they wanted—or felt was needed.

If there were no dramatic life-changing moves to report at Beth Israel, it might also be said that Rabbi Rosenbaum's considerable efforts may have at least held at bay the further assimilation of some of the Jews of Worcester, a not inconsiderable task given the grim assessments of Jewish life I heard when I started my year with the rabbi.

While the rabbi is rarely allowed so much as a glimpse into the souls in his charge, he was afforded an in-depth look when Pat Bizzell gave the sermon for the annual Sisterhood *Shabbat.* She had not converted to Judaism when she married Bruce Herzberg—an English professor like herself—and admitted that while they both led what they considered an ethical life, it was a decidedly secular one. As they went farther in their lives and began a family with the adoption of two Korean girls, they both began to feel that secular ideals were not enough. They hungered, emotionally and spiritually, for more. Pat's workaholism was out of control, although neatly rationalized as service to her students. She had to make an appointment—and her husband had to check his datebook—for a simple conversation.

In Judaism, she felt she "had been picked up by the caravan." The desert of life was still there, but "I was no longer alone." She embraced Judaic practice readily, happily; *Shabbos* observance was hardly a burden; it made her feel wonderful, relaxed, refreshed. She was attracted to Judaism for exactly the same reasons that many turned away: "the detailed, satisfying directions it offers for a spiritual way of life."

It was a heartfelt talk and perhaps the clearest discussion I had heard at Beth Israel about what Judaism might mean to many in the 1990s. What Pat Bizzell was talking about was a specific, prescribed *life-style*. Although she certainly was a woman in pursuit of God, God's name was not mentioned in her half-hour talk. As I looked back at my time at Beth Israel, I realized that God's name must have come up so rarely that I could not remember a specific time I had heard it outside of formal prayer. Christians talk about seeking God; Jews, it seemed, *assume* God—and go on to practice or spurn the life and rituals He has set down. It was a simple, yet amazing revelation to me.

One Friday evening, just before sundown, the Rosenbaums, as usual, lit the *Shabbos* candle on the mantel above their living-room fireplace. After services and the Friday-night meal, they retired, leaving the candle burning. This is proper Judaic practice: lighting the candle is a sacred act and should not be foreshortened, nor is it permitted to light or extinguish a flame once *Shabbos* has begun.

Near midnight, a smoke alarm sounded. The rabbi rushed out to the living room to find Shoshanah's Fisher-Price playhouse aflame on the hearth. The fire was already well advanced; the living room was filled with smoke. The rabbi quickly called the fire department, woke his wife and children, and rushed them outside.

When the rabbi returned to the living room to try to put out the fire, tongues of flames were already climbing the wall. But also in the living room was a young man, a stranger. Together they doused the flames. Later, the rabbi would find that the young man had just dropped off his date down the block, and seeing Janine and the children on the lawn and the flames through the window, had immediately responded.

Once the smoke had cleared somewhat—the smoke damage was eventually found to be extensive in that part of the house—the rabbi saw what had happened. The *Shabbos* candle had burned down and shattered its holder, spilling the tiny, burning wick and hot wax onto the playhouse, which then caught fire.

"I don't know what it all means, but there he was," the rabbi told me not long after as we sat in his office. "I was saved—my home was saved—by a stranger. He wasn't even Jewish, that much I know. And I don't even know his name. What was God saying? What was the message? It's a mysterious thing, this life of ours."

Near the end of the calendar year, the Beth Israel board of directors and finance committee finally ascertained that the year's deficit would be $65,000 and the accumulated deficit, $210,000. Things began to heat up at the synagogue. A number of solutions were proposed, including the closing of the nursery, to which the rabbi responded, "With a fifty-two-percent intermarriage rate, you want to *cut back* on what we do?" The board also proposed eliminating a staff position and giving more administrative responsibilities to Cantor Freedman. They asked the staff to accept an across-the-board 10 percent pay cut.

In response, an ad hoc committee, spearheaded by Dr. Joel Kaufman and Bruce Herzberg, vowed to find money to close the budget gap and to eliminate future shortfalls. In the February issue of the newly designed synagogue newsletter, the committee, evincing a pride in what BI had accomplished, "made a firm commitment not to cut professional staff in order to balance the budget." But then, at a meeting at which the rabbi was not present, the education director's salary was cut by $10,000. She would no longer be responsible for adult education. This would be added to the rabbi's responsibilities.

The rabbi was understandably flabbergasted by this move, and when the education director, Marjorie Holzer, balked, the decision was rescinded.

A flurry of meetings followed, some of them organized by a rump group of dissidents who questioned the rabbi's ability to deal with the continuing fiscal crisis at Beth Israel.

The possible reasons for the growing dissent in the synagogue were the subject of many a conversation. One theory held that a small but significant and vocal number of both leaders and congregants were simply angry at Rabbi Rosenbaum. He had made them uncomfortable with his demands for stricter Judaic observance and practice; he had asked for more than they were willing to give. The second was that the rabbi had simply never developed the ability to schmooze, to make his congregants feel important; that, unlike his predecessor, Rabbi Baruch Goldstein, he failed to ask about children in college, parents in Florida, houses bought and sold. The third was more pragmatic. The many businesspeople on the boards, used to dealing with their own bottom lines, felt that if the money wasn't there, it couldn't be spent. Cuts, unpleasant as they might be, had to be made.

Just about the time Rabbi Rosenbaum received word that the Rabbinical Assembly office in New York was enthused with his "lulav shake" program for Sukkot—they wanted him to make a presentation at the annual convention—a group began advocating another solution to Beth Israel's financial problems. And that was not to renew Rabbi Rosenbaum's contract.

This group did not win over a sufficient number of backers and Rabbi Rosenbaum began his contract negotiations in February.

Because of the "precarious"—an oft-invoked word during those months—state of synagogue finances, the Beth Israel board made it clear from the outset that only a one-year contract could be considered. A tortuous series of meetings followed, with the rabbi presenting his case, defending his stewardship, and restating his vision for Beth Israel before the board and a smaller, three-person negotiating committee.

The Rosenbaums had envisioned a long life in Worcester and now, suddenly, they found their future in doubt. Was this but a precursor of Beth Israel in the years ahead? Would there be a fight for money with every contract, and constant anxiety at every turn as the rabbi tried to employ new approaches to enhance Jewish education, life, and ritual? Would he be asked to tailor his Judiac passion to fit within an unyielding budget? The living room and bedroom on Longworth Street were the scene of many agonized and tearful interchanges between the rabbi and his wife. At one point, in frustration, Rabbi

Rosenbaum shouted at the top of his voice, "I just want to do my god-damn job!"

But when he met with the negotiating committee, he was a study in ministerial composure. He readily acknowledged the current financial constraints; his contract demands would be few. He agreed to work for another year without a raise in pay. But there was one new clause he wanted inserted into the contract. It would grant him two months in severance pay should he not be rehired at the end of the year's contract. The committee was taken aback and initially would not agree to this, but the rabbi felt confident the board of directors would eventually grant it.

At one meeting with the negotiating committee the rabbi was equally stunned when one of his most stalwart backers, a man who had helped him plant flowers and shrubs in his backyard soon after the Rosenbaums' arrival in Worcester, looked up and calmly said, "Maybe our answer is just to get a younger and cheaper version of you, Jay."

The meeting went on. Near its end, the rabbi asked whether, if he did agree to a new contract, at no raise in pay, the synagogue would be in a position to pay his salary the following year.

Two of the three men said Beth Israel would not. Regardless, Jay Rosenbaum readied himself for a new Jewish year—vexed perhaps, without a contract, but hardly defeated. And certainly optimistic. A new committee, the "vision" committee, had risen up, and in it the rabbi saw still more seeds of new life. He still had great hopes for the people of Congregation Beth Israel.

Jay Rosenbaum had enriched the lives of many of his congregants over his eight years as rabbi—certainly I saw many examples of this during the two and a half years I spent with him—playing a crucial role in their spiritual lives, making them more observant Jews and more fulfilled human beings. He had tended to their needs from cradle to grave; he had listened to their problems and shared their triumphs. He was proud of what he had done for his people. And now he was deeply hurt by them.

If there was a "cheaper and younger version" of Jay Rosenbaum out there, such a rabbi would save the synagogue perhaps $20,000 a year. Was this a savings Beth Israel needed to make, or was it something else? To me, the key question came to this: Did the people of Beth Israel want to continue paying a man who, like the prophets of old, would continue to point out their shortcomings? Or had they simply grown tired of Jay Rosenbaum, and wanted to start afresh with a new face, a new voice, one they might find more in keeping with their own comfort level as Jews?

Acknowledgments

When I was in the final days of writing this book, I paid a visit to Rabbi Rosenbaum to go over some questions I had about material that was unclear. I could see, now that the book was becoming a reality in his mind, he was somewhat apprehensive about the outcome.

I was too.

The rabbi and his wife had been most honest and forthcoming with me throughout the year I spent with him and his congregation. I hoped that what I had written was not only accurate, but fair; that I had not placed undue emphasis on minor issues that might have been more compelling, while missing the deeper, more significant themes in his life and the life of his congregation.

I said something to the effect that "I hope I got it right, Jay."

He smiled, walked to the bookcase, and pulled down one of the books of the Torah. I thought he was going to quote something to me. He brought the book over and pointed to a text, in Hebrew.

"See this?" he said. Knowing that I did not understand Hebrew, he quickly followed with, "This is God's word. At least what we *think* He said. Don't worry."

It was this kind of disarming honesty that had attracted me to Jay Rosenbaum in the first place. I was happy to realize he was much the same man I had first talked to in that very office some two years before.

As I owe a great debt to Rabbi Rosenbaum for his patience and honesty with me, I want to thank others who had a hand in this book.

Dr. Howard Fixler, Rabbi Joshua Gutoff—who is now a Hillel chaplain at the University of Minnesota—and a scholar in Israel too modest to be acknowledged were all kind enough to read through my manuscripts and correct mistakes.

Mark Edington—my trusted friend, who wields an awesome pencil, backing it up with a superb grasp of grammar and syntax as well as a unremittingly on-target sense of when ideas are working and when they are not—read through an embarrassingly large number of drafts. Amy Ryan did an excellent copyediting job. Bob Gottlieb originally commissioned this as a long magazine piece, but it soon grew into a book and he was good enough to sustain it nonetheless. And finally, deepest thanks to Anton Mueller, my editor—whose idea this was and whose support and midcourse corrections kept me on track.